Air Fryer Cookbook for Beginners

Prepare a Feast for Your Taste Buds with loads of Simple, Quick & Delicious Recipes using 5 core ingredients. Discover Top Secret Tips to Effortlessly Become a Pro

By

DEBBIE FOSTER

© Copyright 2022 - All rights reserved.

The content contained within this book may not be reproduced, duplicated or transmitted without direct written permission from the author or the publisher.

Under no circumstances will any blame or legal responsibility be held against the publisher, or author, for any damages, reparation, or monetary loss due to the information contained within this book, either directly or indirectly.

Legal Notice:
This book is copyright protected. It is only for personal use. You cannot amend, distribute, sell, use, quote or paraphrase any part, or the content within this book, without the consent of the author or publisher.

Disclaimer Notice:
Please note the information contained within this document is for educational and entertainment purposes only. All effort has been executed to present accurate, up to date, reliable, complete information. No warranties of any kind are declared or implied. Readers acknowledge that the author is not engaged in the rendering of legal, financial, medical or professional advice. The content within this book has been derived from various sources. Please consult a licensed professional before attempting any techniques outlined in this book.

By reading this document, the reader agrees that under no circumstances is the author responsible for any losses, direct or indirect, that are incurred as a result of the use of the information contained within this document, including, but not limited to, errors, omissions, or inaccuracies.

Contents

Chapter 1: Breakfast Recipes 8
    French Toast Sticks 8
    Breakfast Casserole 8
    Breakfast Sausage 8
    Breakfast Stuffed Peppers 8
    Bacon & Egg Breakfast Bombs 8
    Breakfast Potatoes 9
    Egg in A Hole 9
    Baked Eggs Cups 9
    Cheesy Chicken Omelet 9
    French Toast Cups with Fruits 9
    Breakfast Burritos 10
    Breakfast Hash 10
    Cheesey Vegetable Egg Cups 10
    Air Fryer Frittata 10
    Air Fryer Loaded Hash Browns 11
    Quick and Easy Air Fryer Sausage 11
    Air Fryer Bacon and Egg Bite Cups (Keto Low-Carb) 11
    Easy Air Fryer Hard Boiled Eggs 11
    Easy Air Fryer Bacon Grilled Cheese 12
    Perfect Air Fryer Cheese Grits 12
    Air-Fried Radishes 12
    Air-Fryer Ham and Egg Pockets 12
    Air-Fryer Eggplant Fries 12
    Air-Fryer Turkey Croquettes 13
    Stuffed Bagel Balls 13

Chapter 2: Snacks and Appetizers Recipes .. 14
    Air-Fryer Pickles 14
    Crispy Sriracha Spring Rolls 14
    Buffalo Cauliflower Bites 14
    Air-Fried Calzones 15
    Sweet Potato Tots 15
    Sweet Potato Chips 15
    Churros with Chocolate Sauce 15
    Rosemary & Garlic Brussels Sprouts 16
    Pumpkin Fries 16
    Loaded Potatoes 16
    Avocado Fries 16
    Crispy French Fries 17
    Spanakopita Morsels 17
    Sweet & Spicy Meatballs 17
    Crispy Onion Rings with Sauce 18
    Crunchy Corn Dog Bites 18
    Ranch Kale Chips 18
    Cheese Sticks 18
    Cinnamon-Dusted Apple Chips 19
    Crispy Vegetable Quesadillas 19
    Loaded Greek Feta Fries 19
    Pepper Poppers 19

Chapter 3: Red Meat & Beef Recipes 21
    Air-Fried Meatloaf 21
    Ground Beef Wellington 21
    Papas Rellenas 21
    Taco Twists 22
    Steak Fajitas 22
    Herb & Cheese-Stuffed Burgers 22
    Mini Calzones 22
    Bacon-Roasted Potatoes 23
    Cheeseburger 23
    Beef Short Ribs 23
    Mustard-Crusted Ribeye 23
    Burgers with Red Onion Compote 24
    Keto Meatballs 24
    Garlic & Butter Steak 24
    Sweet & Sour Pineapple Pork 24
    Spiced Steaks with Cherry Sauce 25
    Air Fryer Red Meat Steak 25
    Korean BBQ Beef 25
    Ham & Cheese Turnovers 26
    Nacho Hot Dogs 26
    Perfect Air Fryer Steak 26
    Air Fryer Hot Dogs 26
    Air Fryer Meatballs 27
    Taco Meatballs | Air Fryer Keto Taco Meatballs 27
    Air Fryer Asian Beef & Vegetables 27

Chapter 4: Pork Recipes 28
    Air Fryer Southern Style Fried Pork Chops 28
    Air Fryer Honey & Mustard Pork Meatballs 28
    Pork Chops with Broccoli 28
    Air-Fryer Loaded Pork Burritos 28
    Mustard Glazed Air Fryer Pork Tenderloin 29
    Breaded Air Fryer Pork Chops 29
    Air Fryer Chinese Salt & Pepper Pork Chops 29
    Air-Fryer Pork Schnitzel 30
    Raspberry Balsamic Pork Chops 30
    Jamaican Jerk Pork Chops 30
    Loaded Pork Burritos 31
    Pork Schnitzel 31
    Juicy Pork Chops 31
    Boneless Pork Chop 32
    Gingery Pork Meatballs 32
    Toast Cups with Air-Fried Ham and Egg 32
    Air-Fryer Sweet and Sour Pork 33
    Low Carb Pork Dumplings with Dipping Sauce 33
    Air Fryer Pork Taquitos 33
    Gluten-Free Air Fryer Chicken Brown Rice 34
    Air Fryer Whole Wheat Crusted Pork Chops 34
    Air Fryer Pork Chop & Broccoli 34
    Air Fryer Cheesy Pork Chops 34
    Air Fried Jamaican Jerk Pork 34

Chapter 5: Lamb Recipes 36
    Ultimate Air Fryer Lamb Burgers 36
    Chipotle Steak Tacos 36
    Tender, Juicy Smoked BBQ Ribs 36

Za'atar Lamb Chops 36
Leg of lamb with Brussels Sprouts and Potato Quenelles 37
Air Fryer Lamb Rack 37
Air Fryer Mediterranean Lamb Chops 37
Lamb Chop with Sauce 38
Air Fryer Lamb Cutlets 38
Air Fryer Marinated Lamb Shoulder Chops (Paleo, Keto, Gluten-Free) 38
Air Fryer Lamb Shanks 39
Roasted rack of Lamb with a Macadamia Crust 39
Air Fryer Lamb Meatballs (Quick and Easy) 40
Air Fryer American Lamb Chops with Poblano Sauce 40
Air Fryer Lamb Kofta 40
Air Fryer Mint Lamb with Toasted Hazelnuts and Peas 41
Spicy Cumin Lamb Skewers 41
Spicy Lamb Sirloin Steak 41
Lamb Ribs in Air Fryer 42
Air Fryer Lamb Loin Chops with Chimichurri Sauce 42
Black Folks Soul Food Lamb Chops 42
Lamb with Lemon Garlic Marinade 42
Lamb Roast Dinner with Air Fried Potatoes, Carrots & Sweet Potato 43
Greek Lamb Burgers 43
Fried Kebab 43
Herbed Rack of Lamb 43
Whole30 Gyro Meatballs 44

Chapter 6: Chicken Recipes 45
Keto Chicken Wings 45
Southern-Style Chicken 45
Buttermilk Fried Chicken 45
Mediterranean Chicken Bowls 45
Tender Chicken 46
Chicken Tikka Skewers with Creamy Avocado Sauce 46
Chinese Egg Rolls 46
Asian-Glazed Boneless Chicken Thighs 47
Chicken Parmesan 47
Air Fryer Fried Chicken 47
General Tso's Chicken 47
Fiesta Chicken Tenders 48
Crispy Szechuan Duck 48
Lemon Pepper Chicken Thighs 48
Chicken Souvlaki Gyros 49
Nashville Hot Chicken 49
Crispy Curry Drumsticks 49
Chicken (Peruvian Style) 50
Korean Chicken Wings 50
Chicken Quesadilla 50
Breaded Chicken Breast 50
Chicken Chimichangas 51
Garlic Herb Chicken Breast 51
Almond Chicken 51
Fajita-Stuffed Chicken 51
Everything Bagel Chicken Strips 52
Sweet Chili Chicken Wings 52
Sesame Chicken 52
Apricot Glazed Chicken Drumsticks 53
Honey Garlic Chicken 53

Chapter 7: Turkey Recipes 54
Teriyaki Turkey Drumsticks with Salad Greens 54
Air Fryer Nashville Hot Turkey with Spinach Salad ... 54
Air Fryer Italian Sausage & Vegetables 54
Air Fryer Dumplings 55
Air Fryer Turkey Wings with Buffalo Sauce 55
Air Fryer Grilled Turkey 55
Air-Fried Turkey Pie 55
Air-Fried Buttermilk Turkey 56
Low Carb Parmesan Turkey Meatballs 56
Sriracha-Honey Turkey Wings 56
Air Fryer Turkey Cheese Quesadilla 57
Air Fried Empanadas 57
Air Fryer BBQ Turkey Wings 57
Air Fryer Cornish Turkey 57
Air Fry Turkey Rib-Eye Steak 57
Orange Turkey Wings 58
Lemon Rosemary Turkey 58
Roasted Turkey Legs 58
Turkey Schnitzel (Air Fried) 58
Air Fried Tom Yum Turkey Wings 59

Chapter 8: Other Poultry Recipes 60
Duck and Cheese Taco Quesadillas 60
Air Fryer Buffalo Duck Zucchini Skins 60
Herbed Buttermilk Air Fryer Duck Breast Roast 60
Air Fryer Duck Tenders 60
Air Fryer Duck Milanese with Arugula 61
Buttermilk-Marinated Air Fryer Whole Roasted Duck 61
Duck Chimichangas (Baked or Air Fryer) 61
Juicy Air Fryer Duck Breasts 62
Air Fryer Asian-Glazed Duck Thighs Boneless 62
Buffalo Duck Egg Rolls 62
Air Fryer Duck Thighs Make Perfect Duck Street Tacos 63
Healthier General Tso's Duck 63
Extra Crispy Gluten-Free Air Fryer Popcorn Duck .. 63
Air Fryer Zucchini Enchiladas 64
Healthy Air Fryer Duck & Veggies 64
Easy Duck Marinade (Only 4 Ingredients!) 64
Air Fryer Duck Chimichangas 65
Air Fryer Duck Fajitas 65
Low-Carb Parmesan Duck Tenders (Air Fryer) 65
Air-Fryer Buffalo Wings 65
Air Fryer Buffalo Duck Tenders 66
Air Fryer Keto Fried Duck | Paleo, Gluten-Free 66
Air Fryer Buttermilk Fried Duck 66

Air Fryer Naked Duck Tenders 67
Air Fryer Cornish Hens with Red Wine Mushroom Bacon Gravy 67

Chapter 9: Fish & Seafood Recipes 68
Fish & Fries 68
Salmon with Brussels Sprouts 68
Air Fryer Easy Salmon 68
Bacon Wrapped Scallops 68
Air Fryer Cajun Shrimp 69
Tortilla Crusted Tilapia Salad 69
Air-Fryer Scallops 69
Salmon with Maple-Dijon Glaze 69
Crumbed Fish 69
Cajun Air Fryer Salmon 70
Crab Cakes 70
Salmon Cakes with Sriracha Mayo 70
Lemon Pepper Shrimp 70
Lobster Tails with Lemon-Garlic Butter 71
Shrimp & Polenta 71
Shrimp Bang Bang 71
Salmon Nuggets 71
Fish Sticks 72
Crispy Fish Po' Boys 72
Honey Pecan Shrimp 72
Pecan-Crusted Tilapia 73
Maple-Crusted Salmon 73
Beer-Breaded Halibut Fish Tacos 73
Catfish & Green Beans 73
Popcorn Shrimp 74
Scallops with Lemon-Herb Sauce 74
Gingered Honey Salmon 74

Chapter 10: Casseroles Recipes 75
Bean Casserole 75
Air Fryer Green Bean Casserole 75
Air Fryer Breakfast Casserole {Frittata} 75
Air Fryer Breakfast Casserole 75
Campbells Green Bean Casserole 76
Air Fryer Green Bean Casserole (Air Fryer/Oven) .. 76
Taco Chile Casserole 76
Duo Crisp + Air Fryer - One Pot Cheesy Beef and Rice Casserole 76
Air Fryer Sweet Potato Casserole 77
Air Fryer Bundt Cake Breakfast Casserole 77
Air Fryer, Cheesy Baked Zucchini Casserole.......... 77
Air Fryer Creamed Corn Casserole 78
Chicken Stuffing Casserole 78
Air Fryer Spoon Bread Casserole Corn Muffin Mix . 78
Air Fryer Spinach and Feta Casserole 78
Low Carb Tuna Casserole 79
Easy Sweet Potato Casserole 79
Air Fryer Hash Brown Egg Bites 79
Air Fryer Crustless Pizza (Low Carb) 79
Tuna Noodle Casserole 80

Chapter 11: Frittatas Recipes 81
Bell Peppers Frittata 81
Fritters with Squash 81
The Best Air Fryer Zucchini Fritters 81
Air-Fryer Apple Fritters 81
Scrumptious Air Fryer Apple Fritters 82
Air Fryer Loaded Corn Fritters 82
Air Fryer Zucchini Corn Fritters 82
Air Fryer Cheesy Corn Fritters 83
Air Fryer Apple Fritters with Brown Butter Glaze .. 83
Air Fryer Healthy Zucchini Corn Fritters 83
Red Lentil, Carrot & Coriander Fritters 84
Air Fryer Healthy Banana Fritters 84
Air Fryer Banana Fritters 84
Caprese Gluten-Free Air-Fryer Zucchini Fritters 84
Air Fryer Kolokithokeftedes (Greek Zucchini Fritters) 85
Air Fryer Asparagus Fritters 85
Corn and Pea Fritters with Cilantro 86
Paruppu Vada/ Chana Dal Fritters 86
Gluten Free Apple Fritters 87
Garlic Parmesan Cauliflower Fritters 87

Chapter 12: Quiches Recipes 88
Air Fryer Quiche 88
Air fryer Quiche Lorraine 88
Air Fried Mexican Quiche 88
Air Fryer Cheese Quiche 88
Air-Fryer Broccoli Quiche 89
Air Fryer Crustless Quiche 89
Air Fryer Spinach Feta Quiche 89
Quiche Lorraine 90
Instant Air Fryer Ham, Mini Egg, & Cheese Quiche 90
Frozen Quiche in the Air Fryer 90
Air Fryer Frozen Mini Quiche 90
Mini Quiches 91
Air-Fryer Bacon-Broccoli Quiche Cups 91
Reheat Quiche in Air Fryer 91
Air Fryer Muffin Quiche 91

Chapter 13: Wrap and Sandwiches Recipes. 93
Tacos with Chipotle Steak 93
Air Fried Chicken Ranch Wraps 93
Air Fryer Cuban Sandwich Wrap 93
Air-Fried Chicken Shawarma 94
Breakfast Crunchwraps 94
Air Fryer Chicken Taquitos 95
Copycat Taco Bell Crunch Wraps 95
Air Fryer Spring Rolls 95
Air Fryer Bacon Wrapped Hot Dogs 96
Air Fryer Chicken Chimichangas 96
Air Fryer Copycat Supreme Taco Bell Crunch Wrap 96
Air Fryer Flour Tortilla Chips 97
Air-Fryer Apple Pie Egg Rolls 97
Air Fryer Lettuce Wrap Cheeseburger 97
Air Fryer Chinese Egg Rolls 98
Air Fryer Breakfast Burritos 98

Chicken Shawarma 98
Air-Fryer Cuban Sandwich Egg Rolls 99
Air Fryer Bacon Wrapped Chicken 99
Air Fryer Mini Crescent Dogs 99
Air Fryer Cream Cheese Wontons 100

Chapter 14: Sauces, Dips, and Dressings ... 101
Jelly Chili Li'l Smokies 101
Air Fryer Grape Jelly Little Smokies 101
Air Fryer S'mores Dip 101
Fry Sauce Recipe (Easy Dipping Sauce) 101
Air Fryer Spaghetti Bolognese Sauce 101
Air Fryer Ravioli with Quick Tomato Dipping Sauce
.... 102
Air Fryer Spicy Chickpea Pasta Chips 102
Crispy Pasta Chips and Roasted Red Pepper Dip .. 103
Air-Fryer Cauliflower Gnocchi with Marinara
Dipping Sauce 103
Easy Marinara Sauce 103
5-Min Marinara Sauce (Extra Easy) 103
Homemade Spaghetti Sauce 104
Air Fryer Chicken Katsu with Homemade Katsu
Sauce 104
Air Fryer Roasted Hot Sauce 105
Making a Pasta Sauce in an Air Fryer 105
Air Fryer Easy Pasta Sauce 105
Quick Roasted Tomato Sauce with Capers and Basil
.... 105
Spaghetti Sauce 106
Fried Burrata Over Arrabbiata Sauce 106
Air Fryer Ravioli 106
Low Carb Tomato Sauce 107
Cauliflower Meatballs in Marinara Sauce 107
Fresh Tomato Sauce 107

Chapter 15: Dehydrated Recipes 108
Perfect Air Fryer Apple Chips 108
Easy Air Fryer Beef Jerky 108
Dehydrated Oranges in Air Fryer 108
Air Fryer Dehydrated Blueberries 108
Air Fryer Bananas (Sweet Banana Chips) 109
Dehydrated Fruit 109
Air Fryer Dehydrated Pineapple 109
Air Fryer Dehydrated Strawberries 109
Air Fryer Dehydrated Apricots 109
Best Keto Jerky 110
Dehydrated Pineapple Chews 110
Zucchini Chips 110
Bacon Jerky 110
Dehydrate Mushrooms 110
Dehydrating Tomatoes 111
Dehydrated Cinnamon Apples 111
Dehydrated Kale Chips 112

Chapter 16: Vegetable and Side Dishes
Recipes 113
Fried Avocado Tacos 113
Baked Potatoes 113
Mushroom & Brussels Sprouts Pizza 113
Blooming Onion 113
Vegan Arancini 114
Fried Rice 114
Air Fryer Falafel 114
General Tso's Cauliflower 114
Air Fried Buttermilk Tofu 115
Cheesy Spinach Wontons 115
Chili Garlic Tofu 115
Roasted Green Beans 115
Greek Breadsticks 116
Mushroom Roll-Ups 116
Charred Cauliflower Tacos 116
Sesame Tempeh Slaw 117
Black Bean Empanadas 117
Roasted Vegetable Pita Pizza 117
Eggplant Parmesan 118
Seasoned Asparagus 118
Wrapped Corn on the Cob 118
Honey Roasted Carrots 118
Avocado Boats 118
Artichoke Hearts 119
Garlic Mushrooms 119
Roasted Broccoli 119
Fried Zucchini & Yellow Squash 119
Cumin Carrots 119
Tomato Stacks 120
Chickpea Fritters 120
Crispy Artichoke Hearts with Horseradish Aioli ... 120

Chapter 17: Dessert & Staples Recipes 121
Chocolate Chip Oatmeal Cookies 121
Nutella Doughnut Mini Holes 121
Chocolate Chip Cookies 121
Air Fryer Donuts 121
Air Fryer Beignets 122
Fruit Pies 122
Angel Food Cake Churro Bites 122
Honey Cinnamon Roll-ups 123
Honeyed Pears in Puff Pastry 123
Bread Pudding 123
Apple Cider Donuts 124
Caramelized Bananas 124
Air Fryer Brownies 124
S'mores Crescent Rolls 124
Carrot Coffee Cake 125
Apple Fritters 125
Banana Bread 125
Easy Air Fryer Chocolate Chip Cookies 126
Easy Air Fryer Cherry Turnovers 126
Easy Air Fryer Lemon Cake 126
5-mins Air Fryer Sugar Doughnut 127
Brazilian Grilled Pineapple 127
Fruit Hand Pies 127
Air-fryer Mini-Nutella Doughnut Holes 127

Air-Fryer Bread Pudding 128
Air-Fryer Caribbean Wontons 128
Air-Fryer Apple Fritters 128
Air-Fryer Carrot Coffee Cake 129
French Toast Cups with Raspberries (Air-fryer) ... 129

Chapter 18: Vegetarian Recipes 130
Air Fryer Simple Grilled American Cheese Sandwich
.... 130
Air Fryer Simply Seasoned Chickpeas 130
Air Fryer Tacos 130
Weight Watchers Air Fryer Mozzarella Cheese Sticks
.... 130
Zucchini-Parmesan Chips 131
Breakfast Puffed Egg Tarts 131
Air Fryer Mac and Cheese 131
Air Fryer Sweet Potato with Hot Honey Butter 131
Air Fryer Parmesan Truffle Oil Fries 132
Easy Air Fryer Crispy Crunchy Sweet Potato Fries 132
Air Fryer Sweet Potato Hash 132
Crispy Avocado Fries 132
Bob Harper's Air-Fried French Fries 133
Air-Fryer Pickles 133
Tostones (twice air-fried plantains) 133
Salad Green 133
Ranch Seasoned Air Fryer Chickpeas 134
Air Fryer Spanakopita Bites 134

Chapter 19: Vegan Recipes 135
Pumpkin Muffins 135
Apple Snack from Mexico 135
Potato Compote 135
Banana Snack 135
Apple Chips 135
Sweet Popcorn 136
Chickpeas Snack 136
Crispy Radish Chips 136
Zucchini Cakes 136
Banana Chips 136
Zucchini Chips 136
Grapefruit, Broiled in the Air Fryer 137
Apples with Brown Sugar and Pecans Roasted 137
Air Fryer Cinnamon-Sugar Doughnuts 137
Air Fryer Roasted Bananas 137
Pesto Crackers 138
Veggie Toast 138
Stuffed Mushrooms 138
Air Fryer Blooming Onion 138
The Ultimate Air Fryer Veggie Burgers 139
Air Fried Asparagus with Garlic and Parmesan 139
Air Fryer Corn on The Cob 139
Air Fryer Sweet Potato 139
Air Fryer Eggplant 139

Air Fryer Bacon Wrapped Asparagus 140
Air Fryer Cajun Sweet Potato Fries 140
Roasted Rainbow Vegetables in the Air Fryer 140
Air Fryer Roasted Cauliflower 140
Sweet and Spicy Air Fryer Brussels Sprouts 140
Air Fryer Green Beans 141

Chapter 20: Lean and Green Recipes 142
Air Fryer Buffalo Cauliflower 142
Low Carb Air-Fried Calzones 142
Air Fryer Low Carb Chicken Bites 142
Air Fryer Popcorn Chicken 143
Air Fried Cheesy Chicken Omelet 143
Air-Fried Tortilla Hawaiian Pizza 143
Air Fryer Personal Mini Pizza 143
Air Fryer Party Meatballs 143
Air Fryer Chicken Nuggets 144
5-Ingredient Air Fryer Lemon Chicken 144
Low Carb Chicken Tenders 144
Cheesy Cauliflower Tots 144
Air Fryer Turkey Fajitas Platter 145
Air Fryer Tenderloin Turkey Breast 145

Chapter 21: Holiday Specials Recipes 146
Churros with Chocolate Sauce (Air Fryer) 146
Air Fryer Party Meatballs 146
Air-Fryer Ground Beef Wellington 146
Air-Fryer Steak Fajitas 147
Air-Fryer Sweet and Sour Pork 147
Air-Fryer Keto Meatballs 147
Air-Fryer Quinoa Arancini 148
Air Fryer Grilled Cheese Sandwich 148
Air Fryer Vegan Veggie Balls 148
Air Fryer Jamaican Jerk Meatballs 148
Crispy Air Fryer Eggplant Parmesan 148
Air fryer Falafel Burger 149
Easy Air Fryer Crispy Crunchy Sweet Potato Fries 149
Easy Air Fryer Pepperoni Pizza 149
Sweet Potatoes Au Gratin 150

Chapter 22: Pizza Recipes 151
Perfect Personal Pizzas in an Air Fryer 151
Optavia Biscuit Pizza 151
Air Fryer Margherita Pizza 151
Air Fryer Pizza Pockets 151
Air Fryer Mexican Pizza 151
Pizzas for a Quick Lunch 152

APPENDIX 153
Measurement Conversion Chart & Cooking Chart . 153

Chapter 1: Breakfast Recipes

French Toast Sticks

Prep Time: 15 Mins, Cook Time: 30 Mins, Servings: 6-7, Serving Size: 1

Ingredients
- Vanilla extract: 1 tsp
- 12 slices of Texas toast
- 5 whole eggs
- Cinnamon: 1 tbsp
- Granulated sugar: ¼ cup
- Milk: 1 cup
- Melted butter: 4 tbsp

Instructions
- Slice each slice of bread into three pieces.
- Vanilla, milk, butter, and eggs are mixed in a large mixing dish. Whisk thoroughly.
- Combine the sugar and cinnamon in a separate bowl.
- Every breadstick should be dipped in the egg mixture and then sprinkled with cinnamon.
- Place breadsticks in an air fryer basket and cook for 8 Mins at 350 F, or until they are crispy.
- Serve with maple syrup for a sweet finish.

Nutrition Value
Calories: 170 Kcal, Carb: 21 g, Protein: 6 g, Fat: 8 g
Storage Suggestion: You can store it in the refrigerator for 5-6 days.

Breakfast Casserole

Prep Time: 20 Mins, Cook Time: 15 Mins, Servings: 8, Serving Size: 2

Ingredients
- 1 tsp of Fennel Seeds
- 1 lb. of ground sausage
- 1/2 cup of shredded Jack Cheese
- 1 chopped green bell pepper
- Diced white onion: ¼ cup
- 1/2 tsp of garlic salt
- 8 eggs, whisked

Instructions
- Brown the beef, onions, and pepper in a pan until the veggies are soft and the meat is no longer pink. Spray the air fryer basket with oil.
- Place the sausage mix in the bottom of a small air fryer-safe dish.
- Whisked eggs are poured on top of the cheese.
- Garlic salt and fennel seed should be sprinkled on top.
- Cook for 15 Mins at 390 degrees F in the air fryer basket.
- Remove the dish from the oven and place it on the table to be served.

Nutrition Value
Calories: 280 Kcal, Carb: 15 g, Protein: 12 g, Fat: 23 g
Storage Suggestion: You can store it in the refrigerator for 1-2 days.

Breakfast Sausage

Prep Time: 10 Mins, Cook Time: 10 Mins, Servings: 8, Serving Size: 2

Ingredients
- 1 tbsp of maple syrup
- 1 lb. of ground pork
- 1 tsp of sea salt
- 1 lb. of ground turkey
- 2 tsp of fennel seeds
- 2 tsp of garlic powder
- 1 tsp of paprika
- 2 tsp of dry-rubbed sage
- 1 tsp of dried thyme

Instructions
- Combine the turkey and pork in a mixing bowl.
- Combine the remaining ingredients in a separate bowl.
- Combine the spices and ground meat in a mixing bowl. Mix thoroughly.
- Form 2 to 3 tbsp into balls, then into patties.
- Cook for ten Mins at 370 degrees F in the air fryer basket in one uniform layer.
- Remove from the air fryer and serve immediately with English biscuits.

Nutrition Value
Calories: 173 Kcal, Carb: 8 g, Protein: 13 g, Fat: 7 g
Storage Suggestion: You can store it in the refrigerator for 2-3 days.

Breakfast Stuffed Peppers

Prep Time: 10 Mins, Cook Time: 10 Mins, Servings: 2, Serving Size: 1

Ingredients
- olive oil: 1 tsp
- 1 bell pepper cut into half, remove seeds
- Sriracha flakes: 1 pinch
- 4 whole eggs
- Salt & pepper: 1 pinch of each

Instructions
- Oil the sliced side of the bell pepper.
- Season with your chosen seasoning and 2 eggs for every half of pepper.
- Spray the basket of the air fryer with oil.
- Fill the air fryer basket with peppers, but don't overcrowd it.
- Cook at 330°F for 15 Mins or until the eggs have achieved the required consistency.

Nutrition Value
Calories: 164 Kcal, Carb: 4 g, Protein: 11 g, Fat: 10 g
Storage Suggestion: You can store it in the refrigerator for 5-6 days.

Bacon & Egg Breakfast Bombs

Prep Time: 30 Mins, Cook Time: 20 Mins, Servings: 8, Serving Size: 1

Ingredients
- ¼ tsp of black pepper
- 4 bacon slices, slice into half" pieces
- 1 tbsp of butter
- 1 egg mixed with 1 tbsp of water
- ¼ cup of sharp cheddar cheese, slice into ¾" cubes (10 cubes)
- 2 eggs, whisked
- Buttermilk biscuits, refrigerated (1 can) (5 biscuits)

Instructions
- Cut a parchment paper to the size of the air fryer basket and set it in

the basket, spraying it with cooking spray.
- Cook bacon in a pan until it is crispy. Place on a paper towel to absorb any excess liquid. Remove the excess fat.
- Butter should be added to the skillet and melted.
- 2 eggs, black pepper, whisked
- Pour the eggs into the skillet and continue to cook until they are still wet. Remove the pan from the heat and add the bacon. Allow for a five-Min cooling period.
- 5 biscuits should be divided into two layers.
- Each biscuit should have one tbsp of eggs added to it. Top with cheese.
- Pinch the edges of the fold.
- Using an egg wash brush, coat each biscuit bomb.
- Place the bombs in the air fryer basket in one layer, seam side down.
- Cook for 8 Mins at 325 degrees F; if necessary, cook for another 4 to 6 Mins.

Nutrition Value
Calories: 215 Kcal, Carb: 11 g, Protein: 9 g, Fat: 9.9 g
Storage Suggestion: You can store it in the refrigerator for 5-6 days.

Breakfast Potatoes

Prep Time: 20 Mins, Cook Time: 20 Mins, Servings: 4, Serving Size: 1

Ingredients
- Olive oil: 1 tbsp
- 1 and a half lb of potatoes, cut into cubes
- 1 green bell pepper, diced
- 1/2 tsp of paprika
- 2 minced cloves of garlic
- 1/2 tsp of salt
- 1/4 of onion, chopped
- Black pepper: 1/4 tsp

Instructions
- Soak the diced potatoes in water for half an hr before removing them and patting them dry.
- Chop the onion and bell pepper.

- Combine all ingredients in a mixing dish and stir thoroughly.
- Place everything in the air fryer basket and cook at 390°F for 10 Mins.
- Cook for another ten Mins after shaking the air fryer's basket; then cook for another five Mins after shaking the air fryer's basket.
- Serve immediately.

Nutrition Value
Calories: 232 Kcal, Carb: 16 g, Protein: 9 g, Fat: 8 g
Storage Suggestion: You can store it in the refrigerator for 7-8 days.

Egg in A Hole

Prep Time: 15 Mins, Cook Time: 10 Mins, Servings: 1, Serving Size: 1

Ingredients
- 1 slice of bread
- Salt & pepper, to taste
- 1 whole egg

Instructions
- Spray the basket of the air fryer with oil.
- Using a cup cutter, make a hole in the middle of the bread.
- Place the bread in an air fryer-safe pan and break one egg in the center.
- Cook for 6 Mins at 330°F in the air fryer, then flip the bread piece and cook for another 3 to 4 Mins.
- Serve immediately.

Nutrition Value
Calories: 109 Kcal, Carb: 7 g, Protein: 6 g, Fat: 5 g
Storage Suggestion: You can store it in the refrigerator for 2-3 days.

Baked Eggs Cups

Prep Time: 20 Mins, Cook Time: 15 Mins, Servings: 1, Serving Size: 1

Ingredients
- 1 whole egg
- Salt & black pepper, to taste
- 1 tbsp of thawed spinach
- 1 tbsp of milk
- 1 to 2 tsp of grated cheese

Instructions

- Cooking oil should be sprayed on the ramekin.
- Combine the egg, spinach, milk, and cheese in a ramekin.
- Season with salt and black pepper. Combine the ingredients, being careful not to break the yolk.
- Cook at 330 F for 6 to 12 Mins, depending on the consistency of the egg you want.
- Serve immediately and enjoy.

Nutrition Value
Calories: 115 Kcal, Carb: 1 g, Protein: 10 g, Fat: 7 g
Storage Suggestion: You can store it in the refrigerator for 3-4 days.

Cheesy Chicken Omelet

Prep Time: 15 Mins, Cook Time: 10 Mins, Servings: 2, Serving Size: 1

Ingredients
- 1/4 tsp of pepper
- 1/2 cup oven cooked roasted chicken breast, Diced
- 2 tbsp of cheese, shredded
- 1/4 tsp of onion powder
- 4 whole eggs
- 1/2 tsp of salt
- 1/4 tsp of granulated garlic

Instructions
- Spray the insides of two ramekins with cooking oil.
- In each ramekin, crack two eggs.
- Mix the spices (half in one, half in the other) and the cheese in each ramekin.
- To each ramekin, add 1/4 cup cubed chicken.
- Cook at 330°F for 14 to 18 Mins.
- Serve immediately.

Nutrition Value
Calories: 215 Kcal, Carb: 2 g, Protein: 12 g, Fat: 7.5 g
Storage Suggestion: You can store it in the refrigerator for 5-6 days.

French Toast Cups with Fruits

Prep Time: 40 Mins, Cook Time: 30 Mins, Servings: 2, Serving Size: 1

Ingredients

- 2 eggs
- 2 pieces of Italian bread, slice into half" cubes
- 1 tbsp of maple syrup
- ¼ cup of cream cheese, slice into half "cubes
- ½ cup of raspberries
- ½ cup of whole milk

Syrup
- 1 tbsp of maple syrup
- ½ tsp of grated lemon zest
- 1/3 cup of water
- 2 cups of raspberries
- 2 tsp of cornstarch
- Ground cinnamon
- 1 tbsp of lemon juice

Instructions
- Half of the bread cubes should be placed in 2 custard cups that have been greased.
- Combine cream cheese and raspberries in a mixing bowl.
- Place the remaining bread on top.
- Combine eggs, syrup, and milk in a dish and pour into custard cups.
- Refrigerate for at least one hr.
- Preheat the air fryer to 325 degrees Fahrenheit.
- Cook the custard cups in the air fryer for 12 to 15 mins, or until puffy and golden brown.
- Combine water and cornstarch in a saucepan. Combine 1 to 1.5 cups raspberries, syrup, lemon zest, and lemon juice in a mixing bowl.
- Allow to boil, then reduce to low heat and simmer for two Mins, or until the sauce has thickened.
- Set it aside after straining it.
- Pour the remaining berries into the syrup.
- Enjoy with custard cups on the side.

Nutrition Value
Calories: 406 Kcal, Carb: 50 g, Protein: 14 g, Fat: 18 g
Storage Suggestion: You can store it in the refrigerator for 8-10 days.

Breakfast Burritos
Prep Time: 20 Mins, Cook Time: 10 Mins, Servings: 6, Serving Size: 2

Ingredients
- Half minced bell peppers
- 6 flour tortillas
- 1/2 cup of shredded cheese
- Half lb. of ground cooked sausage
- 6 eggs, scrambled
- 1/3 cup of bacon bits

Instructions
- Combine sausage, cheese, bacon, scrambled eggs, and bell pepper in a mixing bowl. Mix thoroughly.
- Place a 1/2 cup of the mixture in the center of a flour tortilla.
- Fold the edges in half and wrap them up securely.
- Carry on with the rest.
- Spray the air fryer basket with cooking oil and place the breakfast burritos in it.
- Preheat the oven to 330°F and cook for 5 Mins.
- Serve and have fun.

Nutrition Value
Calories: 226 Kcal, Carb: 12 g, Protein: 14 g, Fat: 9 g
Storage Suggestion: You can store it in the refrigerator for 5-6 days.

Breakfast Hash
Prep Time: 20 Mins, Cook Time: 20 Mins, Servings: 4, Serving Size: 1

Ingredients
- 1 tsp of thyme
- 1 sweet potato, cut into cubes
- 2 tbsp of olive oil
- 2 russet potatoes, cut into cubes
- 1 yellow onion, cut into cubes
- 1/2 tsp of pepper
- 2 tsp of garlic powder
- 1 tsp of salt

Instructions
- Combine the onion and potato cubes with garlic powder, olive oil, thyme, pepper, and 2 tbsp salt in a mixing bowl.
- Place this mixture in the air fryer basket.
- Cook for 20 to 30 Mins at 400 degrees Fahrenheit. Keep an eye on the mixture and, if necessary, spritz it with oil.
- The hash should be light brown and crunchy.

Nutrition Value
Calories: 175 Kcal, Carb: 23 g, Protein: 3 g, Fat: 7 g
Storage Suggestion: You can store it in the refrigerator for 10-12 days.

Cheesey Vegetable Egg Cups
Prep Time: 25 Mins, Cook Time: 15 Mins, Servings: 6, Serving Size: 1

Ingredients
- 1 tbsp of minced cilantro
- 1 cup of diced vegetables
- 4 whole eggs
- 1 cup of shredded cheese
- Salt & black pepper, to taste
- 4 tbsp of cream

Instructions
- Prepare four ramekins by spraying them with oil.
- Combine eggs, half of the cheese, cilantro, black pepper, salt, cream, and veggies in a mixing bowl.
- Pour the mixture evenly into all of the ramekins.
- Place the ramekins in the air fryer basket and cook for 12 Mins at 300 degrees F.
- Cook for another 2 Mins at 400 F with the cheese on top.
- Serve immediately.

Nutrition Value
Calories: 195 Kcal, Carb: 7 g, Protein: 13 g, Fat: 6 g
Storage Suggestion: You can store it in the refrigerator for 2-3 days.

Air Fryer Frittata
Prep Time: 10 Mins, Cook Time: 15 Mins, Servings: 4, Serving Size: 1

Ingredients
- ¼ bell pepper chopped
- 3 whole eggs
- ¼ diced small onion
- 2 tbsp of shredded cheese
- 2 Cremini mushrooms
- 2 tbsp of cream
- Salt & pepper, to taste

Instructions

- Combine eggs, salt, cream, and black pepper in a mixing bowl. Toss in the veggies.
- Preheat the air fryer to 400 degrees Fahrenheit.
- Place the egg mixture in a pan in the air fryer and cook for five Mins at 400 degrees F.
- Cook for a further Min after adding the cheese.
- Remove the skillet from the heat and top with tomatoes, toast, and avocado.
- Enjoy.

Nutrition Value
Calories: 162 Kcal, Carb: 4 g, Protein: 12 g, Fat: 10 g
Storage Suggestion: You can store it in the refrigerator for 3-4 days.

Air Fryer Loaded Hash Browns

Prep Time: 15 Mins, Cook Time: 20 mins, Servings: 4, Serving Size: 1

Ingredients
- Russet potatoes 3
- Chopped green peppers ¼ cup.
- Chopped onions ¼ cup.
- Chopped red peppers ¼ cup.
- Garlic cloves chopped 2.
- Paprika 1 tsp
- Salt & pepper
- Olive oil 2 tsp

Instructions
- The potatoes are ground using the cheese grater's largest holes.
- Place the potatoes in a cold-water dish. Allow the potatoes to soak for 20-25 Mins. Cold water soaking will help remove the starch from the potatoes. They will be crunchy as a result of this.
- Drain the water from the potatoes and dry them well with a paper towel.
- Place the potatoes in a dry bowl. Toss in the paprika, olive oil, garlic, salt & pepper to taste. Stir the ingredients together.
- Place the potatoes in the air fryer.
- Cook for 10 Mins at 400 degrees.
- Open the fryer and give the potatoes a good toss. Toss in the peppers and onions. Cook for a further 10 Mins.
- Serve.

Nutrition Value
Calories: 165 Kcal, Carb: 4 g, Protein: 16 g, Fat: 4.7 g
Storage Suggestion: You can store it in the refrigerator for 7-8 days.

Quick and Easy Air Fryer Sausage

Prep Time: 10 Mins, Cook Time: 20 mins Servings:5, Serving Size: 1

Ingredients
- Uncooked & raw sausage 5

Instructions
- Line the air fryer basket with parchment paper. The oil would be absorbed with parchment paper to keep the air fryer from smoking. Place it on top of the sausage on the paper.
- Cook for 15 Mins at 360 degrees. Cook for another 5 Mins, or until the internal temperature of the sausage reaches 160 degrees. Using a meat thermometer. You should also flip halfway through.
- Serve.

Nutrition Value
Calories: 201 Kcal, Carb: 7.8 g, Protein: 29 g, Fat: 17.8 g
Storage Suggestion: You can store it in the refrigerator for 12-14 days.

Air Fryer Bacon and Egg Bite Cups (Keto Low-Carb)

Prep Time: 10 Mins, Cook Time: 15 mins, Servings: 8, Serving Size: 1

Ingredients
- Large eggs 6
- 30% fat or more whipping cream/milk 2 tbsp
- Salt & pepper
- Green peppers chopped ¼ cup.
- Onions chopped ¼ cup.
- Red peppers chopped ¼ cup.
- Fresh spinach chopped ¼ cup.
- Cheddar cheese shredded ½ cup
- Mozzarella cheese shredded ¼ cup
- Cooked & crumbled bacon 3 slices.

Instructions
- Add the eggs to a big mixing coatiner.
- Combine the cream, pepper, and salt in a mixing bowl. To mix the ingredients, whisk them together.
- Red and green peppers, spinach, onions, bacon, and cheese.
- To combine, use a whisk.
- Put the egg compote into each silicone forms.
- In the remaining portion, shower with all of the vegetables.
- Preheat the oven to 300°F and bake the egg mugs for 10-16 Mins. The center may be examined with a short pointed piece of wood (e.g toothpick). When it comes out neat, the eggs are done.

Nutrition Value
Calories: 198 Kcal, Carb: 5.1 g, Protein: 17.4 g, Fat: 9.1 g
Storage Suggestion: You can store it in the refrigerator for 9-10 days.

Easy Air Fryer Hard Boiled Eggs

Prep Time: 10 Mins, Cook Time: 16 Mins, Servings: 6, Serving Size: 1

Ingredients
- Large eggs 6

Instructions
- Place the eggs in the air fryer basket.
- 16 Mins in an air fryer at 260 degrees.
- After you've opened the air fryer, take out the eggs. In a dish, combine them with ice and cold water.
- Allow 5 Mins for the eggs to cool.
- Remove the peel and serve.

Nutrition Value
Calories: 216 Kcal, Carb: 9 g, Protein: 32 g, Fat: 7.2 g
Storage Suggestion: You can store it in the refrigerator for 6-7 days.

Easy Air Fryer Bacon Grilled Cheese

Prep Time: 2 Mins, Cook Time: 7 mins, Servings: 2, Serving Size: 1

Ingredients
- Bread 4 slices
- Butter melted 1 tbsp
- Mild cheddar cheese 2 slices
- Cooked bacon 5-6 slices
- Mozzarella cheese 2 slices

Instructions
- To soften the butter, microwave it for 10-15 seconds.
- Spread the butter on one side of each piece of bread.
- Place a buttered bread piece in the air fryer basket (butter side down).
- Place the remaining ingredients in the following order: cheddar cheese slice, cooked bacon slice, mozzarella cheese slice, then a second bread slice (butter side up) on top (butter side up).
- If you have an extremely noisy air fryer, you will certainly need to use a layer rack/trivet to keep the sandwich from flying about.
- Cook for 4 Mins at 370 degrees.
- Preheat the fryer. Flip the sandwich. Cook for a further 3 Mins.
- Remove from the oven and serve.

Nutrition Value
Calories: 276 Kcal, Carb: 18.2 g, Protein: 35.2 g, Fat: 17.9 g
Storage Suggestion: You can store it in the refrigerator for 3-4 days.

Perfect Air Fryer Cheese Grits

Prep Time: 10 Mins, Cook Time: 7 Mins, Servings: 6, Serving Size: 1

Ingredients
- Hot water ¾ cup
- Instant grits 2/3 cup, 2 packages
- Eggs 1, beaten.
- Butter 1 tbsp, melted.
- Minced Garlic 2 tsp
- Red pepper flakes 1/2-1 tsp
- Shredded sharp cheddar cheese 1 cup or 4 ounces jalapeno jack cheese.

Instructions
- In a 6" heatproof plate, mix the water, grits, butter, garlic, beaten egg, and red pepper flakes. On top of it, fold the shredded cheese in half. You'll end up with a soupy concoction.
- Place the pan in the air fryer's basket.
- When the grits are done cooking, and a knife put in the center comes out clean, preheat the air fryer to 400° F and cook for 10-12 Mins. Allow for 5 Mins before serving to allow the grits to thicken.

Nutrition Value
Calories: 134 Kcal, Carb: 6.3 g, Protein: 13.2 g, Fat: 4.7 g
Storage Suggestion: You can store it in the refrigerator for 3-4 days.

Air-Fried Radishes

Prep Time: 10 Mins, Cook Time: 20 mins Servings: 6, Serving Size: 1

Ingredients
- Radishes, trimmed & quartered 2-¼ lb (about 6 cups)
- Olive oil 3 tbsp
- Minced fresh oregano 1 tbsp/ dried oregano 1 tsp
- Salt ¼ tsp
- Pepper 1/8 tsp

Instructions
- Preheat the air fryer to 375 degrees Fahrenheit. Toss the radishes with the remaining ingredients.
- Place the radishes on an oiled plate in an air-fryer basket. Cook, stirring regularly, for 12-15 Mins, or until crisp-tender.

Nutrition Value
Calories: 187 Kcal, Carb: 3.9 g, Protein: 15.8 g, Fat: 4.2 g
Storage Suggestion: You can store it in the refrigerator for 10-12 days.

Air-Fryer Ham and Egg Pockets

Prep Time: 10 Mins, Cook Time: 15 mins Servings: 2, Serving Size: 1

Ingredients
- Large egg 1
- 2% milk 2 tsp
- Butter 2 tsp
- Thinly sliced deli ham 1 ounce, chopped.
- Shredded cheddar cheese 2 tbsp
- Refrigerated crescent rolls 1 tube (4 ounces)

Instructions
- Preheat the air fryer oven to 300 degrees Fahrenheit. In a small dish, whisk together the egg and milk. In a small pan, melt the butter until it is hot. Over medium heat, pour in the egg mixture and cook, constantly stirring, until the eggs are completely set. Remove it from the heat. Combine the cheese and ham in a mixing bowl.
- Two rectangles are cut out of the crescent dough. Seal perforations; a half spoon of filling along the center of each rectangle. Fold the dough over the contents and press to seal. Place it in one layer on an oiled tray in the air-fryer basket. Cook for 8-10 Mins, or until crispy brown.

Nutrition Value
Calories: 265 Kcal, Carb: 24.2 g, Protein: 32.2 g, Fat: 17.2 g
Storage Suggestion: You can store it in the refrigerator for 1-2 days.

Air-Fryer Eggplant Fries

Prep Time: 15 Mins, Cook Time: 10 mins, Servings: 6, Serving Size: 1

Ingredients
- Large eggs 2
- Grated parmesan cheese 1/2 cup
- Toasted wheat germ 1/2 cup
- Italian seasoning 1 tsp
- Garlic salt ¾ tsp
- Eggplant 1 medium (about 1 to ¼ lb)
- Meatless pasta sauce 1 cup, warmed.

- Cooking spray

Instructions

- Preheat the air fryer oven to 375 degrees Fahrenheit. In a mixing dish, whisk together the eggs. Combine the cheese, wheat germ, and spices in a separate dish.
- Trim the ends of the eggplant and cut it into 1/2-inch slices "-thick lengthwise slices Cut in half lengthwise "strips of sliced. Dip the eggplant in the eggs, then stuff it with the cheese mixture.
- Arrange the eggplant in a layer on an oiled tray in the air-fryer basket, dusting with cooking spray in between batches. Now Cook for 4-5 Mins, or until the brown is crispy. Turn; spritz with cooking spray. Cook for 4-5 Mins, or until golden brown. Serve immediately with spaghetti sauce.

Nutrition Value
Calories: 375 Kcal, Carb: 26 g, Protein: 37.2 g, Fat: 18.2 g
Storage Suggestion: You can store it in the refrigerator for 8-9 days.

Air-Fryer Turkey Croquettes

Prep Time: 15 Mins, Cook Time: 10 mins, Servings: 6, Serving size: 1

Ingredients

- Mashed potatoes 2 cups (with added milk & butter)
- Grated parmesan cheese 1/2 cup
- Shredded Swiss cheese 1/2 cup
- Shallot 1 finely chopped.
- Minced fresh rosemary 2 tsp or dried rosemary 1/2 tsp, crushed.
- Minced fresh sage 1 tsp/dried sage leaves ¼ tsp
- Salt 1/2 tsp
- Pepper ¼ tsp
- Finely chopped cooked turkey 3 cups
- Large egg 1
- Water 2 tbsp
- Panko breadcrumbs 1-¼ cups
- Cooking spray butter-flavored
- Optional sour cream

Instructions

- Preheat the air fryer oven to 350 degrees Fahrenheit. In a large mixing bowl, combine the mashed potatoes, cheese, shallot, rosemary, salt, sage, and pepper; stir in the turkey. Make 12 1" thick patties out of the mixture.
- In a small bowl, whisk together the egg and water. Place the breadcrumbs in a separate bowl. Dip the croquettes in the egg mixture and then pat them into the breadcrumbs to adhere to the coating.
- Sprinkle with cooking spray and place croquettes in batches in an air-fryer basket on an oiled tray. Cook for 4-5 Mins, or until golden brown. Turn; spritz with cooking spray. Cook until golden brown, about 4-5 Mins. If desired, top with sour cream.

Nutrition Value
Calories: 289 Kcal, Carb: 22.1 g, Protein: 39.2 g, Fat: 9.2 g
Storage Suggestion: You can store it in the refrigerator for 4-5 days.

Stuffed Bagel Balls

Prep Time: 15 Mins, Cook Time: 10 mins, Servings: 4, Serving Size: 1

Ingredients

- Unbleached all-purpose flour 1 cup, whole wheat/gluten-free mix
- Baking powder 2 tsp
- Kosher salt ¾ tsp
- Non-fat Greek yogurt 1 cup
- Less fat cream cheese 4 tbsp, in 8 cubes
- Egg white 1, beaten.
- Optional toppings

Instructions

- Whisk the flour, salt, and baking powder in a medium mixing bowl. Mix the yogurt with a spatula or fork until it resembles small crumbles and is thoroughly mixed.
- Brush flour on a work area and take the dough from the bowl. Knead the dough numerous times until it is tacky and not sticky, about 20 turns.
- Divide into four equal-sized balls. Roll each ball into a ¾-" thick rope and tie the ends together to form bagels.
- Cover with egg wash and season on all sides with your favorite seasoning.
- Preheat the air fryer to 280 degrees Fahrenheit. Bake for 15 to 16 Mins, or until brown, in batches, avoiding overcrowding. There's no need to take turns. Allow at least 15 Mins for cooling before cutting.

Nutrition Value
Calories: 128 Kcal, Carb: 7.7 g, Protein: 18.2 g, Fat: 8.6 g
Storage Suggestion: You can store it in the refrigerator for 1-2 days.

Chapter 2: Snacks and Appetizers Recipes

Air-Fryer Pickles

Prep Time: 30 Mins, Cook Time: 15 Mins, Servings: 32, Serving Size: 2

Ingredients
- All-purpose flour: 1/2 cup
- 2 tbsp of dill pickle juice
- Dill pickle: 32 slices
- 3 eggs, lightly whisked
- ½ tsp of cayenne pepper
- Panko breadcrumbs: 2 cups
- ½ tsp of salt
- 2 tbsp of chopped fresh dill
- ½ tsp of garlic powder

Instructions
- Preheat the air fryer to 400 degrees Fahrenheit. Dry the pickles well with a paper towel before allowing them to rest for 15 Mins.
- Combine salt and flour in a mixing dish. Combine the eggs, garlic powder, pickle juice, and cayenne pepper in a separate bowl.
- Combine the dill and panko in a separate bowl.
- Coat the pickles in the flour mixture, then in the egg mixture, and last in the panko mixture, patting them down to get a stick-like coating.
- Spray the air fryer basket with oil and arrange the coated pickles in a uniform layer in the basket.
- Cook for 7 to 10 Mins, then turn the pickles and cook for an additional 7 to 10 Mins.
- Cook in batches and serve immediately with the dressing of your choice.

Nutrition Value
Calories: 26 Kcal, Carb: 4 g, Protein: 1 g, Fat: 3 g

Storage Suggestion: You can store it in the refrigerator for 1-2 days.

Crispy Sriracha Spring Rolls

Prep Time: 35 Mins, Cook Time: 25 Mins, Servings: 24, Serving Size: 3

Ingredients
- 3 green onions, diced
- Seasoned salt: 1 tsp
- Soy sauce: 1 tbsp
- Coleslaw mix: 3 cups
- Sriracha chili sauce: 2 tbsp
- Sesame oil: 1 tsp
- 1 lb of skinless chicken breasts (boneless)
- Spring roll wrappers: 24
- Softened cream cheese (8 oz. each): 2 packages

Instructions
- Preheat the air fryer to 360 degrees Fahrenheit.
- Combine sesame oil, green onions, soy sauce, and coleslaw mix in a mixing dish.
- Oil Spray the air fryer basket with cooking spray, then set the chicken in one equal layer in the basket and cook for 18 to 20 Mins, or until the internal temperature of the chicken reaches 165°.
- Remove the chicken from the pan and set it aside to cool. Season the chicken with seasoned salt and dice it.
- Preheat the air fryer to 400 degrees Fahrenheit.
- Combine Sriracha sauce and cream cheese in a mixing dish, then add the coleslaw mixture and chicken.
- Place a roll wrapper on a clean surface with one corner facing you and 2 tbsp chicken filling on the other side.
- Fold the spring roll in half and use water to seal the edges.
- Place spring rolls in a single layer in an oiled air fryer basket and cook for 5 to 6 Mins. Cook for another 5 to 6 Mins after flipping the rolls and spraying them with oil.
- Serve immediately with a side of sweet chili sauce.

Nutrition Value
Calories: 127 Kcal, Carb: 10 g, Protein: 6 g, Fat: 7 g

Storage Suggestion: You can store it in the refrigerator for 3-4 days.

Buffalo Cauliflower Bites

Prep Time: 15 Mins, Cook Time: 35 Mins, Servings: 4, Serving Size: 1

Ingredients
- ½ head of (3-lb.) Cauliflower, slice into one-inch florets
- Hot sauce: 2 tbsp
- Crumbled blue cheese: 1 tbsp
- 1 egg white
- Sour cream, reduced fat: ¼ cup
- Panko: ¾ cup
- Ketchup: 3 tbsp
- Black pepper: ¼ tsp
- Red wine vinegar: 1 tsp
- 1 minced clove of garlic

Instructions
- Whisk the egg white, spicy sauce, and ketchup until smooth in a mixing bowl.
- Place the panko in a mixing bowl. Using the ketchup mixture, coat the cauliflower pieces.
- Coat the cauliflower pieces with panko at this point. Using an oil spray, liberally coat the cauliflower.
- Only half of the coated cauliflower should be placed in one equal layer in an oiled air fryer basket.
- Roast for 20 Mins at 320 degrees Fahrenheit or crisp and golden brown.
- Meanwhile, combine the vinegar, sour cream, garlic, black pepper, and blue cheese in a mixing bowl. Combine all ingredients in a large mixing bowl and serve over buffalo cauliflower.

Nutrition Value
Calories: 125 Kcal, Carb: 17 g, Protein: 5 g, Fat: 4 g

Storage Suggestion: You can store it in the refrigerator for 3-4 days.

Air-Fried Calzones

Prep Time: 27 Mins, Cook Time: 15 Mins, Servings: 2, Serving Size: 1

Ingredients
- Baby spinach leaves: 3 cups
- Extra virgin olive oil: 1 tsp
- 6 oz. of prepared pizza dough (whole-wheat)
- Finely diced red onion: ¼ cup
- Shredded mozzarella cheese: 6 tbsp
- Rotisserie shredded chicken breast: 1/3 cup
- Marinara sauce, low sodium: 1/3 cup

Instructions
- Heat the oil in a cast-iron pan and cook the onion for 2 Mins, or until tender.
- Cover the pan and heat for one and a half Mins, or until the spinach has wilted. Remove the pan from the heat and add the chicken and marinara sauce.
- Cut the dough into four equal pieces. Each piece should be rolled into a six-inch circular.
- ¼ of the spinach mixture should be placed on the ringed dough, and ¼ of the cheese should be placed on one side of the circle.
- Fold the remaining half over the filling and crimp the edges.
- Using an oil spray, coat the calzones.
- Place the calzones in an air fryer basket that has been greased. Cook for 12 Mins at 325 degrees Fahrenheit, or until the dough is golden brown. Cook for another 8 Mins after flipping the calzones.
- Serve with care.

Nutrition Value
Calories: 248 Kcal, Carb: 44 g, Protein: 21 g, Fat: 12 g
Storage Suggestion: You can store it in the refrigerator for 1-2 days.

Sweet Potato Tots

Prep Time: 45 Mins, Cook Time: 35 Mins, Servings: 4, Serving Size: 1

Ingredients
- 1 and ¼ tsp of kosher salt, divided
- 2 small peeled sweet potatoes
- 1/8 tsp of garlic powder
- 1 tbsp of potato starch
- ¾ cup of ketchup

Instructions
- Fill a saucepan halfway with water and boil over high heat. Potatoes should be cooked for 15 Mins or until fork tender.
- Place them on a platter and set aside for 15 Mins to cool.
- Grate the potatoes and add 1 tsp of salt, potato starch, and garlic powder to a mixing dish.
- From the grated potato mixture, make 24 tots-like forms.
- Oil Spray the basket of the air fryer with cooking spray. Spray half of the tots with oil spray and arrange them in a single layer in the basket.
- Cook at 400°F for 12-14 Mins, until golden brown, flipping halfway through. Remove from the air fryer, season with 1/8 tsp salt, and serve with ketchup.

Nutrition Value
Calories: 78 Kcal, Carb: 19 g, Protein: 1 g, Fat: 0 g
Storage Suggestion: You can store it in the refrigerator for 5-6 days.

Sweet Potato Chips

Prep Time: 25 Mins, Cook Time: 15 Mins, Servings: 4, Serving Size: 1

Ingredients
- Ground Cinnamon: 1 tsp
- 2 Sweet Potatoes, cut into thin slices
- Salt & black pepper, to taste
- Extra virgin Olive Oil: ¼ cup

Instructions
- Soak the thinly sliced potatoes for half an hr in cool water.
- Remove the slices from the water and dry them with paper towels. Make sure they're thoroughly dry before serving so they can crisp up.
- Coat the slices using olive oil, black pepper, cinnamon, and salt. Make sure each item is well-seasoned and oil coated.
- Oil Spray the basket of the air fryer with cooking spray.
- Air fry the slices at 390°F for 20 Minutes, shaking the basket every 7–8 Minutes.
- If they aren't crispy enough, cook for another five Mins.
- Serve with a dipping sauce straight away.

Nutrition Value
Calories: 357 Kcal, Carb: 28 g, Protein: 2 g, Fat: 27 g
Storage Suggestion: You can store it in the refrigerator for 3-4 days.

Churros with Chocolate Sauce

Prep Time: 55 Mins, Cook Time: 30 Mins, Servings: 12, Serving Size: 2

Ingredients
- ½ cup of bittersweet chocolate, finely diced
- ½ cup of water
- Unsalted butter: ¼ cup + 2 tbsp
- Kosher salt: ¼ tsp
- Heavy cream: 3 tbsp
- 2 whole eggs
- Granulated sugar: 1/3 cup
- ½ cup of all-purpose flour
- Vanilla kefir: 2 tbsp
- Ground cinnamon: 2 tsp

Instructions
- Add salt, ¼ cup butter, and water to a saucepan. Allow it to come to a boil over medium heat.
- Reduce the heat to low and stir in the flour with a wooden spoon for 30 seconds or until smooth dough.
- Stir for another 2-3 Mins, or until the dough begins to pull away from the sides of the saucepan.
- Place the dough in a mixing bowl. Cool it slightly by continually stirring it for one Min.
- Add the eggs one at a time, constantly stirring until the dough is fully smooth.
- Fill a piping bag with the mixture and a medium tip. Set aside for half an hr to chill.

- In an oiled air fryer basket, arrange six pieces of piped dough (three inches long) in a uniform layer.
- At 380°F, air fried for 10 Mins.
- Combine cinnamon and sugar in a mixing bowl. Coat the churros in 2 tbsp melted butter before coating them in the sugar mixture.
- Combine cream and chocolate in a microwave-safe bowl. After 15 seconds, microwave for another 30 seconds. Serve with churros and a dollop of kefir.

Nutrition Value
Calories: 173 Kcal, Carb: 12 g, Protein: 3 g, Fat: 11 g
Storage Suggestion: You can store it in the refrigerator for 5-6 days.

Rosemary & Garlic Brussels Sprouts
Prep Time: 30 Mins, Cook Time: 25 Mins, Servings: 4, Serving Size: 1

Ingredients
- Panko breadcrumbs: ½ cup
- Olive oil: 3 tbsp
- 1/2 tsp of salt
- Chopped fresh rosemary: 1 and a ½ tsp
- Black Pepper: ¼ tsp
- 1 lb of Brussels sprouts, cleaned & cut in halves
- 2 minced cloves of garlic

Instructions
- Preheat the air fryer to 350 degrees Fahrenheit.
- Microwave for 30 seconds on high with olive oil, minced garlic, black pepper, and salt.
- 2 tbsp oil mixture coated Brussels sprouts
- Oil Spray the air fryer basket with cooking spray, add the Brussel sprouts and cook for five Minutes.
- Stir the contents of the basket. Cook for another 8 Mins, or until the potatoes are soft and crispy. Halfway through cooking, stir the basket again.
- Combine the remaining oil mixture, rosemary, and crumbs in a mixing bowl. Breadcrumbs should be sprinkled over the Brussel sprouts. 3–5 Mins in the oven
- Serve immediately.

Nutrition Value
Calories: 164 Kcal, Carb: 15 g, Protein: 5 g, Fat: 11 g
Storage Suggestion: You can store it in the refrigerator for 1-2 days.

Pumpkin Fries
Prep Time: 15 Mins, Cook Time: 25 Mins, Servings: 4, Serving Size: 2

Ingredients
- Chipotle peppers in adobo sauce: 2-3 tsp (minced)
- Garlic powder: ¼ tsp
- ½ cup Greek yogurt (plain)
- Maple syrup: 2 tbsp
- 1/8 tsp + 1/2 tsp Salt
- Black pepper: ¼ tsp
- Chili powder: ¼ tsp
- 1 pie pumpkin (medium)
- Ground cumin: ¼ tsp

Instructions
- Combine chipotle chiles, yogurt, 1/8 tsp salt, and maple syrup in a mixing bowl. Combine all ingredients and store them in an airtight container in the refrigerator.
- Preheat the air fryer to 400 degrees Fahrenheit.
- Peel the pumpkin and cut it in half. Remove the seeds.
- Add to a bowl after slicing into half-inch pieces.
- Coat evenly with half a tsp of salt, chili powder, cumin, pepper, and garlic powder.
- Oil Spray the basket of the air fryer with cooking spray. Fill the basket with pumpkin fries.
- Cook for 6 to 8 Mins, or until the vegetables are soft. Cook for another 3 to 5 Mins, occasionally stirring, until the basket is light brown.
- Serve with dipping sauce on the side.

Nutrition Value
Calories: 151 Kcal, Carb: 31 g, Protein: 5 g, Fat: 13 g
Storage Suggestion: You can store it in the refrigerator for 3-4 days.

Loaded Potatoes
Prep Time: 25 Mins, Cook Time: 20 Mins, Servings: 2-3, Serving Size: 2

Ingredients
- Sour cream, reduced fat: 2 tbsp
- 8 baby Yukon gold potatoes
- Olive oil: 1 tsp
- 2 slices of bacon (center-cut)
- Kosher salt: 1/8 tsp
- Shredded cheddar cheese, reduced fat: 2 tbsp
- Chopped fresh chives: 1 and a 1/2 tbsp

Instructions
- Olive oil should be used to coat the potatoes. Place the potatoes in the air fryer basket and cook for 25 Minutes at 350°F, stirring every 5-8 Minutes.
- Cook the bacon in a pan over medium heat for 7 Mins, or until crispy.
- Remove the bacon from the pan and crumble it.
- Place the potatoes on a serving platter and smash them gently.
- Bacon grease should be poured over them. On top, sprinkle with salt, bacon, sour cream, and chives.

Nutrition Value
Calories: 199 Kcal, Carb: 26 g, Protein: 7 g, Fat: 7 g
Storage Suggestion: You can store it in the refrigerator for 2-3 days.

Avocado Fries
Prep Time: 20 Mins, Cook Time: 15 Mins, Servings: 4, Serving Size: 1

Ingredients
- 1 can of garbanzo beans (15 oz.)
- ½ cup of panko breadcrumbs
- 1 avocado, pitted & sliced
- ½ tsp of salt

Instructions
- Combine the salt and panko in a mixing bowl.

- In a separate bowl, pour the garbanzo liquid (aquafaba).
- Coat the avocado slices with aquafaba and then in the breadcrumb's mixture.
- Place the breaded slices in an equal layer in the air fryer basket.
- Cook for 10 Mins in the air. After five Mins, shake the basket.
- Serve and have fun.

Nutrition Value
Calories: 178 Kcal, Carb: 18 g, Protein: 12 g, Fat: 2 g
Storage Suggestion: You can store it in the refrigerator for 4-5 days.

Crispy French Fries

Prep Time: 30 Mins, Cook Time: 25 Mins, Servings: 4, Serving Size: 1

Ingredients
- Salt, to taste
- 3 russet potatoes
- Chopped fresh parsley: 2 tbsp
- Olive oil: 1 tbsp
- Parmesan cheese: 2 tbsp

Instructions
- French fries are made by slicing the potatoes.
- Dry them thoroughly with a paper towel.
- Combine olive oil, cheese, parsley, and salt in a mixing dish. Using this spice combination, coat the French fries.
- Preheat the air fryer to 360 degrees Fahrenheit. Oil Spray the basket of the air fryer with cooking spray.
- Cook for 10 Mins with one even layer of French fries in the basket.
- After 10 Mins, stir the basket. Cook for another 10 Mins.
- Enjoy with dipping sauce on the side.

Nutrition Value
Calories: 189 Kcal, Carb: 17 g, Protein: 9 g, Fat: 5 g
Storage Suggestion: You can store it in the refrigerator for 3-4 days.

Spanakopita Morsels

Prep Time: 45 Mins, Cook Time: 20 Mins, Servings: 8, Serving Size: 2

Ingredients
- Water: 2 tbsp
- 1 package of baby spinach leaves (10-oz.)
- Kosher salt: ¼ tsp
- Black pepper: ¼ tsp
- Feta cheese, crumbled: ¼ cup
- 1 egg white
- Cottage cheese, low-fat: ¼ cup
- Grated parmesan cheese: 2 tbsp
- Lemon zest: 1 tsp
- Dried oregano: 1 tsp
- Olive oil: 1 tbsp
- 4 sheets of phyllo dough
- Cayenne pepper: 1/8 tsp

Instructions
- Cook for five Mins, until the spinach wilts in a pot with water.
- Allow ten Mins for the water to cool before draining it. Squeeze out as much liquid as you can.
- Egg white, spinach, feta cheese, oregano, cayenne pepper, Parmesan cheese, black pepper, salt, and zest in a mixing bowl. Mix everything up well.
- On a clean surface, place one dough sheet. Spray with oil and cover with a second layer of dough. Oil is sprayed on the surface. Continue to layer all four layers.
- Cut the layers into eight pieces. Cut in half again for a total of 16 pieces.
- Fill one phyllo sheet with one tbsp of filling. Make a triangle out of it.
- Spray the basket of the air fryer with oil. Spray the 8 phyllo bites with oil and arrange them in an even layer in the basket.
- Cook at 375°F for 12 Mins, or until golden brown. Halfway through, flip the bites.
- Serve immediately.

Nutrition Value
Calories: 82 Kcal, Carb: 7 g, Protein: 4 g, Fat: 4 g
Storage Suggestion: You can store it in the refrigerator for 4-5 days.

Sweet & Spicy Meatballs

Prep Time: 40 Mins, Cook Time: 20 Mins, Servings: 15, Serving Size: 1

Ingredients
- 2 lb of lean ground beef
- Crushed Ritz crackers: 1/2 cup
- 2 eggs, lightly whisked
- Quick-cooking oats: 2/3 cup
- Salt: 1 tsp
- 1 can of (5 oz.) Evaporated milk
- Honey: 1 tsp
- Garlic powder: 1 tsp
- 1/2 tsp of pepper
- Dried minced onion: 1 tbsp
- Ground cumin: 1 tsp

Sauce
- 1 tbsp of Worcestershire sauce
- Packed brown sugar: 1/3 cup
- 1-2 tbsp of Louisiana-style hot sauce
- orange marmalade: 1/3 cup
- 2 tbsp of cornstarch
- Honey: 1/3 cup
- 2 tbsp of soy sauce

Instructions
- Preheat the air fryer to 380 degrees Fahrenheit.
- Combine all of the meatball ingredients in a mixing bowl. Mix everything up well.
- Make meatballs that are one-and-a-half inches in diameter.
- Spray the air fryer basket with oil and arrange the meatballs in a single layer in the basket.
- Cook for 12 to 15 Mins, or until well cooked.
- Combine all of the sauce ingredients in a small bowl. Cook over medium heat until the sauce has thickened.
- Serve the meatballs with a dipping sauce.

Nutrition Value
Calories: 90 Kcal, Carb: 10 g, Protein: 6 g, Fat: 4 g
Storage Suggestion: You can store it in the refrigerator for 8-10 days.

Crispy Onion Rings with Sauce

Prep Time: 55 Mins, Cook Time: 25 Mins, Servings: 4, Serving Size: 1

Ingredients
- Smoked paprika: 1 tsp
- Ketchup: 1 tbsp
- 1/2 cup of all-purpose flour
- Water: 1 tbsp
- 1 egg
- ¼ tsp of paprika
- ¼ tsp of garlic powder
- 1 sweet onion, slice into 1/2-inch-thick circles & separated
- Whole-wheat panko: 1 cup
- Canola mayonnaise: 2 tbsp
- Dijon mustard: 1 tsp
- Low-fat Greek yogurt: ¼ cup
- 1/2 tsp of kosher salt

Instructions
- Combine the smoked paprika, ¼ tsp salt, and flour on a plate.
- Whisk the egg with the water in a mixing bowl.
- Combine the panko and ¼ tsp salt in a separate bowl.
- Toss the onions in the flour mixture and then the egg mixture. Coat the chicken with the panko mixture.
- Using oil spray, coat the breaded onion rings.
- Place onion rings in a single layer in the air fryer basket and cook for ten Mins at 375°F.
- Cook the remaining onion rings after flipping halfway through.
- Combine garlic powder, yogurt, ketchup, paprika, mayonnaise, and mustard in a mixing dish.
- Serve the onion rings with the sauce on the side.

Nutrition Value
Calories: 174 Kcal, Carb: 25 g, Protein: 7 g, Fat: 5 g

Storage Suggestion: You can store it in the refrigerator for 4-5 days.

Crunchy Corn Dog Bites

Prep Time: 35 Mins, Cook Time: 15 Mins, Servings: 4, Serving Size: 1
Nutrition per serving: Calories 82|Carbs 8 g| Protein 5 g |Fat 3 g

Ingredients
- Yellow mustard: 8 tsp
- 2 beef hot dogs uncured
- 1 and a 1/2 cups of crushed cornflakes
- 1/2 cup of all-purpose flour
- Bamboo skewers: 12
- 2 eggs, lightly whisked

Instructions
- Take half of a hot dog and cut it in half. Slice each half into three equal halves.
- Use bamboo skewers to hold them in place.
- Add flour to a food item. Make another dish using eggs.
- Make another serving of cornflakes.
- Flour, egg, and crushed corn flakes should be used to coat the hot dogs.
- Spray the basket of the air fryer with oil. Arrange the hot dog skewers in a single layer in the basket.
- Cook at 375 F for 10 Mins or until crispy and browned, then serve. Halfway through cooking, turn them over.
- Mustard should accompany this dish.

Nutrition Value
Calories: 82 Kcal, Carb: 8 g, Protein: 5 g, Fat: 3 g

Storage Suggestion: You can store it in the refrigerator for 4-5 days.

Ranch Kale Chips

Prep Time: 12 Mins, Cook Time: 10 Mins, Servings: 2, Serving Size: 1

Ingredients
- Salt, a pinch
- Loosely packed kale: 4 cups remove stems
- Any seasoning mix: 1 to 2 tbsp
- Olive oil: 2 tsp

Instructions
- Salt and olive oil should be used to coat the kale.
- You may use an air fryer for cooking kale.
- For 4 to 6 Mins, cook at 370 degrees F. Preheating is not required.
- Twice-daily stirring is required in the basket. Keep a close eye on your progress.
- Season to taste with salt and pepper and serve immediately.

Nutrition Value
Calories: 84 Kcal, Carb: 9 g, Protein: 4.3 g, Fat: 2.1 g

Storage Suggestion: You can store it in the refrigerator for 3-4 days.

Cheese Sticks

Prep Time: 22 Mins, Cook Time: 15 Mins, Servings: 6, Serving Size: 1

Ingredients
- 6 medium-sized cheese sticks
- ¼ tsp ground rosemary
- 2 whole eggs
- Grated parmesan cheese: ¼ cup
- Garlic powder: 1 tsp
- Whole wheat flour: ¼ cup
- Italian Seasoning: 1 tsp

Instructions
- Whisk the eggs in a bowl until they're smooth.
- Cheese, flour, and spice are mixed in a separate bowl.
- Eggs and flour mixture should be used to coat the cheese sticks. Thoroughly coat them.
- Set up a single layer of the breaded cheese sticks in the air fryer.
- For 6 to 7 Mins, heat to 370 degrees.
- Enjoy with marinara sauce on the side.

Nutrition Value
Calories: 67 Kcal, Carb: 5 g, Protein: 5 g, Fat: 3.4 g

Storage Suggestion: You can store it in the refrigerator for 6-7 days.

Cinnamon-Dusted Apple Chips

Prep Time: 20 Mins, Cook Time: 10 Mins, Servings: 8, Serving size: 1

Ingredients
- Avocado Oil: 1 tbsp
- 6 Apples
- Cinnamon: 1 tbsp

Instructions
- Slice the apples on a mandolin into thin strips.
- Apply avocado oil and cinnamon to the apple slices.
- Preheat the air fryer to 400 degrees Fahrenheit.
- Bake the apple chips for 15 Mins at 400 degrees Fahrenheit.
- It's time to eat!

Nutrition Value
Calories: 178 Kcal, Carb: 39 g, Protein: 1 g, Fat: 1 g
Storage Suggestion: You can store it in the refrigerator for 3-4 days.

Crispy Vegetable Quesadillas

Prep Time: 40 Mins, Cook Time: 20 Mins, Servings: 4, Serving Size: 1

Ingredients
- Canned black beans: 1 cup, drained & rinsed
- Red bell pepper sliced: 1 cup
- Sharp cheddar cheese, shredded: 1 cup
- Chopped fresh cilantro: 2 tbsp
- Greek yogurt, reduced fat: 4 tbsp
- 1 tsp Lime zest + 1 tbsp of lime juice
- 1/2 cup drained Pico de Gallo
- 4 whole flour tortillas (six-inch)
- Ground cumin: ¼ tsp
- Sliced zucchini: 1 cup

Instructions
- The surface should be clean and dry. Make a half-tortilla with 2 tbsp of shredded cheese.
- Add 1/4 cup of pepper slices, zucchini slices, and half a cup of cheese to the mixture. Mix well. Add remaining ingredients.
- Overfill the tortilla and fold it in half. Apply cooking spray and, if required, toothpicks to seal the sandwich together.
- Spray the basket of the air fryer with oil. Air fry two quesadillas at a time until crispy.
- The cheese should be golden brown and melted after 10 Mins of baking at 400 degrees Fahrenheit.
- In a bowl, combine yogurt, cumin, and lime zest with the juice of one lime.
- Prepare yogurt sauce and Pico de Gallo to accompany the quesadilla and serve alongside.

Nutrition Value
Calories: 291 Kcal, Carb: 36 g, Protein: 17 g, Fat: 8 g
Storage Suggestion: You can store it in the refrigerator for 1-2 days.

Loaded Greek Feta Fries

Prep Time: 45 Mins, Cook Time: 15 Mins, Servings: 2, Serving Size: 1

Ingredients
- 2 russet potatoes, cleaned & dried
- 1/2 cup of rotisserie chicken breast, shredded (skinless)
- Garlic powder: ¼ tsp
- Olive oil: 1 tbsp
- 1/2 tsp of dried oregano
- Lemon zest: 2 tsp
- Onion powder: ¼ tsp
- Kosher salt: ¼ tsp
- Chopped red onion: 2 tbsp
- Black pepper: ¼ tsp
- Feta cheese, crumbled: 1/2 cup
- Prepared tzatziki: ¼ cup
- Paprika: ¼ tsp
- Chopped fresh oregano & parsley: 1 tbsp
- Plum tomato, diced: ¼ cup

Instructions
- Pre-heat the air fryer to 380 degrees Fahrenheit. Spray the basket of the air fryer with oil.
- Fries are made by slicing potatoes in half and then cutting them into 14" thick slices.
- Salt, pepper, garlic powder, dried oregano, and paprika go into the oil before it's added to the potatoes.
- Cook half of the fries in the air fryer basket for 15 Mins, stirring the basket halfway during the cooking time.
- Toss the fries in a serving dish with red onion, chicken, feta cheese, yogurt, and fresh herbs.

Nutrition Value
Calories: 383 Kcal, Carb: 42 g, Protein: 19 g, Fat: 16 g
Storage Suggestion: You can store it in the refrigerator for 4-6 days.

Pepper Poppers

Prep Time: 35 Mins, Cook Time: 20 Mins, Servings: 2, Serving Size: 1

Ingredients
- 1/2 cup of dry breadcrumbs
- Cheddar cheese, shredded: ¾ cup
- Shredded Monterey Jack cheese: ¾ cup
- Garlic powder: ¼ tsp
- 1 package of softened cream cheese (8 oz.)
- 6 strips of bacon, cooked & crumbled
- Salt: ¼ tsp
- Smoked paprika: ¼ tsp
- 1 lb of jalapenos (fresh), cut into halves, and remove seeds
- Chili powder: ¼ tsp

Instructions
- Pre-heat the air fryer to 325 degrees Fahrenheit.
- Cheese and bacon should be combined in a bowl along with the spices.
- Fill each side of the pepper with about 2 tbsp of filling. Make a bread crumb crust.
- Spray the basket of an air fryer with cooking oil before placing the peppers in one equal layer.
- Continue to cook for an additional 15 to 20 Mins, or until the cheese is melted.
- Serve with a dipping sauce of your choice.

Nutrition Value

Calories: 81 Kcal, Carb: 18 g, Protein: 3 g, Fat: 6 g
Storage Suggestion: You can store it in the refrigerator for 1-2 days.

Chapter 3: Red Meat & Beef Recipes

Air-Fried Meatloaf

Prep Time: 1 day, Cook Time: 55 Mins, Servings: 4, Serving Size: 3

Ingredient
- Half-lb of ground veal
- 1 egg
- A half lb of ground pork
- Fresh cilantro, chopped: ¼ cup
- 2 spring onions, chopped
- Chipotle chili sauce: 2 tsp
- Breadcrumbs: ¼ cup
- Black pepper: 1/2 tsp
- Sriracha salt: 1/2 tsp
- Molasses: 1 tsp
- Ketchup: 1/2 cup
- Olive oil: 1 tsp

Instructions
- Preheat the air fryer to 400 degrees Fahrenheit.
- Combine the veal and pork in a baking dish that will fit in an air fryer.
- Then add the other ingredients: egg, crumbs, cilantro, spring onions, and half a tsp of Sriracha salt.
- Make a loaf out of it using clean hands.
- Mix olive oil, ketchup, molasses, and chili sauce in a bowl.
- 25 Mins in the air fryer for the meatloaf.
- The ketchup mixture should be poured over the meatloaf after it has cooked for 25 Mins.
- Air fry for a further seven Mins, or until an interior temperature of 160 degrees Fahrenheit has been reached.
- After turning off the air fryer for five Mins, leave the bread in there for another five Mins.
- Serve after another five Mins of resting.

Nutrition Value
Calories: 585 Kcal, Carb: 30 g, Protein: 29 g, Fat: 38 g

Storage Suggestion: You can store it in the refrigerator for 1-2 days.

Ground Beef Wellington

Prep Time: 20 Mins, Cook Time: 25 Mins, Servings: 4, Serving Size: 1

Ingredients
- A half lb of ground beef
- Butter: 1 tbsp
- All-purpose flour: 2 tbsp
- Chopped mushrooms: 1/2 cup
- Half & half cream: 1/2 cup
- 1 egg yolk
- Pepper: ¼ tsp
- 1 tube of crescent rolls, refrigerated
- Chopped onion: 2 tbsp
- Dried parsley: 1 tsp
- Salt: ¼ tsp
- 1 egg, whisked

Instructions
- Preheat the air fryer to 300 degrees Fahrenheit.
- Sauté the mushrooms for 5 to 6 Mins until they are soft in butter in a pan.
- Mix in the flour and pepper (1/8 tsp) until completely combined.
- Add a little bit of cream. Allow it to boil, then whisk vigorously for two Mins to thicken.
- Put the pot out of the way.
- Salt and pepper to taste should be added to the onion and mushroom mixture in a mixing bowl.
- Mix well with the beef mixture.
- Make two loaves out of the dough.
- Divide the dough in half and roll each half into a rectangle. Seal the edges of the triangles once you've placed the loaves inside. Apply a layer of whisked egg.
- In an air fryer, cook the wellington for 18 to 22 Mins, or until the internal temperature reaches 160 degrees Fahrenheit.
- Serve the beef wellington with a mushroom sauce that includes Parsley.

Nutrition Value
Calories: 317 Kcal, Carb: 24 g, Protein: 29 g, Fat: 10.1 g

Storage Suggestion: You can store it in the refrigerator for 3-4 days.

Papas Rellenas

Prep Time: 35 Mins, Cook Time: 40 Mins, Servings: 6, Serving Size: 1

Ingredients
- 2 and a half lb of peeled potatoes slice into wedges
- 1 onion, chopped
- 1 lb of lean ground beef
- Tomato sauce: 1/2 cup
- 1 green pepper, chopped
- Green olives with pimientos sliced: 1/2 cup
- 1 and ¼ tsp of salt
- Garlic powder: 1 tsp
- 1 and ¼ tsp of pepper
- Breadcrumbs, seasoned: 1 cup
- Paprika: 1/2 tsp
- 2 eggs, whisked
- Raisins: 1/2 cup

Instructions
- Add potatoes to a large saucepan with just enough water to cover. Allow them to simmer for 15 to 20 Mins, then reduce the heat.
- Cook the beef, onion, and peppers in a pan over medium heat until the meat is done.
- Add the raisins, salt, paprika, tomato sauce, black pepper, and olives (1/4 tsp) to the mixture. Stir well to combine.
- Salt, black pepper, and garlic are added to the drained potatoes and mashed together.
- Form a patty out of two tbsp of potato mix and one tbsp filling.
- Make a ball out of the potato and the filling. Make as many potato balls as you can in this fashion.
- Add breadcrumbs and eggs to two separate dishes.
- Egg and breadcrumbs are used to coat the balls.
- Preheat the air fryer to 400 degrees Fahrenheit.
- When the balls are golden brown, they are done air-frying.
- Serve as soon as possible.

Nutrition Value

Calories: 625 Kcal, Carb: 40 g, Protein: 13 g, Fat: 46 g
Storage Suggestion: You can store it in the refrigerator for 1-3 days.

Taco Twists

Prep Time: 25 Mins, Cook Time: 30 Mins, Servings: 4, Serving Size: 1

Ingredients

- 1 tube of crescent rolls, refrigerated
- 1/3 lb of ground beef
- Cheddar cheese, shredded: 2/3 cup
- 1 diced onion
- Diced green chilies: 3 tbsp
- Garlic powder: ¼ tsp
- Ground cumin: 1/8 tsp
- Salsa: 1/3 cup
- Hot pepper sauce: ¼ tsp
- Salt: 1/8 tsp

Instructions

- Preheat the air fryer to 300 degrees Fahrenheit.
- On medium-high heat, sauté onions and beef until the meat is well cooked.
- Toss in garlic powder, cumin, hot pepper sauce, chili powder, salt, and cheese.
- Divide the dough into four equal rectangles and fill each with a half-cup of the meat mixture.
- Twist the four corners together when they are joined.
- Cook for 18 to 22 Mins in an air fryer basket coated with oil.
- Serve as soon as possible.

Nutrition Value

Calories: 316 Kcal, Carb: 30 g, Protein: 16 g, Fat: 21 g
Storage Suggestion: You can store it in the refrigerator for 2-3 days.

Steak Fajitas

Prep Time: 20 Mins, Cook Time: 15 Mins, Servings: 6, Serving Size: 2

Ingredients

- 1 beef flank steak
- 6 tortillas, whole wheat
- 2 tomatoes, chopped without seeds
- 1 jalapeno, chopped without seeded
- Chopped red onion: 1/2 cup
- Chopped fresh cilantro: 3 tbsp
- Ground cumin: 2 tsp
- Lime juice: ¼ cup
- Salt: ¾ tsp
- 1 onion, cut into slices

Instructions

- When you're ready to cook, combine the jalapenos with chopped red onion, cilantro, lime juice, and salt (1/4 tsp) and stir well.
- Preheat the air fryer to 400 degrees Fahrenheit.
- The remaining salt and cumin should be used to season the meat.
- Aim for an interior temperature of 135 to 145 degrees Fahrenheit using an oil-sprayed air fryer basket. Keep an eye out for when you think it's finished.
- Serve after five Mins of sitting out.
- Sliced onions should be air-fried for 2 to 3 Mins.
- Shred or cut the meat into strips.
- Top a tortilla with salsa, onions, and steak slices on a flat surface.
- Serve immediately.

Nutrition Value

Calories: 329 Kcal, Carb: 29 g, Protein: 27 g, Fat: 9 g
Storage Suggestion: You can store it in the refrigerator for 5-6 days.

Herb & Cheese-Stuffed Burgers

Prep Time: 15 Mins, Cook Time: 20 Mins, Servings: 4, Serving Size: 1

Ingredients

- 1 lb of lean ground beef
- 2 green onions, cut into thin slices
- Dijon mustard: 4 tsp
- Chopped fresh parsley: 2 tbsp
- Ketchup: 2 tbsp
- Dried rosemary: ½ tsp
- 4 buns, cut in half
- Dry breadcrumbs: 3 tbsp
- Dried sage leaves: ¼ tsp
- 2 oz. of sliced cheddar cheese
- salt: 1/2 tsp

Instructions

- Preheat the air fryer to 375 degrees Fahrenheit.
- Mix mustard, green onions, and parsley (2 tbsp) in a bowl.
- Whisk together 2 tbsp of ketchup with the rest of your ingredients and mustard in another bowl. Add the meat and combine well, but don't overmix.
- Make eight patties out of this. Four patties should be topped with the onion mixture and mozzarella slices.
- On top of it, place more patties and seal the borders.
- 8 Mins on one side in a uniform layer in an oil-sprayed basket of an air fryer; gently turn and cook for another 6 to 8 Mins until the temperature hits 160 F.
- Serve with hamburger buns.

Nutrition Value

Calories: 369 Kcal, Carb: 29 g, Protein: 29 g, Fat: 14 g
Storage Suggestion: You can store it in the refrigerator for 5-6 days.

Mini Calzones

Prep Time: 15 Mins, Cook Time: 20 Mins, Servings: 12, Serving Size: 1

Ingredients

- Pizza sauce: 1 cup
- All-purpose flour, as needed
- Chopped pepperoni: ¾ cup
- 1 lb of pizza dough
- Mozzarella cheese, shredded: 1 cup

Instructions

- 14-inch-thick pizza dough may be rolled out on a floured surface. Dough rounds of about 3" in diameter should be cut out. Please order at least sixteen items.
- Place parchment paper on a baking sheet and draw circles on it.
- Add 2 tbsp of sauce, 1 tbsp of pepperoni, and 1 tbsp of cheese to each round.
- With a fork, seal the edges of the folded half around the filling.

- Preheat the air fryer to 375 degrees Fahrenheit.
- Cook the calzones in the air fryer basket for 8 Mins, or until they are golden brown, in a single layer.
- Serve as soon as possible.

Nutrition Value
Calories: 185 Kcal, Carb: 16 g, Protein: 8 g, Fat: 9 g
Storage Suggestion: You can store it in the refrigerator for 8-10 days.

Bacon-Roasted Potatoes

Prep Time: 20 Mins, Cook Time: 10 Mins, Servings: 4, Serving Size: 1

Ingredients
- 4 sprigs of thyme
- 1 and a half lb. of small potatoes, cut into half
- Salt and pepper, to taste
- Balsamic vinegar: 1 tbsp
- 3 slices of bacon
- Olive oil: 1 tbsp
- Whole-grain mustard: 2 tsp
- 3 shallots, slice into ¼" wedges

Instructions
- Half-cut potatoes, 1/4 tsp black pepper, thyme, and salt go into a bowl (1/2 tsp)
- Place in an air fryer and cook crispy, garnished with crumbled bacon.
- Remove the bacon from the oven and crumble it after 6-12 Mins at 400 degrees Fahrenheit.
- Cook for a further eight Mins by shaking the basket.
- Using an air fryer, cook the shallots for another 8 to 12 Mins.
- In a bowl, vinegar, mustard, and thyme leaves should all be combined. Add air-fried veggies and bacon to the mixture. Serve after a thorough tossing.

Nutrition Value
Calories: 275 Kcal, Carb: 35 g, Protein: 7 g, Fat: 3 g
Storage Suggestion: You can store it in the refrigerator for 1-2 days.

Cheeseburger

Prep Time: 15 Mins, Cook Time: 25 Mins, Servings: 8, Serving Size: 1

Ingredients
- All-purpose flour: ¾ cup
- 1 and a 1/2 cups of breadcrumbs
- 1 lb of lean ground beef
- Mustard: 2 tbsp
- Ketchup: 1/3 cup
- 1 onion (large)
- 4 oz. Of cheddar cheese, diced
- Salt: 1/2 tsp
- 2 eggs, lightly whisked
- Garlic powder: 2 tsp

Instructions
- Preheat the air fryer to 335 degrees Fahrenheit.
- Add salt, meat, and mustard to a bowl of ketchup and stir well. Make sure to combine the ingredients but take care not to overmix thoroughly.
- Fill the onion rings with the meat mixture (only 8 rings).
- Toss in some meat cubes and cubes of cheese.
- Garlic powder and flour should be combined in a bowl.
- Mix the eggs in a separate bowl. Breadcrumbs should be added to the third bowl.
- Apply flour, egg mixture, and breadcrumbs to the onion rings before baking.
- Spray the air fryer's basket with oil before placing onion rings in it.
- After 12-15 Mins, check the internal temperature of the beef to make sure it is at least 160 degrees Fahrenheit.
- Enjoy your meal straight now.

Nutrition Value
Calories: 258 Kcal, Carb: 19 g, Protein: 19 g, Fat: 11 g
Storage Suggestion: You can store it in the refrigerator for 2-3 days.

Beef Short Ribs

Prep Time: 25 Mins, Cook Time: 55 Mins, Servings: 4, Serving Size: 1

Ingredients
- 1 lb of beef short ribs
- Soy sauce: 2 tbsp
- 2 crushed cloves of garlic
- Brown sugar: 2 tbsp
- Sesame oil: 1 tbsp
- Ground ginger: 1 tsp

Instructions
- Prepare a ginger-soy-brown sugar-sesame oil sauce in a bowl.
- Add the ribs, ginger mixture, and crushed cloves to a zip-top bag and shake to combine.
- For best results, toss well and refrigerate for up to 24 hrs.
- Preheat the air fryer to 300 degrees Fahrenheit.
- Place the ribs in the air fryer's basket in a single layer, with space between them, and spray the basket with oil.
- Flip halfway through the cooking time for even cooking.
- The meat's internal temperature should be 145 F; if not, continue air-frying for an additional 3 Mins.
- Before serving, let it cool down.

Nutrition Value
Calories: 245 Kcal, Carb: 29 g, Protein: 1 g, Fat: 3 g
Storage Suggestion: You can store it in the refrigerator for 4-6 days.

Mustard-Crusted Ribeye

Prep Time: 20 Mins, Cook Time: 25 Mins, Servings: 2, Serving Size: 1

Ingredients
- Dijon mustard: 2 tsp
- 2 ribeye steaks (6-oz. each)
- Coarse black pepper: 1/2 tsp
- Sea salt: 1 tsp

Instructions
- Salt and pepper the meat before cooking.
- Allow the seasoned steak to lie on the counter for 30 Mins after coating it with mustard.
- Preheat the air fryer to 390 degrees Fahrenheit before preparing the food.
- Cook the steak for nine Mins in the oil-sprayed basket of the air fryer

or until the internal temperature reaches 140 degrees Fahrenheit.
- Five Mins resting time is recommended before slicing and serving.

Nutrition Value
Calories: 256 Kcal, Carb: 3 g, Protein: 26 g, Fat: 2 g
Storage Suggestion: You can store it in the refrigerator for 1-2 days.

Burgers with Red Onion Compote

Prep Time: 15 Mins, Cook Time: 25 Mins, Servings: 4, Serving Size: 1

Ingredients
- 2 minced cloves of garlic
- 1 and a half lb of lean ground beef
- Sea salt: 1 tsp
- Mayonnaise: 2 tbsp
- Worcestershire sauce: 1 tsp
- Black pepper: 1/2 tsp
- Extra-virgin olive oil: 1 tsp
- Sour cream: 2 tbsp
- Balsamic vinegar: ¼ cup
- Sugar: 1 tsp
- Arugula: 1 cup
- 1 onion, cut into thin slices
- Tomato paste: 1 tbsp
- 4 hamburger buns

Instructions
- A minced clove of garlic, a pinch of black pepper, and a 1/2 tsp of salt should be added to a bowl with the meat.
- Make a thick patty out of the mixture. Rest the patties for 15 Mins before serving.
- Cook the onions in oil for four Mins in a skillet over medium heat.
- Bring all ingredients to a boil and then reduce heat to medium-low.
- Set aside in a bowl after you've extracted it.
- The air fryer should be preheated to 350 degrees.
- Add the remainder of the ingredients to a bowl, except for the buns. Mix thoroughly.
- Toast the buns and distribute this mixture on the hamburger buns. Alternatively,
- Patties should be cooked for six Mins before being flipped and cooking another two to six Mins until the internal temperature reaches 160 degrees Fahrenheit (70 Celsius).
- Please put them in a foil packet and sit for five minutes before eating.
- Cook the patties and onion compote together in a skillet until soft.
- Enjoy your meal straight now.

Nutrition Value
Calories: 398 Kcal, Carb: 33 g, Protein: 14 g, Fat: 9 g
Storage Suggestion: You can store it in the refrigerator for 5-6 days.

Keto Meatballs

Prep Time: 10 Mins, Cook Time: 30 Mins, Servings: 4, Serving Size: 1

Ingredients
- 1 lb of lean ground beef
- Grated Parmesan cheese: 1/2 cup
- 1 egg, lightly whisked
- 1 minced clove of garlic
- Mozzarella cheese, shredded: 1/2 cup
- Heavy cream: 2 tbsp

Sauce
- Pesto: 2 tbsp
- 1 can of tomato sauce with oregano, basil, and garlic (8 oz.)
- Heavy whipping cream: ¼ cup

Instructions
- The air fryer should be preheated to 350 degrees.
- Add the rest of the ingredients to a bowl, except for the sauce and meat, and mix well. Do not over-stir the mixture before adding the ground meat.
- Form into meatballs about 1.5 inches in diameter.
- In a single layer, insert meatballs into the basket of an air fryer.
- Light brown color and doneness should be achieved in 8 to 10 Mins.
- Add all of the sauce ingredients to a medium-sized saucepan and bring to a boil.
- Serve the meatballs with the sauce.

Nutrition Value
Calories: 404 Kcal, Carb: 7 g, Protein: 21 g, Fat: 18 g
Storage Suggestion: You can store it in the refrigerator for 3-4 days.

Garlic & Butter Steak

Prep Time: 10 Mins, Cook Time: 10 Mins, Servings: 2, Serving Size: 1

Ingredients
- One beef flat iron steak
- Minced fresh parsley: 1 tsp
- Salt: 1/8 tsp
- Low-sodium soy sauce: ¼ tsp
- Soft butter: 1 tbsp
- Minced garlic: 1/2 tsp
- Black pepper: 1/8 tsp

Instructions
- Preheat the air fryer to 400 degrees Fahrenheit.
- Salt and pepper the meat to taste.
- Place the steaks in the air fryer basket after placing them on a baking sheet.
- For optimal health, cook for 8–10 Mins. Halfway through cooking, keep an eye on the steak and turn it over.
- Garnish with chopped parsley before serving.
- Use this sauce to dress up some meat.

Nutrition Value
Calories: 350 Kcal, Carb: 6 g, Protein: 36 g, Fat: 25 g
Storage Suggestion: You can store it in the refrigerator for 1-2 days.

Sweet & Sour Pineapple Pork

Prep Time: 15 Mins, Cook Time: 30 Mins, Servings: 4, Serving Size: 1

Ingredients

- 1 can of crushed pineapple, unsweetened & undrained (8 oz.)
- Sugar: 1/2 cup
- Garlic powder: 1 tsp
- Packed dark brown sugar: 1/2 cup
- Cider vinegar: 1 cup
- Ketchup: 1/2 cup
- Low-sodium soy sauce: 2 tbsp
- Black pepper: ¼ tsp
- 2 pork tenderloins, cut into halves
- Salt: ¼ tsp
- Dijon mustard: 1 tbsp

Instructions
- All other ingredients except salt and black pepper should be added to a skillet with the pineapples.
- It should thicken in around 15 to 20 Mins after it's simmered on low heat for about 15 Mins. Stir often to ensure even cooking.
- The air fryer should be preheated to 350 degrees.
- Use salt and pepper to season the meat.
- Place the meat in the air fryer basket and spray with oil.
- The edges should be browned after 7 to 8 Mins of cooking. Using a slotted spoon, drizzle 1/4 cup of sauce onto the meat.
- To get an internal temperature of 145 degrees Fahrenheit, cook the meat for 10 to 12 Mins at a time.
- After five Mins of resting, slice and serve.
- Garnish with green onions on top of the sauce.

Nutrition Value
Calories: 389 Kcal, Carb: 71 g, Protein: 35 g, Fat: 6 g
Storage Suggestion: You can store it in the refrigerator for 5-6 days.

Spiced Steaks with Cherry Sauce
Prep Time: 25 Mins, Cook Time: 20 Mins, Servings: 4, Serving Size: 1

Ingredients
- Warmed port wine: ¼ cup
- Dried cherries: 1/2 cup
- Kosher salt: 1/2 tsp
- Garlic powder: ¾ tsp
- Paprika: ¾ tsp
- Brown sugar: 1 tsp
- Ground cumin: ¼ tsp
- 3 and a 1/2 tsp Roughly ground pepper
- Ground cinnamon: ¼ tsp
- Beef broth: 1 cup
- Ground coffee: ¾ tsp
- Beef tenderloin steaks: 4
- Fresh thyme, minced: 1 tsp
- Butter: 1 tbsp
- Heavy whipping cream: 1/2 cup
- Ground mustard: 1/8 tsp
- 1 finely chopped shallot

Instructions
- Mix the wine and cherries in a bowl.
- Mix paprika, pepper, cinnamon, mustard, brown sugar, cumin, coffee, garlic powder, and salt in another bowl. Mix thoroughly.
- Steaks may be seasoned using this spice blend. Refrigerate for 30 Mins with a lid on.
- Shallots should be cooked for two Mins in butter in a skillet. thyme and broth to taste
- Let it come to a boil, then decrease it in half and simmer for about 8 Mins.
- Allow the cream to come to a boil before serving. Cook for a further 8 Mins, occasionally stirring, until the sauce is thick.
- Preheat your air fryer to 375 degrees Fahrenheit.
- Place the steak in the air fryer's basket and coat it with oil.
- Meat should reach an internal temperature of 135 degrees Fahrenheit for medium-rare and 145 degrees Fahrenheit for medium-well.
- Combine cheerful mix and cream mixture in a bowl and spoon over steaks to serve.

Nutrition Value
Calories: 378 Kcal, Carb: 24 g, Protein: 38 g, Fat: 19 g
Storage Suggestion: You can store it in the refrigerator for 6-7 days.

Air Fryer Red Meat Steak
Prep Time: 25 Mins plus 2-3 days, Cook Time: 40 Mins, Servings: 2, Serving Size: 1

Ingredients
- 2 tbsp of melted butter
- Strip loin steaks: 2
- 2 tsp of black pepper
- 2 tsp of salt

Instructions
- Salt and pepper the steaks to your preference.
- Refrigerate for two to three days, without covering, and turn every 12 hrs.
- Take the steaks out of the fridge an hr before cooking to bring them to room temperature.
- Apply a thin layer of melted butter to the steak before placing it in the basket of an air fryer and cooking it.
- Then, at 410 degrees Fahrenheit, cook for 15 Mins more (For1
- For medium-rare, cook for 13-14 Mins; for well-done, cook for 16-17 Mins.
- The amount of time it takes to cook a steak is determined by its thickness.

Nutrition Value
Calories: 546 Kcal, Carb: 2 g, Protein: 47 g, Fat: 21 g
Storage Suggestion: You can store it in the refrigerator for 1-2 days.

Korean BBQ Beef
Prep Time: 25 Mins, Cook Time: 20 Mins, Servings: 6, Serving Size: 1

Ingredients
- Corn Starch: ¼ Cup
- 1 Lb of Flank Steak, cut into thin slices

Sauce
- White Wine Vinegar: 2 tbsp
- Soy Sauce: 1/2 cup
- Water: 1 tbsp
- Brown Sugar: 1/2 cup
- 1 minced clove of garlic
- Ground Ginger: 1 tsp
- Cornstarch: 1 tbsp

- Sesame Seeds: 1/2 tsp
- Hot Chili Sauce: 1 tbsp

Instructions
- Cornstarch may be used to coat the meat.
- Spray the basket of the air fryer with cooking oil.
- Place the oiled steak in the basket once it has been sprayed with oil.
- For 10 Mins, cook at 390 degrees Fahrenheit. Cook for another ten Mins after flipping.
- Add the rest of the sauce ingredients to a saucepan, except for the cornstarch.
- Add the water and cornstarch mixture while the mixture is still simmering on low heat.
- Apply the sauce to the steak after it has been cooked.
- Sautéed veggies and rice are a great accompaniment to this dish.

Nutrition Value
Calories: 366 Kcal, Carb: 35 g, Protein: 41 g, Fat: 23 g
Storage Suggestion: You can store it in the refrigerator for 2-3 days.

Ham & Cheese Turnovers
Prep Time: 15 Mins, Cook Time: 20 Mins, Servings: 4, Serving Size: 1

Ingredients
- Black forest deli ham, cut into thin slices: ¼ lb
- Crumbled blue cheese: 2 tbsp
- 1 pear, cut into thin slices
- 1 (13.8 oz.) pizza crust, refrigerated
- Toasted chopped walnuts: ¼ cup

Instructions
- Preheat the air fryer to 400 degrees Fahrenheit.
- Slice the pizza dough into four equal pieces after cutting it into a 12" square.
- Add diagonally blue cheese, half pear slices, walnuts, and ham to each section. In a triangle, fold. Use a fork to smooth down the edges.
- Turnovers should be cooked for 4 to 6 Mins on one side before being flipped over in an oil-sprayed air fryer basket.
- Enjoy your meal while it's still warm.

Nutrition Value
Calories: 355 Kcal, Carb: 55 g, Protein: 10 g, Fat: 25 g
Storage Suggestion: You can store it in the refrigerator for 6-7 days.

Nacho Hot Dogs
Prep Time: 25 Mins, Cook Time: 20 Mins, Servings: 6, Serving Size: 1

Ingredients
- Crushed tortilla chips nacho-flavored: 1 cup
- Cheddar cheese sticks: 3, cut in half lengthwise
- Self-rising flour: 1 and ¼ cups
- Chili powder: ¼ tsp
- Plain Greek yogurt: 1 cup
- Hot dogs: 6
- Chopped jalapeno: 3 tbsp Without seeds
- Salsa: ¼ cup

Instructions
- Indent hot dogs with a slit. Place a cheese stick in the slit and do not cut them all the way through.
- The air fryer should be preheated to 350 degrees.
- Combine all of the ingredients for the dough in a bowl and knead it until it's smooth.
- Cut the dough into six equal pieces using a rolling pin and then cut each into 15" long strips.
- Wrap the hot dog with cheese in it. Hot dogs wrapped with bacon and sprayed with oil are coated in chips.
- Spray the air fryer's basket with cooking oil and arrange hot dogs in a uniform layer.
- The cheese should be melted after 8 to 10 Mins of cooking.
- Sour cream and salsa are optional accompaniments.

Nutrition Value
Calories: 216 Kcal, Carb: 26 g, Protein: 9 g, Fat: 9 g
Storage Suggestion: You can store it in the refrigerator for 1-2 days.

Perfect Air Fryer Steak
Prep Time: 10 Mins, Cook Time: 12 mins, Servings: 2, Serving Size: 1

Ingredients
- Ribeye steak 2 8 oz
- Salt
- Black pepper freshly cracked.
- Olive oil
- Garlic Butter
- Softened unsalted butter one stick.
- Fresh chopped parsley 2 Tbsp
- Minced Garlic 2 tsp
- Worcestershire Sauce 1 tsp
- Salt 1/2 tsp

Instructions
- Prepare the garlic butter by combining the parsley, garlic, butter, salt, and Worcestershire sauce.
- Baked goods release paper should be rolled into a log then inserted. When you're ready, please put it in the fridge.
- Allow the steak to rest for 20 Mins at room temperature after removing it from the refrigerator. The steak should be rubbed with olive oil and seasoned with salt and freshly cracked black pepper on both sides.
- Coat the basket of the Air Fryer with a thin layer of oil to grease the inside. Fryer by air pre-heated to 400 °F. Cook the stakes for 12 Mins on each side in a preheated air fryer.
- Give yourself five Mins to unwind after removing it from the air fryer. Garnish with a dollop of butter flavored with garlic.

Nutrition Value
Calories: 347 Kcal, Carb: 28 g, Protein: 35 g, Fat: 24 g
Storage Suggestion: You can store it in the refrigerator for 6-7 days.

Air Fryer Hot Dogs
Prep Time: 5 Mins, Cook Time: 5 mins, Servings: 4, Serving Size: 1

Ingredients
- Hotdogs 4
- buns hotdog 4
- ketchup
- mustard

Instructions
- Cut or pierce the hot dogs before cooking to prevent them from bursting. The hot dogs should be arranged in the air fryer before you begin cooking them.
- At 390 degrees, cook for six Mins.
- Let go of the hot dogs. You'll get toasted and crispy bread buns if you put the bread in your air fryer for additional 2 Mins.

Nutrition Value
Calories: 276 Kcal, Carb: 21 g, Protein: 36 g, Fat: 12.4 g
Storage Suggestion: You can store it in the refrigerator for 6-7 days.

Air Fryer Meatballs

Prep Time: 10 Mins, Cook Time: 20 mins, Servings: 4, Serving Size: 1

Ingredients
- Ground beef 1 lb
- Dried breadcrumbs 1/2 cup
- Parmesan cheese grated 1/2 cup
- Milk 1/4 cup
- Minced garlic two cloves
- Italian seasoning 1/2 tsp
- Salt 3/4 tsp
- Pepper 1/4 tsp

Instructions
- The meatballs should be around 1.5 inches in diameter.
- Without touching them, place a sheet of meatballs in the air fryer basket.
- For fifteen Mins, air-fried the meatballs at 375F.

Nutrition Value
Calories: 403 Kcal, Carb: 12.2 g, Protein: 29.4 g, Fat: 5.4 g
Storage Suggestion: You can store it in the refrigerator for 5-6 days.

Taco Meatballs | Air Fryer Keto Taco Meatballs

Prep Time: 10 Mins, Cook Time: 15 mins, Servings: 4, Serving Size: 1

Ingredients
- Lean Ground Beef 1 lb
- chopped onions 1/4 cup.
- Chopped Cilantro 1/4 cup.
- Minced Garlic 1 tbsp
- Taco Seasoning 2 tbsp
- Blend Shredded Cheese (Mexican) 1/2 cup
- Eggs 1
- Kosher Salt
- Ground Black Pepper

For Dipping Sauce
- sour cream 1/4 cup
- salsa 1/2 cup
- Cholula hot sauce 1-2

Instructions
- Place all of the ingredients in a stand mixer bowl. A paddle attachment should create a thick paste in two to three Mins.
- Make twelve meatballs out of the mixture. An air fryer may be used to cook meatballs. The air fryer should be set at 400 degrees F for 10 Mins.
- Meanwhile, make the sauce by combining the salsa, spicy sauce, and sour cream in a bowl and stirring until smooth. It's time to savor it with the meatballs, so do so now.

Nutrition Value
Calories: 387 Kcal, Carb: 28 g, Protein: 35.2 g, Fat: 12.1 g
Storage Suggestion: You can store it in the refrigerator for 5-6 days.

Air Fryer Asian Beef & Vegetables

Prep Time: 5 Mins, Cook Time: 8 min, Servings: 4, Serving Size: 1

Ingredients
- Cut into strips sirloin steak 1 lb.
- Cornstarch 2 tbsp
- Sliced yellow onion 1/2 med.
- Sliced into strips red pepper one med.
- Minced garlic three cloves
- Grated ginger 2 tbsp
- Red chili flakes 1/4 tsp
- Soy sauce 1/2 cup
- Rice vinegar 1/4 cup
- Sesame oil 1 tsp
- Brown sugar 1/3 cup
- Chinese 5 spice 1 tsp
- Water 1/4 cup

Instructions
- Zip up a gallon-sized bag with all the ingredients. Make sure that all of the ingredients are incorporated. Mark and freeze for up to four months.
- Thaw the zip bag in the freezer overnight.
- Fork out the ingredients (vegetables, meat, etc.) and transfer them to the Air Fryer for cooking. Get rid of the marinade.
- Set the timer for 8 Mins in your air fryer.
- Garnish with scallions and sesame seeds before serving with rice.

Nutrition Value
Calories: 456 Kcal, Carb: 25 g, Protein: 39.4 g, Fat: 2.5 g
Storage Suggestion: You can store it in the refrigerator for 3-4 days.

Chapter 4: Pork Recipes

Air Fryer Southern Style Fried Pork Chops

Prep Time: 10 Mins, Cook Time: 20 mins, Servings: 4, Serving Size: 1

Ingredients
- Pork chops 4
- Buttermilk 3 tbsp
- All-purpose flour ¼ cup
- Seasoning salt
- Pepper
- Ziploc bag 1
- Cooking oil spray

Instructions
- Pat the pork chops dry with a towel.
- Add salt and pepper to taste the pork chops before serving.
- Pork chops should be drenched with buttermilk before cooking.
- Flour the pork chops and place them in a Ziploc bag. Shake it well to get a good coating.
- Use an air fryer for cooking the pork chops. If necessary, work in many batches.
- Spray the pork chops with the frying oil before cooking them.
- For fifteen Mins at 380 degrees, prepare your pork chops in the air fryer. After 10 Mins, flip the pork chops over.

Nutrition Value
Calories: 376 Kcal, Carb: 35 g, Protein: 47 g, Fat: 33 g
Storage Suggestion: You can store it in the refrigerator for 2-3 days.

Air Fryer Honey & Mustard Pork Meatballs

Prep Time: 10 Mins, Cook Time: 10 mins, Servings: 4, Serving Size: 1

Ingredients
- Minced Pork 500 g
- Red Onion 1 Small
- Mustard 1 Tsp
- Honey 2 Tsp
- Garlic Puree 1 Tsp
- Pork Seasoning 1 Tsp
- Salt and Pepper

Instructions
- Red onion peeled and finely sliced.
- Make a paste out of all the ingredients in a food processor and season the pork chops.
- Meatballs may be made with a meatball press. Mix them with some oat flour if necessary.
- Air-fry your pork meatballs for 10 Mins at 360 degrees Fahrenheit in an air fryer.
- Serve as soon as possible.

Nutrition Value
Calories: 327 Kcal, Carb: 28 g, Protein: 35 g, Fat: 17.5 g
Storage Suggestion: You can store it in the refrigerator for 6-7 days.

Pork Chops with Broccoli

Prep Time: 10 Mins, Cook Time: 10 min, Servings: 2, Serving Size: 1

Ingredients
- Bone-in pork chops 2 5 ounce
- Divided avocado oil 2 tbsp
- Paprika 1/2 tsp
- Onion Powder 1/2 tsp
- Garlic powder 1/2 tsp
- Divided salt 1 tsp
- Broccoli florets 2 cups
- Minced garlic two cloves

Instructions
- A 350°F air fryer is used. Spray basket with non-stick spray.
- Add a tbsp of oil on each side of the pork chops before cooking.
- Pork chops should be seasoned with onion powder, paprika, garlic powder, and half a tsp of salt on each side.
- Cook the pork chops for five Mins in the air fryer basket.
- Garlic, broccoli, and the remaining 1/2 tsp salt and 1 tbsp oil may be added to the dish while the pork chops cook and then tossed to coat.
- Turn the pork chops in your air fryer.
- Return the broccoli to the air fryer once placed in a basket.
- Stir the broccoli halfway through the cooking time.
- Please remove it from the air fryer to serve the meal and do so safely.

Nutrition Value
Calories: 310 Kcal, Carb: 31.3 g, Protein: 39.4 g, Fat: 17.9 g
Storage Suggestion: You can store it in the refrigerator for 7-8 days.

Air-Fryer Loaded Pork Burritos

Prep Time: 5 Mins, Cook Time: 10 mins, Servings: 6, Serving Size: 1

Ingredients
- Thawed limeade concentrates ¾ cup.
- Olive oil 1 tbsp
- Divided salt 2 tsp
- Divided pepper 1-1/2 tsp
- Boneless pork loin 1-1/2 lb
- Chopped seeded plum tomatoes 1 cup.
- Chopped green pepper, one small.
- Chopped onion, one small.
- Minced fresh coriander ¼ cup + 1/3 cup.
- Seeded & chopped jalapeno pepper, 1.
- Lime juice 1 tbsp
- Garlic powder ¼ tsp
- Uncooked long-grain rice 1 cup
- Shredded Monterey jack cheese 3 cups
- Warmed tortillas six flour
- Rinsed & drained black beans, one can.
- Sour cream 1-1/2 cups
- Cooking spray

Instructions
- Mix the limeade concentrate, oil, 1/2 tsp pepper, and 1 tsp salt with pork in a large dish; season to taste. Refrigerate for twenty Mins after flipping to set the coating.
- The remaining salt and pepper and 1/4 cup of cilantro go into the remaining tomato, onion, and green pepper.
- When it comes to cooking rice, follow the directions on the box.

Keep it warm by adding the remaining coriander.
- Toss the marinade in the trash. A 350°F air fryer is used. Put the pork in an air fryer basket in batches on an oiled tray, one layer at a time. Apply cooking spray to the surface. Cook for 8 to 10 Mins, turning halfway through until the pork is no longer pink.
- Every tortilla should be drizzled with a third of a cup of cheese. Layer each with half a cup of rice mixture, a quarter cup of salsa, a quarter cup of black beans, and a quarter cup of sour cream. Then, top with about half a cup of pork. Fold the edges and the ends of the filling inward. Serve with any remaining salsa.

Nutrition Value
Calories: 276 Kcal, Carb: 29.3 g, Protein: 35.4 g, Fat: 12.5 g
Storage Suggestion: You can store it in the refrigerator for 3-4 days.

Mustard Glazed Air Fryer Pork Tenderloin

Prep Time: 10 Mins, Cook Time: 18 mins, Servings: 4, Serving Size: 1

Ingredients
- Pork tenderloin 1 1.5 lb
- Minced garlic 1 tbsp
- Salt ¼ tsp
- Black pepper fresh cracked ⅛ tsp
- Yellow mustard ¼ cup
- Brown sugar 3 tbsp
- Italian seasoning 1 tsp
- Dried rosemary 1 tsp

Instructions
- Clean and dry the pork tenderloin. Using a sharp knife, slit the top of the tenderloin. Put sliced garlic in the incisions. Add salt and pepper to the meat.
- Small bowl: Whisk together the Italian spice, rosemary & mustard brown sugar. Pour the mustard mixture on the pork and heat it for a few Mins. Marinate it for at least two hrs in the refrigerator.
- Put the pork tenderloin in the air fryer basket that has been greased. When a fast-read meat thermometer reads 145 degrees F, cook for 18 to 20 Mins at 400 degrees Fahrenheit until the internal temperature is reached.
- After removing it from the Air Fryer, allow it to rest for five Mins before slicing.

Nutrition Value
Calories: 312 Kcal, Carb: 25.3 g, Protein: 36.2 g, Fat: 15.3 g
Storage Suggestion: You can store it in the refrigerator for 8-10 days.

Breaded Air Fryer Pork Chops

Prep Time: 10 Mins, Cook Time: 12 Mins, Servings: 4, Serving Size: 1

Ingredients
- Cut pork chops 4, around 24 oz.
- Cooking spray non-fat

Ingredients for Liquid Dredge Station:
- Beaten one egg.
- Water ¼ cup

Ingredients for Dry Dredge Station:
- Panko breadcrumbs 1 cup
- Paprika 4 tsp
- Dried parsley 2 tsp
- Garlic powder 1/2 tsp
- Black pepper 1/2 tsp
- Cayenne pepper ¼ - 1/2 tsp
- Dry mustard ¼ tsp
- Salt 1/2 tsp

Instructions
- Trim the fat off the chops before cooking. Water may be used to remove certain bone fragments.
- Prepare a dredging station: In a dish or baking pan, mix one egg with water and whip it until it becomes a smooth mixture. The spices and Panko breadcrumbs should be mixed in a separate bowl or baking dish.
- If you're using an extra flour dredge, prepare the third pan with flour.
- Coat Your Grizzly Ribs Using the optional flour step, coat a chop in flour first. Remove any excess flour by sifting. Pork chops may be coated in an egg wash using this method. If you don't want to utilize the flour, just go on to the next step.
- Put the chops in the egg wash and turn them over to moist all sides. Finally, coat the chops on both sides with the crumb mixture.
- Put the chops in the Air Fryer: Put the chops in the Air Fryer pan. Use a small amount of non-stick cooking oil to coat the surface lightly. If necessary, add a wire rack and shut the drawer into the fryer for the second stack of pork chops.
- Your Chops are ready: Twelve Mins at 380 degrees Fahrenheit is the ideal cooking time. Set the timer for twelve Mins and the temperature to 380 degrees F for your Chops to be ready to serve. Flip the chops halfway through the cooking time and lightly coat them with cooking spray. Keep cooking with the drawer closed. The chops are done when the internal temperature reaches 145 ° F, and the center is no longer pink.
- Take a break from it all: Serve the chops after 3 Minutes of resting time.

Nutrition Value
Calories: 373 Kcal, Carb: 26.5 g, Protein: 38.5 g, Fat: 24.3 g
Storage Suggestion: You can store it in the refrigerator for 1-2 days.

Air Fryer Chinese Salt & Pepper Pork Chops

Prep Time: 10 Mins, Cook Time: 15 mins, Servings: 1-2, Serving Size: 1

Ingredients
- Pork Chops
- White Egg 1
- Sea Salt 1/2 tsp
- Freshly Ground Black Pepper ¼ tsp
- Potato Starch ¾ cup
- Oil Mister 1
- Stir Fry

- Sliced (stems removed) Jalapeño Pepper 2
- Sliced Scallions 2
- Canola Oil 2 Tbsp
- Sea Salt 1 tsp
- Freshly Ground Black Pepper ¼ tsp
- Chicken Fryer Cast Iron

Instructions

- Apply a thin layer of oil to the air fryer basket.
- Whisk egg whites with salt and pepper into a frothy mixture in a medium-sized bowl. Make cutlets by slicing pork chops in half and patting them dry with paper towels. Place the pork chops in a bowl with the beaten egg whites. Completely encircle. Let it sit for at least 20 Mins before serving.
- Pour Potato Starch over pork chops in a large bowl. Pork chops should be dredged with Potato Starch. Remove the pork from the casing and place it in the Air Fryer Basket. Spray meat with oil.
- At 360 degrees, cook for nine Mins, occasionally shaking the basket and sprinkling the oil between shakes. The pork should be golden and crispy after six further Mins of cooking at 400 degrees.

Nutrition Value

Calories: 237 Kcal, Carb: 19.2 g, Protein: 29.6 g, Fat: 14.3 g
Storage Suggestion: You can store it in the refrigerator for 4-5 days.

Air-Fryer Pork Schnitzel

Prep Time: 10 Mins, Cook Time: 10 Mins, Servings: 4, Serving Size: 1

Ingredients

- All-purpose flour ¼ cup
- Seasoned salt 1 tsp
- Pepper ¼ tsp
- Egg 1
- Milk 2 tbsp
- Dry breadcrumbs ¾ cup
- Paprika 1 tsp
- Sirloin cutlets four pork
- Cooking spray

Dill Sauce
- All-purpose flour 1 tbsp
- Chicken broth ¾ cup
- Sour cream 1/2 cup
- Dill weed ¼ tsp

Instructions

- Preheated air fryer to 375 degrees. Combine the flour, salt, and pepper in a large bowl. In a separate dish, mix the egg and milk until smooth. Combine breadcrumbs and paprika in a third bowl.
- 1 Lb of pork cutlets, hammered to a thickness of 0.25 inches using a meat mallet. Cutlets should be coated on both sides with the flour mixture; brush off any excess. To coat, dip in an egg mixture, then pat the mixture into a crumb mixture until it adheres.
- Place the pork in a single layer on a slippery surface in an air-fryer basket. 4-5 Mins till golden brown. Spray cooking spray on the other side. A golden-brown color may be achieved in 4 to 5 Mins of cooking time. To serve, transfer to a serving dish and keep warm.
- On the other hand, stir flour and broth until smooth in a pot. Stir frequently as you bring the mixture to a simmer; cook and stir for two Mins or until thickened. Turn the thermostat down a notch. Heat through by adding sour cream and dill (do not simmer). Serve it with a pork dish.

Nutrition Value

Calories: 369 Kcal, Carb: 32.1 g, Protein: 39.4 g, Fat: 23.2 g
Storage Suggestion: You can store it in the refrigerator for 4-5 days.

Raspberry Balsamic Pork Chops

Prep Time: 30 Mins, Cook Time: 20 Mins, Servings: 4, Serving Size: 1

Ingredients

- 4 bone-in smoked pork chops
- Balsamic vinegar: 1/3 cup
- Milk: ¼ cup
- Breadcrumbs: 1 cup

- 2 eggs
- Chopped pecans: 1 cup
- Brown sugar: 2 tbsp
- Concentrate orange juice: 1 tbsp
- All-purpose flour: ¼ of cup
- Raspberry jam, seedless: 2 tbsp

Instructions

- Preheat the air fryer to 400 degrees Fahrenheit.
- Combine the milk and eggs in a bowl.
- Mix breadcrumbs and pecans in a separate bowl.
- The chops should be dipped in flour, then egg mixture, and finally pecan mixture.
- Spray the air fryer's basket with oil, then put the pork chops evenly in the basket.
- 145 degrees Fahrenheit should be reached in the meat after 12 to 15 Mins of cooking time. Cook the chops on the other side for about a half hr.
- Add the other ingredients to a saucepan and bring to a boil for 6 to 8 Mins or until thickened.
- Serve immediately.

Nutrition Value

Calories: 579 Kcal, Carb: 36 g, Protein: 32 g, Fat: 36 g
Storage Suggestion: You can store it in the refrigerator for 5-6 days.

Jamaican Jerk Pork Chops

Prep Time: 25 Mins, Cook Time: 10 Mins, Servings: 2, Serving Size: 1
Nutrition per serving: Calories 368 |Carbs 32 g| Protein 28 g |Fat 14 g

Ingredients

- Peach preserves: ¼ cup
- Half of the orange pepper
- 4 thin-cut, boneless pork loin chops
- Softened butter: 1 tbsp
- Caribbean jerk seasoning: 3 tsp
- Half of the red pepper
- Salt: 1/2 tsp
- Pepper: ¼ tsp
- Half of the yellow pepper

Instructions

- The air fryer should be preheated to 350 degrees.
- Set aside a dish to combine the peach preserves and butter.
- Pork chops should be seasoned with herbs and spices. Spray the basket of the air fryer with oil.
- Using an air fryer, cook seasoned chops in batches for 2 to 3 Mins on each side. Keep them warm by bringing them outside.
- Thinly slice the bell peppers.
- Cook for 5 to 6 Mins in an air fryer until golden brown and crisp-tender. Once or twice, give the bin a shake.
- Back in the air fryer, re-apply butter to the steaks and cook until done to your liking.
- Cook for about a Min and a half to two Mins.
- Serve over rice and accompanied with a side of peppers.

Nutrition Value
Calories: 368 Kcal, Carb: 32 g, Protein: 28 g, Fat: 14 g
Storage Suggestion: You can store it in the refrigerator for 3-4 days.

Loaded Pork Burritos

Prep Time: 20 Mins, Cook Time: 25 Mins, Servings: 6, Serving Size: 1

Ingredients
- Olive oil: 1 tbsp
- Salt: 2 tsp
- Concentrate limeade: ¾ cup
- 1 and a 1/2 tsp of pepper
- Chopped plum tomatoes: 1 cup (without seeds)
- 1 diced green pepper
- 1 and a half lb of pork loin, (boneless) thinly cut strips
- 1 diced onion
- 1 can of (15 oz.) Black beans, drained & rinsed
- 1 jalapeno chopped without seeds
- Chopped fresh cilantro: ¼ cup + 1/3 cup
- 6 flour tortillas (12")
- Jack cheese, shredded: 3 cups
- Lime juice: 1 tbsp
- Garlic powder: ¼ tsp
- Uncooked rice, long grain: 1 cup
- 1 and a 1/2 cups of sour cream

Instructions
- Salt (1 tsp), lime concentrate, and a 1/2 tsp of pepper are mixed in a bowl and added to the meat. Cover and refrigerate for about 20 Mins.
- Add the green pepper, jalapeno, black pepper, cilantro (1/4 cup), tomatoes, black pepper, onion, garlic powder, salt, and lime juice to a large bowl. Stir with salt and pepper to taste. Set it away for later use.
- Follow the package instructions for cooking the rice. Stir in the cilantro until it is evenly distributed throughout the mixture.
- The air fryer should be preheated to 350 degrees.
- Place the pork in an equal layer in the air fryer basket and spray with oil. Flipping halfway through, cook for 8 to 10 Mins.
- Place a warmed tortilla on a clean table, top with a third of a cup of cheese, a quarter cup of salsa, a quarter cup of sour cream, a quarter cup of beans, and a quarter cup of pork.
- Serve the rolls hot or cold.

Nutrition Value
Calories: 910 Kcal, Carb: 82 g, Protein: 50 g, Fat: 42 g
Storage Suggestion: You can store it in the refrigerator for 1-2 days.

Pork Schnitzel

Prep Time: 10 Mins, Cook Time: 20 Mins, Servings: 4, Serving Size: 1

Ingredients
- Pork sirloin cutlets: 4 (4 oz. Each)
- All-purpose flour: ¼ cup
- Black pepper: ¼ tsp
- 1 egg
- Paprika: 1 tsp
- Seasoned salt: 1 tsp
- Milk: 2 tbsp
- Breadcrumbs, dry: ¾ cup

Dill sauce
- Chicken broth: ¾ cup
- All-purpose flour: 1 tbsp
- Dill weed: ¼ tsp
- Sour cream: 1/2 cup

Instructions
- Preheat your air fryer to 375 degrees Fahrenheit.
- Mix flour, seasoned salt, and black pepper in a bowl.
- Mix the milk and egg in a separate dish.
- In a separate dish, combine breadcrumbs and paprika.
- First, use flour to coat the pork. Then, use an egg wash and breadcrumbs to finish the coating. Make sure they're well-coated.
- Cutlets should be sprayed with oil before being placed in the air fryer's basket and cooking for 4 to 5 Mins. Flip and cook for another 5 Mins.
- Stir broth and flour together in a saucepan until smooth. Let it simmer for two Mins, then remove from the heat.
- Don't let it come to a boil when you add the dill and sour cream; keep the heat moderate.
- With dill sauce, serve the cutlets.

Nutrition Value
Calories: 309 Kcal, Carb: 17 g, Protein: 30 g, Fat: 13 g
Storage Suggestion: You can store it in the refrigerator for 7-8 days.

Juicy Pork Chops

Prep Time: 25 Mins, Cook Time: 20 Mins, Servings: 4, Serving Size: 1

Ingredients
- Dijon mustard: 1 tbsp
- 4 centers cut, boneless pork chops
- 1 egg
- Onion powder: 1/2 tsp
- Panko breadcrumbs: 1/2 cup
- Garlic powder: 1/2 tsp
- Dry breadcrumbs: ¼ cup
- Kosher salt: 1 tsp
- Parmesan cheese, grated: ¼ cup

Instructions

- Preheat the air fryer to 400 degrees Fahrenheit.
- Rub pork chops gently with salt before cooking.
- Mix mustard and egg in a bowl.
- Garlic powder, breadcrumbs, onion powder, and Parmesan cheese should be combined in a zip-top bag.
- Well, shake the bag.
- Pour egg mixture over pork chops, then coat with breadcrumbs. To ensure an equal coating, shake the bag.
- Put two chops in the air fryer's basket and coat them with oil.
- The internal temperature should be 145 F after six Mins of cooking, so turn them over and cook for another six Mins.
- Serve the remainder of the meal when it has been finished cooking.

Nutrition Value
Calories: 569 Kcal, Carb: 17 g, Protein: 32 g, Fat: 40 g
Storage Suggestion: You can store it in the refrigerator for 6-7 days.

Boneless Pork Chop

Prep Time: 20 Mins, Cook Time: 15 Mins, Servings: 2, Serving Size: 1

Ingredients
- 2 pork chops (boneless and 1.25-inch thick)
- Pork Rub: 2 tsp
- Salt & black pepper, to taste

Instructions
- Preheat the air fryer to 400 degrees Fahrenheit.
- Pork should be seasoned with pork rub, salt, and black pepper.
- Cook the chops for six Mins in the air fryer.
- Cook the chops for 5 to 8 Mins on the other side, or until they reach an internal temperature of 135 to 145 degrees Fahrenheit.
- Before serving, allow the chops to rest.

Nutrition Value
Calories: 258 Kcal, Carb: 19.5 g, Protein: 19 g, Fat: 11 g
Storage Suggestion: You can store it in the refrigerator for 5-6 days.

Gingery Pork Meatballs

Prep Time: 15 Mins, Cook Time: 30 Mins, Servings: 4, Serving Size: 1

Ingredients
Noodles
- Half cucumber, slice into matchsticks
- 6 oz. of rice noodles
- 1 carrot, slice into matchsticks
- Sesame dressing: 1/2 cup
- 1 scallion, cut into thin slices
- Chopped cilantro: ¼ cup

Meatballs
- 1 lb. of ground pork
- Grated lime zest: 2 tsp
- 1 egg
- 1 and a 1/2 tbsp of honey
- Fish sauce: 1 tsp
- Lime juice: 2 tbsp
- Grated ginger: 1 tbsp
- Chopped cilantro: ¼ cup
- Salt, to taste
- 1 jalapeño, chopped without seeds
- 1 minced clove of garlic
- Panko: 1/2 cup
- 2 scallions, chopped

Instructions
- Follow the package instructions for cooking the noodles. Put the items in a bowl and toss to combine. It's time to put it away.
- Add lime juice, salt (1/2 tsp), fish sauce, egg, honey, zest, and panko to a mixing bowl and combine well. Allow the mixture to sit for 60 seconds before sprinkling the powdered sugar.
- Stir in the jalapeño, garlic, ginger, and scallions after they've been cooked down a little. Add meat and cilantro and stir well.
- Air-fry the meatballs in the basket with the oil splashed on top.
- Cook for 8–12 Mins at 400°F.
- With noodles, serve the meatballs.

Nutrition Value
Calories: 620 Kcal, Carb: 60 g, Protein: 22 g, Fat: 31.5 g
Storage Suggestion: You can store it in the refrigerator for 7-8 days.

Toast Cups with Air-Fried Ham and Egg

Prep Time: 6-7 Mins, Cook Time: 15 Mins, Servings: 6, Serving Size: 1

Ingredients
- 4 ramekins
- a dozen eggs
- (8 slices) Toast
- 2 Ham Slicing's
- a stick of butter
- sodium chloride
- cayenne

Instructions
- Butter the interior of the ramekin generously using a frying brush. The toast cups are much simpler to remove from the ramekins if they have extra butter on them.
- You may use a rolling pin or your hand to flatten eight slices of bread. Flatten it out as much as you can.
- You may use a piece of flattened bread to line the insides. Overwhelming amounts of bread are likely to collapse inwards. Pinch the additional folds, on the other hand, to improve the cup's quality.
- Stack two pieces of bread, one flattened and the other pressed flat, on top of each other. Slice two slices of ham into eight pieces.
- Fill each ramekin halfway with ham pieces. See the figure above for a visual illustration.
- Crack an egg into each bread cup.
- Add a dash of salt and freshly ground black pepper to each egg before serving.
- You may also add cheese to the bread cup (as seen above). One tiny piece of cheddar cheese, sliced into slices, was all I needed.
- Use an Air Fryer to cook the ramekins for 15 Mins at 160 degrees Fahrenheit. A pre-heated Air fryer isn't necessary.

- Using tea towels, silicone tongs, or any kind of kitchen contraception that keeps your fingers out of the sun, remove the ramekins from the Air fryer and serve immediately.
- This method was used to remove toast cups that had been lodged in their muffin pans by cutting around the sides of the pans with a small knife, just in case any bread had become lodged there.

Nutrition Value
Calories: 510 Kcal, Carb: 53 g, Protein: 41.6 g, Fat: 26.3 g
Storage Suggestion: You can store it in the refrigerator for 2-3 days.

Air-Fryer Sweet and Sour Pork

Prep Time: 5 Mins, Cook Time: 7-8 Mins, Servings: 2, Serving Size: 1

Ingredients
- 1/2 cup, undrained Unsweetened crushed pineapple
- 1/2 cup Cider vinegar
- 1/4 cup Sugar
- 1/4 cup packed dark brown sugar
- 1/4 cup Ketchup
- 1 tbsp Reduced-sodium soy sauce
- 1-1/2 tsp of Dijon mustard
- 1/2 tsp of Garlic powder
- (3/4 lb) Pork tenderloin (1 halved)
- 1/8 tsp salt
- 1/8 tsp of Pepper
- Optional sliced green onions
- Cooking spray

Instructions
- Add all of the ingredients to a saucepan and heat through. Lower the heat once it reaches a boil. Cook, stirring periodically, for 6 to 8 Mins with the lid off.
- The fryer should be preheated to 350 degrees. Season the pork with salt and pepper. Spray the cooking spray on the pork before placing it in the air fryer basket on a prepared baking sheet. Before the meat begins to brown, cook for 7-8 Mins. Serve the pork with two tsp of the sauce. Cook for another 10 to 12 Mins, or until a thermometer inserted at least 145 degrees Fahrenheit into the pork registers. Slicing pork should be delayed for at least five Mins. Serve with the remaining sauce. Green onion slices may be added as desired.

Nutrition Value
Calories: 376 Kcal, Carb: 28.3 g, Protein: 32.1 g, Fat: 21.2 g
Storage Suggestion: You can store it in the refrigerator for 4-5 days.

Low Carb Pork Dumplings with Dipping Sauce

Prep Time: 30 mins, Cook Time: 20 mins, Servings: 6, Serving Size: 1

Ingredients
- 18 dumpling wrappers
- 1 tsp olive oil
- Bok choy: 4 cups (chopped)
- Rice vinegar: 2 tbsp
- Diced ginger: 1 tbsp
- Crushed red pepper: 1/4 tsp
- Diced garlic: 1 tbsp
- Lean ground pork: 1/2 cup
- Cooking spray
- Lite soy sauce: 2 tsp
- Honey: 1/2 tsp
- Toasted sesame oil: 1 tsp
- Finely chopped scallions

Instructions
- Bok choy should be cooked for six Mins in olive oil in a big pan before adding the garlic and ginger and cooking for one more Min. Pat any remaining oil from the mixture with a paper towel once you've moved it.
- Crush red pepper and add lean ground pork to the bok choy combination. Mix well.
- In the center of each dumpling wrapper, place a tbsp of filling. Seal the edges with water and then crimp them.
- The air fryer basket should be sprayed with a light coat of cooking before the dumplings are placed in the basket and cooked for 12 Mins at 375 degrees Fahrenheit.
- Sauce: in the meantime, combine sesame oil with rice vinegar and scallions in a dish.
- The sauce should accompany the dumplings.

Nutrition Value
Calories: 140 Kcal, Carb: 9 g, Protein: 12 g, Fat: 5 g
Storage Suggestion: You can store it in the refrigerator for 5-6 days.

Air Fryer Pork Taquitos

Prep Time: 10 Mins, Cook Time: 20 Mins, Servings: 10, Serving Size: 1

Ingredients
- Pork tenderloin: 3 cups, cooked & shredded
- Cooking spray
- Shredded mozzarella: 2 and 1/2 cups, fat-free
- 10 small tortillas
- Salsa for dipping
- One juice of a lime

Instructions
- Set the air fryer to 380 degrees Fahrenheit before preparing the food.
- Mix the meat with the lime juice thoroughly.
- To soften the tortilla, microwave it for five seconds with a moist cloth over it.
- Roll up the tortilla firmly after adding the pork mixture and cheese on top.
- Grill or broil tortillas till golden brown.
- Spray the tortillas with oil. Flip the tortillas halfway through the cooking process to ensure even browning.
- This dish is best served with a side of salad greens.

Nutrition Value
Calories: 253 Kcal, Carb: 10 g, Protein: 20 g, Fat: 18 g
Storage Suggestion: You can store it in the refrigerator for 6-7 days.

Gluten-Free Air Fryer Chicken Brown Rice

Prep Time: 10 mins, Cook Time: 20 mins, Servings: 2, Serving Size: 1

Ingredients
- Olive Oil Cooking Spray
- Chicken Breast: 1 Cup, Diced & Cooked &
- White Onion: ¼ cup chopped
- Celery: ¼ Cup chopped
- Cooked brown rice: 4 Cups
- Carrots: ¼ cup chopped

Instructions
- Using a piece of foil, place it on the air fryer's basket and roll it up from the sides to ensure that the air can circulate freely.
- The foil should be sprayed with olive oil. Mix the ingredients.
- Add all ingredients to the air fryer basket on top of the foil.
- Spray the mixture with olive oil.
- At 390F, cook for 5 Mins.
- Toss the mixture in the air fryer after it has been opened.
- At 390F, cook for another five Mins.
- Serve immediately after removing from the air fryer.

Nutrition Value
Calories: 350 Kcal, Carb: 20 g, Protein: 22 g, Fat: 6 g

Storage Suggestion: You can store it in the refrigerator for 1-2 days.

Air Fryer Whole Wheat Crusted Pork Chops

Prep Time: 10 Mins Cook Time: 12 Mins, Servings: 4, Serving Size: 1

Ingredients
- Whole-wheat breadcrumbs: 1 cup
- Salt: ¼ tsp
- Pork chops: 2-4 pieces (center cut and boneless)
- Chili powder: 1/2 tsp
- Parmesan cheese: 1 tbsp
- Paprika: 1½ tsp
- One egg beaten
- Onion powder: 1/2 tsp
- Granulated garlic: 1/2 tsp
- Pepper, to taste

Instructions
- Preheat your air fryer to 400 degrees Fahrenheit.
- Pork chops should be rubbed with kosher salt on both sides and allowed to rest before cooking.
- Add the beaten egg to a large bowl and mix well.
- The following ingredients should be combined well: shredded Parmesan cheese; breadcrumbs; garlic powder; paprika; chili powder; and onion powder
- Egg and breadcrumb mixture on pork chops
- Oil your air fryer and cook it.
- Cook for 12 Mins at 400 degrees Fahrenheit. Halfway through, turn it over. Cook for a further six Mins.
- This dish is best served with a side of salad greens.

Nutrition Value
Calories: 425 Kcal, Carb: 19 g, Protein: 31 g, Fat: 20 g

Storage Suggestion: You can store it in the refrigerator for 4-5 days.

Air Fryer Pork Chop & Broccoli

Prep Time: 20 Mins, Cook Time: 20 Mins, Servings: 2, Serving Size: 1

Ingredients
- Broccoli florets: 2 cups
- Bone-in pork chop: 2 pieces
- Paprika: 1/2 tsp
- Avocado oil: 2 tbsp
- Garlic powder: 1/2 tsp
- Onion powder: 1/2 tsp
- Two cloves of crushed garlic
- Salt: 1 tsp divided

Instructions
- Set the air fryer to 350 degrees Fahrenheit. Cooking oil should be sprayed into the basket.
- Paprika and half-tsp salt is added to a dish along with one tbsp oil and stirred until thoroughly combined. Rub the spice mixture over both sides of the pork chops.
- Cook the pork chops for five Mins in the air fryer basket.
- Meanwhile, combine 1 tbsp oil, 1 clove of garlic, 1/2 tsp salt, and the broccoli in a large bowl and toss to combine.
- After five Mins, flip the pork chop and add the broccoli.
- Serve hot, fresh, and hot from the air fryer.

Nutrition Value
Calories: 483 Kcal, Carb: 12 g, Protein: 23 g, Fat: 20 g

Storage Suggestion: You can store it in the refrigerator for 4-5 days.

Air Fryer Cheesy Pork Chops

Prep Time: 5 Mins, Cook Time: 8 Mins, Servings: 2, Serving Size: 1

Ingredients
- 4 lean pork chops
- Salt: 1/2 tsp
- Garlic powder: 1/2 tsp
- Shredded cheese: 4 tbsp
- Chopped cilantro

Instructions
- Set the air fryer to 350 degrees Fahrenheit.
- Rub the pork chops with salt, garlic, and cilantro. Using an air fryer to cook for Four Mins should be plenty. Cook for a further two Mins on the other side.
- Cook for another two Mins, or until the cheese has melted, on top of them.
- This dish is best served with a side of salad greens.

Nutrition Value
Calories: 467 Kcal, Carb: 8 g, Protein: 61 g, Fat: 22 g

Storage Suggestion: You can store it in the refrigerator for 8-10 days.

Air Fried Jamaican Jerk Pork

Prep Time: 10 Mins, Cook Time: 20 Mins, Servings: 4, Serving Size: 1

Ingredients
- Pork, cut into three-inch pieces
- Jerk paste: ¼ cup

Instructions

- Pork slices should be coated with jerk paste before cooking.
- Refrigerate it for at least four hrs before serving. Or for a longer period.
- Preheat the air fryer to 390 degrees Fahrenheit before preparing the food. Olive oil may be sprayed on.
- Allow the meat to remain at room temperature for 20 Mins before placing it in the air fryer.
- After 20 Mins of air frying at 390 F, turn the food over.
- After removing the chicken from the air fryer, let it rest for 10 Mins before slicing it.
- Include microgreens on the menu.

Nutrition Value
Calories: 234 Kcal, Carb: 12 g, Protein: 31 g, Fat: 9 g
Storage Suggestion: You can store it in the refrigerator for 3-4 days.

Chapter 5: Lamb Recipes

Ultimate Air Fryer Lamb Burgers

Prep Time: 15 Mins, Cook Time: 18 Mins, Servings: 4, Serving Size: 1

Ingredients

Lamb Burgers
- Minced Lamb 650 g
- Garlic Puree 2 Tsp
- Harissa Paste 1 Tsp
- Moroccan Spice 1 Tbsp
- Salt & Pepper

Greek Dip
- Greek Yoghurt 3 Tbsp
- Moroccan Spice 1 Tsp
- Oregano ½ Tsp
- Small Lemon 1 juice

Instructions
- In a medium mixing bowl, combine all lamb burgers and mix well until all lamb mince is well-seasoned.
- Using a burger press, form the minced lamb into burger shapes.
- Cook your lamb patties for 18 Mins at 360°F/180°C in an air fryer.
- While they're cooking, prepare the Greek dip. Lamb burgers are served with a Greek dip that has been combined with a fork.

Nutrition Value
Calories: 256 Kcal, Carb: 13 g, Protein: 25 g, Fat: 7.2 g
Storage Suggestion: You can store it in the refrigerator for 5-6 days.

Chipotle Steak Tacos

Prep Time: 5Mins, Cook Time: 8 Mins, Servings: 4, Serving Size: 1

Ingredients

The Steak
- Flank steak 1.5 lb.
- Red Onion ½ cup
- Garlic 2 cloves crushed & peeled.
- Chipotle Chile in Adobo Sauce 1
- 1 tbsp Ancho Chile Powder
- 1 tsp Ground Cumin
- 1 tsp Dried Oregano
- 1 tbsp Olive Oil
- 1.5 tsp kosher salt
- Ground Black Pepper ½ tsp
- 2 tbsp of water

For Serving
- 1 cup Salsa
- Tortillas 8 flour, tortillas 6-inch, warmed
- ½ cup, Cotija cheese crumbled

Instructions
- Place the beef strips in a large mixing bowl or a resealable plastic bag. Combine chipotle Chili, onion, oregano, chili powder, garlic, cumin, olive oil, water, pepper, adobo sauce, and salt in a blender or food processor. Blend until completely smooth. Put the marinade over the meat, mix it in, close the bag, massage it to coat, and combine it properly. Marinate for thirty Mins at room temperature, then cover and refrigerate for twenty-four hrs.
- Remove the beef strips from the bag with tongs and place them in the air fryer basket. Remove the marinade and minimize the overlap as much as possible. Preheat the air fryer to 400°F for eight Mins, flipping the beef strips halfway through the cooking time. This should be done in batches.

Nutrition Value
Calories: 186 Kcal, Carb: 12 g, Protein: 6 g, Fat: 5 g
Storage Suggestion: You can store it in the refrigerator for 1-2 days.

Tender, Juicy Smoked BBQ Ribs

Prep Time: 10 Mins, Cook Time: 30 Mins, Servings: 4, Serving Size: 1

Ingredients
- One rack of ribs
- 1 tbsp liquid smoke
- 2-3 tbsp Pork rubs
- a pinch of salt and pepper
- ½ cup BBQ sauce

Instructions
- Remove the membrane off the rear of the ribs by peeling it away. It's a thin layer that is tough to remove. Sometimes, it may be peeled straight off. It may be readily cut and peeled away. Cut the ribs in half to make them easier to adjust in the air fryer.
- Brush liquid smoke on both sides of the ribs.
- On both sides, season with pork rub, pepper, and salt.
- Cover the ribs and put them aside at room temperature for thirty Mins.
- In the air fryer, place the ribs.
- Preheat oven to 360 degrees Fahrenheit and bake for 15 Mins.
- A fryer that cooks outside in the open. The ribs should be rotated. Cook for a total of 15 Mins more.
- Remove the ribs from the air fryer and set them aside. Drizzle the ribs with the BBQ sauce.

Nutrition Value
Calories: 476 Kcal, Carb: 28 g, Protein: 19 g, Fat: 12 g
Storage Suggestion: You can store it in the refrigerator for 2-3 days.

Za'atar Lamb Chops

Prep Time: 15 Mins, Cook Time:10 mins, Servings: 4, Serving Size:1

Ingredients
- Lamb loin chops 8, trimmed.
- Garlic three cloves, crushed.
- Extra-virgin olive oil 1 tsp
- Fresh lemon ½
- Kosher salt 1 ¼ tsp
- Za'atar 1 tbsp
- To taste, fresh ground pepper

Instructions
- Garlic and oil rubbed lamb chops
- Squash each side of the lemon and season with zaatar, black pepper, and salt.
- Preheat the air fryer to 400 degrees Fahrenheit. Cook in batches until the desired doneness is reached, about four to five Mins each side.

- Chops must contain 2 ½ oz. Raw meat on per bone.

Nutrition Value
Calories: 396 Kcal, Carb: 36 g, Protein: 24 g, Fat: 8 g
Storage Suggestion: You can store it in the refrigerator for 5-6 days.

Leg of lamb with Brussels Sprouts and Potato Quenelles

Prep Time: 35 Mins, Cook Time: 55 Mins, Servings: 4, Serving Size: 1

Ingredients

For lamb leg:
- 1 kg lamb leg
- 2 spoons oil groundnut
- 16 g of rosemary
- 16 g thyme lemon
- 1 clove garlic
- 600 g sprouts Brussels

For quenelles
- 4 potatoes large
- butter knob
- No milk
- Nutmeg

Instructions
- Stagger some rosemary & lemon thyme on the leg of lamb before roasting it. Put some oil from groundnuts on the thigh and rub it in. Cook your lamb for around 75 Mins within an Air fryer at 150°C.
- Quenelles de Pommes de Terre is a quick and easy side dish that can be made ahead of time and frozen. Add butter, milk, & nutmeg to the mashed potatoes & season to taste. Using two spoons, move the mashed potatoes from 1 spoon to another as you form the quenelles. You may create the quenelles ahead of time and cook them for 15 mins at 200° if you want. It just takes 8 Mins to make them from scratch.
- Mix the Brussels sprouts with honey and a neutral oil after cleaning and tailing them. Add fresh sprouts & frozen quenelles into the Air fryer 75 mins into the cooking time. 15 Mins at 200° for sprouts, lamb, & quenelles. Add the quenelles 7 mins after Brussels sprouts if you made them fresh.

Nutrition Value
Calories: 176 Kcal, Carb: 10.2 g, Protein: 7.9 g, Fat: 3.5 g
Storage Suggestion: You can store it in the refrigerator for 6-7 days.

Air Fryer Lamb Rack

Prep Time: 3 Mins, Cook Time: 12 Mins, Servings: 2, Serving Size: 1

Ingredients
- 2 lamb rack
- 2 tbsp rosemary dried
- 3 tbsp oil olive
- 1 tbsp thyme dried
- 1½ tsp garlic dried
- 1 tsp onion dried
- Salt & Pepper

Instructions
- Gather your ingredients into a small bowl and whisk them together. Mix to create a new substance.
- Racks of lamb should be de-fatted to prevent them from becoming tough. Apply the herb oil combination to the meat before serving.
- Before using the grill pan to place the lamb rack, Air Fryer, preheat your Air Fryer at 360°F for three Mins. You may place the lamb over the parchment-lined basket of Air Fryer.
- For a charred crust, begin by grilling flesh side down, then flip it over halfway through.
- Using a thermometer, check the rack of lamb's internal temperature after cooking it for 12 mins.
- Take the lamb out of your Air Fryer and let it cool. You may soften your meat by wrapping it in Al foil.

Nutrition Value
Calories: 761 Kcal, Carb: 36 g, Protein: 62 g, Fat: 56 g
Storage Suggestion: You can store it in the refrigerator for 6-7 days.

Air Fryer Mediterranean Lamb Chops

Prep Time: 15 Mins, Cook Time: 10 Mins, Servings: 4, Serving Size: 1

Ingredients
- 1 & ¼-1 & ½ lb lamb rack frenched

Marinade
- 1 tbsp Greek yogurt plain
- 2 tbsp avocado oil or olive oil
- 2 tsp garlic minced
- 2 tsp regular paprika
- 1 tsp powder cumin
- ⅛ tsp cinnamon ground
- ½ tsp pepper flakes red
- ¼ tsp pepper skip the cayenne
- 1 tsp lemon juice & zest
- ¾ tsp of salt
- ½ tsp black pepper freshly ground

Instructions
- Lay your lamb rack out on the cutting board and cut it into chops. Trim away any extra weight. Cut the bone into 8 equal-sized chops with a knife, following the contours of the bones as a guide. To remove extra moisture, blot dry chops with a paper towel.
- Add all of the marinade ingredients to a mixing bowl & whisk well.
- To prepare the marinated lamb chops, arrange them in a single layer on a platter or in a big dish. Brush your marinade liberally over lamb chops with a pastry brush, being sure to cover both sides for almost two hrs, cover & store in a cool, dry place.
- Fry the lamb chops in the air fryer as directed below: 390°F (200°C) is ideal for an air fryer. Let some room between lamb chops while laying them down. All of the lamb chops must fit inside one batch.
- For medium-rare, cook for around 7-9 Mins, turning halfway, while for medium-well, cook for around 10-12 Mins, turning halfway through. Be aware that the cooking process continues even when the meat is resting. Use

the meat thermometer to ensure proper doneness.
- According to the USDA guidelines, Lamb Chops should be cooked to a temperature of 125°F for rare, 135°F for medium-rare, and 145°F for medium-well.
- Take a five-Min break, and then continue. Serve: Rest your chops for around 5 Mins on a serving plate. This gives the fluids a chance to redistribute themselves. Serve with some Greek salad, tzatziki, and saffron or lemon rice.

Nutrition Value
Calories: 313 Kcal, Carb: 2 g, Protein: 20 g, Fat: 20 g
Storage Suggestion: You can store it in the refrigerator for 5-6 days.

Lamb Chop with Sauce

Prep Time: 15 Mins, Cook Time: 22 Mins, Servings 4, Serving Size: 1

Ingredients
- 1 bulb garlic
- 3 tbsp oil olive
- 1 tbsp finely chopped fresh oregano
- Sea salt
- black pepper Freshly ground
- 8 chops lamb

Instructions
- Heat your air fryer to around 200°C before using it. Put your garlic in a basket & coat it with olive oil. Set the timer for 12 Mins and put the basket in the air fryer. Roast your garlic unless it's done, then remove it from the oven.
- Add some pepper, sea salt, & olive oil to the herbs while they're still fresh. Allow the lamb chops to rest for five Mins after being thinly rubbed with a half-tsp of herb oil.
- Air fryer pre-heat to 200°C by removing the garlic bulb from the basket.
- Slide your basket into the air fryer with 4 lamb chops within. Time out for five Mins. Lamb chops roasted to perfection. They might still be crimson or pink on the inside. Roast the other lamb chops in the same manner & keep them hot in a dish while you finish the first batch.
- Rub the herb oil with garlic cloves, which should be squeezed between your thumb and index finger. Salt & pepper the mix well before serving.
- Serving suggestion: Garlic sauce over the lamb chops. With couscous & cooked zucchini, this dish is fantastic.

Nutrition Value
Calories: 346 Kcal, Carb: 23 g, Protein: 15 g, Fat: 3 g
Storage Suggestion: You can store it in the refrigerator for 4-5 days.

Air Fryer Lamb Cutlets

Prep Time: 5 Mins, Cook Time: 25 Mins, Servings: 6-8, Serving Size:1

Ingredients
- 600 grams cutlets lamb
- lemon Juice
- 1 tsp oregano dried
- 1 tbsp oil olive
- Salt & pepper

Instructions
- Combine all of the ingredients for the marinade in a mixing bowl & combine well.
- Rest for about five Mins, or place in the refrigerator for up to an hr. In the meanwhile, prepare your air fryer to 190°C/375°F.
- Cook your lamb cutlets within the air fryer basket on 190 deg C/375 deg F for around 10-15 Mins, or as directed by the manufacturer.
- Remove the basket from the air fryer and turn the lamb cutlets over.
- Remove any accumulated fat from the pan. To reduce the amount of smoke produced by the air fryer, do this.
- Return the air fryer basket to the oven & cook for an additional 5-10 Mins, unless the chicken is cooked to your preference.
- Cooked, let lamb cutlets cool for a few Mins inside the air fryer basket, then plate them.

Nutrition Value
Calories: 196 Kcal, Carb: 16 g, Protein: 21 g, Fat: 4.7 g
Storage Suggestion: You can store it in the refrigerator for 1-2 days.

Air Fryer Marinated Lamb Shoulder Chops (Paleo, Keto, Gluten-Free)

Prep Time: 5 Mins, Cook Time: 10 Mins, Servings: 5, Serving Size: 1 Plate

Ingredients
- ¼ cup olive oil extra virgin
- ¼ cup red wine dry
- 1 tbsp thyme leaves fresh
- 1 tbsp rosemary leaves chopped fresh
- 1 tbsp chopped mint leaves or fresh oregano
- 2 finely chopped cloves of garlic
- ½ tsp salt kosher
- 4 shoulder chops lamb
- 4 wedges lemon

Instructions
- Whisk the oil & wine together in a small bowl. Season with salt, rosemary, or oregano and thyme.
- Place your lamb chops inside a baking dish or a big, resealable plastic bag and bake for about 30 Mins. Using a spoon, apply the marinade evenly to the chops. Make sure the dish or bag is well-sealed. For 8-12 hrs, keep the lamb within the refrigerator.
- The lamb should be taken out of the fridge 30 minutes before cooking.
- For around 5 Mins, heat your air fryer to 390°F.
- Remove the lamb chops from the marinade. The marinade should be thrown away. 2 chops should be placed over a crisper plate or within a basket of an air fryer. Allow cooking 3 Mins longer. Cook your chops for a further 3 mins on the other side, or until an instant-

read meat thermometer registers 130–140°F.
- Tent the lamb chops with foil once they've been removed from the oven. Repeat with the remaining two chops.
- Lemon wedges & salad of bitter greens are a great accompaniment to the lamb.

Nutrition Value
Calories: 446 Kcal, Carb: 36 g, Protein: 28 g, Fat: 16.5 g
Storage Suggestion: You can store it in the refrigerator for 5-6 days.

Air Fryer Lamb Shanks

Prep Time: 10 Mins, Cook Time: 1 Hr & 20 Mins, Servings: 4, Serving Size: 1 g

Ingredients
- 4 shanks lamb
- 2 tsp oil olive
- 2 tsp crushed garlic
- 2 tsp of salt
- ½ tsp of pepper
- 1 tsp leaves rosemary
- 2 tsp of oregano
- 8.5 oz stock chicken

Instructions
- In a hot air fryer, raise the temperature to 200° C (390° F). You'll need to wait around five Mins to get the desired temperature.
- It is best to marinate the lamb shanks for at least an hr before cooking them.
- Cook for around 20 Mins in an air fryer.
- Add your chicken stock to an air fryer and lower the temperature to 150° C (300° F). One hr of cooking time.
- Halfway through the cooking time, flip your lamb shanks over.
- Serve!

Nutrition Value
Calories: 348 Kcal, Carb: 2 g, Protein: 55 g, Fat: 0.2 g
Storage Suggestion: You can store it in the refrigerator for 1-2 weeks.

Roasted rack of Lamb with a Macadamia Crust

Prep Time: 10 Mins, Cook Time: 30 Mins, Servings 4, Serving Size: 2

Ingredients
- 1 clove garlic
- 1 tbsp oil olive
- 800 g lamb rack
- salt & pepper
- 75 g macadamia nuts unsalted
- 1 tbsp breadcrumbs
- 1 tbsp fresh rosemary chopped
- 1 large egg

Instructions
- Grind the garlic into a paste. Make your garlic oil by combining olive oil with garlic. Season the lamb rack with pepper and salt after brushing it with oil.
- Set the Air fryer's temperature to 100 degrees Celsius.
- A bowl is all that is needed for this recipe. Add the rosemary & breadcrumbs and mix well. In a separate dish, beat the egg until smooth.
- Dip your lamb into it and shake off any excess using an egg mix. Apply the macadamia crust to the meat before cooking.
- Slide your Air fryer basket inside the Air fryer and put your covered lamb rack inside. The timer should be set for around 25 Mins now. Set a timer for five more Mins and raise the temperature to around 200° C after 25 Minutes. For around 10 mins before serving, take the meat out & cover it with Al foil.

Nutrition Value
Calories: 435 Kcal, Carb: 2 g, Protein: 26 g, Fat: 36 g
Storage Suggestion: You can store it in the refrigerator for 1 week.

Air Fryer Lamb Meatballs (Quick and Easy)

Prep Time: 5 Mins, Cook Time: 12 Mins, Servings: 4, Serving Size: 2

Ingredients
- 1 lb lamb ground
- 1 tsp cumin ground
- 2 tsp onion granulated
- 2 Tbsp parsley fresh
- ¼ tsp cinnamon ground
- Salt & pepper

Instructions
- Gather all ingredients for the dish in a bowl and mix well. Make sure all ingredients are well combined before continuing to mix.
- Assemble into balls of about one inch in diameter.
- In the air fryer basket, place lamb meatballs & cook for around 12-15 mins at 350 deg F. Make a half-shaking motion with the meatballs midway through the cooking process.

Nutrition Value
Calories: 328 Kcal, Carb: 1 g, Protein: 28 g, Fat: 22 g

Storage Suggestion: You can store it in the refrigerator for 2-3 days.

Air Fryer American Lamb Chops with Poblano Sauce

Prep Time: 10 Mins, Cook Time: 20 Mins, Servings: 6, Serving Size: 1

Ingredients

American Lamb
- 1 Lamb rack American
- ½ tsp salt sea
- ½ tsp pepper black
- 1 tsp powder chili
- ¼ tsp powder garlic
- ½ tsp of oregano
- 2 tbsp of oil

Potatoes
- 2 lb baby potatoes bag
- ½ tsp of salt
- ½ tsp of pepper
- 1 tsp powder chili
- ¼ tsp powder garlic
- ½ tsp of oregano
- 2 tbsp of oil

Poblano Sauce
- 3 charred poblano peppers
- 1 charred jalapeno pepper
- 2 & ½ tbsp juice lime
- 2 tbsp oil olive
- ½ tsp salt sea
- 1 chopped avocado
- 2/3 cup of cilantro
- 3 tbsp sour cream or yogurt
- 1 tbsp of honey

Serve
- slices Lime
- cilantro

Instructions
- First, prepare your air fryer potatoes by seasoning them with spices in a big bowl.
- Air fryer: 400°F. Pre-heat two Mins.
- Ten Mins within the air fryer is all that is needed to cook the potatoes. Remove the basket from the air fryer & shake it.
- For a further 6 to 10 Mins, based on the scale of the potatoes, please return them to the oven to air fry.
- Place them over a serving platter, top with cilantro, & serve immediately.
- Preheat your air fryer to 400°F.
- Both sides of the lamb chops should be liberally seasoned with spice and oil. The chops should be laid up in a thin layer on your air fryer tray.
- Remove your basket of air fryer after 8 Mins of air frying.
- Continue air frying your lamb chops for a further 4-8 Mins, based on how often you like your meat.
- In terms of overall time, a medium-rare at 400 degrees Fahrenheit is 12 Mins, whereas a medium at that temperature is 14 Mins.
- Make your poblano sauce as the lamb chops simmer.
- A food processor may combine all of the ingredients & make a creamy sauce.
- Take some time to serve the grilled lamb chops cooked in your air fryer with the poblano sauce & lime wedges.

Nutrition Value
Calories: 386 Kcal, Carb: 4 g, Protein: 28 g, Fat: 9.2 g

Storage Suggestion: You can store it in the refrigerator for 4-5 days.

Air Fryer Lamb Kofta

Prep Time: 15 Mins, Cook Time: 20 Mins, Servings: 4, Serving Size: 1

Ingredients

Tahini Sauce
- ¾ cup paste tahini
- 2 lemons Juice
- 2-3 coarsely chopped garlic cloves
- 1 & ½ tsp divided kosher salt

Lamb Kofta
- 2 tbsp bulgur wheat finely ground
- 1 lb lamb ground
- ½ minced yellow onion
- 1 tsp of coriander
- 1 tsp of cumin
- ½ tsp of pepper black
- ¼ tsp cinnamon ground
- Oil
- for serving Pita bread

Instructions
- Tahini sauce is made by grinding the lemon juice, tahini paste, garlic, and salt in a food processor or blender till the mixture becomes a paste. Add 1/2 cup of cold water to the blender and process it unless your sauce is creamy & pourable, about a Min and a half to two Mins. If the mix is too thick to pour, add up to extra cold water the same way, depending on the thickness of your tahini paste. Keep the sauce in the fridge until you're ready to use it.
- Combine the bulgur with 2 tbsp of extremely hot water in a heatproof dish. Stir using a fork after 7 Mins to ensure that all the water has been absorbed.
- When you're ready to assemble the kofta, add 1 tsp of salt with the

lamb, onion, softened bulgur, & spices in a large bowl & mix well with your hands.
- Form your lamb mix into eight evenly sized, firmly packed oval patties using wet hands to avoid sticking. For best results, refrigerate the patties for almost 30 Mins & up to 24 hrs.
- Preheat your air fryer at 400°F for 3 Mins before you're ideal for cooking the kofta. To keep the patties from sticking to this basket, coat it using oil and spray it down.
- As a precaution against the overburdened air fryer basket, thread patties on metal skewers before placing them in one layer.
- To cook the koftas, place them on a baking sheet and bake at 350 degrees Fahrenheit for 10 Mins, flipping them midway through cooking. Take another set of patties and do the same thing.
- Place your cooked kofta over a paper towel-lined platter to remove excess oil from the surface. Serve heated with a tahini sauce.

Nutrition Value
Calories: 306 Kcal, Carb: 3.1 g, Protein: 19 g, Fat: 7.5 g
Storage Suggestion: You can store it in the refrigerator for 2-3 days.

Air Fryer Mint Lamb with Toasted Hazelnuts and Peas

Prep Time: 5 mins, Cook Time: 35 mins, Servings: 4, Serving Size: 1

Ingredients
- 65 g of hazelnuts
- 650 g lamb shoulder
- 1 tbsp oil hazelnut
- 2 tbsp leaves chopped fresh mint
- 220 g peas frozen
- 85 ml of water
- 100 ml wine white
- sea salt & black pepper freshly cracked

Instructions
- Cook the hazelnuts for 10 minutes at 160 C in the Air Fryer with the lid closed. Air Fry hazelnuts and keep them away for later.
- Salt and pepper the lamb strips liberally in a large bowl, then toss them in the hazelnut oil.
- Arrange the mint leaves on the air fryer pan's handle side, then the seasoned lamb. Finally, top with the roasted hazelnuts.
- Put the lid & add the peas to the opposite side of the pan. Add the wine and water.
- For 25 Mins, cook on setting 7-wok.
- Remove the items from the pan and arrange them on a serving plate whenever they are ready. Serve immediately with your preferred side dishes, garnished with more mint leaves if desired.

Nutrition Value
Calories: 316 Kcal, Carb: 11 g, Protein: 24 g, Fat: 18 g
Storage Suggestion: You can store it in the refrigerator for 1-2 days.

Spicy Cumin Lamb Skewers

Prep Time: 5 Mins, Cook Time: 10 Mins, Servings: 4, Serving Size: 2

Ingredients
- 1 tbsp chili flakes red
- 1 tbsp seed cumin
- 2 tsp seed fennel
- 1 tsp salt kosher
- 2 tsp garlic granulated
- 1 ¼ lb. shoulder chops lamb
- 1 Tbsp oil vegetable
- 2 tsp dry sherry pale

Instructions
- Coarsely crush the cumin, chili flakes, & fennel seeds in the mortar & pestle. When you're done grinding, add your granulated garlic & kosher salt. Make sure all of the ingredients are well mixed.
- Keep a tiny amount of the spice blend in a separate container. Add the lamb to a medium bowl and toss with the leftover spice mixture, oil, & wine.
- Make sure to put the skewers within Air Fryer before cooking. For 10 Mins, air fried the skewers around 340°F on Rotisserie setting.
- Sprinkle the saved spice mixture (optional) on your skewers when they are almost done grilling & let them continue roasting.
- Immediately remove your skewers from the air fryer.

Nutrition Value
Calories: 406 Kcal, Carb: 9.8 g, Protein: 25.1 g, Fat: 12.2 g
Storage Suggestion: You can store it in the refrigerator for 1-2 weeks.

Spicy Lamb Sirloin Steak

Prep Time: 40 Mins, Cook Time: 15 Mins, Servings: 4, Serving Size: 1

Ingredients
- ½ chopped Onion
- 4 Ginger slices
- 5 Garlic cloves
- 1 tsp Masala Garam
- 1 tsp fennel ground
- 1 tsp Cinnamon Ground
- ½ tsp Cardamom Ground
- ½ & 1 tsp Pepper Cayenne
- 1 tsp Salt Kosher
- 1 lb sirloin steaks boneless lamb

Instructions
- In a blender, combine the rest of the ingredients, except for the lamb chops.
- To mince raw onion & combine all the ingredients, pulse & blend for around three or four Mins.
- Into a medium bowl, place your lamb chops. Make slashes in the meat and fat with a knife for the marinade to permeate more deeply.

- Add the mixed spice paste and thoroughly mix it up.
- The longer you leave it in the refrigerator, the better it will taste.
- Place your lamb steaks in such a thin layer within a basket of air fryer and cook for 15 Mins at 330F, turning halfway through.
- To serve medium-well, check the meat using a thermometer to ensure it's at least 150F.

Nutrition Value
Calories: 182 Kcal, Carb: 3 g, Protein: 24 g, Fat: 7 g
Storage Suggestion: You can store it in the refrigerator for 8-10 days.

Lamb Ribs in Air Fryer

Prep Time: 5 Mins, Cook Time: 20 Mins, Servings: 4, Serving Size: 1

Ingredients
- 8 ribs lamb

For seasoning
- ¼ cup oil olive
- 1 tsp fresh Rosemary lives
- 1 tsp fresh thyme
- 1 tsp fresh Oregano
- 1-2 minced garlic clove
- Salt & black pepper

Instructions
- Combine all seasoning ingredients in a bowl and whisk until well combined.
- Rub the meat with the mixture.
- Make a single layer of ribs.
- For 8 to 10 Mins, cook within the air fryer at 360F.

Nutrition Value
Calories: 346 Kcal, Carb: 23 g, Protein: 15 g, Fat: 3 g
Storage Suggestion: You can store it in the refrigerator for 4-5 days.

Air Fryer Lamb Loin Chops with Chimichurri Sauce

Prep Time: 5 Mins, Cook Time: 15 Mins, Servings: 3, Serving Size: 1

Ingredients
For Lamb Chops
- 1 lb chops lamb
- ½ tsp smoked paprika
- Salt & black pepper
- spray oil

Chimichurri Sauce
- ¼ cup oil olive
- 1/3 cup fresh parsley minced
- 1-2 crushed or minced cloves of garlic
- ¼ tsp salt
- ¼ tsp black pepper
- 1-2 pinches pepper flakes red
- 1 tbsp juice lemon

Instructions
- Add salt, pepper, pepper flakes, & lemon juice to a bowl and stir to incorporate. This is chimichurri sauce. Salt & pepper to taste.
- Apply a thin layer of oil to the lamb chops. Salt, smoked paprika, & black pepper are all that are needed to season lamb chops.
- Place the lamb chops in such a thin layer within the air fryer basket/tray, be careful not to overlap the meat. Spray basket/tray using oil spray.
- Air fry for 8 Mins at 380° F/195° C, then turn & air fry for an additional 4-8 Mins, or until cooked to your liking. Chops of lamb are served with a chimichurri sauce.
- Preheating the air fryer or frying in many batches may necessitate shortening the cooking time.

Nutrition Value
Calories: 469 Kcal, Carb: 2 g, Protein: 42 g, Fat: 32 g
Storage Suggestion: You can store it in the refrigerator for 8-10 days.

Black Folks Soul Food Lamb Chops

Prep Time:10 Mins, Cook Time:20 Mins, Servings: 8, Serving Size: 2

Ingredients
- 1 lamb rack
- 1 tbsp oil olive
- ½ tsp of salt
- ½ tsp of pepper
- ½ tsp rosemary dried
- 2-3 fresh sprigs of rosemary

Instructions
- Combine the salt, pepper, olive oil, & dried rosemary.
- Coat the rack of lamb with the mixture, concentrating the rub over the top side (the fat, meaty side).
- Place in your the air fryer lamb rack with the seasonings on it.
- For medium-rare chops, cook at 360° Fahrenheit for 20 Mins.
- Using a pair of scissors, cut the rack in lamb chops by placing a knife between each bone. Perform this step for each of the rack's cooked lamb chops.
- Serve the lamb chops dish right immediately with pure rosemary sprigs & enjoy!

Nutrition Value
Calories: 247 Kcal, Carb: 1 g, Protein: 9 g, Fat: 23 g
Storage Suggestion: You can store it in the refrigerator for 5-6 days.

Lamb with Lemon Garlic Marinade

Prep Time: 15 Min, Cook Time: 1 Hr, Servings: 4, Serving Size: 1

Ingredients
- 6 & ½-inch-thick loin chops lamb
- ½ cup fresh herbs chopped mixed
- ¼ cup garlic chopped
- 2 pits removed lemons sliced
- 1 tsp salt
- 5 tbsp olive oil extra-virgin
- pepper
- ¼ cup wine Cabernet

Instructions
- Add the ingredients above to a jar with a cover and place your lamb inside.
- A minimum of four hrs of marinating is required. Using an air fryer, heat the appliance to 400°F and begin cooking. Add your lamb chops to a basket of the air fryer & cook for around 7-9 Mins, turning halfway through cooking time.

- Cook till the internal temp reaches 135°C for medium-rare, then remove from the air fryer.

Nutrition Value
Calories: 278 Kcal, Carb: 7 g, Protein: 24 g, Fat: 13.2 g
Storage Suggestion: You can store it in the refrigerator for 2-3 days.

Lamb Roast Dinner with Air Fried Potatoes, Carrots & Sweet Potato

Prep Time: 20 Mins, Cook Time: 25 Mins, Servings: 6, Serving Size: 1

Ingredients
- 1.5kg Leg Lamb
- 1 kg Royale Potatoes Red
- 2 Sweet Potatoes medium
- 250 g Carrots Baby
- 1 cup of Peas
- 2 large rosemary sprigs
- 4 Garlic cloves
- Pepper & Salt

Instructions
- A tiny sharp knife may be used to poke Rosemary & sliced Garlic into the meat per 5 cm. The meat is then covered with pepper and salt; after the Veggies are done cooking, set this aside.
- Cut sweet potatoes into chunky wedges, drizzle with a little oil, sprinkle with salt, & Air Fry for around 10 Mins at 200°C on a tray within the base. Do 10 Mins of shaking or flipping till you're satisfied.
- Wrap the carrots in Al foil and bake them for 30 mins at 200°F.
- You just dice them and bake them at 200°C for 30 mins with oil, rosemary, & garlic, stirring the pan every ten Mins or so. The amount of time it takes to cook depends on the size of your potatoes.
- It took an hr at 160°C and an additional 10 Mins at 200°C to crisp up the piece of beef. A temperature of 65°C inside ensured that everything was perfectly cooked to our specifications.
- For 15 Mins, cover this with foil and put the vegetables back in the oven at 180°C while the peas cook up.

Nutrition Value
Calories: 269 Kcal, Carb: 8 g, Protein: 25 g, Fat: 18 g
Storage Suggestion: You can store it in the refrigerator for 4-5 days.

Greek Lamb Burgers

Prep Time: 10 Mins, Cook Time: 20 Mins, Servings: 4, Serving Size: 4

Ingredients
- 1.5 lb lamb ground
- 1 tsp oregano
- 1/3 cup crumbled feta cheese
- 4 buns
- ½ tsp salt & pepper
- ½ lettuce head
- 1 tomato medium
- 1 cup sauce tzatziki

Instructions
- Serve your burgers with tzatziki sauce on the side.
- Air Fryer at 375° Fahrenheit should be turned on.
- Combine the ground lamb, feta cheese crumbles, oregano, & pepper in a small bowl. Make four 6 oz patties of the same thickness once the mixture has been thoroughly pulverized. To finish, salt & pepper the burgers on the outsides once they've been formed.
- Olive oil sprayed on the basket can keep it from sticking. Lay down all of the burgers in a thin layer in the air fryer's basket. If you have a tiny air fryer, you can cook many batches at a time.
- Flip after 10 Mins of cooking for a further 8 to 10 Mins each side. Cook to an interior temp of 160 degrees Fahrenheit by using a thermometer.
- Rest for five Mins after removing the chicken breasts from the air fryer so that the fluids may settle.
- Serve every burger on the brioche bun with lettuce & tomato slices on the side. 2 tbsp of tzatziki sauce over every burger is a nice finishing touch.

Nutrition Value
Calories: 790 Kcal, Carb: 40 g, Protein: 38 g, Fat: 21 g
Storage Suggestion: You can store it in the refrigerator for 10-12 days.

Fried Kebab

Prep Time: 10 Min, Cook Time: 25 Min, Servings: 4, Serving Size: 1

Ingredients
- 2 oz lamb
- 1 chopped Lemon
- 1 tsp chili pepper red
- 2 large Carrots
- 250 ml sauce tomato
- 1 garlic clove
- 6-7 shallots
- 1 olive oil Air Fry spoon
- 1 tsp of salt

Instructions
- A tbsp of lemon juice & a tsp of chili powder is needed to marinate the lamb.
- Cook the shallots & carrots for around 10 Mins after slicing them thinly. For the last ten Mins of cooking, add your marinated lamb.
- Cook for a further 5 Mins after adding tomato sauce. Serve it hot.

Nutrition Value
Calories: 146 Kcal, Carb: 2 g, Protein: 18 g, Fat: 9.2 g
Storage Suggestion: You can store it in the refrigerator for 5-6 days.

Herbed Rack of Lamb

Prep Time: 30 min, Cook Time: 10 Mins, Servings: 2, Serving Size: 1

Ingredients
- 1 tbsp oil olive
- 2 minced garlic cloves
- 1 tbsp fresh parsley minced
- 1 tsp fresh rosemary minced
- 1 tsp fresh thyme minced
- 1 lamb rack French-style

Instructions
- Make a 400°F preheated oven. Mix the parsley, rosemary, oil, garlic, & thyme in a bowl and

whisk to combine. Rub the lamb with the oil mixture.
- In an oiled 11x7-inch baking sheet, place the meat over a rack. When the meat achieves the appropriate doneness, bake for around 20 to 30 mins uncovered.

Nutrition Value
Calories: 241 Kcal, Carb: 1 g, Protein: 20 g, Fat: 17 g
Storage Suggestion: You can store it in the refrigerator for 6-7 days.

Whole30 Gyro Meatballs

Prep Time: 15 Mins, Cook Time: 12 Mins, Servings: 35-40, Serving Size: 5

Ingredients
- 1 lb lamb ground
- 1 lb beef ground
- 1 whisked egg
- 1 tbsp rosemary dried
- 1 tbsp dill dried
- 1 lemon juice
- 1 & ½ tsp Kosher salt or sea salt
- 1 & ½ tsp pepper
- cooking spray nonstick

Instructions
- The components for the meatballs may be added to your food processor and processed.
- Form the mix into balls no larger than one inch in diameter.
- Apply cooking spray to the basket of your air fryer. Cook the meatballs in your air fryer around 350°F for seven Mins until the desired doneness. Shake the meatballs in the basket. Add another 4 Mins to the cooking time. This may have to be done in multiples.
- After cooking, allow the dish to cool for about two Mins before serving.

Nutrition Value
Calories: 42 Kcal, Carb: 3 g, Protein: 6 g, Fat: 3 g
Storage Suggestion: You can store it in the refrigerator for 5-6 days.

Chapter 6: Chicken Recipes

Keto Chicken Wings

Prep Time: 20 Mins, Cook Time: 10 Mins, Servings: 5, Serving Size: 1

Ingredients
- 2 tsp of olive oil
- 3 lb of chicken wings
- 1 tbsp of taco seasoning mix

Instructions
- Add all contents to a resealable bag and seal. Mix thoroughly.
- The air fryer should be preheated to 350 degrees.
- Air fried chicken wings for 12 Mins in an oiled basket.
- Cook for six more Mins on the other side.
- Serve as soon as possible.

Nutrition Value
Calories: 220 Kcal, Carb: 1.2 g, Protein: 18 g, Fat: 15 g
Storage Suggestion: You can store it in the refrigerator for 2-3 days.

Southern-Style Chicken

Prep Time: 15 Mins, Cook Time: 20 Mins, Servings: 6, Serving Size: 1

Ingredients
- Minced fresh parsley: 1 tbsp
- cups of crushed Ritz crackers
- Rubbed sage: ¼ tsp
- Paprika: 1 tsp
- 1/2 tsp of pepper
- 1 broiler chicken (3-4 lb), cut up
- Garlic salt: 1 tsp
- Ground cumin: ¼ tsp
- 1 egg, whisked

Instructions
- Preheat your air fryer to 375 degrees Fahrenheit.
- Add the beaten egg to a mixing bowl.
- In a separate dish, combine the crackers and all the seasonings.
- Afterward, dip the chicken pieces into the cracker mixture. Cooking oil spray should be used to ensure that the chicken is well-coated.
- In the air fryer basket, arrange the chicken pieces in a uniform layer.
- Ten Mins in the oven. Spray the chicken with cooking oil and cook for another 10 to 20 Mins until it reaches 165 degrees and is golden brown and crispy.

Nutrition Value
Calories: 410 Kcal, Carb: 13 g, Protein: 36 g, Fat: 23 g
Storage Suggestion: You can store it in the refrigerator for 1-2 days.

Buttermilk Fried Chicken

Prep Time: 30 Mins, Cook Time: 15 Mins, Servings: 6, Serving Size: 1

Ingredients
- 1 tbsp + 1 tsp of kosher salt
- 1 (3-4 lb) whole chicken
- All-purpose flour: 2 cups
- 1 tsp of cayenne pepper
- 1 tbsp of garlic powder
- 1 tsp of black pepper
- Buttermilk: 2 cups
- 1 tbsp of ground mustard
- tbsp of paprika
- 1 tbsp of onion powder

Instructions
- Ten pieces of chicken should be cut.
- The chicken pieces should be mixed with half a tsp of black pepper and salt in a large bowl.
- Keep the mixture in the fridge for an hr after adding the two cups of buttermilk.
- You'll need another bowl to combine the ground mustard and the rest of the spices.
- Pre-heat the air fryer to 390 degrees Fahrenheit before preparing the food. The flour spice mixture is applied to the chicken after being taken out of the buttermilk.
- The air fryer basket should be filled to the brim with chicken pieces. A temperature of 165 degrees Fahrenheit should be reached in 18 to 20 Mins.
- Serve the remaining chicken.

Nutrition Value
Calories: 435 Kcal, Carb: 9 g, Protein: 35 g, Fat: 23 g
Storage Suggestion: You can store it in the refrigerator for 2-3 days.

Mediterranean Chicken Bowls

Prep Time: 30 Mins, Cook Time: 25 Mins, Servings: 2-4, Serving Size: 1

Ingredients
- 1 lb. of skinless chicken breasts, boneless, cut into one and a half" pieces
- cups of cherry or grape tomatoes
- Dried oregano: 1 tsp
- Olive oil: 1 tbsp
- 1 cup of couscous
- Salt & pepper, to taste
- ¼ cup of fresh dill
- Ground sumac: 1 tsp
- 1 chopped onion
- Grated lemon zest: 1 tsp + 1 Tbsp of lemon juice
- For serving feta (crumbled)

Instructions
- Make an oil-and-salt-and-pepper marinade for the chicken to add the sumac and oregano.
- Mix in the onion and tomato.
- Using an air fryer, place the chicken in the basket and cook for 15-20 Mins, shaking the basket a few times until it's cooked through and browned all over.
- While you wait, prepare the couscous by combining it with the zest and cooking it according to the package directions.
- Add 2 tbsp of dill and 2 tbsp of lemon juice, then fluff it up.
- Add chicken and veggies to the couscous before serving. Top with feta and dill and savor it.

Nutrition Value
Calories: 475 Kcal, Carb: 53 g, Protein: 43 g, Fat: 9 g
Storage Suggestion: You can store it in the refrigerator for 1-2 days.

Tender Chicken

Prep Time: 5 hrs & 20 Mins, Cook Time: 3 Hrs 15 Mins, Servings: 4, Serving Size: 1

Ingredients
- chicken bone-in thighs
- 1 tbsp smoked paprika
- 1 and a 1/2 tbsp of canola oil
- 1 and a 1/2 tsp of dried rosemary
- 1 and a 1/2 tbsp of whole-grain mustard
- Kosher salt & black pepper, to taste
- 1 lemon, juiced & zested

Instructions
- Mix rosemary, mustard, lemon juice, paprika, and zest in a dish before serving
- Spices should be applied to the chicken before cooking. Cover it and put it in the fridge for at least four to eight hrs to keep it fresh.
- Heat to 400 F in the air fryer.
- Remove the marinated chicken from the dish.
- The chicken should be arranged in one layer in the air fryer. Cook for 18 Mins, flipping halfway through until the chicken reaches an internal temperature of 160 to 165 degrees Fahrenheit.
- Rest for five Mins in Al before serving and savoring your meal.

Nutrition Value
Calories: 275 Kcal, Carb: 13 g, Protein: 13 g, Fat: 9 g
Storage Suggestion: You can store it in the refrigerator for 3-4 days.

Chicken Tikka Skewers with Creamy Avocado Sauce

Prep Time: 1 hrs & 20 Mins, Cook Time: 1 Hr 15 Mins, Servings: 4, Serving Size: 1

Ingredients
- 1 lb. of skinless chicken thighs, boneless (slice into bite-size pieces)
- Lemon juice: 1 tbsp
- 1/2 tsp of Sea salt
- 1/2 tsp of Ground cumin
- Avocado mayo: 2 tbsp
- Freshly grated ginger: 1 tbsp
- 1 tsp of Chinese five-spice
- ¼ tsp of Coriander
- 1 tsp of turmeric
- 1 and a 1/2 tsp Smoked paprika
- minced cloves of garlic

Others
- Salt & pepper, to taste
- 1 bell pepper cut julienne style
- 1 onion cut into slices
- Olive oil, as needed

Avocado sauce
- Avocado oil: 2 tbsp
- Half avocado
- Cilantro leaves: ¼ cup
- Salt, to taste
- Lime juice: 1 tbsp
- Water, as needed
- 1 clove of garlic
- Nut milk: ¼ cup

Instructions
- Add the chicken and the rest of the ingredients to a bowl and mix well. Mix well and refrigerate for two hrs before serving.
- 2-3 pieces of chicken per skewer should be used while threading the meat onto the skewers.
- Spray the basket of the air fryer with oil. Arrange the skewers in a single layer in the basket.
- Stack one layer of onion and bell pepper slices in the basket of an air fryer and cook. Season with salt and pepper and drizzle with olive oil.
- Select dual cooking and bake for five Mins at 350 degrees Fahrenheit in the first cycle.
- At 425 degrees Fahrenheit, air fried the second cycle for five Mins.
- The chicken and veggies should be cooked until they are soft.
- Add all of the ingredients for the avocado sauce to a food processor and process until smooth.
- Start with 2 tbsp of water and add as needed while the food processor runs.
- Make your seasonings using salt.
- Cauliflower rice and avocado sauce are a great accompaniment to the chicken.

Nutrition Value
Calories: 232 Kcal, Carb: 12 g, Protein: 11 g, Fat: 8.9 g
Storage Suggestion: You can store it in the refrigerator for 2-3 days.

Chinese Egg Rolls

Prep Time: 1 hr, Cook Time: 15 Mins, Servings: 11, Serving Size: 1

Ingredients
- 1 lb of ground chicken or turkey
- Shredded carrots: 1 cup
- Bean sprouts: 1 cup
- Peanut oil: 2 tbsp
- Soy sauce: 3 tbsp
- minced cloves of garlic
- Minced ginger: 1 tbsp
- Thinly sliced green onions: 1/3 cup
- Shredded Napa cabbage: 2 cups
- Hoisin sauce: 1 tbsp
- Honey: 1 tsp
- Egg roll wrappers: 25
- Black pepper: ¼ tsp

Instructions
- Add one tbsp of peanut oil to a pan and heat it. Two Mins after putting in the Napa cabbage and carrots, keep stirring.
- Toss in the bean sprouts and heat for another 60 seconds.
- Incorporate honey and a tbsp of soy sauce. Remove from heat and place on a plate after cooking for one Min or until liquid has evaporated.
- Sauté ginger and garlic in 1 tbsp oil for 30 seconds.
- Cook the ground beef, breaking it up as it cooks until it is brown.
- Soy sauce, black pepper, and hoisin sauce (two tbsp) welcome additions.
- Toss in a bowl after cooking for 2-3 Mins to let the moisture soak in.
- Mix in the green onion and the other veggies to the meat mixture.

- Place egg roll on a clean surface with one corner facing you and meat in the lower third of an egg roll. Seal the edges with a little water and then securely wrap up the paper.
- Pre-heat the air fryer to 390 degrees Fahrenheit before preparing the food. Place egg rolls in a single layer on the air fryer basket. Cook for 6 Mins on one side, then 5 Mins on the other.
- The sauce should be served as a complement to the dish.

Nutrition Value
Calories: 215 Kcal, Carb: 8 g, Protein: 11 g, Fat: 7 g
Storage Suggestion: You can store it in the refrigerator for 5-6 days.

Asian-Glazed Boneless Chicken Thighs

Prep Time: 1 hrs & 20 Mins, Cook Time: 1 Hr 15 Mins, Servings: 4, Serving Size: 1

Ingredients
- and a 1/2 tbsp balsamic vinegar
- skinless, boneless chicken thighs, cleaned and trimmed
- Honey: 1 tbsp
- minced cloves of garlic
- Freshly grated ginger: 1 tsp
- Low sodium soy sauce: ¼ cup
- 1 scallion, thinly sliced for serving
- Sriracha hot sauce: 1 tsp

Instructions
- Garlic and balsamic vinegar should be combined with the soy sauce mixture. It's time to get down to business.
- Put the chicken in a bowl, add the marinade, and coat the chicken thoroughly. Refrigerate for at least two hrs.
- Keep the remaining marinade in a cool, dry place.
- Preheat the air fryer to 400 degrees Fahrenheit.
- Turn chicken over and cook for a further 14 Mins in the air fryer basket until it is well done.

- Cook the remaining marinade for 1-2 Mins, occasionally stirring, thicken it.
- Serve over chicken thighs with scallions that have been finely sliced.

Nutrition Value
Calories: 297 Kcal, Carb: 5 g, Protein: 45 g, Fat: 9 g
Storage Suggestion: You can store it in the refrigerator for 3-4 days.

Chicken Parmesan

Prep Time: 35 Mins, Cook Time: 15 Mins, Servings: 3, Serving Size: 1

Ingredients
- 1/2 tsp of marinara sauce
- medium chicken breasts
- 1/2 tsp of onion powder
- eggs, lightly whisked
- ¼ cup of parmesan cheese
- 1/2 tsp of Italian seasoning
- ¼ cup of breadcrumbs
- 1/2 tsp of shredded mozzarella cheese
- 1/2 tsp of garlic powder

Instructions
- Whisked eggs should be added to one bowl, while garlic powder, parmesan cheese, onion, and breadcrumbs should be added to the other.
- Mix the breadcrumbs and eggs and coat the chicken breasts before shaking off the excess.
- If necessary, use a mallet to flatten the breasts until they are all the same size.
- Spread oil over the bottom of an air fryer basket and add the breaded chicken.
- At 360 degrees Fahrenheit, cook for 15 to 18 Mins, or until done.
- Top the chicken with marinara sauce and cheese. Two more Mins in the air fryer.
- Mix with some Italian spices before serving.

Nutrition Value
Calories: 462 Kcal, Carb: 14 g, Protein: 23 g, Fat: 17 g

Storage Suggestion: You can store it in the refrigerator for 7-8 days.

Air Fryer Fried Chicken

Prep Time: 35 Mins, Cook Time: 15 Mins, Servings: 6, Serving Size: 1

Ingredients

For Marinade
- 1/2 cup of buttermilk
- Half of the whole chicken cut up (thigh, leg, wing, and breast)
- 1/2 cup of hot sauce

For Seasoning
- Garlic powder: 1 tsp
- All-purpose flour: ¾ cup
- Onion powder: 1 tsp
- Italian seasoning: 1 tsp
- Cayenne pepper: 1/2 tsp
- Seasoning salt: 2 tsp

Instructions
- Coat the chicken in a mixture of spicy sauce and buttermilk.
- Keep in the refrigerator for up to 24 hrs for marinating.
- Set out the spice ingredients in a bowl.
- Place the parchment paper in the air fryer's basket.
- Flour-coated chicken is ready to be served.
- Arrange the breaded chicken breasts in a single layer in the air fryer basket.
- At 390 degrees Fahrenheit, cook the food for 25 Mins.
- Spray the chicken with oil, cook for another 14 Mins, then turn it over and cook for another 12 Mins, or until the chicken reaches an internal temperature of 165 degrees Fahrenheit.
- Serve as soon as possible.

Nutrition Value
Calories: 321 Kcal, Carb: 12 g, Protein: 22 g, Fat: 14 g
Storage Suggestion: You can store it in the refrigerator for 4-5 days.

General Tso's Chicken

Prep Time: 26 Mins, Cook Time: 15 Mins, Servings: 4, Serving Size: 1

Ingredients

For sauce
- 1/2 cup chicken broth
- Sesame oil: 3 tsp
- Soy sauce: 1 tbsp
- Ginger: 1/2 tsp
- 1/2 tsp Sriracha
- Hoisin: 1 tbsp
- Minced garlic: 1 tsp
- Cornstarch: 1 tbsp

For chicken
- Soy sauce: 1 tbsp
- skinless, boneless chicken breasts, slice into one-inch pieces
- Sesame seeds for serving
- Cornstarch: 1 tbsp
- 1 scallion, thinly sliced for serving

Instructions
- Add the ginger, garlic, and sesame oil to a skillet and cook over medium heat until fragrant.
- Low heat for 60 seconds.
- Serve over rice and garnish with sriracha sauce and a sprinkling of hoisin.
- Add the cornstarch and keep stirring until the mixture thickens up slightly.
- Put the pot out of the way.
- Combine cornstarch and soy sauce in a bowl, add the chicken and toss to coat.
- Place the chicken in the basket and coat it with oil.
- At 400 degrees, cook for 16 Mins.
- After the first half, flip the chicken over and coat it with oil before cooking it.
- Serve with sesame seeds and scallions sprinkled on top right away.

Nutrition Value
Calories: 265 Kcal, Carb: 8 g, Protein: 23 g, Fat: 9 g
Storage Suggestion: You can store it in the refrigerator for 3-4 days.

Fiesta Chicken Tenders

Prep Time: 25 Mins, Cook Time: 15 Mins, Servings: 4, Serving Size: 1

Ingredients
- ¾-lb of skinless, boneless chicken breasts
- 1 pack of taco seasoning
- ¼ tsp of pepper
- 1 cup of all-purpose flour
- Salsa, as needed
- 1/2 cup of buttermilk
- cups of crushed corn chips

Instructions
- Preheat your air fryer to 400 degrees Fahrenheit.
- Use a mallet to lb the chicken to a half-inch thickness.
- Cut into "one"-strip sections (wide).
- Mix the buttermilk and pepper in a bowl. Add flour, taco seasoning, and crushed corn chips to a third bowl and stir to combine.
- Apply flour, buttermilk, and corn chips on the chicken before baking it in the oven.
- Spread out the chicken in a uniform layer in an oil-spray-coated basket.
- Heat for 7 to 8 Mins on each side, or until the meat is well cooked through.
- Use a dipping sauce or salsa to accompany.

Nutrition Value
Calories: 676 Kcal, Carb: 45 g, Protein: 24 g, Fat: 36 g
Storage Suggestion: You can store it in the refrigerator for 1-2 days.

Crispy Szechuan Duck

Prep Time: 4 hrs & 40 Mins, Cook Time: 3 Hrs15 Mins, Servings: 5-6, Serving Size: 1

Ingredients
- to 5 lb. of whole duck (Fresh)

For Marinade
- Salt: 2 tbsp
- Chinese five-spice powder: 1 tsp
- Szechuan peppercorns: 2 tbsp

For Seasonings
- green onions (whole), slice into three" lengths
- dry sherry: 3 tbsp
- slices (quarter) of fresh ginger, smashed

Starch solution
- Light soy sauce: 1 tbsp
- Cornstarch: 4 tbsp
- Water: 3 tbsp

Instructions
- Lightly toast the peppercorns over a medium heat source. Put it in a grinder when it's been taken off the heat and ground into a fine powder.
- Ground peppercorns and five different spices should be combined with salt.
- A sharp knife is required for cutting duck feet, tail, neck, and wings.
- Use half of the spice mixture to season the exterior of the duck before massaging it in.
- Rub the interior of the duck with the remaining spice mixture.
- A cooling rack should be placed on a baking sheet, and parchment paper should cover the duck. Refrigerate the duck for 48 hrs.
- Put dry sherry into the duck, along with green onion and ginger.
- Two hrs of steaming are required for the duck to be cooked.
- For the next three hrs, let it dry out in the open air.
- Cut the duck half lengthwise with a well-oiled, straight-edged chef's knife. Add the starch solution ingredients to a dish and coat the duck. Allow 10 Mins for drying.
- Preheat the air fryer to 400 degrees Fahrenheit.
- If your air fryer's basket is tiny, chop the duck in half before placing it in the air fryer.
- For 10 to 15 Mins, air fry. To serve, air-fry the remainder of the duck.

Nutrition Value
Calories: 376 Kcal, Carb: 16 g, Protein: 13 g, Fat: 21.2 g
Storage Suggestion: You can store it in the refrigerator for 3-4 days.

Lemon Pepper Chicken Thighs

Prep Time: 30 Mins, Cook Time: 15 Mins, Servings: 6, Serving Size: 1

Ingredients
- 1/2 tsp Garlic Powder
- 6 skinless, boneless chicken thighs
- 1/4 tsp Black Pepper
- 1 and a 1/2 tbsp lemon juice
- 1/2 tsp Paprika
- 1/2 tbsp Lemon Pepper Seasoning
- 1/2 tsp Italian Seasoning

Instructions
- Except for the chicken, combine all ingredients in a large bowl. Apply the spice blend on the chicken in an even layer.
- Cook for 15 Mins at 360 degrees Fahrenheit in the air fryer's basket. When the meat reaches 165 degrees Fahrenheit, turn it over and continue cooking for another half hr.
- Enjoy your meal straight now.

Nutrition Value
Calories: 243 Kcal, Carb: 6 g, Protein: 21 g, Fat: 9 g
Storage Suggestion: You can store it in the refrigerator for 4-5 days.

Chicken Souvlaki Gyros

Prep Time: 1 hrs & 5 Mins, Cook Time: 1 hr 15 Mins, Servings: 4, Serving Size: 1

Ingredients
- 1-lb skinless, boneless chicken breasts
- 1 minced clove of garlic
- pita bread
- Italian seasoning: 1 tbsp
- Extra-virgin olive oil: 1/4 cup
- Half lemon, cut into slices
- 1/2 cup of chopped tomatoes
- 1/2 tsp of paprika
- 1/4 tsp of salt
- 1/4 cup of yogurt sauce (cucumber)
- Shredded lettuce: 1 cup
- 1/4 cup of chopped red onion

Instructions
- Toss the paprika, lemon juice, and garlic into a zip-top bag with the Italian seasoning. Mix thoroughly, and then add the chicken. Refrigeration is required for two hrs.
- Preheat the air fryer to 360 degrees Fahrenheit.
- Generously oil the air fryer basket.
- Remove the chicken from the package and set it in the air fryer basket.
- Flip it after 10 Mins and cook for another 8 Mins.
- Slice it once it has rested for five Mins.
- Add chicken, additional veggies, and a little yogurt sauce to pita bread that has been cleaned.
- Serve as soon as possible.

Nutrition Value
Calories: 236 Kcal, Carb: 16 g, Protein: 18 g, Fat: 11.2 g
Storage Suggestion: You can store it in the refrigerator for 6-7 days.

Nashville Hot Chicken

Prep Time: 55 Mins, Cook Time: 60 Mins, Servings: 6, Serving Size: 1

Ingredients
- lb of chicken tenderloins
- Slices of Dill pickle
- Dill pickle juice: 2 tbsp
- 1 tsp salt
- Buttermilk: 1/2 cup
- Hot pepper sauce: 2 tbsp
- 1 cup of all-purpose flour
- Pepper: 1/2 tsp
- Chili powder: 1 tsp
- Olive oil: 1/2 cup
- 1 whole egg
- Cayenne pepper: 2 tbsp
- 1/2 tsp Garlic powder
- Dark brown sugar: 2 tbsp
- Paprika: 1 tsp

Instructions
- A tbsp of each spicy sauce and pickle juice, together with half a tsp of salt, should be mixed in a bowl.
- Toss in the chicken and mix well. Refrigerate for an hr before using; after that, toss the marinade.
- Pre-heat the air fryer to 375 degrees Fahrenheit.
- The following ingredients should be combined: flour, pepper, and a 1/2 tsp of salt.
- Combine the egg, spicy sauce, and buttermilk in a separate bowl.
- Using flour and egg as a base, coat the chicken pieces and then re-flour them.
- Generously oil the air fryer basket.
- Spray the chicken with oil and place it in the air fryer's basket in one layer.
- Toss it in oil and cook for another 5 to 6 Mins, flipping it halfway through.
- Cayenne pepper and other ingredients go into a dish with brown sugar.
- Pickle slices are a great accompaniment to the chicken.

Nutrition Value
Calories: 413 Kcal, Carb: 20 g, Protein: 39 g, Fat: 21 g
Storage Suggestion: You can store it in the refrigerator for 3-4s days.

Crispy Curry Drumsticks

Prep Time: 20 Mins, Cook Time: 45 Mins, Servings: 4, Serving Size: 2

Ingredients
- 1/2 tsp of onion salt
- 1 lb of chicken drumsticks
- 3/4 tsp of salt
- 1/2 tsp of garlic powder
- Fresh cilantro, Minced
- 2 tbsp of olive oil
- 2 tsp of curry powder

Instructions
- Put the chicken in a bowl and cover it with water.
- Let it sit for 15 Mins on the counter with a half-tsp of salt. The chicken should be thoroughly dried after draining the water and patting dry with a paper towel.
- Pre-heat the air fryer to 375 degrees Fahrenheit. 14 tsp salt, curry powder, oil, garlic powder, and onion seasoning are mixed in a bowl.
- Toss in chicken and cover well with the spice mix.
- Stack the chicken in a single layer in the air fryer's basket.

- A 170 to 175 degrees Fahrenheit temperature should be reached during 15 to 17 Mins of cooking.
- Halfway through cooking, it's a good idea to turn the chicken over to achieve even cooking.
- Prepare the food and serve it to your guests.

Nutrition Value
Calories: 180 Kcal, Carb: 2 g, Protein: 12 g, Fat: 13 g
Storage Suggestion: You can store it in the refrigerator for 3-4 days.

Chicken (Peruvian Style)

Prep Time: 1 day & 20 Mins, Cook Time: 55 Mins, Servings: 4, Serving Size: 1

Ingredients
- Extra virgin olive oil: 3 tbsp
- 4-5 lb. of chicken cleaned & trimmed
- Lime juice: 2 tbsp
- 6 cloves of garlic
- Dried oregano: 1 tsp
- 1/2 tbsp Kosher salt
- Soy sauce: 2 tbsp
- Brown sugar: 2 tsp
- Paprika: 2 tsp
- Cumin: 1 tbsp
- Black pepper: 1 tsp

Instructions
- Add the rest of the ingredients to a food processor, except for the chicken, and pulse until smooth.
- Apply the spice combination to the outside and interior of the chicken and the skin.
- Marinate for six to twenty-four hrs.
- Cook for 30 Mins at 360 degrees Fahrenheit in the air fryer basket.
- Cook for a further 20 Mins on the other side, or until the chicken reaches an internal temperature of 165 degrees Fahrenheit.
- For 15 to 20 Mins, let the chicken rest. Cut the meat into slices and put them on a plate.

Nutrition Value
Calories: 522 Kcal, Carb: 6 g, Protein: 42g, Fat: 18 g
Storage Suggestion: You can store it in the refrigerator for 2-3 days.

Korean Chicken Wings

Prep Time: 10 Mins, Cook Time: 20 Mins, Servings: 4, Serving Size: 1

Ingredients
- lb. of chicken wings
- 1/2 tsp of salt
- Corn starch: ¾ cup
- Onion powder: 1 tsp
- Garlic powder: 1 tsp

Korean Sauce
- Minced ginger: 1 tsp
- Korean gochujang chili paste: 2 tbsp
- Honey: 3 tbsp
- 1/2 tsp salt
- Soy sauce: 1 tbsp
- Brown sugar: 2 tbsp
- Minced garlic: 1 tsp

Instructions
- Sprinkle with half a tsp each of salt, garlic powder, and onion powder and combine with chicken wings in a bowl.
- Toss in the corn starch and mix well with a pair of tongs.
- Place the wings in the basket of an air fryer and shake off the excess.
- Cook for 30 Mins at 390 degrees Fahrenheit, then turn and cook for another 10 Mins.
- Cook the sauce as you do this.
- Add the sauce's components to a skillet and cook over medium heat until the sauce thickens. Turn the heat down, cover, and simmer for five Mins.
- Serve the fried chicken wings with a Korean sauce.

Nutrition Value
Calories: 421 Kcal, Carb: 36 g, Protein: 45 g, Fat: 23 g
Storage Suggestion: You can store it in the refrigerator for 3-4 days.

Chicken Quesadilla

Prep Time: 15 Mins, Cook Time: 20 Mins, Servings: 1, Serving Size: 1

Ingredients
- 1/2 cup of chicken breast cooked and cubed
- gluten-free, corn tortillas
- Cheddar cheese, grated: 1/3 cup
- Guacamole: 3 tbsp

Instructions
- Preheat your air fryer to 325 degrees Fahrenheit.
- Spray the basket of the air fryer with oil.
- Add chicken, guacamole, cheese, and another tortilla to the basket before closing it up.
- Use a toothpick to keep it in place.
- Depending on how crispy you prefer your food, you may cook it for anywhere from six to ten Mins, flipping halfway through.
- Cut the meat into slices and put them on a plate.

Nutrition Value
Calories: 106 Kcal, Carb: 7 g, Protein: 7 g, Fat: 6 g
Storage Suggestion: You can store it in the refrigerator for 2-3 days.

Breaded Chicken Breast

Prep Time: 20 Mins, Cook Time: 20 Mins, Servings: 2, Serving Size: 1

Ingredients
- Ground mustard powder: 2 tsp
- 1 lb. of chicken breast
- Garlic powder: 2 tsp
- Salt, to taste
- Onion powder: 2 tsp
- Olive oil: 2 tsp
- Paprika: 2 tsp
- 1/2 cup Panko
- Seasoning salt: 2 tsp

Instructions
- Preheat your air fryer to 400 degrees Fahrenheit.
- To achieve the proper thickness, lb the chicken with a mallet and pat dry with a paper towel.
- Add a sprinkle of salt to the oil and coat the chicken.
- Add the other ingredients to a bowl and whisk well.
- Coat the chicken with the seasoning mixture.

- Place the chicken in an air fryer basket that has been coated with oil.
- The chicken should achieve an internal temperature of 165 degrees Fahrenheit after 6 to 8 Mins of cooking on the first side and 6 to 8 additional Mins on the second.

Nutrition Value
Calories: 167 Kcal, Carb: 6 g, Protein: 29 g, Fat: 3 g
Storage Suggestion: You can store it in the refrigerator for 4-5 days.

Chicken Chimichangas

Prep Time: 15 Mins, Cook Time: 25 Mins, Servings: 8, Serving Size: 1

Ingredients
- flour tortillas
- Shredded cooked chicken breast: 4 cups
- 1 can of (16 oz.) red enchilada sauce
- 1 can of (4oz.) green chilies, chopped
- 1 onion, finely diced
- Ground cumin: 1 tsp
- All-purpose flour: 4 tbsp
- Garlic powder: ¼ tsp

Toppings
- Cilantro
- Cheddar Cheese
- Greek Yogurt

Instructions
- Preheat your air fryer to 400 degrees Fahrenheit.
- 1 tsp of oil should be added to a pan.
- Add the chiles and onion to the pan and simmer for two Mins, stirring occasionally.
- Salt and cumin are added to the enchilada sauce. Keep agitating yourself, please.
- If the sauce is too thick, add 2 tbsp of chicken broth.
- Turn the thermostat down to the lowest setting.
- A half-cup of filling should be placed in the center of each tortilla before rolling securely.
- The air fryer should be filled to the brim with tortillas.
- Cook for a further 2 to 3 Mins after flipping at 400 F or until lightly browned.
- Prepare the food and serve it to your guests.

Nutrition Value
Calories: 311 Kcal, Carb: 20 g, Protein: 33 g, Fat: 7 g
Storage Suggestion: You can store it in the refrigerator for 2-3 days.

Garlic Herb Chicken Breast

Prep Time: 35 Mins, Cook Time: 40 Mins, Servings: 6, Serving Size: 1

Ingredients
- 2 lb. of chicken breast, skin on
- Chopped thyme, fresh: 1 tsp
- Kosher salt & black pepper to taste
- Chopped rosemary, freshly: 1 tsp
- Melted butter: 4 tbsp
- 3 minced cloves of garlic

Instructions
- Season the chicken breast with salt and black pepper once it has been dried.
- Combine the other ingredients in a bowl and coat the chicken breasts with a pastry brush.
- For 20 Mins at 375 degrees Fahrenheit, rotate the chicken halfway through the cooking period and cook until the internal temperature reaches 165 degrees Fahrenheit.
- Enjoy your meal straight now.

Nutrition Value
Calories: 358 Kcal, Carb: 23 g, Protein: 32 g, Fat: 11 g
Storage Suggestion: You can store it in the refrigerator for 4-5 days.

Almond Chicken

Prep Time: 30 Mins, Cook Time: 20 Mins, Servings: 2, Serving Size: 1

Ingredients
- 2 skinless, boneless chicken breasts, cut into halves
- Buttermilk: ¼ cup
- 1 whole egg
- Slivered almonds, finely diced: 1 cup
- Garlic salt: 1 tsp
- Black pepper: 1/2 tsp

Instructions
- The air fryer should be preheated to 350 degrees.
- Add the buttermilk, pepper, garlic salt, and one egg to a bowl and mix well to incorporate the ingredients.
- Add almonds to a separate bowl.
- Pat chicken dry after coating it with egg mixture and almonds.
- Spray the chicken with oil after placing it in the air fryer's oil-sprayed basket.
- 165 degrees Fahrenheit should be reached after 15 to 18 Mins of cooking.
- Serve with any kind of sauce.

Nutrition Value
Calories: 341 Kcal, Carb: 6 g, Protein: 53 g, Fat: 18 g
Storage Suggestion: You can store it in the refrigerator for 6-7 days.

Fajita-Stuffed Chicken

Prep Time: 15 Mins, Cook Time: 20 Mins, Servings: 4, Serving Size: 1

Ingredients
- skinless, boneless chicken breast, cut in half
- Ground cumin: 1 tsp
- 1 onion, cut into thin slices
- Ground cumin: 1 tsp
- Olive oil: 1 tbsp
- Half green pepper, cut into thin slices
- 1/2 cup of cheddar cheese, 4 slices
- Garlic powder: ¼ tsp
- Chili powder: 1 tbsp
- 1/2 tsp of salt

Instructions
- Preheat your air fryer to 375 degrees Fahrenheit.
- Slice through the thickest section of the chicken breast to create a cavity. Add green peppers and onions to it.

- Mix the spices and olive oil in a bowl, then coat the chicken in the mixture.
- Cook the chicken for six Mins in the air fryer basket after spraying it with oil.
- When the chicken reaches an internal temperature of 165 F, top it with a few pieces of cheese and continue cooking for another 6 to 8 Mins.
- Prepare the food and serve it to your guests.

Nutrition Value
Calories: 342 Kcal, Carb: 5 g, Protein: 42 g, Fat: 17 g
Storage Suggestion: You can store it in the refrigerator for 3-4 days.

Everything Bagel Chicken Strips

Prep Time: 25 Mins, Cook Time: 20 Mins, Servings: 4, Serving Size: 1

Ingredients
- 1 lb of chicken tenderloins
- Everything bagel, 1 day-old shredded in large pieces
- 1/2 cup of Parmesan cheese, grated
- ¼ tsp red pepper flakes, crushed
- 1/2 tsp salt
- Cubed butter: ¼ cup
- 1/2 cup of panko breadcrumbs

Instructions
- Preheat your air fryer to 400 degrees Fahrenheit. Crush the bagel in a food processor until it resembles a coarse meal.
- Half a cup of bagel crumbs, pepper flakes, cheese, and panko should be combined in a bowl.
- Take the butter out of the fridge and put it in a pan. Add salt and butter to the melted butter and coat the chicken.
- Mix the breadcrumbs and then coat the chicken.
- Place the breaded chicken in the air fryer basket and spray the basket with oil.
- Seven Mins on one side, then seven to eight Mins on the other, or until the chicken is golden brown.
- Serve as soon as possible.

Nutrition Value
Calories: 269 Kcal, Carb: 8 g, Protein: 31 g, Fat: 13 g
Storage Suggestion: You can store it in the refrigerator for 5-6 days.

Sweet Chili Chicken Wings

Prep Time: 30 Mins, Cook Time: 20 Mins, Servings: 4, Serving Size: 1

Ingredient
- Chicken Wings: 12
- Paprika: ¼ tsp
- Baking powder: 1/2 tbsp
- Sea salt: 1/2 tsp
- Onion powder: ¼ tsp
- Black pepper: 1 tsp
- Garlic powder: 1 tsp

Sweet Thai Chili Sauce
- Hoisin Sauce: 1 and a 1/2 tbsp
- Soy Sauce: 1 tbsp
- ½ tbsp sweet chili sauce
- Lime Juice: 1/2 tbsp
- Rice Wine Vinegar: 1/2 tbsp
- Sesame Oil: 1/2 tbsp
- Sea Salt: ¼ tsp
- Brown Sugar: 1 tbsp
- minced cloves of garlic
- Water: ¼ Cup
- Ground ginger: 1/2 tsp

Instructions
- Toss the chicken wings with all spices and baking powder in a resealable plastic bag.
- Mix well by squeezing the bag.
- Oil spray it well before adding the chicken to the air fryer basket.
- At 400 degrees Fahrenheit, cook the wings for 20 Mins, flipping them halfway through.
- Make the sweet chili sauce while you wait.
- Add the sauce ingredients to a skillet and bring to a boil over medium heat.
- Turn up the heat, bring to a boil, and then simmer until the sauce thickens.
- Serve the wings drenched with sauce.

Nutrition Value
Calories: 324 Kcal, Carb: 12 g, Protein: 24 g, Fat: 4 g
Storage Suggestion: You can store it in the refrigerator for 1-2 days.

Sesame Chicken

Prep Time: 30 Mins, Cook Time: 20 Mins, Servings: 6, Serving Size: 1

Ingredients
- 1/2 cup of cornstarch
- 6 skinless, boneless chicken thighs

Sauce
- Cornstarch: 1 tbsp
- Soy Sauce: ¼ Cup
- 1 minced clove of garlic
- Orange Juice: 2 tbsp
- Hoisin Sauce: 5 tsp
- Brown Sugar: 2 tbsp
- Ground Ginger: 1/2 tsp
- Sesame Seeds: 2 tsp
- Cold Water: 1 tbsp

Instructions
- Toss the chicken chunks with cornstarch in a bowl and toss again.
- Pre-heat the air fryer to 390 degrees Fahrenheit before preparing the food.
- Spray oil on the chicken and the air fryer basket. The pieces should be cooked for 24 Mins, flipped halfway through, and sprayed with cooking oil.
- Sauce components, except cornstarch and sesame seeds, should be added to a medium-high temperature in a saucepan before the water is added.
- Whisk it well. Add the rest of the ingredients and bring it to a boil. The last step is to include the seeds.
- Allow it to cool for five Mins after turning off the heat.
- Serve the sauce-coated chicken over hot rice.

Nutrition Value
Calories: 335 Kcal, Carb: 28 g, Protein: 30 g, Fat: 9 g
Storage Suggestion: You can store it in the refrigerator for 2-3 days.

Apricot Glazed Chicken Drumsticks

Prep Time: 17 Mins, Cook Time: 20 Mins, Servings: 2, Serving Size: 1

Ingredients

Spicy Apricot Glaze
- Soy sauce: 1/2 tsp
- 1/2 cup of apricot preserves
- Chili powder: ¼ tsp
- Dijon mustard: 2 tsp

For Chicken
- Seasoned salt: 1/2 tsp
- 4-6 chicken drumsticks
- Pepper: 1/2 tsp
- Salt: 1 tsp

Instructions
- Add all of the sauce ingredients to a skillet and stir on low heat for 5 to 10 Mins until it thickens. Put the pot out of the way.
- Using an air fryer's basket, coat the chicken with oil before placing it in the basket.
- Combine salt, pepper, and seasoned salt in a bowl.
- Place the chicken in the air fryer basket and season with the spice mix.
- For 10 Mins, cook the chicken at 370 degrees Fahrenheit before flipping it over and spraying it with oil.
- A further 10 Mins of cooking time is needed.
- Using a brush, coat the chicken with sauce and cook for two more Mins.

Nutrition Value
Calories: 278 Kcal, Carb: 11 g, Protein: 21 g, Fat: 9 g

Storage Suggestion: You can store it in the refrigerator for 2-3 days.

Honey Garlic Chicken

Prep Time: 15 Mins, Cook Time: 25 Mins, Servings: 4, Serving Size: 1

Ingredients
- 6 skinless, boneless chicken thighs
- Soy Sauce: 1/2 cup
- Potato starch, as needed
- Cornstarch: 1 tbsp
- Ketchup: 2 tbsp
- Honey: 1/2 cup
- Sliced green onions
- Cooked green beans
- 1 minced clove of garlic
- Brown Sugar: 2 tbsp
- Ground Ginger: 1/2 tsp
- Cooked Rice

Instructions
- Coat the chicken with potato starch before slicing it into cubes.
- Flip and cook for another 12 Mins in the air fryer at 390 F.
- Stir up the ketchup with the honey and brown sugar in a saucepan.
- On low heat, bring it to a boil. Make it thicker by sprinkling it with cornstarch.
- Reheat any leftover chicken before adding it to the sauce.
- Top with green onion and serve with green beans and rice.

Nutrition Value
Calories: 629 Kcal, Carb: 76 g, Protein: 40 g, Fat: 13 g

Storage Suggestion: You can store it in the refrigerator for 2-3 days.

Chapter 7: Turkey Recipes

Teriyaki Turkey Drumsticks with Salad Greens

Prep Time: 30 Mins, Cook Time:20 Mins, Servings: 6, Serving Size: 1

Ingredients
- Six Turkey drumsticks
- Teriyaki sauce: one cup
- Salad greens: one cup
- Sesame seeds and chopped green onion for garnish

Instructions
- To get the air fryer to 360F, turn it on.
- Turkey drumsticks should be placed in a large zip-top bag along with the teriyaki sauce.
- Take care not to overdo it. Allow it to marinade for 30 Mins.
- Allow the drumsticks to cook for 20 Mins in the air fryer basket.
- To ensure consistent frying, shake the basket several times.
- Serve with a side of salad greens and green onions, if desired.

Nutrition Value
Calories: 163 Kcal, Carb: 7 g, Protein: 16 g, Fat: 7 g
Storage Suggestion: You can store it in the refrigerator for 1-2 days.

Air Fried Philly Cheesesteak Taquitos

Prep Time: 20 Mins, Cook Time: 6-8 hrs, Servings: 6, Serving Size: 1

Ingredients
- Dry Italian dressing mix: one package
- Super Soft Corn Tortillas: one pack
- Green peppers: two pieces, chopped
- One white onion, diced
- 12 cups of lean beef steak strips
- Beef stock: 2 cups
- Lettuce shredded, one cup
- Provolone cheese: ten slices
- Olive oil

Instructions
- Add onion, meat, stock, pepper, and spices to a slow cooker.
- Make sure the lid is on tightly and cook on low for six to eight hrs.
- Use a microwave to warm tortillas for about a Min.
- Heat the air fryer to 350 degrees Fahrenheit.
- Using a tortilla, scoop 2-3 tbsp of beef into the cheesesteak.
- Roll the tortilla firmly and place it in an air fryer basket before adding part of the cheese.
- If you'd want to make a lot of tortillas, do so.
- Apply a little olive oil swab to the surface.
- Cook for around 6-8 Mins.
- Cook the tortillas on the other side, using additional oil as necessary.
- Enjoy your meal with a side of shredded lettuce.

Nutrition Value
Calories: 210 Kcal, Carb: 20 g, Protein: 23 g, Fat: 14 g
Storage Suggestion: You can store it in the refrigerator for 1-2 days.

Air Fryer Nashville Hot Turkey with Spinach Salad

Prep Time: 30 Mins, Cook Time:25 Mins, Servings: 8, Serving Size: 2

Ingredients
- Buttermilk: 2 cups
- Turkey thighs(bone-in): 8
- Cayenne pepper: 1 tsp
- Hot sauce: ¼ cup
- Garlic powder: 2 Tbsp
- Salt: 1 tsp
- Low-fat butter: 1/2 cup
- Flour: 2 cups
- Black pepper: 1 tsp
- Old bay: 1 tsp
- Paprika: 1 tsp

Instructions
- Add the spicy sauce and buttermilk to a mixing dish and stir well. Then add the turkey chunks.
- Refrigerate for 1 to 24 hrs to allow flavors to blend.
- Garlic powder, flour, salt, black pepper, paprika, cayenne pepper, and old bay are good additions to a bowl of chicken stock. Mix thoroughly.
- When using an air fryer, be sure to cook the turkey in a single layer.
- When you've finished soaking the turkey in buttermilk, drain it and then coat it with the flour mixture. Before placing the turkey in the air fryer, let it cool on a cooling rack for 15 Minutes.
- Air fry the breaded Turkey, allowing space between each piece.
- At 390 F, cook for 25 Mins. During the second half, remove the basket and sprinkle olive oil over the turkey.
- This step is not required. Mix two tbsp of spicy sauce with melted butter. Use it to coat the turkey while it cooks.
- The spinach salad goes well with this.

Nutrition Value
Calories: 330 Kcal, Carb: 19 g, Protein: 26 g, Fat: 20 g
Storage Suggestion: You can store it in the refrigerator for 3-4 days.

Air Fryer Italian Sausage & Vegetables

Prep Time: 5 Mins, Cook Time:14 Mins, Servings: 4, Serving Size: 1

Ingredients
- One bell pepper
- Italian Turkey Sausage: 4 pieces spicy or sweet
- One small onion
- ¼ cup of mushrooms

Instructions
- Let the air fryer heat up to 400 degrees Fahrenheit for three Mins.
- Cook the Italian sausage for six Mins in a single layer in the air fryer basket.
- While the sausages are frying, cut the veggies.
- Reduce the temperature to 360 F after six Mins. The sausage should

be flipped halfway through the process. Mushrooms, onions, and peppers surround sausage in a basket in the oven.
- For 8 Mins, cook at 360 degrees Fahrenheit. Once the meat and veggies have been mixed for four Mins,
- The ideal sausage temperature is 160 degrees Fahrenheit, as measured by an instant-read thermometer.
- If the internal temperature isn't at least 160 degrees Fahrenheit, continue to cook for a few more Mins.
- Remove the veggies and sausage using a fork and serve them over brown rice.

Nutrition Value
Calories: 291 Kcal, Carb: 21 g, Protein: 16 g, Fat: 21 g
Storage Suggestion: You can store it in the refrigerator for 2-3 days.

Air Fryer Dumplings

Prep Time: 5 Mins, Cook Time: 10 Mins, Servings: 3, Serving Size: 2

Ingredients
- One packet of frozen Turkey, vegetable, or pork dumplings
- Salad greens: one cup
- Dipping sauce
- Maple syrup: 1/8 cup
- Soy sauce: ¼ cup
- Red pepper flakes: Pinch
- Garlic powder: 1/2 tsp
- Rice vinegar: 1/2 tsp
- Water: ¼ cup

Instructions
- For four Mins, let the air fryer heat up to 370 degrees.
- Spray the oil into the air fryer basket and add the dumplings.
- Toss the basket and re-apply a little oil coating after letting it cook for five Mins in the oven.
- Allow them to simmer for another six Mins.
- The dipping sauce components should be mixed in a dish before serving.
- Serve the dumplings with salad leaves once they've been drained.

Nutritional value: per serving: Cal 233|FAT: 7g |Carbs: 26g |Protein: 18g

Nutrition Value
Calories: 233 Kcal, Carb: 26 g, Protein: 18 g, Fat: 7 g
Storage Suggestion: You can store it in the refrigerator for 2-3 days.

Air Fryer Turkey Wings with Buffalo Sauce

Prep Time: 5 Mins, Cook Time: 25 Mins, Servings: 6, Serving Size: 2

Ingredients
- Turkey drumettes & flats: 4 cups
- Salt & pepper, to taste

Buffalo Sauce
- Hot sauce: 1/2 cup
- White vinegar: 2 tbsp
- Melted butter: 1/2 cup
- Worcestershire sauce: 2 tsp
- Pinch of garlic powder

Instructions
- The air fryer should be preheated to 380 degrees Fahrenheit.
- Make flat drumsticks by separating the wings and removing the tips.
- Salt and pepper the turkey wings liberally with paper towels, then roast in a preheated oven at 350 degrees Fahrenheit for about an hr.
- Cook for around 22 Mins in an air fryer basket.
- Cook for a further five Mins at a temperature of 400 degrees to crisp up the turkey skin.
- It's time to whip up a batch of Buffalo Sauce!
- Make your buffalo sauce and use it to coat the wings.
- Serve with salad leaves on the side.

Nutrition Value
Calories: 315 Kcal, Carb: 1 g, Protein: 30 g, Fat: 20 g
Storage Suggestion: You can store it in the refrigerator for 1-2 days.

Air Fryer Grilled Turkey

Prep Time: 30 Mins, Cook Time: 20 Mins, Servings: 3, Serving Size: 2

Ingredients
- Turkey tenders: 4 cups

Marinade
- Honey: 2 Tbsp
- Olive oil: ¼ cup
- White vinegar: 2 Tbsp
- Water: 2 Tbsp
- 1/2 tsp salt
- Garlic powder: 1 tsp
- 1/2 tsp of paprika
- Onion powder: 1 tsp
- 1/2 tsp crushed red pepper

Instructions
- Combine all of the marinade's ingredients in a large bowl and stir thoroughly.
- Coat the turkey with the turkey mix you just prepared. Marinate in the refrigerator for 30 Mins before serving.
- Air fried the turkey tenders in one layer in the basket.
- Steak should be cooked for three Mins at 390 degrees Fahrenheit. Turn the tenders over and cook for another five Mins, or until the meat is well cooked.
- Serve with salad leaves on the side.

Nutritional value: per serving: calories 230|fat 14g| protein 20 g| carbs 11g

Nutrition Value
Calories: 230 Kcal, Carb: 11 g, Protein: 20 g, Fat: 14 g
Storage Suggestion: You can store it in the refrigerator for 2-3 days.

Air-Fried Turkey Pie

Prep Time: 10 Mins, Cook Time: 30 Mins, Servings: 2, Serving Size: 1

Ingredients
- Puff pastry: 2 sheets
- Turkey thighs: 2 pieces, cut into cubes
- One small onion, chopped
- Small potatoes: 2, chopped
- Mushrooms: ¼ cup
- Light soya sauce

- One carrot, chopped
- Black pepper, to taste
- Worcestershire sauce: to taste
- Salt, to taste
- Italian mixed dried herbs
- Garlic powder: a pinch
- Plain flour: 2 tbsp
- Milk, as required
- Melted butter

Instructions
- Combine the light soy sauce, pepper, and turkey cubes in a large mixing bowl. Mix thoroughly.
- Sauté the carrots, potatoes, and onion in a medium-sized pan. Cooking the veggies may need the addition of water.
- Add the turkey cubes and mushrooms to the pot and boil them as well.
- Then add the Worcestershire sauce, garlic powder, and dry herbs, and mix everything until combined.
- The turkey should be cooked completely before adding the flour and thoroughly mixing it.
- After a few Mins, add the milk and continue simmering until the veggies are soft.
- Poke holes in the puff pastry with a fork before placing it in the air fryer's baking plate.
- Place the cooked turkey filling, eggs, and a puff pastry top with holes on top of the sauce. Remove any extra pastry by trimming it. Oil spray or melted butter may be used as a finishing touch.
- For six Mins or until golden brown, air fried at 180 F.
- Include microgreens on the menu.

Nutrition Value
Calories: 224 Kcal, Carb: 17 g, Protein: 20 g, Fat: 18 g
Storage Suggestion: You can store it in the refrigerator for 1-2 days.

Air-Fried Buttermilk Turkey

Prep Time: 30 Mins, Cook Time: 20 Mins, Servings: 6, Serving Size: 1

Ingredients
- Turkey thighs: 4 cups skin-on, bone-in

Marinade
- Buttermilk: 2 cups
- Black pepper: 2 tsp
- Cayenne pepper: 1 tsp
- Salt: 2 tsp
- Seasoned Flour
- Baking powder: 1 tbsp
- All-purpose flour: 2 cups
- Paprika powder: 1 tbsp
- Salt: 1 tsp
- Garlic powder: 1 tbsp

Instructions
- At 180 degrees Fahrenheit set the air fryer to cook.
- Pat the Turkey thighs dry with a paper towel.
- Add the paprika, salt, and pepper to a mixing dish and stir well. Then add the turkey cubes. Toss the turkey in buttermilk and thoroughly coat it. For at least six hrs, let it marinade.
- Add baking powder, salt, flour, pepper, and paprika to a separate bowl. Put the turkey pieces one by one in the spice mix and coat them.
- Turkey pieces should be sprayed with oil and placed skin-side up in the air fryer basket. Cook for 8 Mins, then turn the pieces and cook for another 10 Mins.
- To serve, place the meat on a bed of lettuce and toss to coat.

Nutrition Value
Calories: 210 Kcal, Carb: 12 g, Protein: 22 g, Fat: 18 g
Storage Suggestion: You can store it in the refrigerator for 1-2 days.

Low Carb Parmesan Turkey Meatballs

Prep Time: 10 Mins, Cook Time: 12 Mins, Servings: 20, Serving Size: 2

Ingredients
- Pork rinds: 1/2 cup, ground
- Ground Turkey: 4 cups
- Parmesan cheese: 1/2 cup grated
- Kosher salt: 1 tsp
- Garlic powder: 1 tsp
- One egg beaten
- Paprika: 1 tsp
- Pepper: 1/2 tsp

Breading
- Pork rinds: 1/2 cup ground

Instructions
- The Air Fryer should be preheated to 400°F.
- A half-cup of pork rinds and some paprika to the large mixing bowl with the cheese and the rest of the ingredients. Form into 1-inch balls after thoroughly mixing the ingredients.
- Pork rinds may be used to coat meatballs (ground).
- The air fry basket is sprayed with oil, and meatballs are placed uniformly.
- At 400°F, cook for 12 Mins, turning halfway through, until the meat is no longer pink.
- This dish is best served with a side of salad greens.

Nutrition Value
Calories: 240 Kcal, Carb: 12.1 g, Protein: 19.9 g, Fat: 10 g
Storage Suggestion: You can store it in the refrigerator for 1-2 days.

Sriracha-Honey Turkey Wings

Prep Time: 30 Mins, Cook Time: 15 Mins, Servings: 2, Serving Size: 2

Ingredients
- Soy sauce: 1 and 1/2 tbsp
- Turkey wings: 4 cups
- Sriracha sauce: 2 tbsp
- Butter: 1 tbsp
- 1/2 cup honey
- Juice of half lime
- Scallion's cilantro and chives for garnish

Instructions
- Heat the air fryer to a temperature of 360°F.
- Air-fried the turkey wings for 30 minutes, flipping the wings every seven Minutes until they're cooked through.

- Stir together all of the sauce ingredients in a small saucepan and bring to a gentle boil for three Mins.
- Apply sauce generously to the turkey wings before serving.
- Scallions may be added to the dish as a garnish. A microgreen salad is a good accompaniment to this dish.

Nutrition Value
Calories: 207 Kcal, Carb: 10 g, Protein: 22 g, Fat: 15 g
Storage Suggestion: You can store it in the refrigerator for 4-5 days.

Air Fryer Turkey Cheese Quesadilla

Prep Time: 4 Mins Cook Time: 7 Mins, Servings: 4, Serving Size: 2

Ingredients
- Precooked Turkey: one cup, diced
- Tortillas: 2 pieces
- Low-fat cheese: one cup (shredded)

Instructions
- Place one tortilla in the air basket after spraying it with oil. Top with shredded cheese and turkey.
- Add a second tortilla on top of the first. Top with a metal rack.
- 370°F for 6 Mins, flipping halfway through to ensure uniform cooking.
- Serve with salad leaves after slicing.

Nutrition Value
Calories: 171 Kcal, Carb: 8 g, Protein: 15 g, Fat: 8 g
Storage Suggestion: You can store it in the refrigerator for 1-2 days.

Air Fried Empanadas

Prep Time: 10 Mins, Cook Time: 20 Mins, Servings: 2, Serving Size: 1

Ingredients
- Square gyoza wrappers: eight pieces
- Olive oil: 1 tbsp
- White onion: ¼ cup, finely diced
- Mushrooms: ¼ cup, finely diced
- 1/2 cup lean ground beef
- Chopped garlic: 2 tsp
- Paprika: ¼ tsp
- Ground cumin: ¼ tsp
- Six green olives, diced
- Ground cinnamon: 1/8 tsp
- Diced tomatoes: 1/2 cup
- One egg, lightly beaten

Instructions
- Add the oil, onions, and meat to a medium-sized pan and heat for 3 Mins, or until the steak is browned.
- Cook the mushrooms for six Mins, or until they brown on the edges. Cook for 3 Mins or longer after adding paprika, cinnamon, olives, cumin, and garlic to the turkey.
- Add the chopped tomatoes and simmer for a few seconds. Allow it to cool for five Mins after turning off the heat.
- Add one and a 1/2 tbsp of beef filling to each gyoza wrapper. Brush the edges with water or egg, fold the wrappers, and squeeze the edges.
- Using an air fryer basket, arrange four empanadas evenly spaced out and cook for seven Mins at 400°F or until golden brown.
- Serve with a side of sauce and a salad.

Nutrition Value
Calories: 343 Kcal, Carb: 12.9 g, Protein: 18 g, Fat: 19 g
Storage Suggestion: You can store it in the refrigerator for 1-2 days

Air Fryer BBQ Turkey Wings

Prep Time: 5 Mins, Cook Time: 15 Mins, Servings: 4, Serving Size: 1

Ingredients
- BBQ sauce: 1/2 cup
- Turkey wings: 4 cups
- Black pepper, to taste
- Garlic powder: 1/8 tsp
- Ranch
- Celery sticks

Instructions
- Preheat your Air Fryer to 400 degrees Fahrenheit.
- Pat the turkey wings dry with paper towels before sprinkling them with garlic powder. In an equal layer, place the vegetables in the air fryer.
- Flip the wings a few times throughout the 15-Min cooking period. Cook for a further 3 Mins to get a charred exterior.
- Toss them in BBQ sauce after they're out of the air fryer. coat thoroughly
- Ranch dressing, celery sticks, and mixed greens complete this dish.

Nutrition Value
Calories: 197 Kcal, Carb: 14 g, Protein: 11 g, Fat: 10 g
Storage Suggestion: You can store it in the refrigerator for 1-2 days.

Air Fryer Cornish Turkey

Prep Time: 5 Mins, Cook Time: 25 Mins, Servings: 3, Serving Size: 1

Ingredients
- One Cornish Turkey
- Salt & black pepper, to taste
- Olive oil spray
- Paprika, ¼ tbsp

Instructions
- To use, combine all the spices in a bowl and rub them into the Cornish turkey.
- Olive oil may be sprayed into the air fryer basket.
- An Air fryer may be used to cook Cornish Turkey.
- At 390 degrees Fahrenheit, cook the food for 25 Mins. After the first half, switch sides.
- To accompany the meal, serve a mixed greens salad.

Nutrition Value
Calories: 300 Kcal, Carb: 20 g, Protein: 25 g, Fat: 21 g
Storage Suggestion: You can store it in the refrigerator for 1-2 days.

Air Fry Turkey Rib-Eye Steak

Prep Time: 5 Mins, Cook Time: 14 Mins, Servings: 2, Serving Size: 1

Ingredients

- Lean Turkey steaks: 2, medium size
- Salt & freshly ground black pepper, to taste

Instructions
- Preheat the air fryer to 400°F before using. Using paper towels, gently dry the steaks.
- Steaks may be seasoned with any combination of herbs and spices or just salt and pepper.
- On both sides of the steak generously.
- Air fried steaks by placing them in the basket. Cook to your desired level of doneness. Alternatively, cook for 14 Mins before flipping.
- Take the food out of the air fryer and cool for approximately 5 Mins before serving.
- The salad should be served with micro greens.

Nutrition Value
Calories: 470 Kcal, Carb: 23 g, Protein: 45 g, Fat: 31 g
Storage Suggestion: You can store it in the refrigerator for 4-5 days.

Orange Turkey Wings

Prep Time: 5 Mins, Cook Time: 14 Mins, Servings: 2, Serving Size: 1

Ingredients
- Honey: 1 tbsp
- Turkey Wings, Six pieces
- One orange zest and juice
- Worcestershire Sauce: 1.5 tbsp
- Black pepper, to taste
- Herbs (sage, rosemary, oregano, parsley, basil, thyme, and mint)

Instructions
- Rinse and pat dry the wings of the turkey.
- Orange juice and zest should be poured over the turkey wings in a bowl.
- Rub the turkey wings with the remainder of the ingredients. Allow at least 30 Mins of marinating time.
- Pre-heat your Air fryer to 180°C.
- Air fried the wings for 20 Mins at 180 C in an Al foil-wrapped air fryer.
- Then cook the wings for a further 15 Mins with the sauce brushed on once the foil has been removed after 20 Mins. Cook the turkey for a further ten Mins after brushing it with sauce.
- Serve with salad leaves once you've removed them from the air fryer.

Nutrition Value
Calories: 271 Kcal, Carb: 20 g, Protein: 29 g, Fat: 15 g
Storage Suggestion: You can store it in the refrigerator for 1-2 days.

Lemon Rosemary Turkey

Prep Time: 30 Mins, Cook Time: 20 Mins, Servings: 2, Serving Size: 1

Ingredients

For marinade
- Turkey: 2 and ½ cups
- Ginger: 1 tsp, minced
- Olive oil: 1/2 tbsp
- Soy sauce: 1 tbsp

For the sauce
- Half lemon
- Honey: 3 tbsp
- Oyster sauce: 1 tbsp
- Fresh rosemary: 1/2 cup, chopped

Instructions
- Combine the marinade ingredients with the turkey in a large mixing bowl and thoroughly combine.
- Refrigerate for a minimum of 30 Mins before consuming.
- For three Mins, preheat the oven to 200°C.
- One layer of the marinated turkey should go into the air fryer. Also, cook for six Mins at a temperature of 200 degrees Fahrenheit.
- Meanwhile, combine all the sauce ingredients in a bowl and stir thoroughly, except for the lemon wedges.
- Add a good amount of lemon juice to the top of the half-baked turkey.
- Cook for a further 13 Mins at 200 degrees Fahrenheit. Halfway through the cooking process, turn the turkey over and continue cooking it on the other side. Allow the turkey to be brown on both sides.
- Serve with a salad of micro greens.

Nutrition Value
Calories: 308 Kcal, Carb: 7 g, Protein: 25 g, Fat: 12 g
Storage Suggestion: You can store it in the refrigerator for 1-2 days.

Roasted Turkey Legs

Prep Time: 45 Mins, Cook Time: 15 Mins, Servings: 2, Serving Size: 1

Ingredients
- Garlic powder: 1/2 tsp
- 1 and a 1/2 tsp smoked paprika
- Brown sugar: 1 tsp
- 2 turkey legs
- Season salt: 1 tsp

Instructions
- Combine the spices in a large bowl and stir well.
- Paper towels may be used to dry the turkey legs.
- Toss the turkey legs in a seasoning mixture before cooking them.
- Spray the basket of the air fryer with oil.
- In an air fryer, roast turkey legs for 20 Mins at 400 degrees Fahrenheit.
- Cook for another 20 Mins after flipping the turkey.
- Serve as soon as possible.

Nutrition Value
Calories: 257 Kcal, Carb: 11 g, Protein: 29 g, Fat: 18 g
Storage Suggestion: You can store it in the refrigerator for 4-5 days.

Turkey Schnitzel (Air Fried)

Prep Time: 10 Mins, Cook Time: 15 Mins, Servings: 1, Serving Size: 1

Ingredients
- One lean Turkey schnitzel
- Olive oil: 2 tbsp
- Breadcrumbs: ¼ cup
- One egg
- One lemon, to serve

Instructions
- Allow the air fryer to heat up to 180 degrees Fahrenheit.
- Add breadcrumbs and oil to a large bowl and stir well until a crumbly mixture.
- Coat beef steak with breadcrumb mixture after being dipped in beaten egg.
- Air-fried the breaded beef for at least 15 Mins at 180C until it is well done.
- When ready to serve, remove the chicken from the air fryer and serve it with salad leaves and a squeeze of fresh lemon juice.

Nutrition Value
Calories: 340 Kcal, Carb: 14 g, Protein: 20 g, Fat: 10 g
Storage Suggestion: You can store it in the refrigerator for 1-2 days.

Air Fried Tom Yum Turkey Wings

Prep Time: 30 Mins, Cook Time: 20 Mins, Servings: 3, Serving Size: 1

Ingredients
- Tom Yum Paste: 2 tbsp
- Turkey Wings
- Water: 1 tbsp

Coating
- Corn flour: 2 tbsp
- Baking Powder: 1/2 tsp
- Tapioca Starch: 2 tbsp

Instructions
- Combine the Tom Yum paste with water in a small bowl and stir until smooth paste forms.
- For four hrs, marinate the turkey wings in the tom yum sauce by sprinkling them with salt and pepper.
- Pre-heat the Air Fryer to 180°C before using it.
- Mix the tapioca starch, baking powder, and corn flour in a bowl and well combine. Flour the turkey and then bake it. Turkey should be sprayed with the oil.
- Cook the turkey for 10-12 Mins in a uniform layer in the air fryer.
- Then cook them for another 5,8 Mins.
- To serve, remove them from the air fryer and place them on a bed of lettuce with slices of lemon.

Nutrition Value
Calories: 320 Kcal, Carb: 18 g, Protein: 27 g, Fat: 14 g
Storage Suggestion: You can store it in the refrigerator for 1-2 days.

Chapter 8: Other Poultry Recipes

Duck and Cheese Taco Quesadillas

Prep Time: 2 Mins, Cook Time: 6 Mins, Servings: 4, Serving Size: 1

Ingredients
- tortilla shells (soft)
- 8-10 ounces/cubed cooked shredded chicken
- 1 tsp chili powder
- 1 tsp cumin
- 1 cup shredded cheese
- 14 cup chopped onion
- 14 cup chopped tomatoes

Instructions
- Cumin and chili powder are excellent additions to chicken. If rotisserie chicken isn't utilized, salt and pepper will do the trick.
- Fry the tortilla shell in the air fryer until crisp and golden brown. The quesadilla does not stick to the basket since there is no oil.
- On the tortilla, spread out a quarter-cup of cheese.
- Onion, tomatoes, and chicken are all the last components added.
- On top of the other tortillas, add another.
- Bake at 370°F for three Mins.
- Turn the quesadilla out of the air fryer. Allow the food to cook for a final three Mins before serving. Quesadillas should be cooked for a long period for the cheese to melt and for the tortillas to be crispy at the same time.
- It's time to remove the air-quesadilla fryers and put them aside. Cut it into pieces and serve it.

Nutrition Value
Calories: 212 Kcal, Carb: 24.2 g, Protein: 32.1 g, Fat: 19.2 g
Storage Suggestion: You can store it in the refrigerator for 1-2 days.

Air Fryer Buffalo Duck Zucchini Skins

Prep Time: 25 mins, Cook Time: 20 Mins, Servings: 8, Serving Size: 1

Ingredients
- Large zucchini 2 (9 oz each)
- olive oil for spray
- Salt ½ tsp
- Garlic powder ¼ tsp
- Paprika ¼ tsp

Stuffing
- Shredded skinless Duck breasts, from a rotisserie Duck or made in a slow cooker 7 oz
- Softened less fat cream cheese 1 oz 1/3
- Franks hot sauce ¼ cup
- Crumbled blue cheese or gorgonzola 4 tsp
- Blue Cheese or Ranch Dressing ¼ cup
- Chopped scallions 2 tbsp

Instructions
- Combine some cream cheese and spicy sauce in a mixing bowl and whisk until well-combined. In this case, add the duck to the mix.
- Firstly, cut the zucchini in half, and then cut it in half again. Dig out the pulp but leave about 1/4 inch of the shell intact.
- Sprinkle salt, paprika, and garlic powder on both sides of the zucchini before serving.
- Until tender and crispy, cook in 8-Min batches at 350° for 8 Mins. Put 3-4 tbsp of buffalo Duck filling in the zucchini skin, followed by a 1/2 tsp of cheese. Cook until cheese is melted, approximately 2 Mins. Scallions and 12 tsp of blue cheese should be sprinkled on the heated zucchini.

Nutrition Value
Calories: 187 Kcal, Carb: 12.2 g, Protein: 19.2 g, Fat: 8.4 g
Storage Suggestion: You can store it in the refrigerator for 3-4 days.

Herbed Buttermilk Air Fryer Duck Breast Roast

Prep Time: 1 hr, Cook Time: 25 Mins, Servings: 2, Serving Size: 1

Ingredients
- The large bone-in Duck breast about 1 ¼ - 1 ½ lb 1
- 1 percent buttermilk 1 cup
- Dried parsley 1 ½ tsp
- Dried chives or Fresh 1 ½ tsp
- Kosher salt ¾ tsp
- Dried dill ½ tsp
- Onion powder ½ tsp
- Garlic powder ¼ tsp
- Olive oil 1 spray

Instructions
- In a dish, lay the Duck, and coat it with buttermilk to your desired thickness. Marinate the duck for 20 Mins at room temperature or 4 hrs in the refrigerator.
- In the meanwhile, combine all of the seasonings in a large bowl.
- Using a colander, remove any excess batter from the Duck and set it in the air fryer to cook.
- Allow it to sit for at least five minutes to absorb the spices fully.
- Duck should be cooked for around 30 to 35 Mins at 350F until it's golden brown or an instant-read thermometer reaches 160F.
- When ready to serve, allow the Duck to cool for 10 Mins before separating the bones and slicing it into thick slices.

Nutrition Value
Calories: 298 Kcal, Carb: 32 g, Protein: 37.5 g, Fat: 18.2 g
Storage Suggestion: You can store it in the refrigerator for 3-4 days.

Air Fryer Duck Tenders

Prep Time: 35 Mins, Cook Time: 25 Mins, Servings: 4, Serving Size: 1

Ingredients
- Duck tenders (1 ¼ lb) 12
- Large eggs, beaten 2
- Kosher salt 1 tsp
- Black pepper for taste
- Seasoned breadcrumbs ½ cup

- Seasoned panko ½ cup
- Olive oil spray
- Lemon wedges for serving

Instructions
- Sprinkle the Duck with salt and pepper.
- Mix breadcrumbs and panko in a separate shallow bowl while beating the egg in the first.
- Place the duck on a plate or cutting board and brush it with the egg and breadcrumbs. Apply oil to both surfaces.
- Preheat the air fryer to 400°F before using.
- Ensure all sides of the Duck are fully done and golden brown by cooking them in batches for 5-6 Mins. With some lemon slices, it's ready to be devoured.

Nutrition Value
Calories: 237 Kcal, Carb: 25.3 g, Protein: 8.6 g, Fat: 15.4 g
Storage Suggestion: You can store it in the refrigerator for 4-5 days.

Air Fryer Duck Milanese with Arugula

Prep Time: 30 Mins, Cook Time: 25 Mins, Servings: 4, Serving Size: 1

Ingredients
- Boneless, skinless Duck breasts (16 oz) 2
- Kosher salt ¾ tsp
- Black pepper Freshly ground
- Whole wheat Seasoned breadcrumbs, gluten-free or wheat ½ cup
- Parmesan cheese Grated 2 tbsp
- Large egg, beaten 1
- Olive oil 1 spray
- Baby arugula 6 cups
- Lemon's wedge 3

Instructions
- Duck breasts should be chopped into four equal pieces, wrapped in parchment paper or plastic wrap, and lb to a thickness of 1/4 inch.
- Salt and pepper on both sides.
- Mix the egg and water in a small dish (1 tsp).
- Breadcrumbs and Parmesan cheese should be combined in a separate dish.
- Spray oil on both sides of the Duck after it has been dipped in egg and breadcrumbs.
- The air fryer should be set to 400 degrees Fahrenheit before you begin cooking.
- Cook in batches for 7 Mins at a time, flipping halfway through to ensure even browning on both sides.
- Serve it with 1 12 cups of arugula and a squeeze of lemon juice.

Nutrition Value
Calories: 312 Kcal, Carb: 26 g, Protein: 29 g, Fat: 16.2 g
Storage Suggestion: You can store it in the refrigerator for 3-4 days.

Buttermilk-Marinated Air Fryer Whole Roasted Duck

Prep Time: 1 Day, Cook Time: 55 Mins, Servings: 4, Serving Size: 1

Ingredients
- trimmed whole Duck 3 Ibs
- Kosher salt 1 Tbsp
- 1% buttermilk 1 pint

Instructions
- Season the duck with salt (2 tsp) and bake it for 30 minutes the day before you prepare it. Duck legs may be tied together with a butcher's twig.
- In a large bowl, mix the buttermilk with the Duck and marinate for at least an hr. Refrigerate it for the evening by covering it tightly with plastic wrap. To ensure correct margining, flip the side halfway through the timer.
- Remove the duck from the refrigerator one hr before cooking; drain the buttermilk from the duck and discard the marinade.
- Before cooking, set your air fryer to 3500 F for 3 Mins. Put the duck, belly-side down, in the basket (maximum 5.8 quarts). Sprinkle the top with a quarter tsp of sea salt.
- After 25 Mins, flip the Duck over and season it with salt (12 tsp). Cook for another 25 Mins until both sides of the Duck are cooked, golden brown, and crispy, or the juices flow clear when a knife is inserted between the leg and thigh.
- Allow the Duck to cool for ten Mins before slicing.
- You may bake the duck in the oven at 400 degrees Fahrenheit for 60 Mins or more to get a golden brown and crispy exterior and for the fluids to run clear when you put a knife between the thighs and the legs.

Nutrition Value
Calories: 192 Kcal, Carb: 12.2 g, Protein: 18.6 g, Fat: 15.4 g
Storage Suggestion: You can store it in the refrigerator for 3-4 days.

Duck Chimichangas (Baked or Air Fryer)

Prep Time: 35 Mins, Cook Time: 20 Mins, Servings: 4, Serving Size: 1

Ingredients

For the Pico de Gallo
- Diced tomato ½ cup
- Chopped onion 3 tbsp
- Chopped fresh cilantro 1 tbsp + more
- Fresh lime juice 1 tsp
- Kosher salt ¼ tsp
- Freshly ground black pepper

For the Chimichangas
- Shredded leftover or rotisserie Duck breast 12 oz
- Juice of 1/2 navel orange
- Juice of 1/2 lime
- Large garlic, minced 1 clove
- Ground cumin 1 tsp
- Green chiles, Mild diced, drained 1 can (4oz)
- Whole wheat, Low-carb tortillas 4
- Pepper cheese, Shredded ½ cup (2 oz)
- Olive oil spray
- Shredded lettuce 3 cups
- Sour cream 4 tbsp
- Avocado, from 1 small Hass, diced 4 oz

Instructions
- Put all of the ingredients in a small bowl and mix them with salt and pepper to your liking.
- Preparation for Chimichangas: In a large bowl, combine duck, orange juice, lime juice, garlic, cumin, and the drained chiles.
- One at a time, place the tortilla on the area to be worked on. 2 Tbsp of cheese should be added to the lowest part of the tortilla. Wrap the tortilla around the filling by lifting the bottom corner. Make a cylindrical roll by rolling the remaining two edges towards the center. Keep the rest in a separate dish and repeat the procedure.
- The air fryer should be set to 400 degrees Fahrenheit before you begin cooking.
- Make sure to oil both sides of the Chimichangas. Fry them in a basket with the seams down in a deep fryer (ensure that all are tightly wrapped to avoid opening as they cook). To get crispy and golden brown on all sides of the Chimichangas, fry them for 7-8 Mins, turning them halfway through. At 350 degrees Fahrenheit, cook them for 7-8 Mins in an oven or toaster-style fryer. Cook the remaining Chimichangas in the same manner as the first.
- ¾ cup of shredded lettuce, Pico de Gallo, sour cream, and avocado should be placed on a serving platter before serving the Chimichanga. Serve it with fresh cilantro on top.

Nutrition Value
Calories: 286 Kcal, Carb: 23.2 g, Protein: 37.3 g, Fat: 16.4 g
Storage Suggestion: You can store it in the refrigerator for 1-2 days.

Juicy Air Fryer Duck Breasts

Prep Time: 55 Mins, Cook Time: 35 Mins, Servings: 4, Serving Size: 1

Ingredients
- Kosher salt
- Boneless Duck breasts 4
- Olive oil spray
- Garlic powder ¾ tsp
- Onion powder ¾ tsp
- Dried parsley ½ tsp
- Smoked paprika ½ tsp
- Cayenne pepper 1/8

Instructions
- Duck should cook evenly on all sides if leveled by being on the thicker side.
- In a large bowl, combine 1/4 cup kosher salt with 6 cups boiling water.
- Make a brine solution and submerge the duck for 1 to 1 12 hrs. Removing Duck from the solution and blotting off any remaining liquid
- In a bowl, combine the seasonings with 34 tsp salt. Season the whole Duck with the spice combination and spray oil on both sides.
- Before preheating the air fryer, make sure it's ready to go. Cook the duck in batches for 10 minutes at 380 degrees Fahrenheit, turn the bird midway during cooking or until the exterior is golden brown.

Nutrition Value
Calories: 264 Kcal, Carb: 19.2 g, Protein: 23.1 g, Fat: 17.5 g
Storage Suggestion: You can store it in the refrigerator for 1-2 days.

Air Fryer Asian-Glazed Duck Thighs Boneless

Prep Time: 1 hr 35 mins, Cook Time: 1 Hr, Servings, 4, Serving Size: 1

Ingredients
- Duck thighs, Boneless, skinless fat trimmed 8 (32 oz each)
- soy sauce Low sodium ¼ cup
- Balsamic vinegar 2 ½ tbsp
- Honey 1 tbsp
- Garlic, crushed 3 cloves
- Sriracha hot sauce 1 tsp
- Fresh grated ginger 1 tsp
- Scallion, green only sliced for garnish 1

Instructions
- Combine the garlic, honey, soy sauce, balsamic vinegar, and sriracha in a small bowl.
- Put the Duck in a large bowl, add 1/4 cup of spice mix, and distribute the mixture evenly over the Duck. Leave it overnight or for at least two hrs.
- For preheating, set the air fryer at 400 F.
- Remove the meat from the marinade and place it in an air fryer.
- To cook it in batches, heat it for 14 Mins, rotating each side halfway through.
- Meanwhile, cook the remaining mixture for 1-2 Mins on low to medium heat, constantly stirring, until it thickens into a sauce.
- Slaw and sauce should be served with the duck.

Nutrition Value
Calories: 233 Kcal, Carb: 26 g, Protein: 29.1 g, Fat: 12.1 g
Storage Suggestion: You can store it in the refrigerator for 1-2 days.

Buffalo Duck Egg Rolls

Prep Time: 15 Mins, Cook Time: 30 Mins, Servings: 8, Serving Size: 1

Ingredients
- Boneless skinless Duck breasts 2 pieces (16 oz)
- Less fat cream cheese softened 2 oz
- Franks hot sauce or any sauce ½ cup
- Crumbled blue cheese ½ cup
- Shredded carrots, chopped 1/3 cup
- Chopped scallions 1/3 cup
- Egg roll wrappers 16
- Olive oil spray
- Blue cheese dressing, optional for dipping

Instructions
- It's best to cook the duck in a pressure cooker for four hrs at a high temperature. Forks may shred the cooked Duck once the liquid has been removed.
- Use 1 cup water and 1 cup duck or duck broth in an instant pot. Set a

timer for 15 Mins on high pressure and cook the dish until done. Shred the Duck with forks after removing the liquid.
- Make a paste out of the spicy sauce and cream cheese while waiting. Make 3 cups of this mixture and add the carrots, duck, scallions, and blue cheese.
- Make a diamond shape out of the wrapper by placing it on a work surface with its corner facing outwards.
- Place 3 tbsp of the prepared mixture in the lowest third of the wrapper.
- Apply water to the wrapper's corners using your finger. Wrap the filling in the bottom corner of the wrapper and secure it with a little piece of tape.
- Make a cylindrical roll by folding the other two corners of the wrappers toward the middle.
- Use the same method to make more rolls.
- Make sure the egg rolls are evenly coated in oil by spraying them or using your fingertips.
- Fry the egg rolls in batches at 370F for 8 Mins, flipping them over halfway through cooking time for golden and crispy results on both sides.
- They should be served hot, with a sauce to go with them.

Nutrition Value
Calories: 341 Kcal, Carb: 25.3 g, Protein: 28.3 g, Fat: 18.1 g
Storage Suggestion: You can store it in the refrigerator for 3-4 days.

Air Fryer Duck Thighs Make Perfect Duck Street Tacos

Prep Time: 20 mins, Cook Time: 25 Mins, Servings: 8, Serving Size: 2

Ingredients
- Boneless skinless Duck thighs 2 lb
- Avocado oil 2 tsp
- Chili powder 2 tsp
- Cumin 1 tsp
- Garlic powder 1 tsp
- Salt 1 tsp
- Pepper ½ tsp
- Pinch cayenne pepper

Instructions
- An inconspicuous cup is all that's needed to combine the spices mentioned above.
- Brush the Duck with oil and season it evenly on all sides with the spice combination after patting it dry with paper towels.
- Cook the duck for 12-15 Mins at 400° F, or until it reaches an internal temperature of 175°, in a deep fryer basket. You may need to turn halfway through cooking if necessary.
- Before cutting or shredding the Duck, let it cool down a little. Slices of lime may be served on top of lettuce or taco fillings.

Nutrition Value
Calories: 341 Kcal, Carb: 18.2 g, Protein: 34.3 g, Fat: 19.1 g
Storage Suggestion: You can store it in the refrigerator for 1-2 days.

Healthier General Tso's Duck

Prep Time: 30 mins, Cook Time: 25 Mins, Servings: 4, Serving Size: 2

Ingredients
- Duck thighs, boneless and skinless, cut into bite-sized pieces 1.5- 2 lb
- Potato starch 1/3 cup
- Vegetable oil 1 tbsp
- Dried red chilies 6
- Green onions chopped 3
- Garlic minced 2 tsp
- Ginger minced 1 tsp
- Brown sugar ¾ cup
- Duck broth ½ cup
- Soy sauce ½ cup
- Rice vinegar 2 tbsp
- Sesame oil
- Pinch of salt
- Corn starch 2 tsp
- Water ¼ cup

Instructions
- Ensure the air fryer is preheated to 400 degrees Fahrenheit (204 degrees Celsius). Potato starch should be used to coat the duck thighs completely. Aimed at the Fryer basket, place the duck parts with tongs into it. Duck parts should be cooked for 25-30 Mins, shaking the basket every five Mins until they are crispy and golden brown.
- Make the sauce while the oil is heating in a pot over medium heat. After the pan has heated up for about a Min or two, or when the chilies have started to change color, and the onions begin to soften, add the green onions, ginger, and dried chiles.
- Mix all ingredients in a saucepan and bring to a boil. After bringing to a boil, reduce heat to a simmer and cook for three more Mins.
- Add the duck to the sauce when it's finished cooking in the air fryer and mix it up well.
- Corn starch and cold water may be whisked together to thicken a drink. For about a Min, or until the sauce has thickened, stir into the boiling sauce.
- The dish is best served with rice and veggies, so savor it!

Nutrition Value
Calories: 481 Kcal, Carb: 25.3 g, Protein: 43.2 g, Fat: 34.3 g
Storage Suggestion: You can store it in the refrigerator for 6-7 days.

Extra Crispy Gluten-Free Air Fryer Popcorn Duck

Prep Time: 20 mins, Cook Time: 25 Mins, Servings: 2-3, Serving Size: 3

Ingredients
- Skinless Duck tenders, cut into small cubes,1lb
- Corn starch ½ cup
- Unsweetened lite culinary coconut milk 1 cup
- Pickle juice 1 tsp
- Finely crushed corn cereal gluten-free 3 cups
- Garlic powder ½ tsp
- Onion powder ½ tsp
- Paprika ½ tsp

- Black pepper ¼ tsp
- Cayenne pepper (optional) ¼ tsp

Instructions
- Place the cubed Duck tenders to the side as you set up the three coating spots in the sequence.
- Make a tray out of corn flour to get started.
- Coconut milk and pickle juice may also be used in different cuisine.
- Crush the cornflakes and spices in a plastic container first, then transfer them to a pan.
- When placing the Duck piece in the fryer basket, coat it with corn starch, coconut milk, and cornflake crumbs.
- Place the leftover Duck parts in the fryer basket in an even layer.
- For 10 Mins, turn off the air fryer and set the temperature to 400°F (seven-eight mins if doing it in two batches).
- Make the ketchup while the sauce is simmering.

Nutrition Value
Calories: 265 Kcal, Carb: 23.1 g, Protein: 27.5 g, Fat: 18.2 g
Storage Suggestion: You can store it in the refrigerator for 6-7 days.

Air Fryer Zucchini Enchiladas

Prep Time: 15 mins, Cook Time: 35 Mins, Servings: 2, Serving Size: 2

Ingredients
- Zucchini 1 large
- Shredded Duck 1 cup
- Onion diced 1 small
- Ground Cumin 1 tsp
- Chili Powder 1 tsp
- Garlic Powder tsp
- Smoked Paprika 1 tsp
- Red Enchilada Sauce 1 cup
- Shredded Mexican Blend Cheese ¼ cup
- Olive Oil 2 tbsp
- Pepper and salt for taste
- Drizzle of Green Onion & Sour Cream to garnish

Instructions
- Brown the chopped onion in a large skillet of olive oil over medium heat until it's transparent.
- Add salt and pepper to taste, along with the spices such as cumin, garlic powder, chili powder, and smoky paprika.
- Add the shredded duck and mix well.
- The sauce should completely cover the meat, at which point you may remove the pan from the heat. Rechecked the seasoning and, if necessary, adjusted. Before serving, let it cool down a little.
- The zucchini should be cut half lengthwise while the Duck is cooling down. Use a peeler to make thin slices of zucchini. You get 6 to 8 slices from each half.
- Overlap three zucchini slices on a baking sheet.
- A heaping tbsp of the Duck mixture should be placed on one end of each zucchini strip.
- Put it in a fryer basket and bake it on a prepared baking sheet.
- With the remaining Duck mixture and zucchini strips, proceed as before.
- The remaining 1/4 cup of enchilada sauce should be poured over the zucchini strips that have been covered in plastic.
- Then top with melted cheese.
- For ten Mins, cook at 330°F in the oven.
- Serve immediately with a dollop of whipped cream and a sprinkling of green onion on top.

Nutrition Value
Calories: 320 Kcal, Carb: 32.1 g, Protein: 30.3 g, Fat: 25.3 g
Storage Suggestion: You can store it in the refrigerator for 5-6 days.

Healthy Air Fryer Duck & Veggies

Prep Time: 20 mins, Cook Time: 15 Mins, Servings: 4, Serving Size: 2

Ingredients
- Duck breast, chopped into bite-size pieces, 1 lb
- Broccoli florets (fresh or frozen) 1 cup
- Zucchini chopped 1
- Bell pepper chopped 1 cup
- Onion chopped ½
- Garlic minced or crushed 2 cloves
- Olive oil 2 tbsp
- Garlic powder, chili powder, salt, pepper ½ tsp
- Italian seasoning (or spice blend of choice) 1 tbsp

Instructions
- Prepare a 390°F fryer for deep-frying.
- Mix and cut the veggies and duck into small pieces in a large bowl.
- Mix oil and spices in a bowl until well-combined.
- In a preheated air fryer, cook the duck and veggies for 10 Mins, shaking halfway through, or until the duck is crispy and the vegetables are cooked through. You may cook them in two or three batches in an air fryer for smaller amounts.

Nutrition Value
Calories: 276 Kcal, Carb: 29.2 g, Protein: 27.5 g, Fat: 16.5 g
Storage Suggestion: You can store it in the refrigerator for 6-7 days.

Easy Duck Marinade (Only 4 Ingredients!)

Prep Time: 20 mins, Cook Time: 20 Mins, Servings: 4-6, Serving Size: 1

Ingredients
- Boneless, skinless Duck breasts 1-1.5 lb
- Avocado oil 2/3 cup
- Red wine vinegar 1/3 cup
- Minced garlic three cloves
- Honey 2-3 tbsp

Instructions
- Place the Duck in a big plastic bag and seal it.
- Combine the remaining ingredients in a blender.
- To combine it, tighten the seal and give it a quick shake.
- Marinate for 4 to 24 hrs in the refrigerator.

- Remove the marinade and continue cooking as required.

Nutrition Value
Calories: 382 Kcal, Carb: 37.5 g, Protein: 52.2 g, Fat: 19.2 g
Storage Suggestion: You can store it in the refrigerator for 6-7 days.

Air Fryer Duck Chimichangas

Prep Time: 15 mins, Cook Time: 25 Mins, Servings: 8, Serving Size: 1

Ingredients
- Vegetable oil 2 tsp
- Shredded deli rotisserie Duck 2 cups
- Duck taco seasoning mix 1 pack
- Water 3 tbsp
- Traditional refried beans ¾ cup
- Chopped green chiles 1 can
- Flour tortillas (6 inches) 8
- Shredded Cheddar cheese (4 oz) 1 cup
- Butter melted 2 tbsp

Instructions:
- In a 10-inch nonstick pan, heat the oil over medium heat. Stir in the Duck, taco seasoning mix, and water until everything is well combined. Cook for 4 to 5 Mins, uncovered, or until Duck is thoroughly done.
- In a shallow mixing cup, combine the beans and chilies. On the work area, spread roughly 3 tsp bean paste in the middle of the tortilla. Toss in approximately 1/4 cup of Duck and 2 tsp of cheese. Fold the sides of the tortilla inward. Fold the bottom and edges of the envelope over the filling. Roll it up tightly to envelop the filling. Continue with the tortillas that have been left over.
- Brush the outsides of each stuffed tortilla with butter, then place four of them in the air fryer basket, seam side down. Preheat the oven to 400 degrees Fahrenheit and bake for 4 Mins. Cook for another 2 to 3 Mins on the other side, or until golden brown and well cooked. Rep with the last four tortillas.

Nutrition Value
Calories: 298 Kcal, Carb: 21.1 g, Protein: 27.5 g, Fat: 18.2 g
Storage Suggestion: You can store it in the refrigerator for 7-8 days.

Air Fryer Duck Fajitas

Prep Time: 20 mins, Cook Time: 15 Mins, Servings: 2, Serving Size: 2

Ingredients
- Duck breast, sliced into ¼-inch slices 1 large
- Onion, sliced ½ medium
- Green bell pepper, 1/2, sliced
- Red bell pepper, ½, sliced
- Olive or coconut oil 1-1/2 tbsp
- Chili powder 2 tsp
- Cumin 1tsp
- Salt ½ tsp
- Paprika ½ tsp
- Garlic powder ½ tsp
- Onion powder ½ tsp
- Dried oregano ¼ tsp

Instructions
- Combine the Duck, bell peppers, and onion in a medium mixing bowl.
- Season with salt and pepper and drizzle with olive oil. To make sure it's evenly spread, mix it up.
- Place the mixture in an Air Fryer basket. Preheat oven to 350°F and cook for 20 Mins. Open the Air Fryer and shake the basket halfway during the cooking time.

Nutrition Value
Calories: 582 Kcal, Carb: 26.4 g, Protein: 39.3 g, Fat: 17.3 g
Storage Suggestion: You can store it in the refrigerator for 4-5 days.

Low-Carb Parmesan Duck Tenders (Air Fryer)

Prep Time: 17 mins, Cook Time: 15 Mins, Servings: 4, Serving Size: 1

Ingredients
- Boneless, Skinless Duck, 1.5 lb
- Eggs 2
- water 2 cup
- Parmesan cheese Grated 1 cup
- Dried oregano 1 tsp
- Paprika 1 tsp
- Dried thyme ½ tsp
- Dried rosemary ½ tsp
- Garlic salt ½ tsp
- Freshly ground pepper, according to taste
- Canola cooking oil

Instructions
- In a small bowl, whisk together the eggs and water.
- Mix the Parmesan cheese and spices in a shallow dish large enough to dip the Duck tenders in to make the "breading." To make it smooth, whisk everything together.
- Coat the duck tenders in egg wash, brush off the excess, and then dredge one at a time in the Parmesan mixture. Toss to coat evenly. Place the breaded tenders in an air fryer basket. Depending on the size of the basket, you'll have to do it in batches.
- Spray a light coating of cooking oil spray on the Duck. Preheat the oven to 400 degrees Fahrenheit and bake the Duck tenders for 15 Mins in the air fryer. Flip the Duck halfway through the cooking time to brown both sides. Cook until a meat thermometer registers 165 degrees Fahrenheit.
- If desired, serve right away with your favorite dipping sauce.

Nutrition Value
Calories: 302 Kcal, Carb: 17.2 g, Protein: 26.4 g, Fat: 21.2 g
Storage Suggestion: You can store it in the refrigerator for 7-8 days.

Air-Fryer Buffalo Wings

Prep Time: 30 mins, Cook Time: 45 Mins, Servings: 4, Serving Size: 1

Ingredients
- Paprika 1 ½ tsp
- Garlic powder ½ tsp
- Onion powder ½ tsp
- Ground pepper ½ tsp
- Duck wings, 3 ½ to 4 lb

- Buffalo-style hot sauce ½ cup
- Unsalted butter 2 tbsp
- Ranch dressing ¼ cup
- Carrots, cut into sticks 2
- Celery, cut into sticks 1 stalk

Instructions
- Preheat the oven to 200 degrees Fahrenheit. Preheat the air fryer to 375 degrees Fahrenheit. Combine paprika, onion powder, garlic powder, and pepper in a mixing bowl. To coat the wings, toss them in. Allow 10 Mins for relaxation.
- Cook for 15 Mins in the air fryer basket with half of the wings. Cook for 5 Mins more, or until the wings are crisp. Place the wings in a single layer on a baking sheet and keep them heated in the oven. Proceed in the same way with the remaining wings.
- Whisk the hot sauce and butter together in a small saucepan over medium heat for 2 to 3 Mins, or until the butter has melted and the mixture is smooth.
- In a large mixing bowl, place the wings. Toss in the butter sauce to coat the vegetables. Serve with carrots, celery, and ranch dressing.

Nutrition Value
Calories: 187 Kcal, Carb: 12.2 g, Protein: 16.2 g, Fat: 11.2 g
Storage Suggestion: You can store it in the refrigerator for 7-8 days.

Air Fryer Buffalo Duck Tenders

Prep Time: 30 mins, Cook Time: 25 Mins, Servings: 4, Serving Size: 1

Ingredients
- Boneless skinless Duck breasts 1 lb
- Buffalo wing sauce ¼ cup
- Panko breadcrumbs 2/3 cup

Instructions
- Fillets should be cut into 1-inch pieces. Pat your Duck dry with a paper towel.
- Pour the buffalo sauce into a small bowl. Place the Panko breadcrumbs in a separate small dish.
- Dip the duck strips in the buffalo sauce and use your hands to wipe off the excess sauce. Place the dipped Duck in a dish of Panko crumbs and coat evenly.
- Respectfully place the breaded Duck in the Air fryer basket. Cook for 12-20 Mins at 300°F, or until the Duck reaches an internal temperature of 165°F. Serve immediately.

Nutrition Value
Calories: 347 Kcal, Carb: 23.4 g, Protein: 34.2 g, Fat: 15.4 g
Storage Suggestion: You can store it in the refrigerator for 3-4 days.

Air Fryer Keto Fried Duck | Paleo, Gluten-Free

Prep Time: 15 mins, Cook Time: 25 Mins, Servings: 8, Serving Size: 1

Ingredients
- Bone-In, Skin-On Duck 3lb (16 pieces)
- Almond Flour ¾ cup
- Salt or to taste 1-2 tsp
- Tony Chachere's Creole Seasoning 2 tsp
- Paprika ½ tbsp
- Garlic Powder 1 tsp
- Black Pepper 1 tsp
- Avocado or Olive Oil Spray (Optional)

Instructions
- Combine everything except the Duck and the oil mist in a large zip-top container. Seal the bag with four Duck pieces and the spices on top.
- Place the Duck in the air fryer after tossing it in the bag to cover it. Arrange the Duck on a baking sheet in a single layer and drizzle with avocado oil. (The oil helps the almond flour brown, but it's unnecessary.)
- Carry on with the rest of the Duck in the same manner.
- Cook for 30 Mins at 370°F (180°C), or until the Duck reaches an internal temperature of 165°F (75°C), turning halfway through.

Nutrition Value
Calories: 271 Kcal, Carb: 14.2 g, Protein: 19.2 g, Fat: 16.4 g
Storage Suggestion: You can store it in the refrigerator for 7-8 days.

Air Fryer Buttermilk Fried Duck

Prep Time: 10 mins, Cook Time: 30 Mins, Servings: 4, Serving Size: 1

Ingredients
- Low-fat buttermilk 1/3 cup
- Hot sauce ¼ cup
- Boneless, skinless Duck breasts 1 lb (cut in half lengthwise to make 4 equal portions)
- Corn flakes 6 tbsp
- Stone-ground cornmeal 3 tbsp
- Garlic powder 1 tsp
- Paprika 1 tsp
- Salt ¼ tsp
- Coarse-ground black pepper ¼ tsp
- Nonstick cooking spray 1

Instructions
- In a deep dish, combine the buttermilk and hot sauce. Combine the buttermilk and duck in a large mixing bowl. Allow for a 15-Min rest period.
- In a food processor, combine the cornflakes. Blitz until coarse crumbs appear in a food processor. Pulse in the cornmeal, paprika, garlic powder, cinnamon, and pepper until everything is well distributed. Half-fill a small cup with crumbs. (If you don't have a food processor, lb the cornflakes in a plastic bag with a rolling pin.)
- Rinse the duck and re-add the buttermilk to the dish. Coat the Duck bits in an even layer of cornflake mixture. Place the Duck on a wire rack to cool.
- Place the duck in the air fryer basket. Spray with nonstick cooking oil spray for 2 seconds (do not crowd, cook in batches if necessary). Preheat the oven to 375 degrees Fahrenheit and air-fry the duck for 7 Mins. Toss the Duck pieces around a bit. Cook for 7–10 Mins more in the air fryer, or until

the Duck is cooked through and a meat thermometer inserted in the center registers 165°F.

Nutrition Value
Calories: 361 Kcal, Carb: 35.1 g, Protein: 45.3 g, Fat: 14.2 g
Storage Suggestion: You can store it in the refrigerator for 2-3 days.

Air Fryer Naked Duck Tenders

Prep Time: 20 mins, Cook Time: 25 Mins, Servings: 4, Serving Size: 1

Ingredients
- Duck tenderloins 1 lb
- Canola oil 2 tbsp
- Vinegar 1 tbsp
- Butt rub 1 tbsp

Instructions
- Combine the Duck tenders, fat, vinegar, and butt rub in a Ziplock bag or cup. Toss the tenders before they are evenly coated with seasoning.
- Refrigerate for at least 20 Mins before serving.
- Arrange duck tenders on a single sheet in an air fryer basket before the meat is done, air fry it for 10-12 Mins at 400 degrees. Make sure the Duck reaches a minimum internal temperature of 165 degrees.

Nutrition Value
Calories: 375 Kcal, Carb: 31.2 g, Protein: 46.4 g, Fat: 14.2 g
Storage Suggestion: You can store it in the refrigerator for 4-5 days.

Air Fryer Cornish Hens with Red Wine Mushroom Bacon Gravy

Prep Time: 30 mins, Cook Time: 35 Mins, Servings: 2, Serving Size: 1

Ingredients

Cornish Hens
- Cornish hens 2
- Yellow onion, sliced into 1-inch rounds 1 small
- Italian seasoning 1 tbsp
- Paprika 1 tbsp
- Salt

Red Wine Mushroom Bacon Gravy
- strips of thick-cut bacon
- Cremini mushrooms, cleaned and stems trimmed 16 oz
- Dry red wine ¾ cup
- Unsalted butter 2 tbsp
- Garlic, minced 4 cloves
- Heavy cream 1 cup
- Duck broth ½ cup
- parmesan cheese Grated ¼ cup
- Fresh thyme 1 tbsp
- Fresh parsley, chopped 1 tbsp
- Pink peppercorns 1 tbsp
- Corn starch 2 tbsp
- Water 2 tbsp

Instructions
- Preheat the air fryer to 390°F and wrap the outside of the basket with Al foil.
- Place the bacon pieces in the basket after halving them. Cook for 8-9 Mins on each side, flipping midway. Remove the bacon strips from the air fryer and lay them on a platter lined with paper towels to cool. When the bacon is cold enough to handle, dice it and set it aside.
- While the bacon is in the air fryer, melt butter in a skillet with garlic and 1/2 tsp thyme, often stirring for 1-2 Mins until aromatic and butter are melted.
- Increase the heat to high and add the wine and mushrooms. Cook for about 10 Mins, stirring occasionally, or until the mushrooms have weakened and the wine has reduced by half. If the wine boils quickly, turn down the heat. It just has to be brought to a low simmer.
- Combine the maize flour and water in a small cup, then pour it into the pan with the mushrooms. In a large mixing cup, combine the milk, Duck broth, bacon crumbles, parmesan cheese, pepper, and the remaining parsley and thyme. Cook, occasionally stirring, until the sauce has thickened somewhat. Season with salt and pepper to taste and additional herbs and pepper if required.

Nutrition Value
Calories: 361 Kcal, Carb: 32.2 g, Protein: 27.3 g, Fat: 15.3 g
Storage Suggestion: You can store it in the refrigerator for 3-4 days.

Chapter 9: Fish & Seafood Recipes

Fish & Fries

Prep Time: 25 Mins, Cook Time: 15 Mins, Servings: 4, Serving Size:1

Ingredients
- Pepper: ¼ tsp
- medium potatoes
- Salt: ¼ tsp
- Olive oil: 2 tbsp

For Fish
- 1 lb of cod fillets
- Crushed cornflakes: 2/3 cup
- All-purpose flour: 1/3 cup
- Parmesan cheese, grated: 1 tbsp
- Pepper: ¼ tsp
- 1 egg
- Water: 2 tbsp
- Cayenne pepper: 1/8 tsp
- Salt: ¼ tsp

Instructions
- Preheat the air fryer to 400 degrees Fahrenheit.
- Peeled potatoes should be sliced into half-inch-thick slices, then cut into sticks.
- Combine the oil, salt, fries, and pepper in a mixing bowl. Toss it with care.
- Cook for 5 to 10 Mins in an air fryer in one equal layer, then shake the basket and cook for another 5 to 10 Mins.
- Combine pepper and flour in a mixing dish.
- Combine water and egg in a separate dish.
- Combine cornflakes, cayenne, and cheese in the third bowl.
- Season the fish fillets with salt and then coat them in flour, then egg, and finally cornflakes.
- Remove the fries and keep them heated.
- Cook the fillets in one uniform layer in the air fryer for 8 to 10 Mins, or until fork tender.
- Flip halfway during the cooking time.
- Enjoy the fish with the potatoes.

Nutrition Value
Calories: 143 Kcal, Carb: 18 g, Protein: 21 g, Fat: 6 g

Storage Suggestion: You can store it in the refrigerator for 2-3 days.

Salmon with Brussels Sprouts

Prep Time: 15 Mins, Cook Time: 15 Mins, Servings: 4, Serving Size: 2

Ingredients
- 4 fillets of salmon
- Fresh thyme leaves, chopped: 1 tsp
- 4 cloves of minced garlic
- Olive oil: 2 tbsp
- Kosher salt: 2 tsp
- Black pepper: 1 tsp
- Honey: 1 tbsp
- 1 lb of Brussels sprouts
- Balsamic vinegar: 1 tbsp

Instructions
- Add half of the minced garlic to a mixing bowl.
- In a separate dish, combine the remaining minced garlic, olive oil, kosher salt (1 tsp), thyme leaves (1 tsp), lemon juice, and black pepper (1/2 tsp). Brush the fish fillets with the mixture after thoroughly mixing it.
- Preheat the air fryer to 400 degrees Fahrenheit.
- Spray the basket of the air fryer with oil.
- Place the fish skin side down on the final rack of the air fryer. Fillets should have some room.
- Combine 1 tbsp olive oil, 1 tsp salt, the remaining garlic, and 1/2 tsp black pepper in a mixing bowl.
- Cut the Brussel sprouts in half and mix with the remaining garlic bowl.
- Cook for 6 to 8 Mins on the top rack of an air fryer.
- Remove the fish and air fry the sprouts for another 1 to 3 Mins.
- Combine the remaining ingredients in a mixing dish and stir to combine.
- Serve with the fish and sprouts.

Nutrition Value
Calories: 187 Kcal, Carb: 2 g, Protein: 25 g, Fat: 3 g

Storage Suggestion: You can store it in the refrigerator for 4-5 days.

Air Fryer Easy Salmon

Prep Time: 15 Mins, Cook Time: 15 Mins, Servings: 2, Serving Size:1

Ingredients
- Olive oil: 2 tsp
- 2 salmon fillets
- 1 minced clove of garlic
- Black pepper, to taste
- Thyme leaves: 1/2 tsp
- Whole grain mustard: 2 tbsp
- Kosher salt, to taste
- Packed brown sugar: 1 tbsp

Instructions
- Season the salmon with salt and black pepper. Mix the thyme, oil, garlic, mustard, and sugar in a bowl, then brush over the salmon.
- Cook the fish for 10 Mins at 400 degrees Fahrenheit in the air fryer basket.
- Serve and have fun.

Nutrition Value
Calories: 134 Kcal, Carb: 3 g, Protein: 25 g, Fat: 2 g

Storage Suggestion: You can store it in the refrigerator for 1-2 days.

Bacon Wrapped Scallops

Prep Time: 15 Mins, Cook Time: 15 Mins, Servings: 4, Serving Size: 1

Ingredients
- BBQ Sauce: ¼ cup
- 8 center-cut bacon slices
- 16 sea scallops (large)

Instructions
- Half the bacon and air fry it for 3 Mins at 400 degrees F.
- Dry the scallops well.
- Wrap the scallops with bacon slices and secure them with toothpicks.
- Please place them in an equal layer in the air fryer.
- Brush the scallops with BBQ sauce before wrapping them.

Alternatively, spritz with oil, black pepper, and salt.
- At 400 degrees F, air fried for five Mins. Cook for another 5 Mins after flipping them and brushing them with sauce.
- Serve immediately.

Nutrition Value
Calories: 198 Kcal, Carb: 9 g, Protein: 24 g, Fat: 9 g
Storage Suggestion: You can store it in the refrigerator for 1-2 days.

Air Fryer Cajun Shrimp

Prep Time: 30 Mins, Cook Time: 15 Mins, Servings: 4, Serving Size: 1

Ingredients
- 24 peeled shrimp (extra jumbo)
- Cajun seasoning: 1 tbsp
- 1 zucchini, cut into half-moons (¼" thick)
- Olive oil: 2 tbsp
- 1 yellow squash, cut into half-moons (¼" thick)
- Kosher salt: ¼ tsp
- 6 oz. of cooked chicken sausage, cut into slices
- 1 red bell pepper, cut without seeds into 1" pieces

Instructions
- Toss the shrimp in a bowl with the Cajun spice and toss thoroughly.
- Combine the veggies, oil, and sausage in a mixing bowl.
- Preheat the air fryer to 400 degrees Fahrenheit.
- Place the shrimp and veggie combination in an equal layer in the air fryer basket.
- Cook for 8 Mins, then shake the basket after 2-3 Mins.
- Serve immediately.

Nutrition Value
Calories: 215 Kcal, Carb: 3 g, Protein: 26 g, Fat: 9 g
Storage Suggestion: You can store it in the refrigerator for 3-4 days.

Tortilla Crusted Tilapia Salad

Prep Time: 15 Mins, Cook Time: 15 Mins, Servings: 2, Serving Size: 1

Ingredients
- Chipotle lime dressing: 1/2 cup
- 6 cups of mixed greens
- 1/3 cup of chopped red onion
- 1 cup of cherry tomatoes
- 2 Tilapia fillets (tortilla crusted)

Instructions
- Spray the fish fillets with oil on both sides.
- Cook for 15 to 18 Mins at 390 degrees F in an air fryer basket.
- Combine half of the veggies in two dishes and drizzle with the lime dressing.
- Place the fish fillet on top and serve immediately.

Nutrition Value
Calories: 234 Kcal, Carb: 3 g, Protein: 27 g, Fat: 7 g
Storage Suggestion: You can store it in the refrigerator for 4-5 days.

Air-Fryer Scallops

Prep Time: 25 Mins, Cook Time: 15 Mins, Servings: 2, Serving Size: 1

Ingredients
- 6 sea scallops
- 1 egg
- All-purpose flour: 2 tbsp
- Mashed potato flakes: 1/3 cup
- Salt: 1/8 tsp
- Breadcrumbs, seasoned: 1/3 cup
- Pepper: 1/8 tsp

Instructions
- Preheat your air fryer to 400 degrees Fahrenheit.
- Whisk the egg in a bowl.
- Combine breadcrumbs, pepper, potato flakes, and salt in a separate bowl.
- Combine flour and scallops (dry them well) in a mixing dish and toss to coat.
- Then dip it in the egg, and last in the potato mixture.
- Spray the basket of the air fryer with oil. Spray the scallops with oil and place them in the basket. Cook for 3 to 4 Mins before flipping and cooking for another 3 to 4 Mins.

Nutrition Value
Calories: 298 Kcal, Carb: 33 g, Protein: 28 g, Fat: 5 g
Storage Suggestion: You can store it in the refrigerator for 4-5 days.

Salmon with Maple-Dijon Glaze

Prep Time: 35 Mins, Cook Time: 15 Mins, Servings: 4, Serving Size: 1

Ingredients
- 4 salmon fillets
- Butter: 3 tbsp
- Dijon mustard: 1 tbsp
- Maple syrup: 3 tbsp
- Juice of one lemon
- Olive oil: 1 tbsp
- 1 minced clove to garlic
- Salt: ¼ tsp
- Pepper: ¼ tsp

Instructions
- Preheat the air fryer to 400 degrees Fahrenheit.
- Melt the butter in a skillet over medium heat, then add the minced garlic, maple syrup, lemon juice, and mustard.
- Reduce to low heat and simmer for 2 to 3 Mins, or until it thickens. Remove the pan from the heat and put it aside.
- Season the fish fillets with salt, pepper, and olive oil.
- Place the fish in the air fryer basket. Cook until fork-tender, about 5 to 7 Mins.
- Serve with a dollop of sauce on top.

Nutrition Value
Calories: 329 Kcal, Carb: 11 g, Protein: 19 g, Fat: 23 g
Storage Suggestion: You can store it in the refrigerator for 2-4 days.

Crumbed Fish

Prep Time: 22 Mins, Cook Time: 15 Mins, Servings: 4, Serving Size: 1

Ingredient
- Flounder fillets: 4
- Dry breadcrumbs: 1 cup
- 1 lemon, cut into slices
- Vegetable oil: ¼ cup
- 1 egg, whisked

Instructions
- Preheat the air fryer to 350 degrees Fahrenheit.
- Combine the oil and crumbs in a mixing dish.
- Coat the fish fillets in an egg wash and then in breadcrumbs.
- Place the breaded fish in the air fryer basket.
- Cook until fork-tender, about 12 Mins.
- Lemon slices should be placed on top of the dish.

Nutrition Value
Calories: 354 Kcal, Carb: 22 g, Protein: 28 g, Fat: 17 g
Storage Suggestion: You can store it in the refrigerator for 4-5 days.

Cajun Air Fryer Salmon
Prep Time: 20 Mins, Cook Time: 15 Mins, Servings: 2, Serving Size: 1

Ingredients
- Brown sugar: 1 tsp
- 2 skin-on fillets of salmon
- Cajun seasoning: 1 tbsp

Instructions
- Preheat the air fryer to 390 degrees Fahrenheit.
- Using a paper towel, clean and dry the fish. Spray the fish with oil, combine the sugar and Cajun spice in a dish and sprinkle evenly over the fish.
- Spray the air fryer basket with oil and put the fish in the basket.
- Using a little spray of oil, lightly coat the fish.
- Cook for 8 Mins at 390°F.
- Serve immediately and enjoy.

Nutrition Value
Calories: 334 Kcal, Carb: 4 g, Protein: 27 g, Fat: 21 g
Storage Suggestion: You can store it in the refrigerator for 3-4 days.

Crab Cakes
Prep Time: 35 Mins, Cook Time: 55 Mins, Servings: 4, Serving Size: 2

Ingredient
- Mayonnaise: 2 tbsp
- 1 egg, whisked
- Worcestershire sauce: 1 tsp
- Seafood seasoning: 1 tsp
- Dijon mustard: 1 tsp
- Hot pepper sauce: 1/2 tsp
- Baking powder: 1 tsp
- 1 lb of lump crabmeat
- Chopped green onion: 2 tbsp
- Salt & black pepper, to taste
- Milk: 3 tbsp
- 11 crushed saltine crackers

Instructions
- Mix mustard, mayonnaise, green onion, hot pepper sauce, egg, seafood spice, and Worcestershire sauce in a mixing dish. Combine all ingredients in a large mixing bowl and put them aside.
- Add crab meat to a bowl and break it up with a spoon.
- Mix in the pepper, milk, and salt.
- Mix in the baking powder and broken crackers gently.
- Mix thoroughly into the egg mixture.
- Make eight patties out of the mixture. Refrigerate for 1 to 8 hrs.
- Preheat the air fryer to 400 degrees Fahrenheit.
- Spray the crab cakes with oil and throw them in the air fryer basket.
- Cook for five Mins at 400 degrees F, then turn the cakes and cook for another five Mins.

Nutrition Value
Calories: 242 Kcal, Carb: 10 g, Protein: 38 g, Fat: 9 g
Storage Suggestion: You can store it in the refrigerator for 3-4 days.

Salmon Cakes with Sriracha Mayo
Prep Time: 20 Mins, Cook Time: 35 Mins, Servings: 4, Serving Size: 2

Ingredients
Sriracha Mayo
- Sriracha: 1 tbsp
- Mayonnaise: ¼ cup

Salmon Cakes
- 1 and a 1/2 tsp of seafood seasoning
- 1 lb of salmon skinless fillets, slice into one" pieces
- 1 egg, whisked lightly
- Almond flour: ⅓ cup
- 1 chopped green onion

Instructions
- Combine Sriracha and mayonnaise in a mixing dish.
- 1 tbsp Sriracha mayo, green onion, almond flour, seafood spice, egg, and salmon in a food processor Pulse 4-5 times until everything is well blended. Don't overmix the ingredients.
- Refrigerate for 15 Mins after forming eight patties.
- Preheat the air fryer to 390 degrees Fahrenheit.
- Spray the basket of the air fryer with oil.
- Spray the patties with cooking spray and arrange them in an equal layer in the air fryer.
- Cook for a total of 6-8 Mins.
- Serve immediately with spicy mayonnaise.

Nutrition Value
Calories: 434 Kcal, Carb: 4 g, Protein: 40 g, Fat: 25 g
Storage Suggestion: You can store it in the refrigerator for 4-5 days.

Lemon Pepper Shrimp
Prep Time: 15 Mins, Cook Time: 15 Mins, Servings: 2, Serving Size: 2

Ingredients
- 12 oz. of raw medium peeled shrimp, deveined
- Juice and slice of one lemon
- Olive oil: 1 tbsp
- Paprika: ¼ tsp
- Lemon pepper: 1 tsp
- Garlic powder: ¼ tsp

Instructions
- Preheat your air fryer to 400 degrees Fahrenheit.
- Combine all ingredients in a mixing bowl, except the shrimp and lemon slices. Mix well, then add the shrimp and toss to mix.
- Cook for 6-8 Mins in the air fryer basket with seasoned shrimp.

- Lemon slices should be served beside the prawns.

Nutrition Value
Calories: 212 Kcal, Carb: 12 g, Protein: 8 g, Fat: 21.2 g
Storage Suggestion: You can store it in the refrigerator for 3-4 days.

Lobster Tails with Lemon-Garlic Butter

Prep Time: 20 Mins, Cook Time: 15 Mins, Servings: 2, Serving Size: 2

Ingredients
- Butter: 4 tbsp
- 2 lobster tails
- Lemon zest: 1 tsp
- Lemon wedges: 2
- 1 minced clove of garlic
- Fresh parsley, chopped: 1 tsp
- Salt & black pepper, to taste

Instructions
- Using a sharp knife, carve the lobster in the shape of a butterfly. The tail's halves should be spread out.
- Melt butter in a skillet, add garlic, zest, and simmer for 30 seconds.
- tbsp garlic butter brushed on the tail
- Place the lobster in the air fryer's basket with the flesh facing up.
- Season with salt and black pepper.
- At 380 degrees F, air fried for 5-7 Mins.
- Pour the remaining butter over the lobster.
- Serve with lemon wedges and parsley on top of the tails.

Nutrition Value
Calories: 344 Kcal, Carb: 4 g, Protein: 18 g, Fat: 25 g
Storage Suggestion: You can store it in the refrigerator for 4-5 days.

Shrimp & Polenta

Prep Time: 25 Mins, Cook Time: 35 Mins, Servings: 2, Serving Size: 1

Ingredients
- Olive oil: 2 tsp
- Grape tomatoes: 12
- Half tube of polenta, cut into six rounds
- 8 oz. of jumbo peeled shrimp, deveined
- Hot pepper sauce: 1 tsp
- Salt & black pepper, to taste
- Softened unsalted butter: 2 tbsp
- Lemon-pepper seasoning: 1/2 tsp
- Chopped fresh parsley: 2 tsp

Instructions
- Preheat the air fryer to 400 degrees Fahrenheit.
- Place polenta circles on a flat board and brush both sides with 1 tsp olive oil.
- Season with salt and black pepper.
- Toss tomatoes and shrimp in a mixing bowl. Toss in 1 tsp olive oil to mix everything.
- Cook for 2 Mins with the tomatoes in the air fryer basket. Take them out and slam them against the wall.
- Cook the shrimp for 10 Mins in the air fryer basket. Put them in the tomatoes.
- Cook the polenta in the air fryer basket for 15 minutes, then flip the pieces and cook for another 15 Minutes.
- Combine the remaining ingredients in a mixing dish and well combine.
- Place polenta on two dishes, top with shrimp tomatoes, and sprinkle with butter sauce.

Nutrition Value
Calories: 333 Kcal, Carb: 12 g, Protein: 22 g, Fat: 19 g
Storage Suggestion: You can store it in the refrigerator for 3-4 days.

Shrimp Bang Bang

Prep Time: 19 Mins, Cook Time: 15 Mins, Servings: 4, Serving Size: 2

Ingredients
- 1 lb of uncooked peeled shrimp, deveined
- Mayonnaise: 1/2 cup
- Sriracha sauce: 1 tbsp
- 1 head of lettuce leaves
- All-purpose flour: ¼ cup
- Sweet chili sauce: ¼ cup
- Panko breadcrumbs: 1 cup
- 2 chopped green onions

Instructions
- Preheat the air fryer to 400 degrees Fahrenheit.
- Combine the sriracha sauce, mayonnaise, and chili sauce in a mixing bowl. Take some sauce out to use as a dipping sauce.
- Combine flour and panko in two separate bowls.
- Dredge the shrimp in flour, then mayonnaise, and finally panko.
- Arrange the breaded shrimps in a single layer in the air fryer basket.
- Preheat oven to 400 degrees Fahrenheit and bake for 12 Mins.
- Place the cooked shrimps on lettuce leaves and serve with the sauce.

Nutrition Value
Calories: 415 Kcal, Carb: 32 g, Protein: 23 g, Fat: 25 g
Storage Suggestion: You can store it in the refrigerator for 3-4 days.

Salmon Nuggets

Prep Time: 35 Mins, Cook Time: 15 Mins, Servings: 4, Serving Size: 4

Ingredients
- 1 center-cut, skinless, salmon fillet, slice into 1 and a half" pieces
- Maple syrup: ⅓ cup
- Sea salt, one pinch
- Dried ground chipotle pepper: ¼ tsp
- 1 and a 1/2 cups of butter
- 1 egg
- Croutons: garlic-flavored, as needed

Instructions
- Combine the chipotle powder, salt, and maple syrup in a pan. Mix everything and bring to a boil over medium heat. Reduce the heat to a very low setting.
- Add the croutons to a food processor and pulse until they are crumbs. Remove to a dish.
- Whisk the egg in a separate dish.

- Preheat the air fryer to 390 degrees Fahrenheit.
- Season the fish with salt and pepper.
- Coat the salmon in the egg and then in the croutons.
- Spray a baking dish with oil and place it on top.
- Spray the air fryer basket with oil, then stack the fish nuggets in a uniform layer and cook for three Mins.
- Cook for 3-4 Mins after flipping the nuggets and spraying them with oil.
- Serve with maple sauce on the side.

Nutrition Value
Calories: 364 Kcal, Carb: 27 g, Protein: 26 g, Fat: 16 g
Storage Suggestion: You can store it in the refrigerator for 5-6 days.

Fish Sticks

Prep Time: 20 Mins, Cook Time: 15 Mins, Servings: 4, Serving Size: 3

Ingredients
- All-purpose flour: ¼ cup
- Grated parmesan cheese: ¼ cup
- 1 lb of cod fillets
- 1 whole egg
- Paprika: 1 tsp
- Panko breadcrumbs: ½ cup
- Black pepper, to taste
- Parsley flakes: 1 tbsp

Instructions
- Preheat your air fryer to 400 degrees Fahrenheit.
- Make fish sticks out of the fillet.
- Add flour to one bowl and whisk the egg.
- Add pepper, panko, paprika, Parmesan cheese, and parsley to a separate bowl.
- Dip the cod sticks first in flour, then in the whisked egg, and then in the panko mixture. Spray the basket of the air fryer with oil.
- Spray the breaded sticks with oil spray and arrange them uniformly in the air fryer basket.
- Cook for five Mins on one side, then turn and cook for another five Mins.

Nutrition Value
Calories: 200 Kcal, Carb: 16 g, Protein: 25 g, Fat: 4 g
Storage Suggestion: You can store it in the refrigerator for 4-5 days.

Crispy Fish Po' Boys

Prep Time: 20 Mins, Cook Time: 15 Mins, Servings: 4, Serving Size: 2

Ingredients

Fish
- Panko breadcrumbs: ½ cup
- All-purpose flour: ¼ cup
- 4 fillets of white fish
- Black pepper: ½ tsp
- 1 tbsp of water
- Salt: ¼ tsp
- Garlic powder: ¼ tsp
- Cornmeal: ¼ cup
- 1 large egg

Slaw
- Dried ground chipotle pepper: ¼ tsp
- Sour cream: ⅓ cup
- Fresh chopped cilantro: ¼ cup
- Lime juice: 1 tbsp
- Shredded carrot with cabbage: 3 cups
- Salt: ¼ tsp
- Mayonnaise: ¼ cup

Instructions
- Spray the basket of the air fryer with oil.
- Combine salt, flour, garlic powder, and black pepper in a mixing bowl.
- Combine the whipped egg and water in a separate bowl.
- Combine cornmeal and breadcrumbs in a separate bowl.
- Coat the fish with flour, then egg, and finally crumbs.
- Spray the fish with oil and arrange it in a uniform layer in the air fryer.
- Cook at 400°F for 6-10 Mins, or until fork tender.
- Combine chipotle pepper, mayonnaise, salt, sour cream, and lime juice in a mixing bowl.
- Mix in the shredded vegetables and cilantro.
- Serve the fish with chipotle slaw and lime wedges in the bread rolls.

Nutrition Value
Calories: 341 Kcal, Carb: 45 g, Protein: 35 g, Fat: 21 g
Storage Suggestion: You can store it in the refrigerator for 3-4 days.

Honey Pecan Shrimp

Prep Time: 35 Mins, Cook Time: 15 Mins, Servings: 4, Serving Size: 3

Ingredients
- 1 lb of uncooked peeled shrimps, deveined
- Cornstarch: ¼ cup
- Pepper: ¼ tsp
- Sea salt: ¾ tsp
- Chopped pecans: ⅔ cup
- Honey: ¼ cup
- 2 whites from egg
- Mayonnaise: 2 tbsp

Instructions
- Combine half a tsp of salt, pepper, and cornstarch in a mixing bowl.
- Whisk the whites in a separate dish until frothy and soft.
- Add the remaining salt and pecans to a separate bowl.
- Coat the shrimp with cornstarch, then whites, and finally pecan mixture.
- Preheat the air fryer to 330 degrees Fahrenheit.
- Spray the shrimp in the air fryer basket with oil and cook for five Mins.
- Cook for another five Mins on the other side.
- Combine mayonnaise and honey in a mixing bowl.
- Toss the cooked shrimp in the honey sauce until well coated.
- Serve immediately.

Nutrition Value
Calories: 334 Kcal, Carb: 8 g, Protein: 31 g, Fat: 9 g

Storage Suggestion: You can store it in the refrigerator for 3-4 days.

Pecan-Crusted Tilapia

Prep Time: 15 Mins, Cook Time: 15 Mins, Servings: 4, Serving Size: 2

Ingredients

- 1 lb of boneless and skinless tilapia filets
- Melted butter: ¼ cup
- Paprika: ¼ tsp
- Chopped pecans: 1 cup
- Lemon wedges: 4-5
- Dried rosemary: 1 tsp
- Sea salt: 1 tsp
- Chopped parsley: 2 tbsp

Instructions

- Using melted butter, coat the fish.
- Combine paprika, salt, pecans, and rosemary in a mixing bowl.
- Preheat the air fryer to 350 degrees Fahrenheit.
- Place the fish fillet in the air fryer basket and liberally coat with the pecan mixture.
- 6-8 Mins in the air fryer
- Remove the fish from the pan and garnish with lemon wedges and parsley.

Nutrition Value

Calories: 314 Kcal, Carb: 4 g, Protein: 21 g, Fat: 9 g

Storage Suggestion: You can store it in the refrigerator for 3-4 days.

Maple-Crusted Salmon

Prep Time: 45 Mins, Cook Time: 15 Mins, Servings: 2, Serving Size: 4

Ingredients

- Finely chopped walnuts: 1/2 cup
- 12 oz. Of salmon filets
- Worcestershire sauce: 1 tsp
- Dijon mustard: 2 tsp
- Half lemon
- Maple syrup: 1/3 cup
- Sea salt: 1/2 tsp

Instructions

- Mix the mustard, maple syrup, and Worcestershire sauce and coat the fish.
- Refrigerate for at least 30 Mins.
- Preheat the air fryer to 350 degrees Fahrenheit.
- Remove the fish from the sauce and toss it with chopped nuts and salt.
- Cook the salmon in the air fryer basket for 6-8 Mins, or until fork tender.
- Serve the fish with a garnish of parsley.

Nutrition Value

Calories: 334 Kcal, Carb: 8 g, Protein: 21 g, Fat: 8.4 g

Storage Suggestion: You can store it in the refrigerator for 3-4 days.

Beer-Breaded Halibut Fish Tacos

Prep Time: 45 Mins, Cook Time: 15 Mins, Servings: 4, Serving Size: 1

Ingredients

- 1 lb of halibut, slice into one" of strips
- Greek yogurt: ¼ cup
- Light beer: 1 cup
- 1 minced clove of garlic
- 1 finely chopped jalapeño
- Ground cumin: ¼ tsp
- All-purpose flour: ¼ cup
- 1 + ¼ tsp sea salt
- Cornmeal: 1/2 cup
- Chopped onion: ¼ cup
- Juice from one lime
- Mayonnaise: ¼ cup
- Shredded cabbage: 2 cups
- Grape tomatoes: 1 cup, cut into quarters
- Corn tortillas: 8
- Chopped cilantro: 1/2 cup
- 1 whisked egg

Instructions

- Combine the cumin, beer, jalapeño (1 tsp), garlic, and fish in a mixing bowl. Refrigerate for half an hr after thoroughly mixing.
- Combine flour, salt (1/2 tsp), and cornmeal in a mixing bowl.
- Combine lime juice (1 tbsp), salt (1/2 tsp), mayonnaise, cabbage, and yogurt separately.
- To make Pico de Gallo, combine the remaining jalapeño, tomatoes, 14 tsp salt, onion, lime juice, and cilantro in a mixing dish.
- Remove the fish from the pan, coat it with egg, and then cornmeal mixture.
- Preheat the air fryer to 350 degrees Fahrenheit.
- Cook for six Mins after spraying the fish with oil; turn and cook for another four Mins.
- Warm the tortillas in the oven.
- Fill a warmed tortilla with air-fried fish, Pico de Gallo, and slaw.
- Serve immediately.

Nutrition Value

Calories: 214 Kcal, Carb: 4.1 g, Protein: 21.2 g, Fat: 15.3 g

Storage Suggestion: You can store it in the refrigerator for 3-4 days.

Catfish & Green Beans

Prep Time: 25 Mins, Cook Time: 15 Mins, Servings: 2, Serving Size: 2

Ingredients

- Light brown sugar: 1 tsp
- Fresh green beans: 1 and a 1/2 cups, trimmed
- Kosher salt, to taste
- 2 catfish fillets
- Crushed red pepper: 1/2 tsp
- Mayonnaise: 2 tbsp
- 1 egg, whisked
- Panko breadcrumbs: ⅓ cup
- All-purpose flour: ¼ cup
- Apple cider vinegar: 1/2 tsp
- Black pepper: ¼ tsp
- Fresh dill: 1 and a 1/2 tsp
- Granulated sugar: ⅛ tsp
- Dill pickle relish: ¾ tsp

Instructions

- Green beans should be placed in a bowl and liberally sprayed with oil.
- Crushed red pepper, salt (1/8 tsp), and brown sugar are used to season. Toss in the air fryer basket and cook for 12 Mins at 400 degrees F.
- Coat the fish first in flour, then in egg, and last with panko.
- Spray the fish fillet with oil and set it in the air fryer basket.

- Preheat oven to 400°F and bake for 8 Mins.
- Season with salt and black pepper (14 tsp).
- Combine relish, sugar, dill, mayo, and vinegar in a mixing dish.
- Lemon slices and sauces should be served beside the catfish.

Nutrition Value
Calories: 416 Kcal, Carb: 31 g, Protein: 33 g, Fat: 18 g
Storage Suggestion: You can store it in the refrigerator for 3-4 days.

Popcorn Shrimp

Prep Time: 30 Mins, Cook Time: 15 Mins, Servings: 4, Serving Size: 2

Ingredients
- Garlic powder: 1 tbsp
- 2 eggs, whisked
- Water: 2 tbsp
- All-purpose flour: 1/2 cup
- 1 lb of small, peeled shrimp, deveined
- Ground cumin: 1 tbsp
- Ketchup: 1/2 cup
- Fresh cilantro, chopped: 2 tbsp
- Panko breadcrumbs: 1 and a 1/2 cups
- Lime juice: 2 tbsp
- Chipotle chilies chopped: 2 tbsp (in adobo)
- Kosher salt: ⅛ tsp

Instructions
- Oil Spritz the basket of the air fryer.
- Add flour to a mixing bowl.
- Combine water and eggs in a separate dish.
- Combine garlic powder, panko, and cumin in a third bowl.
- Coat the shrimp in flour, then egg, and finally panko.
- Spray the shrimp in the air fryer basket with oil.
- Cook for 8 Mins at 360 degrees Fahrenheit, turning halfway through.
- Combine the remaining ingredients in a dish and serve with shrimp.

Nutrition Value
Calories: 297 Kcal, Carb: 35 g, Protein: 29 g, Fat: 4 g
Storage Suggestion: You can store it in the refrigerator for 3-4 days.

Scallops with Lemon-Herb Sauce

Prep Time: 20 Mins, Cook Time: 15 Mins, Servings: 2|Serving Size:1

Ingredients
- Finely grated lemon zest: 1 tsp
- Black pepper: ¼ tsp
- Salt: ⅛ tsp
- 8 sea scallops, large
- Capers: 2 tsp, chopped
- Olive oil: ¼ cup
- Minced garlic: 1/2 tsp
- Flat-leaf parsley chopped: 2 tbsp

Instructions
- Scallops should be seasoned with salt and black pepper.
- Spray the basket of the air fryer with oil.
- In the air fryer basket, place seasoned scallops.
- At 400°F, cook for six Mins.
- Combine the remaining ingredients in a mixing dish.
- Serve the scallops with the sauce.

Nutrition Value
Calories: 348 Kcal, Carb: 5 g, Protein: 14 g, Fat: 30 g
Storage Suggestion: You can store it in the refrigerator for 5-6 days.

Gingered Honey Salmon

Prep Time: 20 Mins, Cook Time: 15 Mins, Servings: 6, Serving Size: 2

Ingredients
- 1 salmon fillet
- Orange juice: 1/3 cup
- Honey: ¼ cup
- Garlic powder: 1 tsp
- 1 chopped green onion
- Soy sauce: 1/3 cup
- Ground ginger: 1 tsp

Instructions
- Except for the salmon, combine all ingredients in a mixing dish. Mix thoroughly, pour 2/3 cup into a dish, add the salmon, and coat well.
- Refrigerate for at least 30 Mins.
- Preheat the air fryer to 325 degrees Fahrenheit.
- Spray the air fryer basket with oil, then add the fish and cook for 15 to 18 Mins.
- Keep basting with the leftover marinade in the final five Mins of cooking.

Nutrition Value
Calories: 217 Kcal, Carb: 15 g, Protein: 10 g, Fat: 20 g
Storage Suggestion: You can store it in the refrigerator for 3-4 days.

Chapter 10: Casseroles Recipes

Bean Casserole

Prep Time: 10 Mins, Cook Time: 15 Mins, Servings: 4, Serving Size: 1

Ingredients
- 4 tbsp butter unsalted
- ¼ cup yellow onion diced
- ½ cup white mushrooms chopped
- ½ cup whipping cream heavy
- ¼ cup cream cheese low-fat
- ½ cup broth chicken
- ¼ tsp gum xanthan
- 4 cups of fresh edges trimmed green beans
- 1 tbsp finely ground pork rinds

Instructions
- In a medium saucepan over low heat, melt the butter. Before the onion and mushrooms get soft and aromatic, sauté them for 3–5 Mins.
- Combine the hard cream whipping, cream cheese, and broth in a saucepan. Before you start, whisk everything together smoothly. Bring to a boil, then reduce to low heat. Cook for a few Mins after adding the xanthan gum to the pan.
- Green beans should be cut into 2" pieces and placed in a 4-cup circular baking dish. Pour the sauce mixture over them and toss until they are well cooked. Cover the bowl with the ground pork rinds.
- Preheat the oven to 320 degrees Fahrenheit and set the timer for 15 Mins.
- When the top is golden brown, and the green beans are fork soft, it's time to serve. Serve warm.

Nutrition Value
Calories: 267 Kcal, Carb: 6.5 g, Protein: 3.6 g, Fat: 23.4 g

Storage Suggestion: You can store it in the refrigerator for 5-6 days.

Air Fryer Green Bean Casserole

Prep Time: 5 Mins, Cook Time: 15 Mins, Servings: 6, Serving Size: 1

Ingredients
- 14 oz of green frozen or fresh beans canned
- 1 can mushroom soup condensed cream
- 6 oz divided fried onions

Instructions
- Preheat the air fryer at 350°F on the BAKE setting. Using cooking spray, oil a square baking pan.
- Combine your condensed soup, beans, & half of the onions in a mixing dish.
- Fill baking dish halfway with onions & top with leftover onions.
- Bake for around 15 Mins in the air fryer, or till cooked thru & onions have turned brown.

Nutrition Value
Calories: 229 Kcal, Carb: 19 g, Protein: 4 g, Fat: 15 g

Storage Suggestion: You can store it in the refrigerator for 2-3 days.

Air Fryer Breakfast Casserole {Frittata}

Prep Time: 10 Mins, Cook Time: 35 Mins, Servings: 4 Serving Size: 1

Ingredients
- 8 eggs large
- ½ cup of milk
- 15 thinly sliced brown mushrooms
- 1 large thinly sliced bell pepper
- 1/3 cup of thinly sliced red onion
- 2 handfuls kale or baby spinach
- ½ cup shredded Parmesan cheese
- ½ tsp divided salt
- black pepper Ground

Instructions
- Vegetables should be chopped & cheese should be grated.
- Preheat the air fryer for around 5 Mins at 400°F.
- Line your air fryer basket using parchment paper, ensuring it is properly spaced in the middle to contain the egg mix across all sides. Trim any protruding corners.
- Mushrooms, red onion, bell pepper, salt & pepper are added to the pan. Shake and swirl once throughout the 15-Min air fry.
- Meanwhile, whisk together milk, eggs, salt, & pepper in a large mixing dish.
- Remove the basket from the air fryer and mix inside the spinach using a tiny spatula unless it is slightly wilted & uniformly distributed.
- Sprinkle with some Parmesan cheese & pour the egg mixture over it gently. Bake for around 20 Mins at 300°F, or until a toothpick within the center comes out clean.
- Serve cold or hot, cut in 8 pieces with a sharp knife.

Nutrition Value
Calories: 234 Kcal, Carb: 9 g, Protein: 20 g, Fat: 13 g

Storage Suggestion: You can store it in the refrigerator for 3-4 days.

Air Fryer Breakfast Casserole

Prep Time: 15 Mins, Cook Time: 8 Mins, Servings: 4, Serving Size: 1

Ingredients
- 4 large eggs
- 2 tbsp cream heavy
- 1 lb Italian sausage cooked
- 1 cup green chilies & diced tomatoes
- ½ cup cheddar cheese shredded
- 2 tsp seasoning Italian

Instructions
- Combine the diced tomatoes, Italian sausage, & Italian seasoning in a wide mixing bowl. Mix thoroughly.
- Place the crumbled cheese on top.
- Whisk together the eggs & heavy cream. This will aid in the frothiness of the eggs.
- Fill the ramekins with egg ingredients, then top with extra shredded cheese.

- Preheat the air fryer to 340°F and cook for 5-8 Mins. Because each air fryer is unique, ensure the eggs are fully cooked before removing them.
- Plate, serve, & have a good time!

Nutrition Value
Calories: 560 Kcal, Carb: 9 g, Protein: 32 g, Fat: 43 g
Storage Suggestion: You can store it in the refrigerator for 5-6 days.

Campbells Green Bean Casserole

Prep Time: 5 Mins, Cook Time: 15 Mins, Servings: 6, Serving Size: 1

Ingredients
- 1 can Mushroom soup condensed Cream
- ½ cup of milk
- 1 tsp sauce soy
- 4 cups of cut beans, green
- 1 & 1/3 cup crispy divided French-fried onions
- to taste pepper

Instructions
- If using green beans (Fresh), clean, cut, & blanch them for around 2 Mins in a saucepan of boiling water. Drain your green beans inside a colander if you're using green beans (canned).
- In a mixing dish, combine the soup & milk. Stir it until it's completely smooth & free of lumps. Then add the soy sauce and mix well.
- Combine green beans & onions in a mixing bowl. Toss in some pepper and thoroughly combine everything.
- In your Air Fryer, cook to 350°F and bake for around 10 Mins. Stir the casserole again, then top with the leftover onions & heat for another 2 mins to brown them.

Nutrition Value
Calories: 279 Kcal, Carb: 10 g, Protein: 24 g, Fat: 15.1 g
Storage Suggestion: You can store it in the refrigerator for 7-8 days.

Air Fryer Green Bean Casserole (Air Fryer/Oven)

Prep Time: 10 Mins, Cook Time: 15 Mins, Servings: 4, Serving Size:1

Ingredients
- 1 Lb Green Beans Fresh
- 1 Can Mushroom Soup Condensed Cream
- ½ Cup Half & Half or Milk
- 1 tsp Sauce Soy
- ½ Cup Parmesan Cheese Shredded
- 1 & 1/3 Cups Onions French Fried

Instructions
- Preheat the air fryer at 350°F.
- Combine Mushroom Soup Cream, Soy Sauce, Milk, Fried Onions, & Parmesan Cheese in a wide mixing bowl.
- Toss in the green beans & coat well. Put in a baking dish & air fry for 12-15 Mins.
- Top with the remaining onions & Parmesan cheese, then Air Fry in almost 5-Min intervals unless golden brown on top.

Nutrition Value
Calories: 301 Kcal, Carb: 3 g, Protein: 23 g, Fat: 10.8 g
Storage Suggestion: You can store it in the refrigerator for 1-2 weeks.

Taco Chile Casserole

Prep Time: 10 Mins, Cook Time: 5 Mins, Servings: 4, Serving Size: 1

Ingredients
- 1 lb 85 percent ground beef lean
- 1 tbsp taco seasoning salt-free
- 1 tsp salt kosher
- cooking spray vegetable oil

Topping
- 2 eggs large
- ½ cup of milk
- 2 tbsp flour all-purpose
- 1 can green chilies diced mild
- 1 cup blend cheese shredded Mexican
- ½ tsp salt kosher

Instructions
- Combine the taco seasoning, meat, & salt in a big mixing bowl to make ground beef. Mix thoroughly.
- Use veg's oil spray to grease a baking pan. In a large skillet, brown your seasoned ground meat.
- To make the topping, whisk together milk, eggs, & flour in a medium bowl unless no lumps are left. Combine the chilies & cheese in a large mixing bowl and stir until thoroughly blended. Over your ground beef mixture, add the topping.
- In your air-fryer basket, place a pan. Preheat your air fryer at 350 degrees Fahrenheit for around 15 Mins. Make sure that meat has achieved a core temp of 160°F using a thermometer.
- The fat & liquid should be drained from the pan. Allow for a 5-Min rest before slicing.

Nutrition Value
Calories: 198 Kcal, Carb: 7.2 g, Protein: 23 g, Fat: 15.1 g
Storage Suggestion: You can store it in the refrigerator for 2-3 days.

Duo Crisp + Air Fryer - One Pot Cheesy Beef and Rice Casserole

Prep Time: 5 Mins, Cook Time: 40 Mins, Servings: 6-8, Serving Size: 1

Ingredients
- 1 lb of ground 93% beef, preferably
- 1 & ¼ cup broth beef
- 1 cup rice rinsed uncooked grain
- 1 cup carrots chopped
- 1 cup peas frozen
- 11 oz mushroom soup condensed cream
- 1 & ½ cups Cheddar cheese shredded

Instructions

- Fill your Instant Pot halfway with ground beef. Select a SAUTE function over the LCD screen, change to HIGH, then press START.
- Select CANCEL after browning the meat unless no pink appears. Fat should be drained. Cover loosely using foil the browned meat in a small bowl.
- Deglaze with broth by scraping the brown pieces from the saucepan with a wooden spoon.
- Stir in some rice that has been washed.
- Add the veggies, cooked meat, & soup to a pot in that sequence. Stirring is not allowed. Place Pressure Lid on top of the pressure cooker.
- Select on PRESSURE COOK option from the display panel. Set the timer for 15 Mins and then press START.
- Allow 10 Mins for pressure to naturally dissipate once the timer has expired, then quickly release the excess pressure.
- Stir to blend the ingredients, level on top & sprinkle with cheese in a uniform layer.
- Now secure the ==> strong ==> Air Fryer Lid by selecting CANCEL.
- Select your BROIL function from the display panel. Set the temperature to 400 degrees Fahrenheit and the timer to 5 minutes, then press START.
- Remove your lid & set it on the protecting pad after the cheese has melted & begun to color. Serve hot, scooped into separate bowls.

Nutrition Value
Calories: 198 Kcal, Carb: 9.9 g, Protein: 17.4 g, Fat: 12.5 g
Storage Suggestion: You can store it in the refrigerator for 6-7 days.

Air Fryer Sweet Potato Casserole

Prep Time: 10 Mins, Cook Time: 25 Mins, Servings: 10, Serving Size: 2

Ingredients
- 2 & ½ Lb Cooked & peeled Sweet Potatoes
- ½ Stick unsalted Butter Softened
- ½ Cup Dark Tightly packed Brown Sugar
- ½ Cup Milk Evaporated
- 2 Beaten Eggs
- 2 tsp of Vanilla
- 1 Cup of Pecans Chopped
- 1 Cup of Raisins

Topping
- 1 Cup of Dark Tightly packed Brown Sugar
- ½ Cup Flour All Purpose
- ⅓ Cup Melted Butter

Instructions
- Prepare your air fryer by preheating it. Oil an oven-safe baking dish that will fit in the air fryer. Remove the topping from the oven and put it aside.
- In a wide mixing bowl, mash potatoes with butter. Lightly beat using an electric mixer on medium speed till frothy.
- After every addition, whisk in the milk, eggs, sugar, and vanilla extract. Within the prepared baking dish, evenly spread. Spread the topping over the potatoes, then top with some pecans & raisins.
- Bake at 310° for around 25 mins or unless set.

Nutrition Value
Calories: 426 Kcal, Carb: 70 g, Protein: 7 g, Fat: 14 g
Storage Suggestion: You can store it in the refrigerator for 7-8 days.

Air Fryer Bundt Cake Breakfast Casserole

Prep Time: 8 Mins, Cook Time: 32 Mins, Servings: 4, Serving Size: 1

Ingredients
Breakfast Cake Bundt
- 2 Peppers Medium
- 1 Sweet Potato Medium
- 3 Sausages Medium
- Onion Spring
- 1 tbsp Olive Oil Extra Virgin
- 1 tbsp of Oregano
- Pepper & Salt

Breakfast Batter
- 4 Large Eggs
- 2 tbsp Cream Sour
- 2 Cups Cheddar Cheese Grated
- 2 Cups Mozzarella Cheese Grated
- 1 tbsp of Basil
- 1 tbsp Chives
- Pepper & Salt

Instructions
- The sweet potato should be peeled and diced. Remove the seeds from the pepper and slice them into bits. Cut the fresh spring onion into thin slices. Toss with oregano, salt, olive oil, & pepper in a mixing bowl.
- After 5 Mins of air frying at 360°F/180°C, add sausages, which were quartered.
- Cook for another 6 Mins within the air fryer at a similar temperature until the sausages are fully cooked.
- Prepare the remaining ingredients while your air fryer is at work. Crack the eggs into a mixing dish with the sour cream & whisk together using a fork. Season with spices & grated cheese.
- When your air fryer sounds, add the contents into the Bundt pan & pour some batter over the top.
- Cook for around 15 Mins at 180°C/360°F with the Bundt pan in the air fryer basket. Reduce the temp to 320°F/160°C for the last 6 Mins of cooking to ensure the center is properly done.

Nutrition Value
Calories: 759 Kcal, Carb: 17 g, Protein: 43 g, Fat: 57 g
Storage Suggestion: You can store it in the refrigerator for 6-7 days.

Air Fryer, Cheesy Baked Zucchini Casserole

Prep Time: 10 Mins, Cook Time: 10 Mins, Servings: 4, Serving Size: 1

Ingredients
- 3 cups zucchini sliced
- ½ cup onion diced

- 2 tsp of parsley
- 1 tsp of oregano
- 1 tsp of salt
- ½ tsp of pepper
- 4 eggs large
- ½ cup of oil vegetable
- 1 cup Bisquick or Baking mix
- ½ cup cheese Parmesan

Instructions
- To begin, chop the zucchini into tiny pieces.
- Finish slicing the zucchini unless you've 3 cups. Next, chop your onion.
- Toss in your spices (parsley, salt, pepper, & oregano)
- Combine all of the ingredients.
- Add the eggs and mix well.
- Add your vegetable oil to the pan.
- Combine the baking powder and baking soda in a mixing bowl.
- Combine the cheese & the other ingredients in a mixing bowl.
- Fill an oiled, air fryer-safe pan halfway with the mixture.
- Preheat the oven to 320°F.
- 15 Mins has been set as the timer.
- Examine your casserole after 15 Mins. Does it seem to be cooked? If you require additional time, just add it. Otherwise, remove it from the oven & set it aside to cool somewhat.
- Plate & serve

Nutrition Value
Calories: 326 Kcal, Carb: 28 g, Protein: 19 g, Fat: 12.2 g
Storage Suggestion: You can store it in the refrigerator for 1-2 days.

Air Fryer Creamed Corn Casserole

Prep Time: 5 Mins, Cook Time: 45 Mins, Servings: 6, Serving Size: 1

Ingredients
- ½ cup melted butter
- ¼ cup flour AP
- ⅓ cup of sugar
- 2 beaten eggs
- ½ tbsp salt garlic
- ½ cup of milk
- 1 can drained corn
- 1 can corn creamed

Instructions
- Combine flour & melted butter in a large mixing bowl. Combine combined ingredients in a mixing bowl and whisk unless smooth.
- Combine the beaten eggs, milk, & sugar in a mixing bowl. To mix the ingredients, whisk them together.
- Combine garlic salt, kernel corn, & creamed corn in a large mixing bowl. To blend, stir everything together.
- Fill an oven-safe bowl halfway with the ingredients. In the basket of the air fryer, place that bowl. Air fry for around 40-45 Mins on 320F/160C.
- Allow 10 mins for the dish to rest before serving.

Nutrition Value
Calories: 365 Kcal, Carb: 46 g, Protein: 7 g, Fat: 19 g
Storage Suggestion: You can store it in the refrigerator for 5-6 days.

Chicken Stuffing Casserole

Prep Time: 15 Mins, Cook Time: 30 Mins, Servings: 2, Serving Size: 1

Ingredients
- 1 & ½ cups shredded rotisserie chicken
- 11 oz cream of condensed soup bacon
- 1/3 cup milk whole
- 1 box of stovetop cooked stuffing

Instructions
- Set your oven or air fryer to 350 degrees Fahrenheit.
- Add the chicken to the bottom of a Pyrex baking dish that has been lightly sprayed using olive oil.
- Add the milk to the sour bacon cream in a small bowl and stir well. Spritz it all over the meat.
- To finish your casserole, prepare some filling and place it on top.
- 30 Mins in an air fryer or oven, with a flip at the halfway point. To avoid overcooking or burning, keep an eye on the top & avoid overcooking or overcooking.

Nutrition Value
Calories: 300 Kcal, Carb: 3 g, Protein: 16 g, Fat: 1 g
Storage Suggestion: You can store it in the refrigerator for 2-3 days.

Air Fryer Spoon Bread Casserole Corn Muffin Mix

Prep Time: 10 Mins, Cook Time: 20 Mins, Servings: 6-8, Serving Size: 1

Ingredients
- 1 pkg Muffin Mix "JIFFY" Corn
- 6 Tbsp melted butter or margarine
- 1 can whole drained kernel corn
- 1 can corn cream style
- ½ cup cream sour
- 2 beaten eggs

Instructions
- Set your air fryer at 310°F. Oil an 8-½-inch ring mold.
- Add the ingredients and mix well. Add to pot. Bind using Al foil.
- Continue to cook for extra 20 Mins after the first 20 have expired. Allow it cool for 10 Mins before slicing into it to see whether it's done cooking.

Nutrition Value
Calories: 276 Kcal, Carb: 23 g, Protein: 18 g, Fat: 38 g
Storage Suggestion: You can store it in the refrigerator for 3-5 days.

Air Fryer Spinach and Feta Casserole

Prep Time: 10 Mins, Cook Time: 20 Mins, Servings: 4, Serving Size: 1

Ingredients
- spray cooking
- 1 can drained & squeezed spinach
- 1 cup cheese cottage
- 2 beaten eggs
- ¼ cup feta cheese crumbled
- 2 tbsp flour all-purpose
- 2 tbsp melted butter
- 1 minced clove garlic
- 1 & ½ tsp powder onion
- ⅛ tsp nutmeg ground

Instructions
- The air fryer should be preheated to 375 deg Fahrenheit. Set aside

a pie tin that's been greased using cooking spray.
- Gather all of the ingredients for the dish in a large bowl and mix them. Stirring is necessary to ensure that all of the components are well combined. Pour into the pie pan that has been prepared.
- Fry in an air fryer for 18-20 Mins unless the center is set.

Nutrition Value
Calories: 211 Kcal, Carb: 9.3 g, Protein: 14.8 g, Fat: 13.4 g
Storage Suggestion: You can store it in the refrigerator for 2-3 days.

Low Carb Tuna Casserole

Prep Time: 5 Mins, Cook Time: 5 Mins, Servings: 2, Serving Size: 2

Ingredients
- 2 cans drained & fluffed tuna
- ¼ cup Mexican blend shredded cheese
- ¼ cup panko Japanese
- ¼ cup chopped celery finely
- ¼ cup onion chopped
- 2 tbsp of mayonnaise
- 2 tbsp pickled jalapeno chopped
- 1 tbsp cheese Parmesan
- ¼ tsp of salt
- ¼ tsp pepper black
- ¼ tsp powder onion
- ¼ tsp pepper cayenne
- Some green onion thinly sliced

Instructions
- Preparation: Oil a shallow baking dish or a pizza pan generously.
- Mix all ingredients, excluding green onion, in a medium bowl until well-combined.
- Cook for 5 to 6 mins at 380 deg F on a pizza pan with the ingredients inside. After approximately 2 Mins within the air fryer, if you'd want to top it with more cheese, do so.
- To serve, garnish with shaved green onion.

Nutrition Value
Calories: 338 Kcal, Carb: 9 g, Protein: 39 g, Fat: 16 g
Storage Suggestion: You can store it in the refrigerator for 1-2 days.

Easy Sweet Potato Casserole

Prep Time: 10 Mins, Cook Time: 30 Mins, Servings: 8, Serving Size: 1

Ingredients
- 1 drained cooked yam
- ¼ cup melted unsalted butter
- ¼ cup sugar brown
- 1 egg large
- ½ tsp of cinnamon
- ¼ tsp of salt
- 8 oz marshmallows miniature
- ¼ cup pecans chopped

Instructions
- The oven should be preheated to 350°F. The baking dish should be sprayed using cooking spray & placed on the counter.
- To mash the canned yams, use a wooden spoon or potato masher to move them to a wide mixing bowl. Pour in the egg, cinnamon, brown sugar, melted butter, & salt. Mix thoroughly.
- In the wide baking dish that has been prepared, spread potato mash equally. 30 Mins in the oven, uncovered. Add marshmallows & chopped pecans on top of the dish after it has come out of the oven.
- Place the dish over an upper-middle rack of the oven & turn the broiler on. 1-2 Mins of broiling time, or when the marshmallows are just beginning to brown.
- Take it out of the oven & eat it up!

Nutrition Value
Calories: 215 Kcal, Carb: 34 g, Protein: 2 g, Fat: 9 g
Storage Suggestion: You can store it in the refrigerator for 5-6 days.

Air Fryer Hash Brown Egg Bites

Prep Time: 35 Mins, Cook Time: 10 Mins, Servings: 7, Serving Size: 1

Ingredients
- cooking spray Nonstick
- 4 eggs large
- ¼ cup cream heavy
- salt Kosher
- 2/3 cup Cheddar shredded
- ¼ cup bell peppers diced
- 1 sliced scallion, white & green parts
- ½ cup of shredded frozen-thawed hash browns

Instructions
- Nonstick spray the mold's seven cavities before using it to make egg bites. In a big measuring glass cup, whisk together eggs, heavy cream, & salt till no white streaks are left.
- You'll need to fill each cavity with a third of Cheddar cheese & a few slices of sliced bell pepper. A spoon and some gentle stirring will do. A six-quart air fryer may be used to cook the mold for three Mins at a temperature of 300° F.
- Separately in a separate dish, mix the hash browns with the remaining 1/3 cup cheese. Your hash brown-cheese mix should be gently topped on every egg bite.
- Cook for a further 12 Mins at 300°F within the air fryer. A light golden top & set egg are required for each mouthful. After removing the mold, let your egg bits sit for around 10 mins before removing them from the mold. Serve hot.

Nutrition Value
Calories: 249 Kcal, Carb: 29 g, Protein: 5 g, Fat: 12.2 g
Storage Suggestion: You can store it in the refrigerator for 6-7 days.

Air Fryer Crustless Pizza (Low Carb)

Prep Time: 10 Mins, Cook Time: 10 Mins, Servings: 4, Serving Size: 1

Ingredients
- 1 lb cooked browned & drained ground beef
- 2 cups of shredded divided mozzarella cheese
- 7 oz sauce marinara
- pizza toppings Your favorite

Instructions
- Mix the meat with 1 cup of mozzarella in a medium bowl.

- In barrel pan or pizza pan, evenly distribute the ground beef mixture.
- Spread your marinara sauce equally over the top of the pizza.
- Add the rest of the cheese & toppings on the top. If you're using pepperonis, be sure to sprinkle some cheese on top before baking; otherwise, your pizza may end up flying apart.
- Use your basket of air fryers to hold the pan.
- Using an instant-read thermometer, monitor the cheese's crispiness in an oven preheated to 360° F (or 350°F if 360° F is not possible). Pizzas baked around 15 Mins might satisfy the need for crispy cheese.

Nutrition Value
Calories: 457 Kcal, Carb: 3 g, Protein: 41 g, Fat: 31 g
Storage Suggestion: You can store it in the refrigerator for 6-7 days.

Tuna Noodle Casserole

Prep Time: 10 Mins, Cook Time: 40 Mins, Servings: 8, Serving Size: 1

Ingredients
- 8 oz egg noodles wide
- 3 tbsp butter unsalted
- ½ finely diced yellow onion or large white
- 1 diced celery rib
- 3 minced garlic cloves
- ¼ cup flour all-purpose
- 1 & ½ cups stock chicken
- 1 cup of milk
- salt & pepper
- 1 tbsp seasoning Italian
- 1 & ½ cups divided shredded cheese
- 5 oz drained tuna
- 1 cup peas frozen
- ½ cup ritz crackers crushed

Instructions
- Salted water should be used to cook your egg noodles till they are al dente. Stop the cooking by rinsing using cold water & draining again. Set aside the casserole dish with cooled noodles in it.
- Medium heat is ideal for melting butter in a big pan or air fryer. For 3-4 Mins, sauté the celery, onion, & garlic until they are soft.
- Cook for 2 to 3 Mins, constantly stirring, after adding flour. Whisk in the chicken broth & milk when the heat is reduced to low. Toss in the Italian seasoning & pepper/salt before heating through. The mixture will thicken if you keep whisking it.
- Preheat the air fryer to 350°F. Then add shredded cheese & stir until it's completely melted. Tuna and beans should be mixed until well-combined.
- Toss the noodles with sauce mixture & mix well to coat them in the sauce
- The leftover shredded cheese may be topped with a final sprinkle. Crush Ritz crackers and sprinkle them on top. Bake covered for 25 mins at 350°F. Bake for a further 5 to 10 Mins, or unless the cheese is browned & bubbling, after removing the lid.

Nutrition Value
Calories: 380 Kcal, Carb: 30.6 g, Protein: 28.6 g, Fat: 16.5 g
Storage Suggestion: You can store it in the refrigerator for 2-3 days.

Chapter 11: Frittatas Recipes

Bell Peppers Frittata

Prep Time: 10 Mins, Cook Time: 20 Mins, Servings: 4, Serving Size: 2

Ingredients
- 2 Tbsp oil olive
- 2 cups casings removed & chopped chicken sausage
- 1 chopped sweet onion
- 1 red chopped bell pepper
- 1 orange, chopped bell pepper
- 1 green chopped bell pepper
- Salt & black pepper
- 8 whisked eggs
- ½ cup shredded mozzarella cheese
- 2 tsp chopped oregano

Instructions
- In your air fryer, pour 1 tbsp of oil, add bacon, heat at 320°F, then brown for around 1 Min.
- Remove the leftover butter, stir in the onion, orange, bell pepper, & white, then continue to cook for around 2 Mins more.
- Stir in pepper, oregano, salt, & eggs after 15 Mins of cooking.
- Add the mozzarella, set aside for a few Mins, then divide & serve amongst plates.
- Enjoy.

Nutritional Value Nutrition Value
Calories: 212 Kcal, Carb: 8 g, Protein: 12 g, Fat: 4 g
Storage Suggestion: You can store it in the refrigerator for 6-7 days.

Fritters with Squash

Prep Time: 15 Mins, Cook Time: 10 Mins, Servings: 5, Serving Size: 1

Ingredients
- 4 tbsp of olive oil extra-virgin
- 1 cup breadcrumbs baking
- 2/3 cup carrot grated
- 2 summer squash grated yellow
- salt & black pepper
- 1 tsp oregano dried
- 2 eggs whisked
- 5 oz cheese cream

Instructions
- Combine your carrot, breadcrumbs, cream cheese, egg, oregano, pepper, salt, & squash in a large mixing bowl.
- Form your mixture into little patties & coat them with oil.
- Cook for around 7 Mins on 400°F in your air fryer with the squash patties.
- For lunch, serve them hot. Have a blast!!

Nutrition Value
Calories: 279 Kcal, Carb: 25 g, Protein: 18 g, Fat: 7.8 g
Storage Suggestion: You can store it in the refrigerator for 5-6 days.

The Best Air Fryer Zucchini Fritters

Prep Time: 5 Mins, Cook Time: 15 Mins, Servings: 8, Serving Size: 1

Ingredients
- 2 large Zucchini
- 1 cup cheddar shredded
- 1 large egg
- ½ cup of flour
- 2 tbsp chives
- 1 tsp salt
- 1 tsp pepper

Instructions
- Zucchini should be shredded, and the excess water squeezed out using a cheesecloth.
- Combine the zucchini, chives, salt, egg, flour, & pepper in a mixing dish.
- Combine all of the ingredients.
- Form the mixture into 8 patties.
- Store it within the freezer for around 5-10 Mins to retain the shape.
- Preheat the air fryer to 350 degrees.
- Preheat your air fryer to 350°F and cook the zucchini patties for around 5 Mins.
- Cook for a further 5-10 Mins on the other side, unless brown.

Nutrition Value
Calories: 104 Kcal, Carb: 8 g, Protein: 6 g, Fat: 6 g
Storage Suggestion: You can store it in the refrigerator for 2-3 days.

Air-Fryer Apple Fritters

Prep Time: 10 mins, Cook Time: 10 mins, Servings: 15, Serving Size: 2

Ingredients
- 1 & ½ cups flour all-purpose
- ¼ cup of sugar
- 2 tsp powder baking
- 1 & ½ tsp cinnamon ground
- ½ tsp salt
- 2/3 cup milk2%
- 2 room temperature large eggs
- 1 tbsp juice lemon
- 1 & ½ tsp divided vanilla extract
- 2 medium peeled & chopped Honeycrisp apples
- ¼ cup of butter
- 1 cup sugar confectioners'
- 1 tbsp milk 2%

Instructions
- Preheat the air fryer to 410 degrees. Combine flour, cinnamon, baking powder, sugar, and salt in a wide mixing bowl. Combine the lemon juice, milk, eggs, & vanilla extract in a mixing bowl and whisk just until combined. Apples should be folded in.
- Spray the air-fryer basket and line it is using parchment paper (cut to fit). Drop dough apart on parchment paper in batches. Using cooking spray, spritz the surface. Cook for 5 to 6 Mins, or unless golden brown. Continue to air-fry fritters unless golden brown, about 1-2 Mins.
- In a shallow saucepan on medium-high heat, melt the butter. Cook, constantly stirring, unless the butter begins to brown & froth, approximately 5 Mins. Remove from the heat and let it cool slightly. Toss the browned butter with the confectioner sugar, milk, and vanilla extract, whisk unless smooth. Before serving, drizzle the glaze over the fritters.

Nutrition Value
Calories: 145 Kcal, Carb: 24 g, Protein: 3 g, Fat: 4 g
Storage Suggestion: You can store it in the refrigerator for 5-6 days.

Scrumptious Air Fryer Apple Fritters

Prep Time: 5 Mins, Cook Time: 5 Mins, Servings: 12, Serving Size: 1

Ingredients
- 1 can flakey biscuits refrigerated
- 1 medium peeled & diced apple
- ½ tsp of cinnamon
- ½ tsp sugar

glaze
- ½ cup sugar powdered
- 1 tbsp of milk

Instructions
- Place all biscuits on the cookie sheet split them in half.
- Then put chopped apples, cinnamon, & sugar in a large mixing bowl.
- Combine all ingredients in a mixing bowl and pour over biscuit dough.
- Your apple mixture should be pressed into the dough.
- Use parchment paper to line your Air Fryer basket or rack.
- Place your fritters within Air Fryer into batches.
- Air fry for around 5 mins at 390°F.
- Combine powdered milk & sugar in a medium bowl and stir unless a glaze appears.
- Drizzle over the fritters & serve immediately.

Nutrition Value
Calories: 45 Kcal, Carb: 9 g, Protein: 0 g, Fat: 1 g
Storage Suggestion: You can store it in the refrigerator for 6-7 days.

Air Fryer Loaded Corn Fritters

Prep Time: 10 Mins, Cook Time: 20 Mins, Servings: 10, Serving Size: 1

Ingredients
- 1 can of corn
- 2 large eggs
- 1-2 tsp sugar
- 1 tsp salt
- ½ tsp pepper
- ½ cup flour all-purpose
- 1 tsp powder baking
- ¾ cup cheddar cheese shredded
- 2 tbsp of butter
- 2 tbsp vegetable oil or olive
- ¼ cup crumbled and cooked bacon
- 1 jalapeno diced
- as garnish Chives
- your choice Dipping sauce

Instructions
- In a medium-sized mixing bowl, whisk the pepper, sugar, eggs, salt, & baking powder.
- Whisk in the flour until it is completely combined.
- Combine the corn, bacon, shredded cheese, & diced jalapeno in a large mixing bowl.
- Form patties from the mixture.
- Place for around 30 Mins in the freezer
- Preheat the air fryer at 400 degrees Fahrenheit.
- Spray the Air Fryer using cooking oil & cook for around 10 Mins before flipping it over for another 5 Mins.
- Enjoy with your favorite condiments!

Nutrition Value
Calories: 172 Kcal, Carb: 11 g, Protein: 7 g, Fat: 11 g
Storage Suggestion: You can store it in the refrigerator for 5-6 days.

Air Fryer Zucchini Corn Fritters

Prep Time: 15 Mins, Cook Time: 15 Mins, Servings: 10-12, Serving Size: 2

Ingredients
- 1 lb medium zucchini
- 1 cup frozen or canned corn kernels
- ¼ cup parmesan cheese grated
- ¼ cup grated yellow onion
- 1 finely minced clove garlic
- 1 tbsp parsley dried
- 1 tsp of salt
- ½ tsp black pepper freshly ground
- ½ tsp basil dried
- ½ tsp oregano dried
- ¼ tsp of paprika
- 2 lightly beaten eggs
- 1 cup flour almond, & flour all-purpose
- 1 tsp powder baking
- Spray cooking oil

Instructions
- Preheat the Air Fryer at 360 degrees Fahrenheit.
- Using the box grater with big holes, shred your zucchini; transfer shredded zucchini to the kitchen towel.
- Wrap your zucchini inside a kitchen towel & squeeze out as enough liquid as you can. Place zucchini inside a large mixing bowl.
- Combine corn kernels, oregano, paprika, garlic, parsley, salt, cheese, onion, pepper, basil, & beaten eggs in a large mixing bowl with zucchini.
- Stir in the flour & baking powder unless everything is thoroughly combined. Add extra flour if the mixture is too moist. Less the flour you use, the dried the zucchini is.
- Make 10-12 patties out of the mixture.
- OPTIONAL: To retain the form of the uncooked patties, place them in the fridge for 5-8 Mins.
- Using cooking spray, coat the basket of an air fryer.
- Working in batches to avoid overcrowding the air fryer basket, arrange the patties in a thin layer within the air fryer & spray each one using cooking spray. 6 Mins in the oven
- Cook for around 6-8 Mins longer, or unless browned, after flipping the patties & spraying them using cooking spray.
- Serve immediately after removing from the air fryer.

Nutrition Value

Calories: 95 Kcal, Carb: 7 g, Protein: 5 g, Fat: 6 g
Storage Suggestion: You can store it in the refrigerator for 6-7 days.

Air Fryer Cheesy Corn Fritters

Prep Time: 5 Mins, Cook Time: 8 Mins, Servings: 12, Serving Size: 2

Ingredients

- 1 cup stripped off corn
- ½ cup cheddar cheese shredded
- ¼ cup breadcrumbs panko
- 1 tbsp of flour
- 1 large egg
- 3 diced green onions
- 1 tbsp of mayonnaise, Greek yogurt, or sour cream
- 1 tsp of salt
- ½ tsp pepper
- ½ tsp powder garlic
- ½ tsp powder onion

Instructions

- Preheat the air fryer to 375°F.
- In a large mixing bowl, combine all fritter ingredients. Make sure everything is properly mixed, but don't overdo it. Add more sour cream or mayonnaise if the mix is too dry. If it's too moist, add a little flour at a time until it's the right consistency. The consistency should be sticky.
- Form balls of mix using a cookie scoop. Flatten into a disc using the palm. Cook for around 8 Mins in a hot air fryer, flipping at 4 min mark.
- Serve right away with your favorite dipping sauce.

Nutrition Value

Calories: 249 Kcal, Carb: 25 g, Protein: 6 g, Fat: 23 g
Storage Suggestion: You can store it in the refrigerator for 4-5 days.

Air Fryer Apple Fritters with Brown Butter Glaze

Prep Time: 10 Mins, Cook Time: 10 Mins, Servings: 10, Serving Size: 1

Ingredients

Brown Butter Glaze
- 1 cup Sugar Powdered
- ¼ cup of Butter
- ½ tsp of Vanilla
- 1 tbsp of Milk

Apple Fritters
- 1 & ½ cups Flour All Purpose
- ¼ cup Sugar Granulated
- 2 tsp Powder Baking
- ½ tsp of Salt
- 1 ½ tsp Cinnamon Ground
- ⅓ cup of Milk
- 1 tsp of Vanilla
- 1 tbsp fresh Lemon Juice
- 2 large Eggs
- 2 peeled, cored large Apples
- Vegetable or Canola Oil

Instructions

Brown Butter Glaze

- In a medium saucepan on medium heat, melt the butter. Continue to melt the butter unless it foams and becomes a golden-brown color. Remove from burner once browned and let to cool slightly. Your butter must have a nutty fragrance & brown fleck in it.
- In a medium bowl, sift the powdered sugar. Whisk together the milk, browned butter, & vanilla extract unless smooth.

Apple Fritters

- Preheat the air fryer at 400 degrees F (adjust the setting and wait 3-4 Mins for the interior basket to become nice & hot).
- In a medium mixing bowl, combine flour, sugar, salt, baking powder, & cinnamon.
- Make the well in the middle of the bowl and pour in the lemon juice, milk, vanilla, and eggs. Stir in some apples unless they are uniformly distributed.
- Using parchment paper, carefully line your basket of the preheated air fryer. So, there is no bulging over the sides; cut your parchment to suit the bottom. Apply a light coat of oil or use an oil sprayer to apply a light coat of oil.
- Pour roughly a quarter cup of batter into the prepared air fryer basket. You would be able to place two fritters within the air fryer once at a time, varying according to the size of the air fryer.
- Using an oil sprayer, lightly dab the tops of your fritters using oil. Preheat your air fryer at 400°F and cook the fritters for around 4-5 Mins, unless golden brown. Repeat with the other fritters.
- Drizzle some brown butter glaze over apple fritters while they're still warm over a cooling rack.
- Serve right away & enjoy!

Nutrition Value

Calories: 168 Kcal, Carb: 29.95 g, Protein: 3.12 g, Fat: 4.13 g
Storage Suggestion: You can store it in the refrigerator for 7-8 days.

Air Fryer Healthy Zucchini Corn Fritters

Prep Time: 10 Mins, Cook Time: 12 Mins, Servings: 4, Serving Size: 1

Ingredients

- 2 zucchinis medium
- 1 cup kernels corn
- 1 medium cooked potato
- 2 tbsp flour chickpea
- 2 to 3 minced garlic finely
- 1 to 2 tsp oil olive
- salt & pepper

For Serving

- Yogurt or Ketchup tahini sauce

Instructions

- Using a food processor, grate the zucchini. Mix shredded zucchini with a pinch of salt in a mixing dish and let aside for 10 to 15 Mins. Then, squeeze out any extra water from the zucchini using a cheesecloth.
- Grate cooked potato as well.
- Combine garlic, salt, zucchini, corn, potato, chickpea flour, & pepper.

- Take about the batter, shape it into a patty, and set it on parchment paper.
- Apply a little coat of oil over the surface of every fritter. Preheat the Air Fryer at 360 degrees Fahrenheit.
- Place your fritters over Air Fryer mesh, ensuring they don't touch. Cook for around 8 Mins.
- Then flip the fritters & cook for the next 3-4 Mins, unless well-cooked or the desired color is achieved.
- Serve with tahini sauce or ketchup while still heated.

Nutrition Value
Calories: 118 Kcal, Carb: 12 g, Protein: 6 g, Fat: 3.8 g
Storage Suggestion: You can store it in the refrigerator for 5-6 days.

Red Lentil, Carrot & Coriander Fritters

Prep Time: 15 Mins, Cook Time: 25 Mins, Servings: 6, Serving Size: 1

Ingredients
- 150 g lentils red
- 1 carrot large
- 1 garlic clove
- 2 tbsp flour plain
- 2 tbsp of olive oil
- 2 tbsp of tahini
- 1 tsp of paprika
- 6 g coriander fresh
- pepper & Salt

Instructions
- After rinsing the lentils in cold water, place them in a pot with 200 ml of water. Simmer for around 12 mins, or unless lentils have absorbed all of the liquid. Remove from the oven and set aside to cool.
- Peel your carrot, grate it, then combine it with lentils & the additional ingredients in the food processor.
- Pulse unless the material is fully blended & broken down but not pureed.
- Warm 1 tbsp of olive oil into your frying pan on medium heat.
- Place the ingredients within the frying pan & form in fritters.
- Cook for around 3-4 Mins on one side before switching and cooking for another 3-4 Mins.
- Eat right away or store within the fridge for up to 3 days.

Nutrition Value
Calories: 320 Kcal, Carb: 27.3 g, Protein: 19.3 g, Fat: 6.5 g
Storage Suggestion: You can store it in the refrigerator for 7-8 days.

Air Fryer Healthy Banana Fritters

Prep Time: 20 Mins, Cook Time: 20 Mins, Servings: 2, Serving Size: 1

Ingredients
- 2 large, diced bananas
- ½ cup of flour
- 2 large eggs
- ½ cup desiccated coconut or almond meal
- 1 tbs melted butter
- 1 tsp of cinnamon
- to sprinkle Sugar
- to drizzle Honey
- to serve Ice cream

Instructions
- Bananas should be peeled and sliced in half.
- Flour your bananas and roll them in them.
- Eggs should be whisked together. Toss the banana inside the egg and cover it fully.
- In a large bowl, combine the butter, desiccated coconut/almond meal & cinnamon. Roll your bananas within a mixture, pressing any residual mix into the banana with your fingers.
- Cook for around 8 Mins at 180°C in an air fryer.
- Take the bananas out of your air fryer. Divide the mixture into 2 bowls. Drizzle with some honey & sprinkle with some sugar. Serve with ice cream.

Nutrition Value
Calories: 346 Kcal, Carb: 23 g, Protein: 15 g, Fat: 3 g
Storage Suggestion: You can store it in the refrigerator for 5-6 days.

Air Fryer Banana Fritters

Prep Time: 5 Mins, Cook Time: 7 Mins, Servings: 2, Serving Size: 1

Ingredients
- 3 halved Banana
- ½ cup starch Corn
- 1 beaten Egg
- ½ cup of Breadcrumbs
- 1 tbsp oil olive

Instructions
- In a large saucepan over medium heat, pour in the oil.
- Stir in the breadcrumbs unless they are golden brown. Remove this from the pan and place it in a large mixing bowl.
- One after another, coat your bananas with corn starch, then within egg mix, and last with breadcrumbs.
- Set aside your bananas that have been covered. Preheat the air fryer at 360 degrees Fahrenheit for around 5 Mins.
- Oil your basket of air fryer lightly. Arrange the covered bananas in a thin layer within the basket.
- 5 Mins in the oven. Shake your basket a little bit. Cook for the next 2 Mins, or unless golden brown on the outside.
- Place your air-fried banana over a serving platter after removing it from your air fryer. Allow it to cool completely before eating since the inside may be quite hot.

Nutrition Value
Calories: 210 Kcal, Carb: 13 g, Protein: 23 g, Fat: 5 g
Storage Suggestion: You can store it in the refrigerator for 2-3 days.

Caprese Gluten-Free Air-Fryer Zucchini Fritters

Prep Time: 15 Mins, Cook Time: 20 Mins, Servings: 16, Serving Size: 4

Ingredients
For Zucchini Fritters

- 4 cups zucchini shredded
- 2/3 cup all-purpose flour Gluten-free
- 2 eggs large
- ¼ cup pesto prepared
- ½ cup mozzarella cheese shredded
- ½ tsp salt Kosher
- 1/8 tsp pepper black
- Cooking Spray Non-stick

For balsamic roasted tomatoes topping

- 2 cups tomatoes cherry
- 3 tbsp of vinegar balsamic
- 2 tbsp of olive oil or olive oil garlic-infused
- Salt & pepper

Instructions

- Preheat the air fryer to 400 degrees Fahrenheit for roasting tomatoes.
- Using a food processor, shred the zucchini. Place your zucchini in a strainer, season with salt, and then let aside for around 10 Minutes. This will aid in the removal of moisture from the zucchini.
- Transfer your zucchini to the high-quality paper towels & set over a medium bowl after it has rested for around 10 Mins. Squeeze water out of zucchini as you want to into a small bowl.
- Combine the mozzarella, salt, eggs, pesto, zucchini, flour, & pepper in a wide mixing bowl & toss until well incorporated.
- Put cherry tomatoes over a baking pan coated using cooking spray. Season with pepper & salt, then drizzle with balsamic vinegar & olive oil. Toss to coat evenly. Roast for around 15-20 mins at 400° F, unless they are soft & have burst a bit.
- While tomatoes are cooking, coat the air fryer's basket using nonstick cooking spray. Using one serving spoon, form the fritters into little patties with your hands, then arrange them within the basket. The batter is sticky & will result in a thick fritter. Coat the fritters well using cooking spray.
- To avoid overcrowding the basket, fry your fritters into batches. Cook for around 12 Mins at 360° F, turning halfway through.
- Serve with baked balsamic tomatoes as soon as they're done.

Nutrition Value
Calories: 307 Kcal, Carb: 25 g, Protein: 11 g, Fat: 19 g
Storage Suggestion: You can store it in the refrigerator for 3-4 days.

Air Fryer Kolokithokeftedes (Greek Zucchini Fritters)

Prep Time: 30 Mins, Cook Time: 25 Mins, Servings: 16-18, Serving Size: 4

Ingredients

- 1 & ½ g grated zucchini
- 1 tsp salt kosher
- ½ cup white & green chopped scallion
- 1 grated garlic clove
- 1 cup of breadcrumbs
- 1 cup of cheese feta
- 1 tsp powder baking
- ¼ cup kefalotiri shredded
- 1 egg large
- 2 tbsp fresh dill finely chopped
- olive oil or baking spray

Instructions

- Grate zucchini using a grater blade in the food processor. Place your zucchini inside the fine-mesh strainer, season with salt, toss well, then drain for around 30 Mins within the sink.
- Squeeze liquid out as you can. This will be simpler if you wrap the sieve with a cheesecloth.
- Combine zucchini, feta, breadcrumbs, scallion, garlic, baking powder, kefalotiri cheeses, beaten egg, & dill in a large mixing bowl. Add one extra egg if your mixture is too dry to cling together.
- Spray the air fryer basket with a brush with some olive oil.
- Make 1" balls out of the zucchini mix. Place your patties on your prepared basket after lightly smashing the balls in patties. Using the leftover olive oil, brush the tops.
- Cook for around 20-25 mins at 375°F, monitoring halfway through to ensure uniform cooking. Since the patties over the edge were frying quicker, flip some of them from the side to the center.
- Set aside for 5 to 10 mins to allow flavors to meld. Then take it out of the basket & serve it.

Nutrition Value
Calories: 146 Kcal, Carb: 16 g, Protein: 19 g, Fat: 4 g
Storage Suggestion: You can store it in the refrigerator for 1-2 days.

Air Fryer Asparagus Fritters

Prep Time: 10-15 mins, Cook Time: 15-20 mins, Servings: 4, Serving Size: 3

Ingredients

Lemon Dill Aioli

- ¼ cup Greek yogurt plain
- 3 tbsp of mayonnaise
- 1 lemon medium Juice
- 2 tbsp chopped fresh dill
- 1 peeled & minced clove garlic
- ½ tsp powder onion
- ½ tsp sugar granulated
- ¼ tsp salt coarse
- ¼ tsp black pepper ground

Asparagus Fritters

- ½-lb of fresh thinly sliced asparagus spears
- ½ cup Panko breadcrumbs or all-purpose flour
- ¼ cup of milk or Greek yogurt plain
- ¼ cup of flat leaf chopped parsley leaves
- 2 tbsp chopped fresh chives
- 2 beaten large eggs
- medium lemon 1
- 1 tsp salt coarse
- ½ tsp black pepper ground

- ½ tsp oregano leaves dried
- ¼ tsp pepper cayenne

Instructions
- Whisk aioli ingredients in a medium bowl until smooth. Refrigerate unless ready to prepare, covered.
- Preheat your air fryer at 375°F.
- A big pot of water should be brought to a boil. Cook for around 2-3 Mins unless the asparagus is fork tender. Transfer your asparagus to the bowl full of cold water using a slotted spoon. Use a slotted spoon for transferring the asparagus over a paper towel-lined dish after the ice has melted. Allow to air dry.
- Stir the asparagus, breadcrumbs or flour, Greek yogurt or milk, parsley, chives, oregano, eggs, salt, lemon zest, black pepper, & cayenne pepper together in a medium mixing bowl unless well blended.
- Using cooking spray, coat your air fryer basket. In batches, drop 1" dollops of fritter batter in the basket air fryer using a cookie scoop. Cook for 8-12 mins unless the fritters are cooked through. Rep with the rest of the batter.
- Serve your asparagus fritters along with aioli made with lemon and dill.

Nutrition Value
Calories: 204 Kcal, Carb: 18 g, Protein: 8 g, Fat: 11 g
Storage Suggestion: You can store it in the refrigerator for 1-2 days.

Corn and Pea Fritters with Cilantro

Prep Time: 10 Mins, Cook Time: 12, Servings: 8, Serving Size: 2

Ingredients
- ¾ cup flour all-purpose
- 1 & ½ tbsp powder baking
- ¼ tsp of salt
- ½ tsp pepper black
- 3 tbsp diced onion
- ¼ cup cheese parmesan
- 1 large egg
- 4 tbsp milk
- olive oil drizzle
- 1 cup corn sweet
- ½ cup of peas
- 1 & ½ tbsp chopped cilantro
- 1 minced jalapeño

Dipping Sauce
- ½ cup sour cream or yogurt
- a lime juices
- 1 minced jalapeno
- ¼ cup leaves cilantro

Instructions
- Put the dry ingredients to a large mixing bowl to prevent lumps, then whisk to combine.
- Finally, include milk & olive oil into the mixture. Once those ingredients are combined (onion through jalapeño), the dish is complete. Mix until a homogeneous mixture is formed.
- Add some olive oil to a medium-sized pan & simmer for a few Mins until the oil is sizzling.
- Spoon out fritter mixture onto the pan & cook it for a few Mins until it's done. For a golden-brown finish, cook for 2 to 3 Mins every side.
- Make your dipping sauce while you're preparing the main dish. Add all sauce ingredients to a medium bowl & whisk them together.
- The dipping sauce may be served on the sides or over top of the fritter.

Nutrition Value
Calories: 143 Kcal, Carb: 10 g, Protein: 13 g, Fat: 5 g
Storage Suggestion: You can store it in the refrigerator for 3-4 days.

Paruppu Vada/ Chana Dal Fritters

Prep Time: 10 Mins, Cook Time: 30 Mins, Servings: 10, Serving Size: 2

Ingredients
- ¼ Cup Finely Chopped Onions
- Cilantro/Coriander Leaves
- ¼ tsp Seeds Fennel
- Salt
- To Brush Oil

To Grind Coarsely
- ½ Cup of Dal Chana / Soaked Kadala Paruppu
- 2 Nos Chili Green
- ¼-Inch Ginger

Instructions
- Pulverize all of the 'To grind' components in a food processor or blender until they are roughly ground without adding water.
- Toss it into a dish and store it.
- Add all the other ingredients, excluding the oil.
- Using your hands, knead the dough. Flatten a tiny lime-sized piece in your hand and hold it in your fingers. Place it on a platter and serve.
- Using up all of the leftover dal mixtures, do it again a second time. Oil every vada.
- Heat the oil in the air fryer to 400 degrees Fahrenheit. Heat for around 2 Mins before using.
- Make sure the vadas are arranged within the basket of the air fryer. Avoid overcrowding the container. Air circulation is best achieved by placing the vadas close together. In 1 batch, my vadas occupied five of them.
- Set the timer for 15 Mins & put the basket within the Air fryer. To make it crispy, turn the vadas over twice.
- Remove your vadas from the basket when the timer goes off. That way, it's not overcooked.
- Once you've finished all of the vadas, repeat the process. Make a chutney to go along with it.

Nutrition Value
Calories: 35.7 Kcal, Carb: 6.9 g, Protein: 1.6 g, Fat: 0 g
Storage Suggestion: You can store it in the refrigerator for 5-6 days.

Gluten Free Apple Fritters

Prep Time: 10 Mins, Cook Time: 12 Mins, Servings: 9, Serving Size: 2

Ingredients
- 1 & ¼ cups of free flour gluten
- ¼ cup of sugar
- 2 tsp cinnamon ground
- 2 tsp powder baking
- ¼ tsp of salt
- ⅓ cup melted butter
- 1 tsp vanilla extract pure
- 1 tbsp juice lemon
- 2 large eggs
- ½ cup peeled & chopped apples

For Glaze
- 1 cup sugar powdered
- ¼ cup melted butter
- 1 tbsp of milk
- 1 tsp vanilla extract pure

Instructions
- For around 5 Mins, preheat the air fryer at 375°F. Keep it closed to keep the heat in.
- Whisk together dry ingredients for the apple fritters in a large bowl.
- Add the remaining wet ingredients to the melted butter, ensuring it isn't too hot. Blend with a whisk.
- Your apple pieces should be poured into dry ingredients.
- Combine wet & dry ingredients in a batter. HINT: Overmixing your dough would result in denser fritters. Avoid this at all costs.
- Use coconut oil to coat parchment paper. Drop dough balls for apple fritters upon parchment paper using a cookie scooper. See down for oil frying instructions if you plan on cooking in oil.
- Cut a circle around each fritter using scissors. You need to do it so that the fritters can breathe. As a result, they'll cook more evenly.
- Put the fritters within the basket of your air fryer and cook them for a few Mins. Use similar coconut oil to coat the fritters' tops as well.
- In an air fryer, cook a batch of fritters for around 10 Mins at 375 deg F. Check to see whether they're done by opening the air fryer. On the exterior, they should have a golden sheen.
- In a small dish, combine all of the glaze's components.
- Mix thoroughly. Your glaze should be a little runny. On a cooling rack, sprinkle every fritter with glaze. You may eat the glaze after it has hardened.

Nutrition Value
Calories: 258 Kcal, Carb: 33 g, Protein: 3 g, Fat: 14 g
Storage Suggestion: You can store it in the refrigerator for 1-2 days.

Garlic Parmesan Cauliflower Fritters

Prep Time: 10 Mins, Cook Time: 16 Mins, Servings 4, Serving Size: 2

Ingredients
- 4 cups florets cauliflower
- ½ cup flour almond
- ¼ cup flour tapioca
- ¾ cup parmesan cheese grated
- 1 tsp powder garlic
- Salt & pepper
- 2 large eggs
- lightly coating Oil
- freshly parmesan cheese chopped parsley
- marinara sauce

Instructions
- Garlic powder, salt & pepper go into a bowl with the above ingredients. In a separate dish, combine the eggs. Set up the assembly line along with eggs, cauliflower, & flour mixture, then assemble the dish.
- Dip your cauliflower into the egg mix and bread it. When you're done, make sure it's well covered with flour before dipping it back in. Repeat with the rest of the cauliflower.
- Add oil to a big nonstick skillet and cook the chicken in batches unless it is golden brown and cooked through.
- Get crispy & delicious results without all the extra oil & fat by cooking within an Air fryer!
- Cauliflower should be spread out & spaced out inside the basket air fryer. Dot the surface with a thin layer of oil. For 16 to 17 Mins, close your drawer and put the air fryer to manual on 375 degrees, stopping to stir them halfway through. Continue to spread them out once you've stirred them. To avoid overcrowding, you may have to bake in 2 batches.
- If preferred, garnish with chopped parsley & additional parmesan cheese. Serve with a dipping sauce of marinara sauce.

Nutrition Value
Calories: 136 Kcal, Carb: 12 g, Protein: 17 g, Fat: 4 g
Storage Suggestion: You can store it in the refrigerator for 1-2 days.

Chapter 12: Quiches Recipes

Air Fryer Quiche

Prep Time: 10 Mins, Cook Time: 10 Mins, Servings: 1, Serving Size: 1

Ingredients
- 1 egg
- 3 to 4 tbsp cream
- 4 to 5 tiny florets broccoli
- 1 tbsp cheddar cheese finely grated

Instructions
- Combine the egg & cream in a bowl, then whisk until smooth. The dish should be lightly sprayed with nonstick cooking spray. Place your broccoli florets in the bottom of the pan. In a large bowl, whisk together the egg and milk until smooth. Grate some cheddar cheese on top.
- For around 10 Mins, air fried at 325 deg F (162 deg C).

Nutrition Value
Calories: 656 Kcal, Carb: 18 g, Protein: 21 g, Fat: 2 g
Storage Suggestion: You can store it in the refrigerator for 1 week.

Air fryer Quiche Lorraine

Prep Time: 20 Mins, Cook Time: 40 Mins, Servings: 4, Serving Size:

Ingredients
- 1 sheet puff pastry frozen
- 2 tsp oil olive
- 175 g bacon rindless
- 1 finely chopped brown onion
- 5 large eggs
- ½ cup cream thickened
- ½ cup milk
- 1 cup Swiss-style cheese coarsely grated

Instructions
- Puff pastry should be used to line an 18cm round fluted tart pan with a detachable base. It should be pushed into the bottom and up the sides of the tin. You'll need to use baking paper and weights to keep the crust from crumbling.
- The air fryer's sliding rack should be taken out. Place your lined tart pan inside the rack and close the lid tightly around it. Incorporate a new grate into the oven. Cook for six Mins at 180C. Remove the baking paper & rice or pastry weights. Prick the pastry all over with a fork. Return the pastry to an air fryer & cook for the next 6 Mins unless it is extremely dry. Allow the pasty to cool gently on the rack.
- To prepare the oil for cooking, heat it to medium-high in a big frying pan Stir often for around 5 Mins or unless the bacon begins to brown. Toss in the onion and sauté until the onion is softened and the bacon is browned. Remove from heat and let cool slightly.
- Before serving, the cream, eggs, and milk should all be beaten together in a mixing bowl. Pepper to taste. The pastry foundation should be spooned with the bacon mixture. Add the cheese and mix well. Pour your egg mixture on top of it. Slide your air fryer's rack back in. To ensure that the filling is set, bake for around 30 Mins at 160°C. Remove from heat and let cool slightly.
- Serving suggestion: Sliced and served either hot or cold.

Nutrition Value
Calories: 453 Kcal, Carb: 19 g, Protein: 17 g, Fat: 7 g
Storage Suggestion: You can store it in the refrigerator for 1 week.

Air Fried Mexican Quiche

Prep Time: 10 Mins, Cook Time: 8 Mins, Servings: 4, Serving Size: 1

Ingredients
- 3 large eggs
- ¼ diced bell pepper
- ¼ cup diced onions
- 2 tbsp milk
- 2 to 3 halved grape tomatoes
- 1 tbsp tomatoes sun-dried
- 2 tbsp shredded cheese
- ¼ tsp thyme
- ¼ tsp salt
- 1/8 tsp black pepper
- spray olive oil

Instructions
- For 5 mins, heat the air fryer at around 360 Deg F.
- Whisk the eggs in a small bowl, then add the rest of the ingredients and mix well.
- Use nonstick spray to coat a 4" pie pan. It is then time to pour the egg mixture into the dish.
- For an 8-Min cook time, place in the air fryer basket and turn halfway through.
- Remove from heat and let sit inside pan for three Mins before removing from pan.

Nutrition Value
Calories: 93 Kcal, Carb: 3 g, Protein: 7 g, Fat: 6 g
Storage Suggestion: You can store it in the refrigerator or fridge for 2-3 days.

Air Fryer Cheese Quiche

Prep Time: 15 mins, Cook Time: 18 mins, Servings: 4, Serving size: 2

Ingredients
- 300 g Pie Crust Air Fryer
- 300 g Cheddar Cheese Grated
- 4 Tomatoes Cherry
- 75 ml Milk Whole
- 2 Tsp Herbs Mixed
- 3 Eggs Large
- 1 Tbsp Oregano
- Pepper & Salt

Instructions
- Make your pie crust first. To improve the crust's flavor, sprinkle it with a mixture of dried herbs. In small dishes, such as ramekins, spoon out the rolled-out mixture.

- Whip the milk and eggs together using a mixer jug, then season with pepper and salt.
- Pour the milk & egg mixture over the cheese in your ramekins, filling them about three-quarters of the way. Load the cherry tomatoes into the mix, then top with a generous sprinkling of more grated cheese & fresh oregano.
- For 8 Mins at 180 deg C/360 deg f, then another 10 mins at 160 deg C/320 deg f, air-fry for around 8 Mins.

Nutrition Value
Calories: 715 Kcal, Carb: 40 g, Protein: 29 g, Fat: 49 g
Storage Suggestion: You can store it in the fridge and refrigerator for 3 to 7 days.

Air-Fryer Broccoli Quiche
Prep Time: 10 Mins, Cook Time: 20 Mins, Servings: 2, Serving Size: 1

Ingredients
- 4 chopped bacon strips
- ¼ cup broccoli florets small fresh
- ¼ cup onion chopped
- 1 minced garlic clove
- 3 eggs large
- 1 tbsp parsley flakes dried
- 1/8 tsp salt seasoned
- pepper Dash
- ¼ cup cheddar cheese shredded
- 2 tbsp tomato chopped

Instructions
- Preheating the air fryer at 400 degrees is a simple process. Cook the bacon unless crisp in a pan over moderate heat, turning periodically. Drain the bacon using paper towels after removing this with a spoon. Reserving 2 tsp of the drippings in the pan, drain the rest of the drippings.
- Cook and toss the broccoli & onion in the pan drippings for 2-3 mins until they are soft. Add garlic and cook for an additional Min.
- Pour the eggs, seasoned salt, parsley, & pepper into a bowl & whisk to combine. Add the broccoli combination to the tomato, bacon, cheese, and onion.
- Using greased 10-oz custard cups or ramekins, divide the mixture equally between the two cups. To use an air fryer, put ramekins over a tray in the basket. As long as a knife falls out clean, it's done cooking!

Nutrition Value
Calories: 301 Kcal, Carb: 5 g, Protein: 19 g, Fat: 23 g
Storage Suggestion: You can store it in the refrigerator for 1 week.

Air Fryer Crustless Quiche
Prep Time: 8 Mins, Cook Time: 12 Mins, Servings: 2, Serving Size: 1

Ingredients
- 4 links of sausage
- 3 oz spinach
- 1 tbsp water
- 1 small cheese handful
- ⅓ cup of milk
- 3 to 4 beaten eggs
- ¼ tsp salt
- ½ tsp salt
- pepper dash
- nutmeg pinch

Instructions
- At 350° F/ 175° C, cook sausage for around 3 Mins in an air fryer. 370° F/185° C for 3 more Mins, and flip.
- Cover a microwave-safe bowl with spinach & water, then microwave for around 2 Mins.
- Toss the eggs and milk with the nutmeg, then season to taste.
- Top the cooked sausage with spinach & cheese on an air fryer pizza pan that has been gently sprayed. Then, on top of it, pour the egg & milk combination.
- A toothpick put into the cake should fall out clean after 12 Mins of cooking at 350° F/175° C.

Nutrition Value
Calories: 137 Kcal, Carb: 4 g, Protein: 11 g, Fat: 8 g
Storage Suggestion: You can store it in the refrigerator for almost 1 to 2 weeks.

Air Fryer Spinach Feta Quiche
Prep Time: 10 Mins, Cook Time: 15 Mins, Servings: 5, Serving Size: 1

Ingredients
- 6" round crust dough pie
- 1 tbsp fresh spinach finely chopped
- ⅛ cup cheddar cheese grated
- 1 tbsp feta cheese crumbled
- 1 egg large
- 1 tbsp cream heavy
- salt & pepper Pinch

Instructions
- Before making the quiche, let the chilled pie crust come to room temperature for approximately 15 Mins.
- Place the tart pan over top of the crust after unrolling the dough. The circle you cut doesn't have to be exact; it may be as large as 1 inch beyond the tart pans outside edge.
- Tuck the crust's edges into the sides of the tart pan & trim off any extra dough to ensure that your crust is level with the pan's surface.
- In your air fryer, cook a tart pan for around 5 Mins, around 300°F.
- Chop the spinach and spread it out within a tart pan to provide a bed.
- Cheeses may be added to the mix.
- Egg & heavy cream should be whipped together unless they form a smooth paste. Take a few seconds to add a little additional air to the egg mix.
- Pour the egg mix over the crust's contents slowly and carefully. The top of the crust must be completely covered with an egg mixture. Avoid cramming. A little salt & pepper would be nice here.
- The egg should be set in the middle when you return the prepared quiche to your air fryer basket & cook it for an

additional 10 Mins at around 300° F.
- Allow the quiche to settle for around 1-2 Mins before removing it from the tart pan with care. You may serve your quiche immediately or put it over the rack for cooling down after removing the bottom plate from the pastry pan.
- Put the food on a plate and serve!

Nutrition Value
Calories: 676 Kcal, Carb: 77 g, Protein: 59 g, Fat: 38 g
Storage Suggestion: You can store it in the fridge for up to 3 weeks.

Quiche Lorraine

Prep Time: 40 Mins, Cook Time: 45 Mins, Servings 8, Serving Size: 1

Ingredients
- 250 g wheat flour fine
- 100 g butter
- 5 g dried yeast
- 5 g of salt
- 5 g sugar super-fine
- 100 ml milk whole
- 1 large egg
- 255 g lean bacon
- 255 g ham cubes lean
- 110 g mushrooms
- 110 g onion
- 310 g cheese grated
- 3 large eggs
- 310 ml cream
- pepper & Salt
- finely chopped Chives

Instructions
- Refrigerate the mixture after combining the cream, eggs, & chives with a little pepper and salt.
- The yeast & sugar should be mixed with lukewarm milk in a large bowl. Sift the flour while the mixture sits for a few Mins and then proceed with the recipe. Using a bowl or work surface, spread the flour out and form a well within the midst of it. Add the beaten egg, butter, & yeast mixture to the other ingredients. From the inside out, knead the dough.
- Continue to add flour to a wet mix until it is the correct consistency. Make the dough thoroughly.
- Place your dough in a small bowl that has been lightly oiled and let it rise for about an hr. The oil keeps the dough from sticking to the bowl. Just let the dough rise for around an hr under a wet towel.
- Clean and thinly slice the mushrooms and bacon before cutting them into cubes. Slice the onion very thinly.
- Divide the dough into 4 equal pieces if you have an Air fryer Viva. Place a layer of parchment paper over the top of the greased spring forms. Put your dough in the pan by rolling it out. To stop bubbles from developing, prick the dough with a fork.
- Stack the ingredients into the tin(s). Afterward, pour inside the egg mix & fold the leftover dough toward the center. Bake the quiche in the Air fryer springform pan (s).
- Cooking time: 30 Mins around 160 deg in the Air Fryer

Nutrition Value
Calories: 243 Kcal, Carb: 28 g, Protein: 17 g, Fat: 12 g
Storage Suggestion: You can store it in the fridge for around 2 weeks.

Instant Air Fryer Ham, Mini Egg, & Cheese Quiche

Prep Time: 5 Mins, Cook Time: 25 Mins, Servings: 6, Serving Size: 1

Ingredients
- 4 large eggs
- 2 tbsp of milk
- ½ cup ham bacon diced
- 1 bread piece
- ½ cup of cheese
- ½ tsp pepper & salt

Instructions
- Prepare the Air Fryer by setting the temperature to bake for around 350°F.
- Slice the ham, bread, & cheese finely.
- In a bowl, add all ingredients & mix well.
- Pour about 3/4 of the contents into each cup onto a cooling rack.
- It's important to shovel the delicacies into cups so that you receive cheese and ham, not just egg.
- Bake for around 20 Mins, then remove the foil. Uncover & cook for another five Mins.
- Cook for another few Mins, then top with more cheese.

Nutrition Value
Calories: 106 Kcal, Carb: 3 g, Protein: 8 g, Fat: 7 g
Storage Suggestion: You can store it in your refrigerator for around 2 to 3 days.

Frozen Quiche in the Air Fryer

Prep Time: 15 Mins, Cook Time: 15 Mins, Servings: 2, Serving Size: 1

Ingredients
- 4 Quiche Frozen

Instructions
- Within a basket of air fryer, put your frozen quiche that has been defrosted.
- For around 15-20 Mins, cook at around 350 degrees.
- Take a bite out of it!

Nutrition Value
Calories: 210 Kcal, Carb: 14 g, Protein: 18 g, Fat: 6 g
Storage Suggestion: You can store it in the refrigerator for 1-2 weeks.

Air Fryer Frozen Mini Quiche

Prep Time: 15 Mins, cook time: 10 MINS, Servings: 12, Serving Size: 2

Ingredients
- 10 to 14 mini quiches frozen

Instructions
- Preheating your air fryer at 325 deg F is a good idea.
- Make sure your air fryer is heated before putting in all frozen mini quiches.

- For a core temperature of 165° Fahrenheit, cook all frozen quiches for around 8-11 Mins. Your air fryer & the brand of mini quiche you're using will affect the frying time.
- Remove the tiny quiche from the air fryer & allow it to cool for 2 Mins before serving. Then have a good time!

Nutrition Value
Calories: 220 Kcal, Carb: 18 g, Protein: 21 g, Fat: 2 g
Storage Suggestion: You can store it in the refrigerator for 1 week.

Mini Quiches

Prep Time: 10 Mins, Cook Time: 15 Mins, Servings: 6, Serving Size: 1

Ingredients
- 9-inch pie dough prepared
- 3 large eggs
- 1/3 cup of heavy cream
- ½ tsp salt
- ¼ tsp black pepper
- 1 tbsp butter unsalted
- ½ cup of each meat, veggies, & cheeses

Instructions
- To begin, gently dust the work surface and set the pie dough over its top. Cut a rim around the ramekin by placing it face down over the pie crust and cutting around it with a knife. With one 9" pie crust, you must be able to make 3-4 small pie crusts. Place pie weights in the ramekins after placing the prepared dough in them. Heat the crust within the air fryer oven for 3 to 5 Mins to 400°F. Preparation of the quiche components may be done in conjunction with baking the crust.
- Mix the eggs, salt, heavy cream, & pepper in a small bowl. In a skillet, brown the meat and vegetables. Remove from heat and put aside.
- Remove all ramekins from your air fryer, take the pie weights, & let them cool for the next few Mins. Fill every ramekin to its top with egg mix, then top with the grated cheese. Ten Mins of air-frying at 350 degrees Fahrenheit.

Nutrition Value
Calories: 189 Kcal, Carb: 18 g, Protein: 11 g, Fat: 8 g
Storage Suggestion: You can store it in the fridge for around 1-2 weeks.

Air-Fryer Bacon-Broccoli Quiche Cups

Prep Time: 10 mins, Cook Time: 20 mins, Servings: 2, Serving Size: 1

Ingredients
- 4 chopped bacon strips
- ¼ cup broccoli florets small fresh
- ¼ cup onion chopped
- 1 minced garlic clove
- 3 eggs large
- 1 tbsp parsley flakes dried
- 1/8 tsp salt seasoned
- pepper Dash
- ¼ cup cheddar cheese shredded
- 2 tbsp tomato chopped

Instructions
- Preheating the air fryer at around 400 degrees F is a simple process. Cook the bacon unless crisp in a pan over moderate heat, turning periodically. Drain the bacon using paper towels after removing it with the slotted spoon. Reserving 2 tsp of the drippings in the pan, drain the rest of the drippings.
- Cook and toss the broccoli & onion in the pan drippings for 2-3 Mins until soft. Add garlic and cook for an additional Min.
- Pour the eggs, seasoned salt, parsley, & pepper into a bowl & whisk to combine. Add the broccoli combination to the bacon, cheese, tomato, and onion.
- Using greased 10-oz custard cups or ramekins, divide the mixture equally between the two cups. To use an air fryer, put ramekins over a tray in the basket. As long as a knife falls out clean, it's done cooking!

Nutrition Value
Calories: 301 Kcal, Carb: 5 g, Protein: 19 g, Fat: 23 g
Storage Suggestion: You can store it in the fridge for almost 1 week.

Reheat Quiche in Air Fryer

Prep Time: 1 min, Cook Time: 8 mins, Servings: 2, Serving Size: 1

Ingredients
- 500 g Quiche Leftover

Instructions
- Use silver foil to cover the inside of the air fryer basket.
- In the basket of air fryer, put 2 remaining quiche pieces. Fry for around 8 Mins in an air fryer at 160° C/320° F.
- Optionally, you may serve with your favorite quiche dip dressing.

Nutrition Value
Calories: 250 Kcal, Carb: 40 g, Protein: 29 g, Fat: 23 g
Storage Suggestion: You can store it in the fridge for around 3-4 days.

Air Fryer Muffin Quiche

Prep Time: 4 mins, Cook Time: 12 mins, Servings: 8, Serving Size: 1

Ingredients
- 3 large eggs
- ¼ cup cheese shredded
- 2 cooked & crumbled patties sausage
- Salt & pepper

Instructions
- Mix cheese & sausage crumbles with cracked eggs inside a bowl.
- Season to taste with salt & pepper.
- Fill muffin tins with the mixture.

- Place inside the basket of an air fryer.
- For 12 Mins, bake at around 350°F/177°C.
- Take a bite out of it!

Nutrition Value
Calories: 193 Kcal, Carb: 23 g, Protein: 14 g, Fat: 10 g

Storage Suggestion: You can store it in the fridge for around 5-6 days.

Chapter 13: Wrap and Sandwiches Recipes

Tacos with Chipotle Steak

Prep Time: 4 Mins, Cook Time: 8 Mins, Servings: 4, Serving Size: 1

Ingredients
- 1.5-lb steak flank
- ½ cup onion red
- peeled & crushed garlic cloves
- Chipotle Sauce Adobo Chile
- 1 tbsp chili powder ancho
- 1 tsp powder cumin
- 1 tsp oregano dried
- 1 tbsp oil olive
- 1.5 tsp salt kosher
- ½ tsp pepper black
- 2 tbsp of water

For Serving
- 1 cup of salsa
- warmed flour tortillas
- ½ cup Cotija cheese crumbled

Ingredients
- Place the meat strips in a large mixing bowl or resealable plastic bag. In a blender or food processor, combine chipotle chili, onion, oregano, chili powder, garlic, cumin, olive oil, water, pepper, adobo sauce, and salt. Blend until the mixture is completely smooth. Combine the marinade into the meat, close the bag, massage it to coat and fully mix. Refrigerate for twenty-four hrs after marinating for thirty Mins at room temperature.
- With tongs, remove the beef strips from the bag and place them in the air fryer basket. Remove the marinade and try to keep the overlap to a minimum. Preheat the air fryer to 400°F and cook the beef strips for eight Mins, turning halfway through. It's possible to do it in batches.
- Cooking in the air fryer.
- On a sheet pan, arrange the steaks in a single layer.
- Preheat the oven to broil and cook the steak for 3–4 Mins.
- Cook for another two Mins on the other side.

Nutrition Value
Calories: 197 Kcal, Carb: 12 g, Protein: 10 g, Fat: 7 g

Storage Suggestion: You can store it in the fridge for around 5-6 days.

Air Fried Chicken Ranch Wraps

Prep Time: 5 Mins, Cook Time: 22 Mins, Servings: 5, Serving Size: 2

Ingredients
- 1 package Chicken Breast Tenders
- 4 12" wheat wraps whole
- 2 Heads chopped romaine lettuce
- ½ cup mozzarella cheese Shredded
- 4 tbsp dressing Ranch

Instructions
- Both baskets should have a crisper plate installed. Placing baskets in place, divide your chicken tenders into half & place them in Zones 1 & 2.
- Zone 1, AIR FRY, 390° F, & 22 Mins are all you need to cook a chicken breast properly. To make Zone 2's settings match Zone 1, choose MATCH COOK. To start cooking, just press the PAUSE/START button.
- After 11 Mins, push the PAUSE/START button to stop the device from running. Flip the chicken over after removing the baskets. Press the PAUSE/START button to restart the cooking process.
- Remove the chicken from the pan and cut it up after it's done cooking. Add chicken, cheese, lettuce, & ranch dressing on a smooth surface and roll it up. Seal the wrap by rolling it up securely once the 2 ends have been folded in. Continue with the rest of the ingredients.

Nutrition Value
Calories: 232 Kcal, Carb: 16 g, Protein: 13 g, Fat: 9.5 g

Storage Suggestion: You can store it in the fridge for around 5-6 days.

Air Fryer Cuban Sandwich Wrap

Prep Time: 10 Mins, Cook Time: 10 Mins, Servings: 2, Serving Size: 1

Ingredients
- 1 10" tortilla flour
- 1-oz cubed cooked pork
- 1 oz Ham Virginia
- 1½ oz shredded Swiss cheese
- 1 Tbsp mustard Cuban-style
- ¼ cubed dill pickle
- 1 Tbsp room temp butter

Instructions
- Preheat an air fryer for around 10 Mins at 375° F/190° C with the cooking area within the air fryer. Set your air fryer to 425°F/220°C for 10 Mins if you're using an oven-style model.
- Cooked pork may be cut or shredded. Grate some Swiss cheese & chop the ham into tiny pieces before assembling the sandwich. Slice the pickle into cubes using a mandolin.
- The flour tortilla should be placed on a dry, clean surface. Using roughly a mustard, spread it in the middle of the wrap. Plan to depart at least two hrs early "without mustard around the edges; it will seep out.
- Starting at approximately 2 inches from the edge of the tortilla, begin layering the ingredients "from the side closest to you in this order; the ham, pickles, shredded cheese, & pork are placed on top of the grated cheese, followed by the rest of it. The filling should be tucked under the tortilla's closest edge. Pull the wrap back toward you and gently tuck it beneath the contents. To make a wrap, fold every end toward the center, then roll out from you.
- Apply a small butter coating to the wrap's outside, focusing on the seam area, to ensure a tight seal. Place your wrap seam within the

air fryer when it has completed preheating. For around 10 Mins, air fry at the preheating temperature, turning halfway during the cooking time.
- Serve immediately after being removed from the oven and cool over a rack. It's time to savor!

Nutrition Value
Calories: 299 Kcal, Carb: 17 g, Protein: 15 g, Fat: 10 g
Storage Suggestion: You can store it in the fridge for around 1-2 days.

Air-Fried Chicken Shawarma

Prep Time: 25 Mins, Cook Time: 10 Mins, Servings: 4, Serving size: 1

Ingredients
- 2 tbsp oil olive
- 2 minced garlic cloves
- 1 lemon Juice
- 1 tsp cumin ground
- 1 tsp of paprika
- ½ tsp allspice ground
- ¼ tsp turmeric
- ¼ tsp cinnamon ground
- 1 tsp salt
- ½ tsp black pepper freshly ground
- 1½ lb chicken breast boneless
- 4 pieces pita bread of naan bread

Tahini Sauce
- ½ Cup sesame paste tahini
- 1/3 cup water warm
- ½ lemon Juice
- 1 clove minced garlic
- ¼ tsp cumin ground
- ¼ tsp of salt
- 2 tsp fresh parsley chopped

Tomato-Cucumber Salad
- 1 cup tomatoes diced
- 1 English cucumber small
- 2 tbsp red onion minced
- ½ lemon juice
- 1 tsp wine vinegar red
- 2 tsp oil olive
- 2 tbsp fresh parsley chopped
- salt & black pepper freshly ground

Instructions

- Mix the lemon juice, garlic, olive oil, & spices. Do not forget to do this with the chicken breasts! Add your marinade to a zipper-sealed plastic bag & seal it. The marinade should be applied to the chicken on all sides by massaging it in the bag. Refrigerate the chicken for at least six hrs or maybe overnight while preparing the marinade.
- Please make sure the air fryer is pre-heated to 380°F before using it.
- Using an air fryer basket, place the seasoned chicken breasts into the basket and cook for 8-10 Mins at 380oF, turning halfway during the cooking period.
- Prepare the Tahini Sauce by whisking together the first four ingredients in a small bowl. Put all of the ingredients into a blender or food processor: water, tahini paste, garlic, lemon juice, cumin & salt. The mixture should be smooth and creamy at this point. If it's too thick, just add a little extra warm water. Add salt and pepper to taste, and then toss in the parsley.
- Preparation of the Tomato-Cucumber Salad is the next step. Toss the vegetables together in a bowl with lemon juice, wine vinegar, olive oil, and herbs. Salt & black pepper should be sprinkled over the mixture before serving. Refrigerate the sandwiches until you're ready to assemble them.
- To put the shawarma together. The naan should be brushed with oil on both sides & fried at 400° F for 2 mins on all sides in your air fryer. Toast the naan in a pan with some olive oil on both sides.
- Thinly slice the chicken breasts. Warm the naan bread and drizzle it with a little tahini sauce. Spread some cucumber-tomato salad over naan bread & top with the cut chicken. Drizzle some extra tahini sauce over the top. The bread should be rolled or folded around the filling. Wrap the shawarma in foil or parchment paper to hold it together. Prepare the food and serve it right away.

Nutrition Value
Calories: 173 Kcal, Carb: 9 g, Protein: 6 g, Fat: 7.8 g
Storage Suggestion: You can store it in the fridge for around 1-2 days.

Breakfast Crunchwraps

Prep Time: 2 Mins, Cook Time: 10 Mins, Servings: 1, Serving Size:1

Ingredients
- 2 eggs large
- 1 flour tortilla large
- 1 tbsp green onions chopped
- 4 slices ham deli
- 2 slices cheese American
- 2 oz cheese blend shredded cheddar
- 1/8 tsp weed dill

Instructions
- Whisk together green onion, eggs, & dill weed. Taste and adjust the salt & pepper with a pinch of each.
- Place your nonstick pan over medium heat & spray it well using cooking spray.
- Add the egg mixture & immediately cover, then simmer for approximately 2 Mins, or until the eggs are well cooked.
- Remove the eggs from the pan onto a big tortilla.
- Seconds later, a piece of American cheese is placed on the cheese and ham, followed by the shredded cheddar and another slice of American cheese.
- Make 5 to 6 folds by folding one edge of the egg inward its center and repeating this process around it. Once you've done this, fold the tortilla in the same way.
- Spray cooking spray on the folded tortilla while keeping it closed with your finger. Using a spatula, flip the wrap over and spray the opposite side while holding it in place with the folded edge of your wrap.
- Cook the wrap for four Mins in a hot air fryer set to 390 degrees Fahrenheit (198 degrees Celsius).

Cook for a further 4 Mins after flipping the wrap.
- Take a few mins to let the crunch wrap cool down a little since it would be really hot.

Nutrition Value
Calories: 206 Kcal, Carb: 17 g, Protein: 21 g, Fat: 9 g
Storage Suggestion: You can store it in the fridge for around 2-3 days.

Air Fryer Chicken Taquitos

Prep Time: 15 mins, Cook Time: 20 mins, Servings: 6, Serving Size: 1

Ingredients
- 1 tsp oil vegetable
- 2 tbsp onion diced
- 1 clove minced garlic
- 2 tbsp green chiles chopped
- 2 tbsp tomato sauce Mexican-style
- 1 cup rotisserie chicken shredded
- 2 tbsp cheese Neufchatel
- ½ cup cheese blend shredded Mexican
- 1 pinch of salt & black pepper
- 6 each tortillas corn
- 1 serving cooking spray avocado oil

Instructions
- In a large pan, bring oil to a boil. Add the onion and cook for 3 to 5 Mins, occasionally stirring, until tender and translucent. Cook for approximately a Min after adding the garlic to ensure that it is aromatic. Then, add green chilies and tomato sauce, then mix well. Add Neufchatel cheese, chicken, & Mexican cheese mix to the casserole. Cook and stir for approximately 3 Mins until the cheeses have melted & the mixture has warmed through. Salt & pepper to taste.
- To make the tortillas more malleable, place them in a pan or straight on the gas stove grates. Each tortilla should have 3 tsp of the chicken mixture in the middle. Taquitos are made by folding a tortilla in half and rolling it up.
- An air fryer should be heated to 400° F. (200 deg C).
- When using an air fryer, put taquitos within the basket & spritz them with avocado oil. If necessary, work in many batches. Cook for 6-9 Mins, or until golden & crispy. After 3-5 Mins, flip the taquitos over & finish cooking in the air fryer for 3-5 more Mins.

Nutrition Value
Calories: 174 Kcal, Carb: 12.9 g, Protein: 10.3 g, Fat: 9.2 g
Storage Suggestion: You can store it in the fridge for around 3-4 days.

Copycat Taco Bell Crunch Wraps

Prep Time: 15 Mins, Cook Time: 4 Mins, Servings: 6, Serving Size: 1

Ingredients
- 2 lb beef ground
- 2 Servings Taco Seasoning Homemade
- 1 cup water
- 6 flour tortillas large
- 3 tomatoes Roma
- 12 oz cheese nacho
- 2 cup shredded lettuce
- 2 cup blend cheese Mexican
- 2 cup cream sour
- 6 shell tostadas

Instructions
- Make a list of all the items you'll need.
- Set the temperature of the air fryer at 400 degrees Fahrenheit.
- Stir-fry ground beef in a skillet until no longer pink, about 5 Mins.
- Bring water & taco seasoning to a boil.
- Allow the mixture to thicken by lowering the heat to a simmer.
- Tostada, sour cream, lettuce, and meat in the middle of every flour tortilla. 3 1/3 oz. Cheddar & the tomatoes.
- To finish, flood the outside borders up and over the center to resemble a pinwheel.
- Repeat steps 2 & 3 with the rest of the wraps you have.
- Apply oil to a fry basket.
- Put it in the air fryer with the seam facing down.
- Spray some more oil on it.
- Cook for around 2 Mins, or till golden brown.
- Turn it over with a spatula & spray again.
- Repeat this process with the remaining wraps.
- After a few Mins of cooling, serve.

Nutrition Value
Calories: 1025 Kcal, Carb: 47 g, Protein: 62 g, Fat: 65 g
Storage Suggestion: You can store it in the fridge for around 5-6 days.

Air Fryer Spring Rolls

Prep Time: 20 mins, Cook Time: 16 mins, Servings: 8, Serving Size: 1

Ingredients
- 2 tbsp oil sesame
- ½ tsp garlic minced
- 2 cups cabbage shredded
- 1 cup carrots matchstick
- ½ cup bamboo shoots thinly sliced
- 1 tbsp lime juice fresh
- 2 tsp sauce fish
- 1 tsp sauce soy
- 8 square roll wrappers spring
- seal wrappers water

Instructions
- Preheat the air fryer to a 390° F (200° C) temperature before you begin cooking.
- In a medium-sized pan, heat sesame oil on medium heat and sauté garlic for approximately 30 seconds, or till fragrant.
- Simmer for approximately five Mins until the vegetables are somewhat soft.
- Stir in the fish sauce, lime juice, & soy sauce to the vegetable mixture once removed from the heat.

- Place a little amount of the veggie filling in the middle of every spring roll wrapper. Tuck the bottom tip under & over the filling. Make a tight roll by folding in both ends and rolling firmly. The wrapping should be sealed with water. Repeat this process with the leftover vegetable mixture & wrappers.
- Cooking spray for the air fryer basket is recommended. Spray the spring rolls using cooking spray before placing them in the basket.
- Cook the spring rolls for around 5 Mins in the air fryer, then flip them over & cook for an additional 5 Mins, or till they are well fried on both sides.

Nutrition Value
Calories: 256 Kcal, Carb: 13 g, Protein: 12 g, Fat: 16 g
Storage Suggestion: You can store it in the fridge for around 3-4 days.

Air Fryer Bacon Wrapped Hot Dogs

Prep Time: 10 Mins, Cook Time: 15 Mins, Servings: 8, Serving Size: 1

Ingredients
- 8 Dogs Hot
- 8 Bacon strips

Instructions
- Use as much bacon as you want to cover every hot dog.
- Stack four hot dogs over a Foodi steamer rack at once. The hot dogs should be arranged to allow for air to flow around them.
- Cook for around 15 Mins at 360 degrees in your air fryer or foodi.
- Check the doneness of hot dogs. Cook the hot dogs & bacon for a further 1-2 Mins in increments unless the desired doneness is achieved.

Nutrition Value
Calories: 203 Kcal, Carb: 9 g, Protein: 8 g, Fat: 15 g
Storage Suggestion: You can store it in the fridge for around 2-3 days.

Air Fryer Chicken Chimichangas

Prep Time: 35 Mins, Cook Time: 10 Mins, Servings: 8, Serving Size: 1

Ingredients
- 2 tsp oil vegetable
- 2 cups rotisserie chicken shredded deli
- 1 packet seasoning mix chicken taco
- 3 tbsp of water
- ¾ cup beans traditional refried
- 1 can green chiles chopped
- 8 tortillas flour
- 1 cup Cheddar cheese shredded
- 2 tbsp melted butter

Instructions
- Medium-high heat in a 10" nonstick skillet is ideal. Pour water into a large bowl and add taco seasoning mix, stirring until everything is thoroughly combined. Stirring often, cook for a further 4-5 Mins, uncovered, until the chicken is well cooked.
- In a small bowl, combine beans and chilies and toss well. Spread some bean mix in the center of the tortilla on the workspace. A quarter cup of the chicken and two tsp of cheese should be sprinkled on top. Fold in the tortilla's long edges. Fold the bottom & sides over the filling. The filling should be securely rolled up. Repeat with the rest of the tortillas.
- Put 4 filled tortillas in an air fryer basket and brush the outsides with some melted butter. Cook for 4 mins at 400°F. Set the timer to 4 mins. Turn & cook another 2-3 Mins, unless the meat is no longer pink in the middle. Re-fill the leftover 4 tortillas in the same way.

Nutrition Value
Calories: 167 Kcal, Carb: 14 g, Protein: 12 g, Fat: 10.2 g
Storage Suggestion: You can store it in the fridge for around 3-4 days.

Air Fryer Copycat Supreme Taco Bell Crunch Wrap

Prep Time: 15 Mins, Cook Time: 15 Mins, Servings: 4, Serving Size: 1

Ingredients
- 1 lb beef ground
- 2 tbsp seasoning taco
- 2 tsp cumin ground
- 1 tsp powder onion
- 1/3 cup of water
- 4 tortillas flour
- ½ cup of cheese nacho
- 4 shells tostada
- 1 diced tomato
- ½ cup lettuce shredded
- ½ cup cream sour
- 4 flour tortillas
- Spray Olive Oil

Instructions
- The meat should be browned in a large pan over medium-high heat, breaking this into small pieces. When there is no longer any pink in the meat, drain the liquid and put it back in the pan.
- Be careful to cover the meat well with taco seasoning before adding it to the pan.
- Add the water, whisk to blend, lower the heat towards a low simmer, & let the sauce thicken unless most of the water has evaporated, about an hr and fifteen Minutes. Remove the heat and put it away.
- To begin, set the temperature of your air fryer on the "air fryer" preset to 400 degrees Fahrenheit for 5 Mins.
- Lay out a 12" tortilla on a clear work area and start rolling it up. Add a quarter cup of a meat mixture.
- Add a tostada, tomatoes, lettuce, nacho cheese, & sour cream over the top. On top of it, place a 6" tortilla.
- Warp the bigger bottom tortilla all around edges as firmly as you can, turning it over each time.

- Use olive oil spray to coat the interior of the air fryer.
- When using an air fryer, put the wrap seam in the appliance.
- Cooking spray on the top is a good idea.
- Spray extra olive oil and cook for 2 Mins on the second side.
- Re-use the leftover crunch wraps in the same manner.

Nutrition Value
Calories: 165 Kcal, Carb: 13 g, Protein: 12 g, Fat: 11 g
Storage Suggestion: You can store it in the fridge for around 3-4 days.

Air Fryer Flour Tortilla Chips

Prep Time: 5 mins, Cook Time: 10 mins, Servings: 4, Serving Size: 1

Ingredients
- 6 Wraps Tortilla
- 1 Tbsp Olive Oil Extra Virgin
- 1 Tbsp Seasoning Cajun

Instructions
- Inside a ramekin, combine your olive oil & seasonings.
- A pastry brush is all that is needed to coat all sides of your tortillas.
- You may use a pair of kitchen scissors to cut your tortillas into eight equal halves.
- Cook for five Mins at 180° C/360° F in your air fryer.
- Continue to cook the opposite side for an additional 5 mins at the same temperature.

Nutrition Value
Calories: 171 Kcal, Carb: 24 g, Protein: 4 g, Fat: 7 g
Storage Suggestion: You can store it in the fridge for around 4-5 days.

Air-Fryer Apple Pie Egg Rolls

Prep Time: 25 min, Cook Time: 15 min, Servings: 8, Serving Size: 1

Ingredients
- 3 cups tart apples chopped peeled
- ½ cup brown sugar packed light
- 2 & ½ tsp divided ground cinnamon
- 1 tsp of cornstarch
- 8 wrappers egg roll
- ½ cup cream cheese spreadable
- cooking spray Butter-flavored
- 1 tbsp of sugar
- 2/3 cup ice cream hot caramel

Instructions
- Preheat your air fryer at 400°F. Combine the brown sugar, apples, 2 tsp cinnamon, & cornstarch in a medium bowl. Spread a scant dollop of cream cheese within an inch of the corners of the egg roll wrapper. Place a third of the apple mixture in the middle of the wrapper, right below the center.
- Moisten the remaining corners of the wrapper using water and fold the bottom corner over the filling. Stack the filling in the middle of the two corners and fold the corners toward the center. Seal the end of the egg roll by pushing firmly on it. Repeat.
- Place egg rolls in bunches on a greased tray and coat them using cooking spray before placing them in the basket of an air-fryer. Cook for 5-6 Mins, or until golden brown. Then, sprinkle the pan with cooking spray; shake to distribute evenly. Cook for another 5-6 Mins, or till golden brown & crispy. Sugar and the remaining cinnamon may be mixed and coat the heated egg rolls. Serve with warm caramel sauce.

Nutrition Value
Calories: 273 Kcal, Carb: 56 g, Protein: 5 g, Fat: 4 g
Storage Suggestion: You can store it in the fridge for around 3-4 days.

Air Fryer Lettuce Wrap Cheeseburger

Prep Time: 5 Mins, Cook Time: 20 Mins, Servings: 4, Serving: 1, Serving Size:1

Ingredients
- 1 lb beef Ground
- 1 tbsp rub Burger
- 2 tbsp sauce Worcestershire
- 4 slices jack cheese American, cheddar
- 4 leaves lettuce iceberg

Instructions
- It's time to get your air fryer up to snuff!
- Mix the Worcestershire sauce, ground beef, & burger rub in a bowl, then form into patties
- Dividing the ground beef into 4 equal portions is easy if you have a kitchen scale handy.
- Patty forms may be formed by flattening the balls & pressing hard.
- To cook the patties, place them in the basket of a grill or air fryer and broil.
- Turn on your oven's broiler, then set the timer for around 10 Mins.
- To flip the burger, use long-handled tongs & use extreme caution since the air fryer would be very hot when you do so.
- Set the timer for around 5 Mins, then broil some more.
- Make sure the internal temperature of the burgers is 145°F or above for medium well-doneness before adding the cheese. Broil for five Mins if the internal temperature is below 140 degrees Fahrenheit.
- Open the cover and add the cheese slices after the five Mins are up. Allow the air fryer to continue cooking for an additional five Mins with the lid closed.
- Serve after five Mins of letting the food settle once it has finished cooking.
- Single-patty or Double-decker burgers may be wrapped with lettuce.
- Enjoy!

Nutrition Value
Calories: 466 Kcal, Carb: 4 g, Protein: 39 g, Fat: 32 g
Storage Suggestion: You can store it in the fridge for around 2-3 days.

Air Fryer Chinese Egg Rolls

Prep Time: 20 Mins, Cook Time: 25 Mins, Servings: 12, Serving Size: 1

Ingredients

For egg rolls
- 1 tbsp oil olive
- 1 lb of ground chicken of pork
- 1 minced clove garlic
- 1 tbsp fresh ginger grated
- 1 shredded medium carrot
- 3 chopped scallions
- 3 cups green cabbage shredded
- 1 tbsp sauce soy
- 1 tbsp vinegar rice wine
- 12 wrappers egg roll
- for brushing Oil

For dipping:
- Plum sauce
- Duck sauce
- Soy sauce

Instructions

Cook Filling
- Add some olive oil and ground chicken or pork to a large pan on medium heat. As the meat cooks, use a wooden spoon or spatula to break it into smaller pieces. Cook for 6-8 Mins or unless the meat is well done.
- You may also add carrots & cabbage to the mix. Continue to simmer for another 3-4 Mins, often stirring, until the cabbage is wilted and tender. Soy sauce & rice wine vinegar are used to season your filling, which is allowed to cool. It's possible to make the filling ahead of time.

Assemble Egg Rolls
- Put one egg roll wrap over the dry surface so that the square tip is towards your work direction. Your filling mix of egg rolls should be placed around the wrapper in the center of the egg roll wrapper.
- Using your fingertips, run water along the wrapper's edges. To make a cylinder, roll your egg roll far from you, tucking in the ends of the wrapper. Repeat the process until you've used up all of the fillings. Dozens of egg rolls are a good starting point.

Air fry
- In the air fryer, put your egg rolls within the basket. Apply a little coat of oil on them. Be careful not to overlap any of the egg rolls as you add as much as possible without creating a towering pile. They need to be surrounded by moving air. Lightly grease the egg rolls.
- Set your air fryer at 350° F & put the basket inside. After 6-7 Mins of cooking, turn the egg rolls over and cook for the next 4-5 Mins on the opposite side.
- Golden brown & crispy is the goal for finished egg rolls! Prepare the food and serve it right away.

Nutrition Value
Calories: 387 Kcal, Carb: 29 g, Protein: 18 g, Fat: 22 g

Storage Suggestion: You can store it in the fridge for around 3-4 days.

Air Fryer Breakfast Burritos

Prep Time: 20 Mins, Cook Time: 3 Mins, Servings: 8, Serving Size: 1

Ingredients
- 1 lb sausage breakfast
- 1 chopped bell pepper
- 12 beaten eggs
- ½ tsp pepper black
- 1 tsp salt sea
- 8 burrito size flour tortillas
- 2 cups jack cheese shredded Colby

Instructions
- In a big pan, brown the sausage by crumbling it and cooking it. Add the peppers cut finely. Sausage should be drained, then placed on a platter lined with paper towels, covered, and left aside.
- Over moderate flame, add the eggs, salt & pepper to a medium-sized pan; constantly whisk until the eggs are mostly set & no longer runny, about 8 to 10 Mins.
- Remove from fire and add sausage that has been cooked.
- Place part of the egg & sausage mix in the center of a tortilla, sprinkle with cheese, fold the edges in, and wrap up the tortilla.
- The air fryer should be heated to 390 degrees.
- Lightly mist burritos using olive oil spray before serving.
- For a basket of air fryers, cook burritos for around 3 mins at 390 deg F, and for Instant Pot trays, cook for around 2 Mins at 220 deg F, rotating the trays halfway through. Cook your burritos within Vortex for a further three mins for darker, crispier results.
- Wrap tightly and store in an airtight container for later use if desired.

Nutrition Value
Calories: 283 Kcal, Carb: 16 g, Protein: 16 g, Fat: 17 g

Storage Suggestion: You can store it in the fridge for around 3-4 days.

Chicken Shawarma

Prep Time: 10 Mins, Cook Time: 10 Mins, Servings: 6, Serving Size: 1

Ingredients
- 1 & ½ lb boneless & skinless fat trimmed chicken
- 3 minced cloves garlic
- 2 tbsp olive oil extra virgin
- 1 tbsp juice lemon

Shawarma Spices
- 1 tsp of salt
- 1 tsp paprika smoked
- 1 tsp paprika regular
- 1 tsp pepper flakes crushed red
- 2 tsp coriander ground
- 2 tsp cumin ground
- ¼ tsp cinnamon ground

For Chicken Shawarma Wrap
- wraps or pita pockets
- store-bought or tzatziki homemade
- hummus roasted pepper hummus
- tomato & lettuce
- Kalamata olives pitted baby
- garlic sauce or Sambal Oelek

Instructions

Marinate Chicken

- Chicken thighs should be trimmed of extra fat before being placed in a big mixing bowl or a gallon-sized ziplock bag for storage (easy clean-up). Toss the chicken with olive oil, minced garlic, & lemon juice after sealing the bag carefully.
- Salt, paprika (regular and smoked), coriander, cumin, red pepper flakes, and cinnamon are mixed in a small bowl. Seal your bag firmly & toss the chicken in the spices to ensure that they are properly distributed. Refrigerate for 30mins-2 hrs before using.
- EITHER use an oven, air fryer, or instant pot to prepare the chicken.

Air Fryer Chicken Shawarma

- Cook your chicken for 12 to 14 Minutes at 360° F in a thin layer within the air fryer basket. Check after 12 Mins because air fryer timings vary. It's done when the chicken's exterior is crispy, and the interior temperature reaches 165° F or higher.

Nutrition Value

Calories: 185 Kcal, Carb: 2 g, Protein: 22 g, Fat: 10 g
Storage Suggestion: You can store it in the fridge for around 4-5 days.

Air-Fryer Cuban Sandwich Egg Rolls

Prep Time: 15 Mins, Cook Time: 20 Mins, Servings: 16, Serving Size: 1

Ingredients

- 8 wrappers egg roll
- 16 slices Smoked Ham
- 2 Tbsp Mustard HEINZ Yellow
- 4 Slice Cheese Slices Aged Swiss
- 8 CLAUSSEN Pickle Spears Kosher Dill
- ¼ cup of oil

Instructions

- 400°F is the ideal temperature for an air fryer.
- Place one egg roll wrap on a work surface, with the pointed corner facing you. Distribute 2 ham slices equally on top. About a tsp of mustard is spread on the ham. Add 2 pickle slices & 1 cheese slice on the top. Roll the wrapper up securely after folding in the opposite edges. Seal your egg roll by pressing firmly on the top corner of the wrapper after it has been lightly moistened with water. Fill & roll the remaining egg rolls.
- Cooking spray for the air fryer basket is recommended. Toss the egg rolls in a little amount of oil. In the prepared basket, arrange four egg rolls in a thin layer. Crispy & golden-brown egg rolls are done after 8-10 Mins of cooking. To use up all of the egg rolls, you must repeat the process.
- Serve your egg rolls by slicing them in half.

Nutrition Value

Calories: 130 Kcal, Carb: 10 g, Protein: 8 g, Fat: 6 g
Storage Suggestion: You can store it in the fridge for around 4-5 days.

Air Fryer Bacon Wrapped Chicken

Prep Time: 5 Mins, Cook Time: 30 Mins, Servings: 2, Serving Size: 1

Ingredients

- 2 boneless skinless chicken breasts
- 4 bacon pieces
- ⅓ tsp paprika smoked
- ⅓ tsp pepper black
- ⅓ tsp powder garlic

Instructions

- The Air Fryer should be preheated to 400°F. Use nonstick olive oil or cooking spray to coat the air fryer's basket.
- Set up a small bowl with the spices.
- After thoroughly cleaning and drying your chicken breasts, equally, apply the seasoning rub on both sides.
- Using two slices of bacon for each chicken breast, be sure to keep the bacon ends tucked under the meat.
- In a pre-heated basket of air fryer, place your bacon-wrapped chicken breasts.
- 15 Mins at 400°F, then 10-15 Mins at 370°F, or unless the chicken reaches a core temperature of 165°F.
- Make sure to serve all your favorite sides right away!

Nutrition Value

Calories: 270 Kcal, Carb: 1 g, Protein: 49 g, Fat: 7 g
Storage Suggestion: You can store it in the fridge for around 3-4 days.

Air Fryer Mini Crescent Dogs

Prep Time: 10 Mins, Cook Time: 10 Mins, Servings: 24, Serving Size: 1

Ingredients

- 1 can Crescent Rolls refrigerated
- 24 link sausages cocktail-size smoked

Instructions

- The parchment paper should be cut into an 8-inch circle. Use as a base in the basket of an air fryer. Place in the basket.
- Unwrap the dough and cut it into 8 equal halves. Cut every triangle into three thin triangles by slicing it lengthwise.
- Each triangle should have a sausage placed on the shortest side. Place 12 tiny crescent dogs on parchment paper in a basket of air fryer; roll each up beginning at the shortest side of the triangle & rolling to the opposite tip.
- Cook for 3 to 4 Mins, or until the tops of the crescents are light golden when using an air fryer set at 325°F. Turn each over with a pair of tongs and bake for a further 3-4 Mins, till golden brown. Unplug the air fryer. Repeat with the remainder of the 12 small crescent dogs. Serve at room temperature.

Nutrition Value

Calories: 234 Kcal, Carb: 11 g, Protein: 12.2 g, Fat: 7.8 g

Storage Suggestion: You can store it in the fridge for around 4-5 days.

Air Fryer Cream Cheese Wontons

Prep Time: 10 mins, Cook Time: 10 Mins, Servings: 4, Serving Size: 1

Ingredients
- 8 oz softened cream cheese
- 2 tbsp finely chopped green onion
- ½ tsp powder garlic
- ¼ tsp of salt
- wrappers wonton
- spray olive oil

Instructions
- The garlic powder, green onions, cream cheese, and salt should be mixed in a medium bowl & whipped until smooth and creamy.
- To begin cooking, a wonton wrapper should be laid out on a non-stick surface. Wet all edges of a wonton wrapper using your finger. Each corner should be brought up and sealed securely with a spoonful of cream cheese filling.
- The air fryer basket may be sprayed using olive oil. Spray all wontons using olive oil before placing them in the basket. For around 8 Mins, cook the food at 370°F. A further 2 Mins of cooking time may be required when they're not golden.

Nutrition Value
Calories: 195 Kcal, Carb: 3 g, Protein: 3 g, Fat: 19 g

Storage Suggestion: You can store it in the fridge for around 3-4 days.

Chapter 14: Sauces, Dips, and Dressings

Jelly Chili Li'l Smokies

Prep Time: 5 Mins, Cook Time: 10 Mins, Servings: 4, Serving Size: 1

Ingredients
- Eckrich Li'l Smoked Sausages Smokies Cocktail
- ½ cup Grape jelly
- ½ cup Chili sauce

Instructions
- Set your air fryer timer to 5 mins at 350°F & add the Li'l Smokies Cocktails Smoked Sausages to the basket.
- Move to a dish by removing.
- Mix in chili sauce & grape jelly.
- SERVE & take pleasure in!

Nutrition Value
Calories: 436 Kcal, Carb: 28 g, Protein: 20 g, Fat: 12 g
Storage Suggestion: You can store it in the refrigerator for 1-2 weeks.

Air Fryer Grape Jelly Little Smokies

Prep Time: 30 Mins, Cook Time: 1 Hr 30 Mins, Servings: 6, Serving Size: 1

Ingredients
- 28 oz cocktail sausages Little smokies
- 1 cup sauce BBQ
- 1 cup jelly grape

Instructions
- In an air fryer, combine all of the ingredients.
- Put the lid on. Cook for around 2 to 3 hrs over high.
- Removing the cover allows you to combine the ingredients easily.

Nutrition Value
Calories: 436 Kcal, Carb: 25 g, Protein: 29 g, Fat: 15 g
Storage Suggestion: You can store it in the refrigerator for 7-8 days.

Air Fryer S'mores Dip

Prep Time: 3 Mins, Cook Time: 5 Mins, Servings: 10, Serving Size: 1

Ingredients
- 12 oz bag semi-sweet chocolate chips
- 30 marshmallows large
- Graham crackers

Instructions
- Preheating your air fryer is the 1st step. For around 3 Mins, set the temp to 350°F.
- Make sure that chocolate chips are evenly distributed in the cake pan before proceeding. Bake the cake in a cake pan, which was easy to clean.
- These photographs show how the marshmallows should be placed on a chocolate chip upright. Use precisely 30 marshmallows. Whether you're using a big or small cake pan, you might need some more or maybe less.
- To get a golden-brown top & jiggly marshmallow, air fried for 4 to 5 Mins on 350°F.
- S'more's dip may be served with some graham crackers as dipping but be careful while removing it from your air fryer.

Nutrition Value
Calories: 236 Kcal, Carb: 93 g, Protein: 1 g, Fat: 2 g
Storage Suggestion: You can store it in the refrigerator for 4-5 days.

Fry Sauce Recipe (Easy Dipping Sauce)

Prep Time: 5 Mins, Cook Time: 20 Mins, Servings: 24, Serving Size: 1

Ingredients
- 2-3 cups Mayonnaise Real
- ½ cup of Ketchup
- 1 tbsp Franks Buffalo Sauce Red Hot
- 1 tbsp bread & butter pickle juice
- 2 tsp sauce Worcestershire
- ¼ tsp ancho powder chili
- ½ tsp salt seasoned
- ¼ tsp paprika

Instructions
- Combine all the ingredients in a medium bowl and whisk until smooth.
- Heat in your air fryer at 225 deg F for around 3 to 4 mins.

Nutrition Value
Calories: 149 Kcal, Carb: 2 g, Protein: 1 g, Fat: 16 g
Storage Suggestion: You can store it in the refrigerator for 2-3 days.

Air Fryer Spaghetti Bolognese Sauce

Prep Time: 5 Mins, Cook Time: 35 Mins, Servings: 2, Serving Size: 1

Ingredients
- 8 oz lean beef ground
- 3 oz of onion
- 1 oz of carrot
- 1 oz celery
- 1 minced clove garlic
- 1 tbsp olive oil
- 15 oz tomatoes crushed
- ½ tbsp parsley dried
- ½ tbsp oregano dried
- ½ tbsp basil dried
- salt & pepper
- cooked spaghetti squash or grain pasta
- 2 tbsp Parmesan cheese grated

- 2 tbsp basil leaves fresh

Instructions
- As coarsely as possible, pulverize the ground beef into crumbs. It won't cook if you keep it in large bits.
- It's time to slice up the onion & mince the garlic. Cut the celery & carrots into dice no larger than ¼ inch. The celery & carrots must be finely chopped to cook more quickly.
- Preheat your air fryer to 375° F (190° C) for five Mins.
- Place your ground beef over half of an air fryer tray that has been preheated. On the opposite side of the tray, arrange the celery, carrots, onions, & garlic. Pour olive oil on the vegetables and toss to coat. The air fryer oven's top rack should be used for the tray.
- At 375 degrees Fahrenheit (190 degrees Celsius), air fried for five Mins. If necessary, break up the beef with a meat mallet until crumbly. The sauce won't soften the celery and carrots too much. If necessary, continue to cook them in the air fryer for some more Mins.
- Use parchment paper to cover an Al pan 8 inches by 8 inches. Add the meat & veg to the pan. Add salt & pepper to taste, along with the parsley, oregano, crushed tomatoes, & dried basil.
- Wrap the pan in foil so that no air can get in. Air fry at 375° F (190° C) for around 35 to 45 Mins over the rack within the air fryer. Take a 5-Min break and let your sauce cool.
- Your favorite spiralized vegetables or pasta can be topped with the Bolognese sauce for a hearty meal. Fresh basil & Parmesan cheese can be added to the dish if desired.

Nutrition Value
Calories: 256 Kcal, Carb: 19 g, Protein: 23 g, Fat: 15 g
Storage Suggestion: You can store it in the refrigerator for 4-5 days.

Air Fryer Ravioli with Quick Tomato Dipping Sauce

Prep Time: 10 Mins, Cook Time: 8 Mins, Servings: 18, Serving Size: 1

Ingredients
For Ravioli
- ½ cup breadcrumbs plain
- ½ tsp oregano dried
- ½ tsp basil dried
- ¼ cup freshly grated parmesan
- 1 cayenne pepper pinch
- ½ cup lightly beaten egg or buttermilk
- 1 9-oz ravioli thawed package cheese
- 1 cup store-bought marinara sauce

Tomato Dipping Sauce
- 8 oz sauce tomato
- ½ tsp oregano dried
- ½ tsp basil dried
- ½ tsp powder garlic
- ½ tsp powder onion

Instructions
- Defrost the ravioli first if they've been frozen.
- Make sure your air fryer is preheated to 350°F. Set the temperature & let your air fryer run for 3-5 Mins before you begin cooking.
- Mix the parmesan cheese, oregano, basil, breadcrumbs, & cayenne pepper.
- Set aside a medium-sized shallow bowl for the buttermilk.
- Toss the breadcrumbs with ravioli at once after dipping them within the egg.

For Air Fryer
- Rinse and dry your ravioli before cooking them in your air fryer. Continue to fill the basket unless it is overflowing with food. Ensure each ravioli is separated by at least 14 inches (1.25 centimeters) before cooking. More than 1 batch may be required at a time.
- Place your ravioli on a basket within your air fryer that has been warmed. Cook for 4-8 Mins, depending on the thickness of the potatoes, at 350°F. To cook the ravioli, continue the cycle.

Nutrition Value
Calories: 78 Kcal, Carb: 10 g, Protein: 4 g, Fat: 3 g
Storage Suggestion: You can store it in the refrigerator for 3-4 days.

Air Fryer Spicy Chickpea Pasta Chips

Prep Time: 5 Mins, Cook Time: 10 Mins, Servings: 6, Serving Size: 1

Ingredients
- 1 cup Pasta Chickpea
- 1 & ½ cups of water
- 1 tsp salt
- 1 & ½ tbsp Olive oil
- 1 tsp powder garlic
- 1 tsp powder red chili

Instructions
Cooking Pasta
- Add pasta, olive oil, water, & salt to the saucepan and bring to a boil. Ensure that the spaghetti is completely submerged before moving on.
- Pressure cook for 2 Mins with the vent within sealing position & the lid closed.
- Just as quickly as the countdown expires, gently release the spool pin. Rinse your pasta under cold water after draining it.

Air Frying Pasta
- Drain your pasta and place it in a small bowl. Add the rest of the oil, garlic powder, chili powder, & salt to the pan.
- To make air-fried pasta, place the pasta within the air fryer & cook for around 10-15 Mins on 370°F or unless it is crispy. Every five Mins, shake your basket & stir the pasta.

Nutrition Value
Calories: 320 Kcal, Carb: 54 g, Protein: 12 g, Fat: 6 g
Storage Suggestion: You can store it in the refrigerator for 3-4 days.

Crispy Pasta Chips and Roasted Red Pepper Dip

Prep Time: 20 Mins, Cook Time: 15 Mins, Servings: 2, Serving Size: 1

Ingredients

- 200 g tube pasta or Dry rigatoni
- 30 g cheddar cheese or Vegan parmesan
- 15 g of Breadcrumbs
- ½ tsp Paprika
- Salt pinch
- Pepper pinch
- 1 tbsp pesto or Oil

Spice Mix

- ½ tsp onion/garlic salt or Sea salt
- ¼ tsp Cayenne pepper
- 3 tsp Toasted crushed sesame seeds

Red Pepper Dip

- 175 g cashew nuts Raw
- 2 tsp Powder Garlic
- 50 g red pepper Roasted
- 1 chopped Lemon
- ½ tsp Salt
- ½ tsp Pepper Black
- pinch Flakes Chili
- 100 ml of Water

Instructions

- Prepare the pasta as directed on the package, then drain well.
- Cook the cashews for ten Mins in the broth. Drain & then rinse thoroughly.
- Cooked pasta is ready to eat. Add the cheese, herbs, & breadcrumbs to the oil/pesto mixture.
- Bake at 160 deg C for around 15 Mins or unless golden brown in your air fryer or a conventional oven for another 15 Mins.
- The sesame seeds should be heated in a big dry non-stick skillet over a moderate flame for around 3 to 4 Mins unless they begin to brown & pop while being careful not to burn. For this step, just put the sesame seeds into a sealed bag & beat them about with a kitchen utensil or rolling pin unless they become more powder-like in consistency. Combine with the other ingredients for the spice blend.
- A blender is needed to prepare the pepper dip: soak softened cashews, add the rest dip ingredients, & mix until smooth. Take your time and mix until it's completely smooth. Toss with chopped olives, red peppers, & basil before serving in a dish.
- Prepare air fryer or oven chips, then quickly throw in spice mixture & serve with delicious dip. Enjoy!

Nutrition Value

Calories: 346 Kcal, Carb: 23 g, Protein: 15 g, Fat: 3 g

Storage Suggestion: You can store it in the refrigerator for 4-5 days.

Air-Fryer Cauliflower Gnocchi with Marinara Dipping Sauce

Prep Time: 10 mins, Cook Time: 20 mins, Servings: 8, Serving Size: 1

Ingredients

- 2 packages frozen-thawed, divided cauliflower gnocchi
- 3 tbsp extra-virgin divided olive oil
- ½ cup of grated, divided Parmesan cheese
- 2 tbsp flat-leaf parsley chopped fresh
- 1 cup of reduced sodium warmed marinara sauce

Instructions

- Ensure that the air fryer is preheated to 375°F before using. Combine gnocchi, olive oil, & Parmesan cheese.
- Spray the cooking spray on the basket of an air fryer. Cook your gnocchi for around 5 Mins, flipping once halfway inside the basket. Make a big bowl for it all. The leftover gnocchi, oil, & Parmesan cheese should all be used in this recipe. Add the left Parmesan & parsley to cooked gnocchi. Marinara should be served alongside.

Nutrition Value

Calories: 160 Kcal, Carb: 14.1 g, Protein: 3 g, Fat: 9.3 g

Storage Suggestion: You can store it in the refrigerator for 2-3 days.

Easy Marinara Sauce

Prep Time: 10 Mins, Cook Time: 20 Mins, Servings: 8, Serving Size: 1

Ingredients

- 3 tbsp oil olive
- 1 cup finely diced onion
- ⅓ cup shredded carrot
- 3 minced garlic cloves
- ¼ cup of fresh chopped basil
- ½ tsp oregano dried
- salt & pepper
- 28 oz canned whole tomatoes
- 28 oz canned crushed tomatoes
- 2 tbsp paste tomato
- 1 to 2 tsp sugar
- ½ cup of water

Instructions

- Olive oil should be heated at medium-high heat in a big saucepan. Add onion, carrots, & garlic. Cook for 5 Mins or so, or until tender.
- Toss in the tomatoes, breaking them up with the back of a spoon as you go. The remaining components should be mixed in.
- Stirring occasionally will help the sauce thicken more quickly.
- Use in your favorite pasta dishes or as a side dish with pasta. Store in the freezer or the refrigerator by freezing or refrigerating.

Nutrition Value

Calories: 156 Kcal, Carb: 21 g, Protein: 15 g, Fat: 4.3 g

Storage Suggestion: You can store it in the refrigerator for 3-4 days.

5-Min Marinara Sauce (Extra Easy)

Prep Time: 5 mins, Cook Time: 15 mins, Servings: 8, Serving Size: 1

Ingredients

- 28 oz diced tomatoes canned
- 1 tbsp olive oil light
- 3 cloves garlic
- 1 tbsp of sugar

- ¼ cup marsala wine dry
- ½ tbsp of salt
- 1 tsp black pepper ground
- 8 basil leaves fresh

Instructions
- Prepare the marinara sauce by gathering all of the necessary ingredients. Remember that canned tomatoes are required for the sauce, not fresh ones.
- In a blender or food processor, puree your canned tomatoes until smooth. Cut the basil into small pieces.
- To begin, warm up in an air fryer with a pot of water and a little olive oil. Sauté chopped garlic inside the oil unless it becomes a golden-brown color, then remove from heat. You may also add the chopped basil & black pepper if you want to spice things up a little.
- Boil & simmer the sauce for five Mins. The sauce may be used on pasta, breadsticks, pizza, as a dip. Enjoy!

Nutrition Value
Calories: 53 Kcal, Carb: 7 g, Protein: 1 g, Fat: 2 g
Storage Suggestion: You can store it in the refrigerator for 3-4 days.

Homemade Spaghetti Sauce
Prep Time: 15 Mins, Cook Time: 1 Hr 30 Mins, Servings: 7, Serving Size: 1

Ingredients
- 1 tbsp oil olive
- 1 cup yellow onion finely diced
- 3 minced cloves garlic
- 2 tbsp paste tomato
- 1 can tomatoes crushed
- 1 can sauce tomato
- 1 can diced tomatoes & their juice petite
- 1 tbsp sugar white
- 1 tbsp oregano dried
- ½ tsp thyme dried
- ¼ tsp pepper flakes red
- 1 leaf bay
- ¼ cup fresh basil chopped
- ¼ cup fresh parsley chopped
- 1 tbsp of butter

Instructions
- In a big, deep-pan, heat the oil to medium-high heat. The onion should be added to the pan and cooked for 4 to 5 minutes unless it becomes translucent. Stir in the garlic & cook for another Min or unless it begins to smell good.
- Onion rings are coated with tomato paste as they cook.
- You'll also want to include chopped oregano & thyme, as well as the flakes & bay leaves from your dried herbs.
- Combine all ingredients in a bowl using a whisk. Add water and bring to a boil, then lower the heat and simmer for almost an hr, or 3 hrs, slightly covered. Stir now and then. Make sure your sauce isn't clinging to the pan's bottom. If necessary, reduce or increase the heat.
- Take care to remove the bay leaf & stir in the basil, butter, & parsley unless the butter is completely melted.
- Serve after tasting and seasoning with pepper and salt.

Nutrition Value
Calories: 48 Kcal, Carb: 7 g, Protein: 1 g, Fat: 2 g
Storage Suggestion: You can store it in the refrigerator for 2-3 days.

Air Fryer Chicken Katsu with Homemade Katsu Sauce

Prep Time: 20 Mins, Cook Time: 20 Mins, Servings: 4, Serving Size: 1

Ingredients

Katsu Sauce
- ½ cup of ketchup
- 2 tbsp sauce soy
- 1 tbsp sugar brown
- 1 tbsp of sherry
- 2 tsp sauce Worcestershire
- 1 tsp garlic minced

Chicken
- 1 lb chicken breast boneless skinless
- 1 pinch of salt & black pepper ground
- 2 large beaten eggs
- 1 & ½ cups breadcrumbs panko
- 1 serving spray cooking

Instructions
- Garlic & ketchup are combined in a bowl with brown sugar, Worcestershire sauce, sherry, & soy sauce. Make room for the katsu sauce.
- The temperature of your air fryer should be set to 350°F.
- Lay the chicken pieces out in the clean work area while you're waiting. Use salt & pepper to taste.
- Beat the eggs in the dish and spread them out on a level surface. In a separate flat plate, add breadcrumbs to the mixture. Chicken should be dredged in egg & then breadcrumbs before serving. Press down on the breadcrumbs as you dredge the chicken within egg & then again within breadcrumbs.
- Place your chicken within the fry basket of your air fryer preheated. Apply cooking spray on the tops of the cakes.
- Cook 10 mins in the air fryer. Spray the tops of the chicken pieces with cooking spray after flipping them overusing a spatula. Continue cooking for an additional 8 Mins. Slice the chicken when it has been transferred to a chopping board. Serve with some katsu sauce on the side for dipping.

Nutrition Value
Calories: 318 Kcal, Carb: 41.2 g, Protein: 32 g, Fat: 6.7 g

Storage Suggestion: You can store it in the refrigerator for 1-2 days.

Air Fryer Roasted Hot Sauce

Prep Time: 2 Mins, Cook Time: 10 Mins, Servings: 4, Serving Size: 1

Ingredients
- 3 tomatoes Roma
- 1 onion yellow
- 2 jalapeños
- 2 Tbsp cilantro
- 2 Tbsp garlic
- 2 Tbsp salt kosher

Instructions
- In a basket of air fryer, add all vegetables except cilantro & garlic.
- Re-insert basket in air fryer & cook at 385°F for the specified time at the recommended temperature.
- Blend the contents of the basket once the timer has expired. Remove from heat and serve with a sprinkle of salt & a sprinkling of chopped cilantro. Refrigerate & serve chilled.

Nutrition Value
Calories: 25 Kcal, Carb: 5 g, Protein: 1 g, Fat: 0 g

Storage Suggestion: You can store it in the refrigerator for 4-5 days.

Making a Pasta Sauce in an Air Fryer

Prep Time: 10 Mins, Cook Time: 1 Hr 35 Mins, Servings: 6, Serving Size: 1

Ingredients
- 1 tbsp oil olive
- 1 large onion
- 2 peppers bell
- 250 g of mushrooms
- 1-2 kg tomatoes
- 150 ml paste tomato
- herbs

Instructions
- Slice the mushroom and place it in a bowl. Set aside the washed, seeded, and sliced bell peppers. Slice the onion in rings, then cut each ring in halves lengthwise. Set away for later.
- Air fry 2 Mins for heating the oil.
- Add the onion and simmer for around 5 Mins more.
- Cook for a further 10 Mins after adding the peppers.
- Cook your mushrooms for the next 15 Mins.
- In the blender, puree the tomatoes & add them to the air fry.
- To taste, include any other herbs you like.
- When the herbs are buried, add some tomato paste and stir to ensure that they might not get blown about by the wind.
- Cook for a further 65 Mins at a low to medium heat.

Nutrition Value
Calories: 143 Kcal, Carb: 7.3 g, Protein: 6.3 g, Fat: 3.8 g

Storage Suggestion: You can store it in the refrigerator for 2-3 days.

Air Fryer Easy Pasta Sauce

Prep Time: 5 Mins, Cook Time: 18 Mins, Servings: 4, Serving Size: 1

Ingredients
- 1.5 lb quartered tomatoes, halved
- 1 tsp oregano dried
- ½ tsp allspice ground
- 2 finely sliced green onions
- salt
- ½ tsp vinegar balsamic
- 1 tsp syrup maple

Instructions
- Start by preheating the Air Fryer at 350 degrees Fahrenheit (180 degrees Celsius).
- Cut your tomatoes into halves on a chopping board if they are big (if small).
- Add the ground allspice, tomatoes, dry oregano, & salt to a bowl and combine well.
- Place the tomatoes inside the Air Fryer once they've been transferred to a cake barrel pan.
- They should be roasted for around 18 Mins, with occasional stirrings.
- Stir in green onions & balsamic vinegar approximately 3 mins before the end of the cooking time and enjoy.
- You may then use an immersion blender to get the appropriate degree of chunkiness or smoothness by removing the cake barrel dish from Air Fryer & allowing it to cool. You may also use a fork to mix it up.

Nutrition Value
Calories: 40 Kcal, Carb: 9 g, Protein: 2 g, Fat: 1 g

Storage Suggestion: You can store it in the refrigerator for 3-4 days.

Quick Roasted Tomato Sauce with Capers and Basil

Prep Time: 15 Mins, Cook Time: 20 Mins, Servings: 4, Serving Size: 1

Ingredients
- 1 & ½ pints halved cherry tomatoes
- 2 tbsp oil olive
- 1 tbsp vinegar white wine
- 1 minced clove garlic
- 1 diced shallot
- 2 tbsp of capers
- 1 tsp seasoning Italian
- ½ lb of dried, cooked pasta
- ¼ cup fresh basil chopped
- parmesan cheese Grated

Instructions
- Set your air fryer at 400 degrees Fahrenheit before cooking anything in it.
- Combine the shallots, capers, cherry tomatoes, wine vinegar, olive oil, garlic, & Italian spice. Salt & black pepper should be sprinkled on top. Using a slotted spoon, transfer all ingredients to an air fryer basket.
- When air-frying, move the basket or shake it several times to break the tomatoes somewhat. Cook for around 20 Mins.
- Pasta and tomato sauce should be combined. To loosen your sauce, pour in the liquid from the air fryer's bottom drawer. Add fresh basil & sprinkle with salt to taste.

Parmesan cheese should be sprinkled over the top.

Nutrition Value
Calories: 102 Kcal, Carb: 7 g, Protein: 3 g, Fat: 2.4 g
Storage Suggestion: You can store it in the refrigerator for 1-2 days.

Spaghetti Sauce

Prep Time: 15 Mins, Cook Time: 20 Mins, Servings: 8, Serving Size: 1

Ingredients
- 1 can tomatoes whole peeled
- 1 sausage roll spicy
- 8 oz sauce tomato
- 6 oz of water
- 6 oz paste tomato
- 1 diced onion
- 1 can diced tomatoes petite
- 1 tbsp garlic minced
- 1 tbsp salt garlic
- 1 tbsp of basil
- 1 tsp of oregano
- salt

Instructions
- Sauté medium in the Instant Pot. Spritz the pot using non-stick spray. Then, add the sausage & onions.
- Cook the sausages until they are fully cooked.
- Pressing the cancel button will turn off the Instant Pot. To avoid receiving a burn notice, deglaze the pot by scratching stuck over meat from the bottom with a small amount of water.
- Stir in the remaining ingredients within the pot.
- Turn on the soup setting on the stove and cook for around 20 Mins with the lid closed and the steam valve partially open.
- Add 8 oz of spaghetti noodles, cover with liquid, & cook over the high manual for around 8 Mins to bring everything together.

Nutrition Value
Calories: 46 Kcal, Carb: 10 g, Protein: 2 g, Fat: 1 g
Storage Suggestion: You can store it in the refrigerator for 1-2 days.

Fried Burrata Over Arrabbiata Sauce

Prep Time: 10 Mins, Cook Time: 45 Mins, Servings: 4, Serving Size: 1

Ingredients

Arrabiata Sauce
- 3 tbsp oil olive
- 2 to 3 tsp flakes chili
- 2 tbsp tomato paste Pomi concentrated
- 1 diced small onion
- 4 gently smashed garlic cloves
- 24 oz. Tomatoes Pomi Rustica
- ½ cup roughly torn basil leaves

Fried Burrata
- 8 oz. burrata fresh
- ½ cup flour all-purpose
- 1 lightly beaten large egg
- 1 cup of breadcrumbs
- frying Oil

Instructions
- In a saucepan, heat olive oil to medium-high heat. Add the chili flakes & cook for a further one Min. Add onions & tomato paste. Simmer for approximately 5 to 6 Mins, or until the onions are transparent. Make a fragrant sauce with the addition of garlic. Break up any big bits of tomato using a spoon as you add them to the dish. Reduce the temperature to a low-medium setting. 25 to 35 mins or unless desired consistency is reached. Add ¼ cup basil to the mix. Fried burrata & fresh basil complete the dish. Salt & pepper to your liking. Serve with warm, freshly sliced bread.
- Prepare your fried burrata while the sauce is simmering. Fill large saucepan using oil, almost 4 inches. Raise the temperature of the oil to 350 degrees Fahrenheit. Prepare your burrata by dredging it in breadcrumbs, flour, egg, & breadcrumbs. Prepared burrata may be kept in the refrigerator or freezer for up to 30 Mins. Drop the burrata into the heated oil in a gentle manner. To get a golden-brown color, fry for around 3-4 Mins. Using paper towels, remove the burrata from the oil. Burrata cheese and fresh basil should be placed on the arrabbiata sauce.

Nutrition Values
Calories: 51 Kcal, Carb: 5.6 g, Protein: 2.3 g, Fat: 3.4 g
Storage Suggestion: You can store it in the refrigerator for 3-4 days.

Air Fryer Ravioli

Prep Time: 10 Mins, Cook Time: 5 Mins, Servings: 6, Serving Size: 1

Ingredients
- 1-2 packages of frozen ravioli
- 2 large eggs
- 1 cup breadcrumbs or Panko
- ¼ cup grated Parmesan cheese
- 1 tsp powder garlic
- 1 tsp seasoning Italian
- ½ tsp salt kosher
- ¼ tsp pepper black
- 2 cups sauce marinara
- chopped Parsley

Instructions
- Prepare egg wash by beating the eggs in a small bowl until they are smooth and thoroughly blended; add some water.
- Mix dry ingredients in a separate small bowl. Fork together parmesan cheese, breadcrumbs, and all other spices.
- To make cleanup a cinch, preheat your air fryer at 400°F and prepare the baking sheet with parchment paper before placing the food within the fryer. Prepare a second baking sheet by covering it with parchment paper and preheating the oven to 275 degrees F. While your air fryer is heating up and the portions of ravioli are toasting, you may continue breading.
- Once you've reached the required quantity of toasted portions of ravioli, transfer them to a sheet pan & reheat them in the air fryer.
- Rao's marinara sauce may be warmed up and served in a dish with toasted ravioli sprinkled with minced Italian Parsley as preferred.

Nutrition Value
Calories: 56 Kcal, Carb: 4.3 g, Protein: 2.7 g, Fat: 1.3 g
Storage Suggestion: You can store it in the refrigerator for 1-2 days.

Low Carb Tomato Sauce

Prep Time: 5 Mins, Cook Time: 5 Mins, Servings: 8, Serving Size: 2

Ingredients
- 28 oz. tomatoes canned
- ¼ cup oil olive
- 1 tsp kosher salt
- ½ tsp black pepper fresh cracked
- 1 tsp powder garlic
- ½ tsp powder onion
- 2 tsp dried herbs
- ½ tsp pepper flakes

Instructions
- Blend all the ingredients until smooth (canned tomatoes, herbs, olive oil, garlic powder, salt, pepper, onion powder, & optional pepper flakes). Pulse until it's smooth.
- Now heat for around 1-2 mins in your air fryer.
- You may change the seasonings to suit your tastes if you prefer.
- Refrigerate for up to two weeks in a tightly sealed jar.

Nutrition Values
Calories: 81 Kcal, Carb: 5 g, Protein: 1 g, Fat: 7 g
Storage Suggestion: You can store it in the refrigerator for 3-4 days.

Cauliflower Meatballs in Marinara Sauce

Prep Time: 5 Mins, Cook Time: 20 Mins, Servings: 5, Serving Size: 1

Ingredients
Cauliflower Meatballs
- 3 Cups Rice Cauliflower
- 1 Cup of Breadcrumbs
- 5 Tbsp Flour Chickpea
- Ginger & Garlic Powder
- Salt & Pepper
- Seasoning Italian
- Flakes Chili
- Oil air-frying

Marinara Sauce:
- Marinara Sauce
- Seasoning Italian
- Salt & Pepper
- Cheese
- Oil

Instructions
Cauliflower Meatballs:
- Mix all meatball ingredients in a big bowl.
- Scoop 1-2 tbsp of the batter and mold it into a meatball with your hands when it has been well combined.
- Preparation time: 15-20 mins to tighten up all of the meatballs.
- At 350 degrees Fahrenheit, place the meatballs inside the basket of the air-fryer & drizzle with oil.

Marinara Sauce:
- Add your Marinara sauce to a pan & heat it up.
- After a few Mins of simmering, remove the sauce from the heat.
- Serve the meatballs over top of the sauce inside a serving dish.
- Add more grated cheese & chopped cilantro/basil on the top.
- Serve immediately.

Nutrition Value
Calories: 457 Kcal, Carb: 90 g, Protein: 23 g, Fat: 23 g
Storage Suggestion: You can store it in the refrigerator for 1-2 weeks.

Fresh Tomato Sauce

Prep Time: 10 Mins, Cook Time: 20 Mins, Servings: 6, Serving Size: 1

Ingredients
- 2 tsp oil olive
- ½ diced yellow onion
- 5 cloves minced garlic
- 6 cups roughly chopped fresh tomatoes
- 1 peeled & roughly chopped carrot
- 1 can paste tomato
- 2 Tbsp fresh basil chopped
- pepper & salt

Instructions
- Sauté the vegetables in olive oil in the Air Fryer. Then, add the onion & sauté until it becomes translucent.
- Add garlic & continue to cook for another Min.
- Add the tomatoes & carrots to the stew and mix well. Adding water is unnecessary because the tomatoes produce plenty of liquid during the cooking process.
- The cover of the Air Fryer should be locked, and the cooking time should be set at 20 Mins. Ten Mins of NPR after the end of the cooking time is recommended.
- Add up to ½ c. of tomato paste.
- Sauce may be blended to a silky smoothness using an immersion blender. After that, add the basil and mix well. Taste and adjust the spices to your liking.
- This sauce would be thin because of the use of fresh tomatoes. If the sauce becomes too thin, you may thicken it using the Air Fryer to sauté.

Nutrition Values
Calories: 67 Kcal, Carb: 4.5 g, Protein: 1.8 g, Fat: 5.3 g
Storage Suggestion: You can store it in the refrigerator for 5-6 days.

Chapter 15: Dehydrated Recipes

Perfect Air Fryer Apple Chips

Prep Time: 5 Mins, Cook Time: 15 Mins, Servings: 2, Serving Size: 10

Ingredients
- 1 diced apple
- 1 tsp juice lemon
- 1 tsp of cinnamon or pie spice pumpkin

Instructions
- Heat your air fryer at 320°F.
- Make sure the apples have been well cleaned. Peeling the apples isn't necessary, but it's an option. Core your apple if you like, but it's not required. Slice your apples as thin as possible; approximately 1/8" thick would do.
- Prevent browning of apples by sprinkling with some lemon juice. You may also add a dash of cinnamon spice to your apples.
- The basket of air fryer may be used to arrange apples. Avoid overlapping the apples. For 5 Mins, cook your apples within the air fryer until they are soft and mushy.
- Flip your apples over & remove them from the container. As a result, sticking is avoided, and even more, dehydration occurs. Rotate these trays if you've them. Cook for an additional 5 Mins.
- Bake for an additional 2 to 10 Mins if necessary. Hardened and with some of the adaptabilities are considered finished. As they dry, they will get crispier.
- To avoid softening, keep it in a sealed jar.

Nutrition Value
Calories: 95 Kcal, Carb: 25 g, Protein: 0.5 g, Fat: 0.3 g
Storage Suggestion: You can store it in the refrigerator for 3-4 days.

Easy Air Fryer Beef Jerky

Prep Time: 24 Hrs 10 Mins, Cook Time: 1 Hr, Servings: 24, Serving Size: 2

Ingredients
- 1 & ½ lb tip steak sirloin
- 1/3 cup of sauce soy
- 1 tsp sauce Worcestershire
- ½ cup sweetener brown
- 1 tsp smoke liquid
- 1 tsp paprika smoked
- 1 tsp powder garlic
- 1 tsp powder onion
- ½ tsp pepper black
- 1 tsp cayenne red pepper

Instructions
- Make thin strips of steak, approximately the thickness of an eighth of an inch. Jerky would be more delicate if sliced against the grain. It'll be chewier if you cut it against the grain.
- Add steak to a medium bowl. Add your marinade ingredients & mix well.
- Refrigerate for around 30 mins to overnight, or as long as necessary. Jerky gains flavor as marinating time increases.
- Jerky may be placed within the air fryer in 2 ways. It is possible to utilize bamboo skewers & thread meat lengthwise through the skewer. Several pieces of beef may be added but ensure they don't come into contact. Drying the meat will be easier using this method. In an air fryer, place the skewers along its upper borders.
- You may also use the basket air fryer for cooking the meat. First, use an olive oil spray. The basket should not be stacked or overstuffed. Cooking time will be longer.
- If you use skewers, air fry the beef at 180°F for 60-75 Mins.
- If you're using an air fryer basket, plan on cooking the beef for two to three hrs at 180 degrees.
- Keep an eye on the beef while you cook it both ways to ensure that it gets the correct texture. After 60 Mins of cooking with the bamboo sticks, the jerky would be firm but tender. The longer you cook it, the more it will become chewy.
- It will take around 2 hours to get firm and tender using just your air fryer technique, but more time is required for chewy jerky.

Nutrition Value
Calories: 156 Kcal, Carb: 10 g, Protein: 7.8 g, Fat: 4.7 g
Storage Suggestion: You can store it in the refrigerator for 3-4 weeks.

Dehydrated Oranges in Air Fryer

Prep Time: 5 Mins, Cook Time: 3 Hrs, Servings: 4, Serving Size: 15

Ingredients
- 3 large Oranges

Instructions
- Using an air fryer, cut the oranges into medium-sized pieces and remove their stems.
- Air fried for three hrs at 130°F/55°C in an air fryer over the top rack (or all shelves).
- Before storing in containers, allow the mixture to cool.

Nutrition Value
Calories: 46 Kcal, Carb: 12 g, Protein: 1 g, Fat: 1 g
Storage Suggestion: You can store it in the refrigerator for 1-2 weeks.

Air Fryer Dehydrated Blueberries

Prep Time: 5 Mins, Cook Time: 10 Mins, Servings: 2, Serving Size: 1

Ingredients
- 1 lb of blueberries

Instructions
- Washing the blueberries is the first step.
- Dehydrate the food at 125°F for 12-18 hrs. During the cooking time, shake your basket many times.
- Retain in a tight container.

Nutrition Value
Calories: 121 Kcal, Carb: 7.9 g, Protein: 5.8 g, Fat: 2.2 g
Storage Suggestion: You can store it in the refrigerator for 3-4 weeks.

Air Fryer Bananas (Sweet Banana Chips)

Prep Time: 10 Mins, Cook Time: 10 Mins, Servings: 1, Serving Size: 1

Ingredients
- 1 banana medium
- 1 tsp fresh squeezed lemon juice
- ⅛ tsp of cinnamon
- salt
- cooking non-aerosol oil spray

Instructions
- Slice your banana into 1/8-¼-inch-thick slices, then remove the core. Make sure they are all the same thickness.
- If you haven't already, squeeze one lemon to extract the juice. On a serving dish, arrange the banana pieces in a thin layer, turn them over and finish sprinkling with the remaining lemon juice.
- Apply frying spray to a tray of an air fryer. Using a thin piece, arrange the banana slices on the baking sheet.
- Cooking spray your banana slices. Cinnamon & salt should be sprinkled over them. Use a cinnamon dusting wand, but you may just use your fingertips.
- Using an oven temperature of 350°F, bake bananas for 10 to 12 Mins. To avoid browning, remove chips from the dish before they've had a chance to harden.
- Before you consume them, allow them to cool fully. As they cool, they'll solidify even more. You may air fry them for around 2 to 4 Mins longer at 350°F if you think they need extra crispiness. Enjoy!

Nutrition Value
Calories: 234 Kcal, Carb: 28 g, Protein: 27 g, Fat: 14 g
Storage Suggestion: You can store it in the refrigerator for almost 20 days.

Dehydrated Fruit

Prep Time: 10 Mins, Cook Time: 4 Mins, Servings: 4, Serving Size: 15

Ingredients
- 2 thinly sliced mangoes
- 1 thinly sliced kiwi
- 2 thinly sliced bananas
- 6 thinly sliced strawberries
- 1 thinly sliced apple, cored

Instructions
- Prepare your fruit by peeling (if desired) and slicing it very thinly. Dehydrate or air fry fruit in trays.
- Dehydrate to 130°F for four hrs in your Air Fryer using dehydrate option.

Nutrition Value
Calories: 343 Kcal, Carb: 35 g, Protein: 20 g, Fat: 18 g
Storage Suggestion: You can store it in the refrigerator for 1 week.

Air Fryer Dehydrated Pineapple

Prep Time: 10 Mins, Cook Time: 35 Mins, Servings: 1, Serving Size: 1

Ingredients
- 1/3 peeled & cored Whole Pineapple
- ¼ tsp of Cinnamon

Instructions
- Pineapple should be trimmed off and sliced into quarter inch to one-eighth-inch slices.
- Cinnamon-sprinkled pineapple slices go into the air fryer basket after being placed within the basket. To prevent the pineapples from being stacked on top of one another, you'll probably need to work into 2 batches.
- Using an air fryer, cook every batch of pineapple for 30-40 mins, or unless it is completely dry. After around 30 mins, you should see whether it needs further time. Remove when finished & enjoy!

Nutrition Value
Calories: 151 Kcal, Carb: 4.5 g, Protein: 1.5 g, Fat: 0.5 g
Storage Suggestion: You can store it in the refrigerator for 1-3 weeks.

Air Fryer Dehydrated Strawberries

Prep Time: 5 Mins, Cook Time: 1 Hr, Servings: 6, Serving Size: 1

Ingredients
- 1 lb fresh strawberries

Instructions
- To begin, turn the air fryer on and let it warm up for five Mins at the lowest feasible temperature. If you're looking for an air fryer that can go as lower as 180 degrees Fahrenheit, you'll have to go elsewhere.
- Slice the strawberries into 1/8-inch-thick slices after washing and removing the stems. Paper towels work well for this.
- In your air fryer, cook your slices at 180-200°F for one hr. After around 30 Mins, turn them over.
- After they've desiccated to the point where they resemble leather, take them out of the air fryer.
- Top your favorite snacks & breakfast dishes with these delicious sprinkles.

Nutrition Value
Calories: 24 Kcal, Carb: 6 g, Protein: 1 g, Fat: 1 g
Storage Suggestion: You can store it in the refrigerator for 1-2 weeks.

Air Fryer Dehydrated Apricots

Prep Time: 5 Mins, Cook Time: 12 Hrs, Servings: 4, Serving Size: 1

Ingredients
- 15 oz halves apricot

Instructions
- Pat your apricot halves dry using a paper towel after draining them.
- In an air fryer, separate the apricots from each other.
- For around 12 hrs, keep the temperature at 120 degrees F. The air fryer may include an option to dehydrate food.

- When done, the apricots would still have tiny moisture content in the core, but the outside should be dry.
- Cook at 135 degrees F for around 6 to 8 hrs, often monitoring if the air fryer doesn't get below 120 degrees F.

Nutrition Value

Calories: 3 Kcal, Carb: 1 g, Protein: 1 g, Fat: 1 g

Storage Suggestion: You can store it in the refrigerator for 1-2 weeks.

Best Keto Jerky

Prep Time: 15 Min, Cook Time: 10 Mins, Servings: 6, Serving Size: 1

Ingredients

- ¾ cup sauce soy
- 1 tbsp Golden Lakanto
- 1 tsp smoke liquid
- 1 tsp of salt
- ¼ tsp powder garlic
- ¼ tsp ginger ground
- ½ tsp pepper ground
- 1 lb sliced meat

Instructions

- Except for the meat, combine all ingredients in a large bowl. For the flavors to meld, allow the ingredients to sit for at least fifteen Mins.
- Toss in the meat strips & marinate for around 1 hr or for as long as three days.
- Place the beef strips on the dehydrator rack after removing them from the marinade.

Nutrition Value

Calories: 60 Kcal, Carb: 1 g, Protein: 6 g, Fat: 0 g

Storage Suggestion: You can store it in the refrigerator for 3-4 days.

Dehydrated Pineapple Chews

Prep Time: 7 Mins, Cook Time: 15 Mins, Servings: 6, Serving Size: 1

Ingredients

- 1 cored & sliced pineapple, peeled
- 1 tbsp palm sugar coconut
- 2 tsp cinnamon ground
- ½ tsp ginger ground
- ½ tsp pink salt Himalayan

Instructions

- Toss your pineapple pieces with cinnamon, ginger, sugar, & salt before serving them.
- On 3 Air Flow Racks, arrange the pineapple slices so that each is a single layer thick. Ensure that the Racks are placed on the oven's bottom, middle, & top shelves.
- For around 12 hrs, power button & then Dehydrator Button, then raise the cooking temp to 120°F.

Nutrition Value

Calories: 56 Kcal, Carb: 8 g, Protein: 1 g, Fat: 2.3 g

Storage Suggestion: You can store it in the refrigerator for 1-2 weeks.

Zucchini Chips

Prep Time: 15 Mins, Cook Time: 20 Mins, Servings: 6, Serving Size: 2

Ingredients

- 4-5 thinly sliced medium zucchini
- 2 Tbsp oil olive
- garlic salt & black pepper

Instructions

- Pour garlic salt, olive oil, & pepper over the zucchini. A thin layer over the dehydrator screen is all that is needed to dry & crisp up the food in roughly 3 hrs of cooking time.
- Please keep it in a plastic jar in the fridge for two weeks.

Nutrition Value

Calories: 66 Kcal, Carb: 6 g, Protein: 2 g, Fat: 3.1 g

Storage Suggestion: You can store it in the refrigerator for 2-3 weeks.

Bacon Jerky

Prep Time: 5 Mins, Cook Time: 2 Hrs, Servings: 10, Serving Size: 2

Ingredients

- 10 slices bacon thick
- ½ cup brown sugar lightly packed
- 2 tbsp of Sriracha
- ¼ tsp of cayenne pepper
- ¼ cup brown sugar lightly packed

Instructions

- Preheat the air fryer to 200°F.
- Make cleaning a breeze by lining on the baking sheet using Al foil.
- Place on a baking rack over the top to let the bacon fat drain.
- Add cayenne & cayenne sauce to the brown sugar mixture.
- To coat the bacon, separate it into strips and combine it.
- Place the bacon on the baking sheet or rack that can be used in the air fryer.
- For the best results, bake the bacon jerky in the air fryer for around 3 to 4 hrs, or until the required chewiness is achieved.
- Adding a little brown sugar & flipping the pancakes halfway through the cooking process. You may skip this step and still have jerky that's full of bacon flavor.

Nutrition Value

Calories: 192 Kcal, Carb: 11 g, Protein: 5 g, Fat: 14 g

Storage Suggestion: You can store it in the refrigerator for 2-3 weeks.

Dehydrate Mushrooms

Prep Time: 30 Mins, Cook Time: 4 Hrs, Servings: 32, Serving Size: 2

Ingredients

- 4 lb fresh rinsed & drained mushrooms washed
- 3-4 cups of water

Instructions

- Under cold running water, thoroughly rinse the entire mushrooms. Remove any dirt you see with a soft brush to avoid hurting the mushroom. Using paper towels, if necessary, gently pat the surface dry.
- Cut each mushroom into 14- to 12-inch-thick slices using a sharp knife.
- Dehydrate the sliced mushrooms inside an air fryer dehydrator using a plastic mesh liner placed inside a dehydrator tray.

- Slice and fill your dehydrator trays as many times as you want unless you run out of mushrooms.
- First, lay the trays over the dehydrator base & secure the cover with the included screws.
- Make sure that the dehydrator is turned on.
- The dehydrator's temperature and the slices' thickness will determine how long it takes.
- Ensure that the mushrooms are drying evenly by checking in on them every hr and flipping them over. Each hr, check your mushroom slices for signs of decay.
- Dehydrating 14-inch-thick slices in a dehydrator will take anywhere from four to four and a half hrs. At a lower temperature, this would take longer to dehydrate.
- You may let them cool over a paper towel while you wait for them to finish drying in the dehydrator.
- Use an airtight glass jar to keep the dried mushroom pieces fresh.

Nutrition Value
Calories: 12 Kcal, Carb: 2 g, Protein: 2 g, Fat: 1 g
Storage Suggestion: You can store it in the refrigerator for 6-7 days.

Dehydrating Tomatoes
Prep Time: 10 Mins, Cook Time: 8 Hrs, Servings: 10, Serving Size: 2

Ingredients
- 3 Diced Tomatoes

Instructions
- Tomatoes of all varieties, including Roma, cherry, and plum, are cut in half.
- Cut tomatoes into 3/4" thick slices for slicing. Make sure the slices are all the same size.
- Dehydrate your tomatoes by placing them on the trays. Please don't allow them to get too close and not crowd them.
- A temperature of 135 deg Fahrenheit should be used in the dehydrator.
- Check on their progress after four hrs of dehydration. Rotate the trays so that the ones at the base are over the top if they're movable.
- Allow the tomatoes to air dry for a further 4 to 6 hrs, or unless they are completely dry & chewy to touch.
- Refrigerate or freeze for almost six months, then store inside a jar or zip-top bag at room temp for three to four months.

Nutrition Value
Calories: 33 Kcal, Carb: 1 g, Protein: 2 g, Fat: 2 g
Storage Suggestion: You can store it in the refrigerator for 4-5 days.

Dehydrated Cinnamon Apples
Prep Time: 20 Mins, Cook Time: 12 hrs, Servings: 8, Serving Size: 1

Ingredients
- 5 apples, Fuji, Honeycrisp, Gala,
- 1 lemon
- 2 Tbsp granulated sugar
- 2 tsp ground cinnamon
- ½ tsp ground nutmeg
- 1 tsp extract vanilla

Instructions
- Slice your apple into 14-inch-thick rings once it has been cored.
- Serve with a dollop of whipped cream and a sprinkle of powdered sugar. Whip until smooth. A little lumpiness is expected, but it's not a dealbreaker.
- Rinse your apples in the colander. Ziploc bags may be used to store apples. Seal the bag with a combination of lemon juice & cinnamon.
- The apples should be properly covered with the mixture by shakily shaking the bag. Allow the apples to sit on the countertop for around 10 Mins before serving.
- Dehydrate the apples one at a time on the dehydrator's wire rack. Apples shouldn't even be near one other or overlapping in any way.
- Close your dehydrator's door after inserting the wire racks. Temperatures should be set at 135°F.
- Dehydrating apples for a certain length of time depends on desired texture.
- Remove your apples from the dehydrator when they are totally dry and cool.
- Use a container with a tight-fitting lid to keep fresh.

Nutrition Value
Calories: 78 Kcal, Carb: 20 g, Protein: 1 g, Fat: 1 g
Storage Suggestion: You can store it in the refrigerator for 4-5 days.

Dehydrated Kale Chips
Prep Time:10 Mins, Cook Time: 0 Mins, Servings: 4, Serving Size: 1

Ingredients
- 1 bunch kale large
- 2-3 tsp olive oil extra-virgin
- ¾ tsp salt
- pepper Dash cayenne
- 2 tbsp yeast nutritional

Instructions
- To prepare your kale, remove the leafstalks & stiff midribs from kale leaves. The midribs, which are not edible if dried whole, will have the appearance of twigs if dried whole. Leave stalks may be composted or used as soup stock.
- Spin your kale leaves in the salad spinner and gently wrap them in the dish towel to dry them thoroughly.
- The leaves would shrink somewhat as they dry, so cut them into pieces that are a little bigger than chips.
- Combine the olive oil, kale, and salt in a medium bowl. Clean the hands & thoroughly massage the leaves. The oil should be uniformly applied to all leaves.
- Adding a sprinkle of cayenne pepper can amp up the heat if you want it.
- For a cheese taste, you may also add nutritious yeast.
- Lay the leaves out in a thin layer over the dehydrator trays. Leaves would not dry uniformly if they were crowded together. It's okay if your leaves rub against one other, but don't let them get too closely intertwined.
- After that, the chips should be dried out.

Nutrition Value
Calories: 44 Kcal, Carb: 3 g, Protein: 1 g, Fat: 4 g
Storage Suggestion: You can store it in the refrigerator for 3-4 weeks.

Chapter 16: Vegetable and Side Dishes Recipes

Fried Avocado Tacos

Prep Time: 40 Mins, Cook Time: 15 Mins, Servings: 4, Serving Size: 3
Nutrition per serving: Calories 407|Carbs 48 g| Protein 9 g |Fat 21 g

Ingredients
- Fresh cilantro minced: ¼ cup
- Coleslaw mix: 2 cups
- Honey: 1 tsp
- Salt: ¼ tsp
- Pepper: ¼ tsp
- 1 egg, whisked
- Ground chipotle pepper: ¼ tsp
- peeled avocados, sliced
- Plain Greek yogurt: ¼ cup
- Lime juice: 2 tbsp
- Cornmeal: ¼ cup
- Salt: 1/2 tsp
- Garlic powder: 1/2 tsp
- 1 chopped tomato
- Ground chipotle pepper: 1/2 tsp
- tortillas (6")

Instructions
- Preheat the air fryer to 400 degrees Fahrenheit.
- Add the egg to a mixing bowl.
- Combine garlic powder, chipotle pepper, salt, and cornmeal in a separate bowl.
- Coat avocado slices in the egg, then in the cornmeal mixture.
- Combine the other ingredients in a large mixing dish, except the tortilla and tomato, and stir thoroughly. Refrigerate.
- Spray the basket of the air fryer with oil.
- Arrange the breaded avocado slices in an equal layer in the air fryer basket.
- Cook for four Mins, then turn and cook for another three to four Mins, until golden brown.
- Combine avocado slices, coleslaw mix, and tomatoes in a tortilla.
- Serve immediately.

Nutrition Value
Calories: 320 Kcal, Carb: 12 g, Protein: 29 g, Fat: 21 g
Storage Suggestion: You can store it in the refrigerator for 4-5 days.

Baked Potatoes

Prep Time: 55 Mins, Cook Time: 15 Mins, Servings: 2, Serving Size: 2

Ingredients
- 1 tsp neutral oil
- 2 russet potatoes
- Kosher salt: 1/2 tsp
- Black pepper, to taste

Instructions
- Preheat the air fryer to 375 degrees Fahrenheit.
- The potatoes should be washed and dried.
- Using a fork, pierce the potatoes all over.
- Oil the pierced potatoes and season with half a tsp of salt.
- In the air fryer basket, place the potatoes.
- Cook for 40 Mins in an air fryer.
- Remove them and split them in half lengthwise.
- Serve with butter, black pepper, and salt on top.

Nutrition Value
Calories: 407 Kcal, Carb: 48 g, Protein: 9 g, Fat: 21 g
Storage Suggestion: You can store it in the refrigerator for 3-4 days.

Mushroom & Brussels Sprouts Pizza

Prep Time: 25 Mins, Cook Time: 15 Mins, Servings: 4, Serving Size:1

Ingredients
- 2 tbsp of olive oil
- 1 lb. of pizza dough
- Fresh thyme: 6 sprigs
- 1 and a 1/2 tbsp of balsamic vinegar
- 4 Brussels sprouts, cut into thin slices
- 1 sliced red onion
- 1/3 cup of grated fontina cheese
- 1/2 cup of shiitake mushrooms, remove stems
- ¼ cup of fresh goat cheese
- Salt & pepper, to taste

Instructions
- Preheat the air fryer to 400 degrees Fahrenheit.
- Place the parchment paper on a baking pan.
- Make a huge oval out of the pizza dough.
- Place a 1/2 cup of cheese fontina on the parchment paper and spread it out on the pizza dough.
- Combine the balsamic vinegar and mushrooms in a bowl. Mix the onion, Brussels sprouts, salt, pepper, and oil, then distribute over the pizza dough.
- Top with the remaining cheese and herbs.
- Spray the basket of the air fryer with oil.
- Preheat oven to 350°F and bake for 10-12 Mins.
- Serve and have fun.

Nutrition Value
Calories: 485 Kcal, Carb: 58 g, Protein: 16 g, Fat: 19 g
Storage Suggestion: You can store it in the refrigerator for 5-6 days.

Blooming Onion

Prep Time: 30 Mins, Cook Time: 15 Mins, Servings: 2, Serving Size: 4

Ingredients

For Onion
- Olive oil: 3 tbsp
- 3 whole eggs
- Breadcrumbs: 1 cup
- Onion powder: 1 tsp
- Paprika: 2 tsp
- 1 yellow onion (large)
- Garlic powder: 1 tsp
- Kosher salt: 1 tsp

Sauce
- Ketchup: 2 tbsp
- Dried oregano: ¼ tsp
- Horseradish: 1 tsp
- Mayonnaise: 2/3 cup
- Paprika: 1/2 tsp

- Kosher salt, to taste
- Garlic powder: 1/2 tsp

Instructions
- Remove the onion's stem and set it on a flat surface.
- From the root down, slice into 12-16 pieces, but don't go all the way through.
- Separate the layers by turning them over.
- 1 tbsp water + eggs in a mixing bowl
- Combine the spices and breadcrumbs in a separate bowl.
- Coat the onion in egg, then dip it in the breadcrumbs mixture and coat it well with a spoon.
- Using a pastry brush, coat the breaded onion in oil.
- Cook for 20-25 Mins at 375°F in an air fryer basket.
- Combine all sauce ingredients in a dish, stir well, and serve with blossoming onion.

Nutrition Value
Calories: 191 Kcal, Carb: 11 g, Protein: 3 g, Fat: 4 g
Storage Suggestion: You can store it in the refrigerator for 2-3 days.

Vegan Arancini

Prep Time: 40 Mins, Cook Time: 15 Mins, Servings: 12, Serving Size: 1

Ingredients
- Panko breadcrumbs: 1 cup
- Mozzarella, as needed
- Sea salt: ¼ tsp
- 2 and a 1/2 cups of leftover risotto
- Black pepper: ¼ tsp
- Garlic powder: ¼ tsp

Instructions
- Combine breadcrumbs and shredded mozzarella in a mixing bowl.
- Make risotto balls using the risotto.
- Using the panko mixture, coat the risotto balls.
- Refrigerate these breaded balls for half an hr.
- Preheat the air fryer to 450 degrees Fahrenheit.
- Spray the breaded balls with oil and arrange them uniformly in the air fryer basket.
- Serve after 8 Mins of cooking.

Nutrition Value
Calories: 181 Kcal, Carb: 9 g, Protein: 2 g, Fat: 2.3 g
Storage Suggestion: You can store it in the refrigerator for 5-6 days.

Fried Rice

Prep Time: 20 Mins, Cook Time: 15 Mins, Servings: 8, Serving Size:1

Ingredients
- 1/3 cup of coconut aminos
- 3 cups of cooked rice
- 2 eggs whisked
- 1 cup of frozen mixed vegetables
- 1 tbsp of oil

Instructions
- Add cold cooked rice to a mixing bowl.
- Toss in the veggie mixture.
- Combine rice and veggies with whisked eggs, oil, and coconut aminos.
- Mix thoroughly and put in an air fryer-safe dish.
- Cook for 15 Mins at 360 degrees F in an air fryer.
- During the 15-Min cooking period, stir the rice at least three times.

Nutrition Value
Calories: 680 Kcal, Carb: 121 g, Protein: 14 g, Fat: 7 g
Storage Suggestion: You can store it in the refrigerator for 4-5 days.

Air Fryer Falafel

Prep Time: 1 hr & 5 Mins, Cook Time: 15 Mins, Servings: 18, Serving Size: 3

Ingredients
Falafel
- Flour: 1/2 cup
- 1 can of drained chickpeas (15 oz.)
- White onion chopped: 1 cup
- Parsley leaves: 1 cup
- Lemon juice: 1 tbsp
- 6 cloves of garlic
- Baking powder: 1 tsp
- Cumin: 2 tsp
- Cilantro leaves: 1/2 cup
- Salt: 1 tsp
- Fresh dill leaves: ¼ cup

Instructions
- Combine all ingredients in a food processor. Pulse on high until a crumbly mixture develops.
- Continue scraping the bowl as needed.
- Place in a bowl and place in the refrigerator for one hr.
- Take 1 tbsp dough and shape it into falafels using a scooper.
- Spray the air fryer basket with oil and warm to 375 degrees F.
- Arrange the falafels in a single layer in the air fryer basket.
- Cook for 15 Mins at 375 degrees Fahrenheit.
- Remove them from the oven and set them aside to cool somewhat.
- Serve with hummus and tahini sauce.

Nutrition Value
Calories: 34 Kcal, Carb: 6 g, Protein: 1 g, Fat: 1 g
Storage Suggestion: You can store it in the refrigerator for 5-6 days.

General Tso's Cauliflower

Prep Time: 45 Mins, Cook Time: 15 Mins, Servings: 4, Serving Size: 2

Ingredients
- Cauliflower florets: 6 cups
- All-purpose flour: 1/2 cup
- Club soda: ¾ cup
- Salt: 1 tsp
- Cornstarch: 1/2 cup
- Baking powder: 1 tsp

Sauce
- Sugar: 3 tbsp
- 3 minced cloves of garlic
- Soy sauce: 3 tbsp
- Orange juice: ¼ cup
- Rice vinegar: 2 tbsp
- Sesame oil: 2 tsp
- Grated gingerroot: 1 tsp
- Vegetable broth: 3 tbsp
- Canola oil: 2 tsp
- Orange zest: 1/2 tsp

- Cornstarch: 2 tsp

Instructions
- Preheat the air fryer to 400 degrees Fahrenheit.
- Combine baking powder, flour, salt, and cornstarch in a mixing dish.
- Mix in the soda well; the batter should be thin.
- Place the florets on a wire rack after coating them in the batter. Allow for a five-Min rest period.
- Spray the air fryer's tray with oil. Cook for 10 to 12 Mins with the florets in the tray.
- Combine all sauce ingredients in a bowl at a medium temperature and simmer for 2 to 4 Mins.
- If desired, add some crushed chili pepper.
- Serve the cauliflower with rice after coating it in the sauce.

Nutrition Value
Calories: 246 Kcal, Carb: 34 g, Protein: 8 g, Fat: 6 g
Storage Suggestion: You can store it in the refrigerator for 3-4 days.

Air Fried Buttermilk Tofu
Prep Time: 55 Mins, Cook Time: 1 Hr 15 Mins, Servings: 2, Serving Size: 1

Ingredients
- Salt: 1 tsp
- Block of firm tofu (8 oz.) Slice into 4 slices
- Black pepper: 1/2 tsp
- Cornstarch: 1/3 cup
- Salt: 1 tbsp
- Garlic powder: 1 tbsp
- All-purpose flour: 1 and a 1/2 cups
- Cayenne: 2 tsp
- Onion powder: 1 tbsp
- Paprika: 1 tbsp
- 1 Egg whisked with 1 tbsp of water
- Hot sauce: 1 tbsp
- Soymilk: 1 cup mix with two tsp of apple cider
- Bourbon: 2 tbsp

Instructions
- Season the tofu slices with salt and pepper and set aside for an hr to rest.
- Combine all dry ingredients in a mixing bowl.
- Combine all of the wet ingredients in a separate bowl.
- Toss the tofu in the dry ingredients first, then in the wet ingredients.
- To apply the flour mixture to the wet tofu, sprinkle it on top and pat it down.
- Refrigerate for at least 30 Mins. Spray the breaded tofu with oil.
- Air fried them for 10 Mins at 400 degrees F, turning halfway through.
- Serve immediately with rice.

Nutrition Value
Calories: 435 Kcal, Carb: 46 g, Protein: 14 g, Fat: 6 g
Storage Suggestion: You can store it in the refrigerator for 5-6 days.

Cheesy Spinach Wontons
Prep Time: 14 Mins, Cook Time: 15 Mins, Servings: 16-20, Serving Size: 2

Ingredients
- 1 and a 1/2 cups of chopped baby spinach
- Wonton wrappers: 16 to 20
- Softened cream cheese: 1/2 cup
- Salt & pepper, to taste

Instructions
- Combine spinach and cream cheese in a mixing bowl.
- Salt and black pepper to taste.
- Place 1 tsp of spinach mixture in the center of wonton wrappers on a flat surface.
- Make a triangle with the edges by moistening them and sealing them.
- Cook for 6 Mins at 400 F in the air fryer basket in one equal layer.
- Serve with a dipping sauce of your choice.

Nutrition Value
Calories: 281 Kcal, Carb: 32 g, Protein: 12 g, Fat: 12 g
Storage Suggestion: You can store it in the refrigerator for 3-4 days.

Chili Garlic Tofu
Prep Time: 25 Mins, Cook Time: 15 Mins, Servings: 5, Serving Size: 1

Ingredients
- Cornstarch: 1/2 cup
- Chili garlic sauce: 2 tbsp
- Olive oil: 1 tbsp
- 1 pack of firm tofu
- Soy sauce: ¼ cup
- 1 and a 1/2 tbsp of brown sugar
- Sesame oil: 1 tsp
- 2 minced cloves of garlic
- Two green onions, cut into slices
- Rice vinegar: 1 tbsp
- Grated ginger: 1 tsp
- Sesame seeds, toasted: 1/2 tsp

Instructions
- Place a cast-iron on top of the tofu covered in a paper towel for half an hr to press it.
- Tofu should be diced into tiny bits.
- In a resealable bag, combine tofu chunks and cornstarch. Shake the tofu and place it in a mixing bowl. Drizzle 1 tbsp of olive oil over it and stir.
- Cook the tofu in the air fryer for 15 minutes at 370 degrees Fahrenheit, spray it with oil halfway through.
- Place the tofu in a mixing bowl.
- Combine garlic, soy sauce, brown sugar, ginger, chili garlic sauce, and vinegar in a pan.
- Allow for 60 seconds of simmering time.
- Cook for 60 seconds after adding the tofu and sesame oil.
- Serve with green onions and seeds on top.

Nutrition Value
Calories: 135 Kcal, Carb: 21 g, Protein: 7 g, Fat: 7 g
Storage Suggestion: You can store it in the refrigerator for 3-4 days.

Roasted Green Beans
Prep Time: 35 Mins, Cook Time: 15 Mins, Servings: 6, Serving Size: 2

Ingredients
- 1 red onion, cut into thin slices
- 1 lb of fresh green beans, slice in half
- Italian seasoning: 1 tsp
- A half lb of mushrooms, cut into slices
- Pepper: 1/8 tsp
- Olive oil: 2 tbsp
- Salt: ¼ tsp

Instructions
- Preheat the air fryer to 375 degrees Fahrenheit.
- Combine all ingredients in a mixing bowl and combine well.
- Spray the air fryer basket with oil and arrange the veggies in it.
- Cook for a total of 8 to 10 Mins. Halfway through cooking, give the basket a good shake.

Nutrition Value
Calories: 76 Kcal, Carb: 8 g, Protein: 3 g, Fat: 5 g
Storage Suggestion: You can store it in the refrigerator for 1-2 days.

Greek Breadsticks
Prep Time: 35 Mins, Cook Time: 15 Mins, Servings: 32, Serving Size: 2

Ingredients
- Parmesan cheese, grated: 2 tbsp
- Marinated artichoke hearts: ¼ cup, quartered & drained
- 1 pack of puff pastry (17.3 oz.)
- Greek olives pitted: 2 tbsp
- Sesame seeds: 2 tsp
- 1 can of (6 and a half oz.) artichoke & spinach cream cheese, spreadable
- 1 egg
- Water: 1 tbsp

Instructions
- Preheat the air fryer to 325 degrees Fahrenheit.
- Add the olives and artichoke to a food processor. Pulse until the ingredients are finely minced.
- Place one sheet of dough on a floured board and top with half of the cream cheese mixture.
- Spread half of the Parmesan cheese on top of the artichoke mixture, then cover with the other half of the dough. The edges should be sealed.
- Restart the procedure with the remaining materials.
- Brush the top of the dough with a mixture of water and egg.
- Sesame seeds are sprinkled on top.
- Sesame seeds are sprinkled on top, and the strips are cut into 16 pieces. Make twisted strips out of them.
- Cook for 12 to 15 Mins in an air fryer basket sprayed with oil.
- The tzatziki sauce is served on the side.

Nutrition Value
Calories: 76 Kcal, Carb: 17 g, Protein: 1 g, Fat: 5 g
Storage Suggestion: You can store it in the refrigerator for 3-4 days.

Mushroom Roll-Ups
Prep Time: 40 Mins, Cook Time: 15 Mins, Servings: 10, Serving Size: 2

Ingredients
- 4 oz. of ricotta cheese
- Olive oil: 2 tbsp
- Dried oregano: 1 tsp
- Flour tortillas: 10
- Dried thyme: 1 tsp
- 8 oz. of Portobello mushrooms, chopped without gills
- Red pepper flakes: 1/2 tsp
- 1 pack of softened cream cheese (8 oz.)
- Salt: ¼ tsp

Instructions
- Sauté mushrooms in a skillet for four Mins, then season with salt, thyme, oregano, and pepper flakes. Cook for another 4 to 6 Mins, or until browned. Allow time for it to cool.
- Combine all cheeses in a mixing bowl, then add the mushroom mixture.
- Place 3 tbsp of the mushroom mixture on the bottom end of each tortilla and roll firmly, securing with toothpicks.
- Preheat the air fryer to 400 degrees Fahrenheit.
- Spray the air fryer basket with oil and lay the tortilla inside.
- Cook for 9–11 Mins, then remove toothpicks and serve.

Nutrition Value
Calories: 291 Kcal, Carb: 31 g, Protein: 8 g, Fat: 16 g
Storage Suggestion: You can store it in the refrigerator for 1-2 days.

Charred Cauliflower Tacos
Prep Time: 25 Mins, Cook Time: 15 Mins, Servings: 4, Serving Size: 2

Ingredients
- Black pepper: ¼ tsp
- Avocado oil: 2 tbsp
- 1 avocado
- Red onion chopped: 2 tbsp
- 1 head of cauliflower, cut into florets
- Garlic powder: 1/2 tsp
- Salt: ¼ tsp
- Taco seasoning: 2 tsp
- Corn tortillas: 8
- Lime juice: 2 tsp
- Purple cabbage, shredded: 1/2 cup
- Chopped cilantro: ¼ cup
- Cooked corn: 1/2 cup

Instructions
- Preheat the air fryer to 390 degrees Fahrenheit.
- Combine cauliflower, taco spice, and avocado oil in a mixing bowl.
- Spray the basket of the air fryer with a large amount of oil.
- Cook for 10 Mins with the cauliflower in the basket. After every 4 Mins, continue shaking the basket.
- Mash the avocado with the onion, pepper, cilantro, garlic powder, lime juice, and salt in a mixing bowl.
- Put 1 tbsp avocado sauce in each tortilla, then top with cabbage, corn, and air-fried cauliflower.
- Serve immediately.

Nutrition Value
Calories: 287 Kcal, Carb: 19 g, Protein: 19 g, Fat: 6 g

Storage Suggestion: You can store it in the refrigerator for 5-6 days.

Sesame Tempeh Slaw

Prep Time: 60 Mins, Cook Time: 1 Hr 15 Mins, Servings: 2, Serving Size: 3

Ingredients
- 8 oz. of tempeh, cut into 1" pieces
- Hot water: 2 cups
- Salt: 1 tsp
- Rice vinegar: 2 tbsp
- Cabbage slaw: 4 cups
- Water: 1 tbsp
- Soy sauce: 2 tbsp
- Ginger: 1/2 tsp
- Chopped cilantro: 2 tbsp
- Peanut dressing: 4 tbsp
- Black pepper: ¼ tsp
- Sesame oil: 2 tsp
- 1 minced clove of garlic
- Half jalapeño, thinly sliced
- Chopped peanuts: 2 tbsp

Instructions
- Combine the salt, boiling water, and tempeh in a mixing dish. Mix well and set aside for ten Mins.
- Remove the tempeh from the water and drain it.
- Combine jalapeño, sesame oil, soy sauce, pepper, vinegar, garlic, water, and ginger in a mixing bowl.
- Mix thoroughly and pour over tempeh, covering it with plastic wrap. Refrigerate for 2 hrs.
- Preheat the air fryer to 370 degrees Fahrenheit.
- Remove the tempeh and toss out the remainder.
- Place tempeh in the air fryer basket after spraying it with oil.
- Cook for four Mins on one side, then flip and cook for another four Mins.
- Toss the slaw with the Peanut Dressing, add the peanuts and cilantro, divide among four plates, and top with tempeh to serve.

Nutrition Value
Calories: 267 Kcal, Carb: 7 g, Protein: 19 g, Fat: 6 g
Storage Suggestion: You can store it in the refrigerator for 3-4 days.

Black Bean Empanadas

Prep Time: 45 Mins, Cook Time: 15 Mins, Servings: 12, Serving Size: 2

Ingredients
- Salt: 1 tsp
- Cold unsalted butter: 1/2 cup
- Purple cabbage, shredded: 1 cup
- 1 whole egg
- Milk: 1/2 cup
- Jack cheese, shredded: 1 cup
- Salsa: ¼ cup
- One can of black beans (14.5-oz.) Drained & rinsed
- All-purpose flour: 1 and a 1/2 cups
- Whole-wheat flour: 1 cup
- Chopped cilantro: ¼ cup

Instructions
- Add butter, all flours, and salt to a food processor. Two Mins of pulsing
- Process for half a Min after adding the egg.
- While the machine is working, add 1 tbsp of milk, just using as much as is needed. Make a dough that can be rolled into a ball.
- Allow the dough to rest for half an hr on the counter.
- Combine cabbage, salsa, cheese, cilantro, and beans in a mixing dish.
- Cut the dough in half and divide it into two balls; each ball should yield six pieces, for a total of 12 pieces.
- Make each piece into a six-inch circle and fill with 4 tbsp filling. Fold the other half over the filling. The edges should be crimped and sealed.
- Make a small slit in the top. Rep with the remaining dough and filling.
- Preheat the air fryer to 350 degrees Fahrenheit.
- Place empanadas in a single layer in the air fryer basket and spray with oil. Cook for 3 to 4 Mins.
- Cook for 3 to 4 Mins longer after flipping and spraying with oil.
- Serve with Greek yogurt on the side.

Nutrition Value
Calories: 237 Kcal, Carb: 19 g, Protein: 21 g, Fat: 8 g
Storage Suggestion: You can store it in the refrigerator for 6-7 days.

Roasted Vegetable Pita Pizza

Prep Time: 30 Mins, Cook Time: 15 Mins, Servings: 4|Serving Size:1

Ingredients
- Olive oil: 1 tsp
- Shredded mozzarella cheese: 1/2 cup
- Black pepper: 1/8 tsp
- Pesto sauce: 6 tbsp
- Salt: 1/8 tsp
- 1 red bell pepper, slice into quarters without seeds
- ¼ red onion, cut into thin slices
- Two pita bread (6")

Instructions
- Preheat the air fryer to 400 degrees Fahrenheit.
- Combine the bell peppers, salt, oil, and black pepper in a mixing bowl.
- Cook the bell peppers in an air fryer for 15 minutes, shaking the basket every five Minutes.
- Remove the peppers from the recipe. Preheat the air fryer to 350 degrees Fahrenheit.
- Spread pesto sauce over each pita bread, then top with veggies and cheese.
- Spray the basket of the air fryer with oil.
- Place the pita bread in the air fryer basket.
- Cook for a further 5-8 Mins, or until the cheese has melted.
- Serve immediately.

Nutrition Value
Calories: 287 Kcal, Carb: 20 g, Protein: 11 g, Fat: 6 g
Storage Suggestion: You can store it in the refrigerator for 1-2 days.

Eggplant Parmesan

Prep Time: 40 Mins, Cook Time: 15 Mins, Servings: 4, Serving Size: 2

Ingredients
- Dried oregano: 1/2 tsp
- Salt: 2 tsp
- All-purpose flour: 1/2 cup
- Dried thyme: 1 tsp
- 1 round eggplant, cut in half "thick circles
- 2 whole eggs
- Marinara sauce: 2 cups
- Breadcrumbs: 1 cup
- Grated parmesan: ¼ cup

Instructions
- Place eggplant slices on a baking pan and season with salt (1 and a 1/2 tsp)
- Using a skillet and paper towels, press the eggplant slices. Allow for a half-hr respite in this state.
- Combine 14 tsp salt, flour, and thyme in a mixing bowl.
- Beat the eggs in a separate bowl.
- Combine salt (14 tsp), parmesan cheese (1/4 cup), breadcrumbs, and oregano in a separate bowl.
- Preheat the air fryer to 370 degrees.
- Remove the eggplant slices from the pan.
- Coat in the flour mixture first, then the egg and the bread crumb mixture.
- Place the coated slices in a uniform layer in the air fryer basket and cook for five Mins. Cook for another five Mins after turning them and spraying them with oil.
- On a medium burner, add marinara sauce to a pan.
- Serve with 1 tsp heated marinara and mozzarella on top of the eggplant pieces.

Nutrition Value
Calories: 189 Kcal, Carb: 11 g, Protein: 5 g, Fat: 7.1 g

Storage Suggestion: You can store it in the refrigerator for 2-3 days.

Seasoned Asparagus

Prep Time: 13 Mins, Cook Time: 15 Mins, Servings: 4, Serving Size:1

Ingredients
- Garlic Salt, to taste
- 1 bunch of asparagus

Instructions
- 2" from the stem, cut off the asparagus.
- In the air fryer basket, place the asparagus.
- Season with garlic salt after spraying with oil.
- Preheat the oven to 390°F and cook for five Mins.
- Cook for another five Mins after shaking the basket.

Nutrition Value
Calories: 32 Kcal, Carb: 0 g, Protein: 0 g, Fat: 3 g

Storage Suggestion: You can store it in the refrigerator for 2-3 days.

Wrapped Corn on the Cob

Prep Time: 13 Mins, Cook Time: 15 Mins, Servings: 4, Serving Size: 2

Ingredients
- 8 bacon slices
- 4 Corn on the Cob

Instructions
- In the air fryer basket, place the foil piece.
- Wrap the corns with bacon strips.
- At 355 F, air-fried them for 10 Mins.
- Serve immediately.

Nutrition Value
Calories: 220 Kcal, Carb: 22 g, Protein: 10.2 g, Fat: 6.5 g

Storage Suggestion: You can store it in the refrigerator for 3-4 days.

Honey Roasted Carrots

Prep Time: 15 Mins, Cook Time: 15 Mins, Servings: 4, Serving Size:1

Ingredients
- Salt & pepper, to taste
- Olive oil: 1 tbsp
- Baby carrots: 3 cups
- Honey: 1 tbsp

Instructions
- Combine all ingredients in a mixing bowl and toss to combine.
- Cook the carrots in the air fryer for 12 to 20 Mins at 390 degrees F.
- Serve with a garnish of fresh herbs.

Nutrition Value
Calories: 176 Kcal, Carb: 2 g, Protein: 5 g, Fat: 5 g

Storage Suggestion: You can store it in the refrigerator for 3-5 days.

Avocado Boats

Prep Time: 15 Mins, Cook Time: 15 Mins, Servings: 4, Serving Size:1

Ingredients
- 2 avocados, cut in halves
- 4 eggs
- 2 plum tomatoes, diced without seeds
- Fresh cilantro, chopped: 2 tbsp
- Black pepper: ¼ tsp
- Diced red onion: ¼ cup
- Lime juice: 1 tbsp
- Salt: 1/2 tsp

Instructions
- Remove the pulp from the avocado and discard the peel.
- Place the pulp in a bowl and dice it. Combine salt, tomato, black pepper, cilantro, and onion in a mixing bowl. Cover and store in the refrigerator.
- Preheat the air fryer to 350 degrees Fahrenheit.
- To give each avocado shell more support, wrap it in foil and throw it in the air fryer.
- Add an egg to each shell and air fry for 5-7 Mins.
- Remove them from the pan and serve with salsa.

Nutrition Value
Calories: 211 Kcal, Carb: 15 g, Protein: 9 g, Fat: 5 g

Storage Suggestion: You can store it in the refrigerator for 5-6 days.

Artichoke Hearts

Prep Time: 15 Mins, Cook Time: 15 Mins, Servings: 4, Serving Size: 2

Ingredients

- 2 to 3 cans of Artichokes, quartered drained
- Salt and black pepper, to taste
- Panko breadcrumbs: 1 cup
- Mayonnaise: 1/2 cup
- Grated Parmesan: 1/3 cup

Instructions

- Using paper towels, pat the artichokes dry.
- Toss all ingredients in a bowl, except the breadcrumbs, and coat thoroughly.
- Combine breadcrumbs and seasoned artichokes in a zip-top bag and shake thoroughly.
- At 370 F, air fried the artichokes for 10 to 15 Mins.
- Serve with a garnish of parsley and parmesan cheese.

Nutrition Value

Calories: 342 Kcal, Carb: 35.2 g, Protein: 14.3 g, Fat: 9.4 g

Storage Suggestion: You can store it in the refrigerator for 6-7 days.

Garlic Mushrooms

Prep Time: 25 Mins, Cook Time: 15 Mins, Servings: 2, Serving Size:1

Ingredients

- Olive oil: 1 to 2 tbsp
- Chopped parsley: 1 tbsp
- 1 cup of mushrooms
- Soy sauce: 1 tsp
- Salt & pepper, to taste
- Garlic powder: 1/2 tsp

Instructions

- Cut the mushrooms in half or quarters.
- Toss the mushrooms with the other ingredients in a large mixing bowl.
- Place them in the air fryer basket and cook for 10 to 12 Mins at 380 degrees F.
- After halftime, shake the basket.
- Serve with a squeeze of lemon juice over the top, if preferred.

Nutrition Value

Calories: 92 Kcal, Carb: 4 g, Protein: 3 g, Fat: 7 g

Storage Suggestion: You can store it in the refrigerator for 2-3 days.

Roasted Broccoli

Prep Time: 25 Mins, Cook Time: 15 Mins, Servings: 4, Serving Size: 1

Ingredients

- Avocado Oil: 2 tbsp
- 2 minced cloves of garlic
- Black Pepper: 1/8 tsp
- 2 Broccoli heads
- Lemon juice: 2 tbsp
- Sea Salt: 1/2 tsp

Instructions

- Broccoli should be cut into tiny florets.
- Toss florets and remaining ingredients in a mixing bowl to blend.
- At 375 degrees F, air fried the broccoli for 20 Mins.
- Change the temperature to 400 degrees Fahrenheit in the final 3 to 5 Mins.
- Serve with 2 tbsp lemon juice drizzled over all of the broccoli.

Nutrition Value

Calories: 70 Kcal, Carb: 5 g, Protein: 2 g, Fat: 4 g

Storage Suggestion: You can store it in the refrigerator for 2-3 days.

Fried Zucchini & Yellow Squash

Prep Time: 30 Mins, Cook Time: 15 Mins, Servings: 8, Serving Size:1

Ingredients

- 1 Zucchini, cut into thin slices
- Breadcrumbs: 2 Cups
- 1 Yellow Squash, cut into thin slices
- All-Purpose Flour: 2 Cups
- Salt, to taste
- 2 Eggs whisked
- Buttermilk: 1 Cup

Instructions

- Combine the squash, zucchini, and buttermilk in a mixing bowl.
- Allow 10 to 15 Mins for the mixture to rest.
- In three separate dishes, combine flour, eggs, and breadcrumbs with a touch of salt.
- Coat the veggies with flour, then eggs, and finally the bread crumb mixture.
- Place equally in the air fryer basket.
- At 390 F, cook for five Mins on each side.
- Serve with a pinch of salt.

Nutrition Value

Calories: 334 Kcal, Carb: 62 g, Protein: 12 g, Fat: 4 g

Storage Suggestion: You can store it in the refrigerator for 3-4 days.

Cumin Carrots

Prep Time: 15 Mins, Cook Time: 15 Mins, Servings: 4, Serving Size:1

Ingredients

- Pepper: 1/8 tsp
- Cumin seeds: 2 tsp
- 1 lb of peeled carrots, cut into sticks
- Coriander seeds: 2 tsp
- Melted butter: 1 tbsp
- fresh cilantro chopped
- 2 minced cloves of garlic
- Salt: 1/4 tsp

Instructions

- Preheat the air fryer to 325 degrees Fahrenheit.
- Toast the cumin and coriander seeds in a pan over medium heat for 45 to 60 seconds. Allow time for it to cool.
- Grind them finely with a spice grinder.
- Combine carrots, salt, oil, garlic, ground spices, and pepper in a mixing bowl. Toss everything together.
- Place carrots in the air fryer basket after spraying them with oil.
- Cook for 12 to 15 Mins, then serve with cilantro on top.

Nutrition Value

Calories: 86 Kcal, Carb: 12 g, Protein: 1 g, Fat: 4 g

Storage Suggestion: You can store it in the refrigerator for 5-6 days.

Tomato Stacks

Prep Time: 35 Mins, Cook Time: 15 Mins, Servings: 8, Serving Size:1

Ingredients

- Lime zest: ¼ tsp
- 2 red tomatoes
- Lime juice: 2 tbsp
- 2 egg whites, whisked
- Chopped fresh thyme: 1 tsp
- Pepper: 1/2 tsp
- 2 green tomatoes
- Mayonnaise: ¼ cup
- Salt: ¼ tsp
- All-purpose flour: ¼ cup
- 8 bacon slices
- Cornmeal: ¾ cup

Instructions

- Preheat the air fryer to 375 degrees Fahrenheit.
- Combine the thyme, pepper (14 tsp), lime juice, and zest in a mixing bowl. Keep refrigerated.
- Combine flour, egg whites, and cornmeal in three separate bowls with 14 tsp salt and pepper.
- Each tomato should be cut into four wedges.
- Coat the slices with flour, egg, then cornmeal, in that order.
- Place in an equal layer in the oil-sprayed air fryer basket, cook for 4 to 6 Mins, turn, and cook for another 4 to 6 Mins.
- Serve by stacking tomatoes in alternating hues.

Nutrition Value

Calories: 118 Kcal, Carb: 14 g, Protein: 6 g, Fat: 2 g

Storage Suggestion: You can store it in the refrigerator for 4-5 days.

Chickpea Fritters

Prep Time: 25 Mins, Cook Time: 15 Mins, Servings: 24, Serving Size: 1

Ingredients

- 1 can of (15 oz.) chickpeas, rinsed
- Sugar: 2 tbsp
- Plain yogurt: 1 cup
- Salt: 1/2 tsp
- Pepper: 1/2 tsp
- Ground ginger: 1/2 tsp
- Honey: 1 tbsp
- Red pepper flakes: 1/2 tsp
- Ground cumin: 1 tsp
- Baking soda: 1/2 tsp
- Salt: 1/2 tsp
- 1 egg
- Garlic powder: 1/2 tsp
- 2 green onions, cut into thin slices
- Fresh cilantro: 1/2 cup

Instructions

- Preheat the air fryer to 400 degrees Fahrenheit.
- Seasonings and chickpeas in a food processor, pulse until finely chopped.
- Pulse in the baking soda and egg one more.
- Remove to a bowl and mix with green onions and cilantro.
- Mix the remaining ingredients in a separate dish and put it aside.
- Spray the air fryer basket with oil, pour a tbsp chickpea mixture on the tray, and cook for 5 to 6 Mins.
- Enjoy the sauce you've made.

Nutrition Value

Calories: 37 Kcal, Carb: 6 g, Protein: 2 g, Fat: 1.2 g

Storage Suggestion: You can store it in the refrigerator for 1-2 days.

Crispy Artichoke Hearts with Horseradish Aioli

Prep Time: 15 Mins, Cook Time: 50 mins, Servings: 2, Serving Size: 2

Ingredients

- Frozen artichoke hearts 3 cups (1 to 12-ounce bag)
- Olive oil 2 tbsp
- Homemade seasoned salt 1/2 tsp
- Coarsely ground black pepper ¼ tsp
- Fresh squeezed lemon juice 1 tbsp

Instructions

- Preheat the oven to 425 degrees Fahrenheit. Using parchment paper, line a cookie sheet.
- Open the bag of frozen artichoke hearts; sprinkle with olive oil and lemon juice; toss to coat the heart. Toss with black pepper and seasoned salt and toss one more to combine.
- Arrange artichoke hearts in a single layer on a parchment-lined cookie sheet and bake for 45 Mins in the middle of the oven, occasionally stirring, until gently brown.
- Remove the hearts from the oven and allow them to cool before crisping them further. Transfer to a platter and serve with cold horseradish sauce as a dip.

Nutrition Value

Calories: 112 Kcal, Carb: 26.4 g, Protein: 12.1 g, Fat: 7.3 g

Storage Suggestion: You can store it in the refrigerator for 4-5 days.

Chapter 17: Dessert & Staples Recipes

Chocolate Chip Oatmeal Cookies

Prep Time: 30 Mins, Cook Time: 15 Mins, Servings: 6, Serving Size: 1

Ingredients
- Softened butter: 1 cup
- Semisweet chocolate chips: 2 cups
- Sugar: ¾ cup
- Packed brown sugar: ¾ cup
- Quick-cooking oats: 3 cups
- 2 whole eggs at room temperature
- 1 and a 1/2 cups all-purpose flour
- Vanilla extract: 1 tsp
- Baking soda: 1 tsp
- Chopped nuts: 1 cup
- 1 pack of (3.4 oz.) Vanilla pudding instant mix
- Salt: 1 tsp

Instructions
- Preheat the air fryer to 325 degrees Fahrenheit.
- In a mixing bowl, cream the sugars and butter for 5 to 7 Mins, or until frothy and light. Combine the vanilla and eggs in a mixing bowl.
- Combine baking soda, oats, salt, dry pudding mix, and flour in a separate bowl.
- Carefully incorporate the cream mixture, as well as the nuts and chocolate chips.
- Place the dough on a baking pan and set it aside. Divide the mixture into tbsp and gently flatten each one.
- Place cookies in a single layer in an oiled air fryer basket.
- Cook for a total of 8 to 10 Mins.
- Remove them from the oven and set them aside to cool before serving.

Nutrition Value
Calories: 102 Kcal, Carb: 13 g, Protein: 2 g, Fat: 5 g
Storage Suggestion: You can store it in the refrigerator for 2-3 days.

Nutella Doughnut Mini Holes

Prep Time: 35 Mins, Cook Time: 15 Mins, Servings: 32, Serving Size: 1

Ingredients
- Nutella: 2/3 cup
- 1 whole egg
- 1 tube of flaky biscuits, refrigerated (8 biscuits)
- 1 tbsp water

Instructions
- Preheat the air fryer to 300 degrees Fahrenheit.
- In a mixing dish, whisk together the water and the egg.
- Sprinkle some flour on a clean surface, shape each biscuit into a six-inch circle, and then slice into four triangles.
- Apply an egg wash to the surface. To make the Nutella triangles, spread 1 tsp of Nutella on each one.
- In each wedge, fold the filling in half and close the edges.
- There's no need to spray the air fryer basket with oil. Place small doughnuts in a single layer in the basket and bake for 8 to 10 Mins, flipping once.
- Serve with a dusting of confectioners' sugar on top.

Nutrition Value
Calories: 94 Kcal, Carb: 10 g, Protein: 1 g, Fat: 6 g
Storage Suggestion: You can store it in the refrigerator for 6-7 days.

Chocolate Chip Cookies

Prep Time: 35 Mins, Cook Time: 15 Mins, Servings: 30, Serving Size: 2

Ingredients
- Unsalted butter: 1 cup
- Granulated sugar: ¾ cup
- 2 whole eggs
- Chocolate chunks: 2 cups
- Vanilla extract: 1 tbsp
- Kosher salt: 1 tsp
- Flaky sea salt, for serving
- Packed dark brown sugar: ¾ cup
- Chopped walnuts: ¾ cup
- Baking soda: 1 tsp
- 2 and 1/3 cups of all-purpose flour

Instructions
- With the paddle attachment, add softened butter to a stand mixer bowl.
- Add the dark brown sugar and granulated sugar and mix on medium speed for 3-4 Mins, or until fluffy and blended.
- Mix in the salt, eggs, and vanilla essence until just combined.
- Gradually add all-purpose flour and baking soda, being careful not to overmix.
- With a spatula, combine the chopped nuts and chocolate bits.
- Preheat the air fryer to 350 degrees Fahrenheit.
- In the air fryer basket, put parchment paper so that air may circulate freely and allow some room on the sides.
- tbsp dough, 2 tbsp parchment paper, 2 tbsp dough, 2 tbsp parchment paper, 2 tbsp dough, 2 tbsp parchment paper, 2 tbsp parchment paper, 2 tbsp parchment paper, 2
- Bake for five Mins after sprinkling flaky sea salt on the scoops.
- Allow them to cool for 3-5 Mins in the basket.
- Serve immediately and enjoy.

Nutrition Value
Calories: 87 Kcal, Carb: 8 g, Protein: 2.1 g, Fat: 4 g
Storage Suggestion: You can store it in the refrigerator for 5-6 days.

Air Fryer Donuts

Prep Time: 15 Mins, Cook Time: 15 Mins, Servings: 8, Serving Size: 2

Ingredients
- 1 can of large flaky biscuits (16.3-oz.)
- Granulated sugar: 1/2 cup
- Melted unsalted butter: 4 tbsp
- Ground cinnamon: 1 tbsp

Instructions
- Combine cinnamon and sugar in a mixing bowl.

- Cut one" round holes in the middle of each biscuit on a parchment-lined baking sheet.
- Spray the basket of the air fryer with oil.
- Cook for 5-6 Mins at 350 F, until doughnuts are golden brown, leaving one" inch between them in one even layer.
- Brush the doughnuts with melted butter and then roll them in the sugar-cinnamon mixture.
- Serve immediately.

Nutrition Value
Calories: 132 Kcal, Carb: 14 g, Protein: 2 g, Fat: 9 g
Storage Suggestion: You can store it in the refrigerator for 3-4 days.

Air Fryer Beignets

Prep Time: 38 Mins, Cook Time: 25 Mins, Servings: 9, Serving Size: 1

Ingredients
- Melted unsalted butter: 2 tbsp
- Plain Greek yogurt: 1 cup
- Vanilla extract: 1 tsp
- Powdered sugar: 1/2 cup
- Granulated sugar: 2 tbsp
- Self-rising flour: 1 cup

Instructions
- Combine vanilla, yogurt, and granulated sugar in a mixing dish. Mix thoroughly.
- Mix in the flour until it is barely combined and dough forms.
- Sprinkle some dough in a clean work area. Knead the dough two or three times until smooth and mixed.
- Place dough within a 4 by 5" rectangle and slice into nine pieces.
- Divide the pieces into thirds and lightly sprinkle them with flour. Allow 15 Mins for resting.
- Preheat the air fryer to 350 degrees Fahrenheit.
- Spray the basket of the air fryer with oil.
- Brush the beignets with melted butter.
- Place in a uniform layer in the air fryer. Do not allow them to get into contact with one other.
- Brush with melted butter once more. Cook for 7 Mins, or until they seem dry and brown.
- Cook for another six Mins on the other side.
- Place on a paper towel to absorb excess liquid and sprinkle with confectioners' sugar.
- Warm it up and enjoy it.

Nutrition Value
Calories: 186 Kcal, Carb: 26 g, Protein: 4 g, Fat: 6.8 g
Storage Suggestion: You can store it in the refrigerator for 2-3 days.

Fruit Pies

Prep Time: 10 Mins, Cook Time: 35 Mins, Servings: 12, Serving Size: 1

Ingredients
- Raspberries: 3/4 cup
- 1 and a 1/2 tsp cornstarch with 1 tsp of water
- Granulated sugar: 1 tbsp
- Fuji apples: 2, peeled, remove core & slice into 1/4" dice
- Ground cinnamon: 1/4 tsp
- A pinch of kosher salt
- 1 egg yolk with 1 tsp of water
- Apple juice: 1 tbsp
- Light brown sugar: 2 tbsp
- 1 pack of pie crusts (2 rounds)

Instructions
- Toss raspberries, apple juice, apples, salt, sweeteners, or cinnamon into a saucepan.
- Allow it to simmer on medium heat for a few Mins before covering it and turning the heat down to low. Cook for 15 Mins, occasionally stirring, until apple is cooked but not too soft.
- Toss the fruit mixture with cornstarch. Increase the heat to medium-high and cook for 1 to 2 Mins, or until it thickens. Turn off the heat and let the room cool down.
- Meanwhile, take the pie crusts out of the freezer and cut them with a 4" cookie cutter before rolling them out again. There will be 12 rounds in all.
- Fill each round with 1 spoonful of fruit filling. Brush the edges of the rounds with water, then fold and seal the edges.
- Crimp the sides of the pie with a fork, then cut two slits in the top and brush with the egg mixture.
- Sugar is sprinkled on top.
- Preheat the air fryer to 320 degrees Fahrenheit.
- Cook for 15 Mins, or until the pies are light brown, adding 5-6 fruit pies to the basket.
- Remove them from the oven and serve.

Nutrition Value
Calories: 213 Kcal, Carb: 21 g, Protein: 7 g, Fat: 9 g
Storage Suggestion: You can store it in the refrigerator for 5-6 days.

Angel Food Cake Churro Bites

Prep Time: 10 Mins, Cook Time: 15 Mins, Servings: 2, Serving Size: 1

Ingredients

For bites
- Granulated sugar: 1/4 cup
- Cinnamon: 1 tbsp
- Half cake loaf of angel food

For dipping sauce
- Milk: 1-2 tsp
- Softened cream cheese: 1/4 cup
- Butter at room temperature: 2 tsp
- Confectioners' sugar: 2 tbsp

Instructions
- Cut the cake into 1.5-inch chunks.
- Combine the sugar and cinnamon in a mixing bowl.
- Spray the air fryer basket with oil and place the cake cubes inside.
- Cook for five Mins at 350 degrees F, or until golden brown.
- Remove the cake cubes and toss them with a sugar-cinnamon mixture.

- Combine the butter, cream cheese, milk, and confectioners' sugar in a mixing bowl. Mix everything up well.
- Make it to your desired consistency and serve with cake bits.

Nutrition Value
Calories: 171 Kcal, Carb: 21 g, Protein: 4.6 g, Fat: 8.1 g
Storage Suggestion: You can store it in the refrigerator for 5-6 days.

Honey Cinnamon Roll-ups

Prep Time: 25 Mins, Cook Time: 35 Mins, Servings: 24, Serving Size: 1

Ingredients
- 12 sheets of phyllo dough
- Toasted ground walnuts: 2 cups
- Ground cinnamon: 2 tsp
- Honey: 1/2 cup
- Melted butter: 1/2 cup
- Sugar: 1/4 cup+ 1/2 cup
- Lemon juice: 1 tbsp
- Water: 1/2 cup

Instructions
- Preheat the air fryer to 325 degrees Fahrenheit.
- Combine cinnamon, walnuts, and sugar in a mixing bowl.
- Brush one sheet of dough with butter and place it on parchment paper.
- Brush the second piece of dough with butter before placing it on top.
- Place 1/4 cup of the walnut mixture on the baking sheet. Start with the long side and roll it up firmly.
- Cut the roll into four smaller pieces. Brush them with butter and toothpicks to keep them together.
- Repeat with the walnut mixture and phyllo dough.
- Spray the air fryer basket with oil and drop the rolls inside.
- Cook for 9–11 Mins at 350°F. Remove the toothpicks and set them aside to cool.
- To make the syrup, combine all ingredients in a skillet, stir well, and bring to a boil. Reduce the heat to low and cook for five Mins. Allow five Mins for cooling.
- Serve with syrup-soaked buns.

Nutrition Value
Calories: 140 Kcal, Carb: 19 g, Protein: 2.6 g, Fat: 7.9 g
Storage Suggestion: You can store it in the refrigerator for 6-7 days.

Honeyed Pears in Puff Pastry

Prep Time: 10 Mins, Cook Time: 45 Mins, Servings: 4, Serving Size: 1

Ingredients
- Water: 4 cups
- 1 sheet of puff pastry
- Small pears: 4
- 1 lemon, cut into half
- 3 cinnamon sticks of (3")
- Sugar: 2 cups
- 1 egg, lightly whisked
- 6-8 cloves
- Honey: 1 cup
- 1 vanilla bean

Instructions
- Remove the core from peeled pears, leave the stems in place, and chop off the bottom 14 inches.
- Add half of the lemons, water, cloves, sugar, cinnamon, and honey to a saucepan.
- Remove the seeds from the vanilla bean and cut them half before adding them to the honey mixture.
- Please bring it to a boil. Reduce the heat to low, add the pears to the saucepan, and poach them without a cover for 16 to 20 Mins, or until soft.
- Remove the pears from the pan without the syrup and set them aside to cool for a few Mins.
- Save ½ cup of the syrup after straining it.
- Preheat the air fryer to 325 degrees Fahrenheit.
- On a floured board, roll out the puff pastry. In width, cut into half-inch strips.
- Brush the egg with a whisked egg.
- Start wrapping the pear in pastry dough from the bottom up, adding extra strips as needed.
- All of the pears should be wrapped in dough sheets.
- Spray the air fryer basket with cooking spray and arrange the pears in an equal layer in the basket. Cook for 12 to 15 Mins, until golden brown.
- Bring the syrup to a boil, then reduce to low heat for ten Mins.
- Serve the pears with a sprinkle of maple syrup on top.

Nutrition Value
Calories: 536 Kcal, Carb: 87 g, Protein: 23 g, Fat: 18.2 g
Storage Suggestion: You can store it in the refrigerator for 2-3 days.

Bread Pudding

Prep Time: 30 Mins, Cook Time: 15 Mins, Servings: 2, Serving Size: 1

Ingredients
- Vanilla extract: 1 tsp
- 2 oz. of chopped semisweet chocolate
- Sugar: 2/3 cup
- 2% milk: 1/2 cup
- 4 slices of old bread, cut into cubes (remove the crust)
- Half & half cream: 1/2 cup
- 1 egg at room temperature
- Salt: ¼ tsp

Instructions
- Melt the chocolate in a microwave-safe dish until smooth, then add the cream and put it aside.
- Combine the salt, sugar, egg, and vanilla in a mixing dish. Combine all ingredients in a mixing bowl, then stir in the chocolate mixture.
- Allow the bread cubes to soak up the chocolate mixture for 15 Mins.
- Preheat the air fryer to 325 degrees Fahrenheit.
- Take two ramekins, brush them with oil, and fill them with bread cubes.
- Cook for 12 to 15 Mins in the air fryer basket using these ramekins.

- Serve with a dollop of whipped cream and a dusting of confectioners' sugar on top.

Nutrition Value
Calories: 779 Kcal, Carb: 87 g, Protein: 14 g, Fat: 22 g
Storage Suggestion: You can store it in the refrigerator for 6-7 days.

Apple Cider Donuts

Prep Time: 55 Mins, Cook Time: 15 Mins, Servings: 18, Serving Size: 1

Ingredients
- Apple cider: 2 cups
- Packed light brown sugar: 1/2 cup
- Baking powder: 2 tsp
- Ground ginger: 1 tsp
- Cold unsalted butter: 1 stick
- All-purpose flour: 3 cups
- Ground cinnamon: 1 tsp
- Cold milk: 1/2 cup
- Baking soda: 1/2 tsp
- Kosher salt: 1/2 tsp

For finishing
- Ground cinnamon: 1 tsp
- Unsalted butter: 8 tbsp
- All-purpose flour: ¼ cup
- Granulated sugar: 1 cup

Instructions
- Add apple cider to a pan and boil over medium heat.
- Boil for 10-12 Mins, or until it has reduced by half; add a splash of apple cider if it becomes too dry.
- Allow for a half-hr cooling period.
- Light brown sugar, ground ginger, kosher salt, all-purpose flour, baking soda, powdered cinnamon, and baking powder should all be combined in a mixing dish.
- Grate the butter stick into the flour mixture and work it with your fingertips until it resembles pebbles.
- Mix in the cooked (but cooled) apple cider and chilled milk until a dough forms.
- Place the dough on a floured, clean surface. Make a one-inch-thick layer of dough. Continue folding into itself to create one" of thickness. Repeat the process six times.
- Make a half-inch thick rectangle out of the dough, which should be springy.
- Cut the doughnuts using a donut cutter. Make 18 donuts out of the whole dough and chill them.
- Preheat the air fryer to 375 degrees Fahrenheit.
- 2 tbsp butter, melted in a bowl Mix in the other finishing ingredients, except the flour, using a fork.
- Cook for 12 Mins in the air fryer, flip halfway through and allow some space between doughnuts.
- Serve the doughnuts warm after coating them in the butter mixture.

Nutrition Value
Calories: 318 Kcal, Carb: 45 g, Protein: 3.6 g, Fat: 13.4 g
Storage Suggestion: You can store it in the refrigerator for 2-3 days.

Caramelized Bananas

Prep Time: 10 Mins, Cook Time: 15 Mins, Servings: 2, Serving Size: 1

Ingredients
- Coconut sugar: 1 tbsp
- 2 bananas
- Juice of a ¼ lemon

Instructions
- Cut the bananas in half lengthwise after cleaning them but without peeling them.
- Lemon juice should be poured over the bananas.
- Using coconut sugar, coat the bananas.
- Place bananas in the air fryer basket lined with parchment paper.
- Air fry for 6–8 Mins at 400°F.
- Serve with granola, trail mix, and other toppings.

Nutrition Value
Calories: 354 Kcal, Carb: 38 g, Protein: 9 g, Fat: 17.4 g
Storage Suggestion: You can store it in the refrigerator for 1-2 days.

Air Fryer Brownies

Prep Time: 40 Mins, Cook Time: 15 Mins, Servings: 5, Serving Size: 1

Ingredients
- All-purpose flour: ¼ cup
- Butter: 1/2 cup
- 2 whole eggs
- Salt: ⅛ tsp
- Vanilla extract: 2 tsp
- Chopped walnuts: 1/2 cup
- Cocoa powder: ¼ cup
- Brown sugar: 1 cup

Instructions
- Spray ramekins with cooking oil.
- Microwave cocoa powder and butter in a bowl until melted. Mix thoroughly.
- Allow cooling before adding the vanilla essence and eggs.
- Combine the salt, flour, brown sugar, and nuts in a mixing bowl.
- Pour into the ramekins and bake for 20 to 30 Mins at 320 degrees F, or until lightly moist in the center.
- Allow cooling before serving.

Nutrition Value
Calories: 281 Kcal, Carb: 21.1 g, Protein: 6.4 g, Fat: 8.9 g
Storage Suggestion: You can store it in the refrigerator for 1.2 days.

S'mores Crescent Rolls

Prep Time: 15 Mins, Cook Time: 25 Mins, Servings: 8, Serving Size: 1

Ingredients
- Nutella: ¼ cup
- Miniature marshmallows: 2/3 cup
- 2 graham crackers, crushed
- 1 tube of crescent rolls (refrigerated)
- Milk chocolate chips: 2 tbsp

Instructions
- Preheat the air fryer to 300 degrees Fahrenheit.
- Make eight triangles out of crescent dough.
- Place 1 tsp of Nutella on the triangle's broad side. Graham crackers, marshmallows, and

chocolate chips are sprinkled on top.
- To form a crescent, fold them in half.
- Spray the air fryer basket with oil and arrange the vegetables in one layer in the basket.
- Cook for a total of 8 to 10 Mins.
- Serve with a dollop of warm Nutella.

Nutrition Value
Calories: 191 Kcal, Carb: 26 g, Protein: 5.1 g, Fat: 13.2 g
Storage Suggestion: You can store it in the refrigerator for 3-4 days.

Carrot Coffee Cake

Prep Time: 15 Mins, Cook Time: 35 Mins, Servings: 6, Serving Size: 1

Ingredients
- Dark brown sugar: 2 tbsp
- Buttermilk: 1/2 cup
- Baking raising agent: 1 tsp
- Sugar: 1/3 cup + 2 tbsp
- 1 egg, whisked at room temperature
- Canola oil: 3 tbsp
- Shredded carrots: 1 cup
- White whole wheat flour: 1/3 cup
- Grated orange: 1 tsp
- Vanilla extract: 1 tsp
- All-purpose flour: 2/3 cup
- Toasted chopped walnuts: 1/3 cup
- bicarbonate-of-soda for baking: 1/4 tsp
- Salt: 1/4 tsp
- Pumpkin pie spice: 2 tsp
- Dried cranberries: 1/4 cup

Instructions
- Preheat your air fryer to 350 degrees Fahrenheit.
- Spray an air fryer-safe pan with cooking oil.
- Combine orange zest, egg, 1/3 cup sugar, vanilla, oil, buttermilk, and brown sugar in a mixing bowl.
- Combine salt, pumpkin pie (1 tsp), flours, baking soda, and baking powder in a separate bowl.
- Fold the cranberries and carrots into the egg.
- Pour the mixture into the cake.
- Combine the sugar (2 tbsp), pumpkin spice (1 tsp), and walnuts in a mixing bowl.
- Toss on top of the batter.
- Place in the air fryer for a few Mins. Serve after 35 to 40 Mins of cooking.

Nutrition Value
Calories: 316 Kcal, Carb: 46 g, Protein: 8 g, Fat: 13 g
Storage Suggestion: You can store it in the refrigerator for 2-3 days.

Apple Fritters

Prep Time: 18 Mins, Cook Time: 15 Mins, Servings: 15, Serving Size: 1

Ingredients
- 2 Honey crisp peeled apples, diced
- 2 tsp of baking powder
- 1/4 cup of butter
- 1 and a 1/2 cups of all-purpose flour
- 1 and a 1/2 tsp of ground cinnamon
- 1/2 tsp of salt
- 1 cup of confectioners' sugar
- 2 eggs, at room temperature
- 1/4 cup of sugar
- 1 tbsp of lemon juice
- 2/3 cup + 1 tbsp of milk
- 1 and a 1/2 tsp of vanilla extract

Instructions
- Spray the parchment paper in the air fryer basket with oil.
- Preheat the air fryer to 410 degrees Fahrenheit.
- Combine cinnamon, flour, salt, sugar, and baking powder in a mixing dish.
- Mix in 1 tsp vanilla essence, milk, lemon juice, and eggs until well combined. Toss in the apples.
- Place 1/4 cup of dough in the basket of an air fryer, two inches apart.
- All of them were sprayed with oil. Cook for 5 to 6 Mins on one side, then turn and cook for another 2 Mins until golden brown.
- Melt butter in a pan until it begins to brown. Remove the pan from the heat and allow it to cool slightly.
- Mix in the vanilla essence, 1 tbsp milk, and confectioners' sugar until smooth.
- Serve the fritters with the sauce.

Nutrition Value
Calories: 145 Kcal, Carb: 24 g, Protein: 3 g, Fat: 4.5 g
Storage Suggestion: You can store it in the refrigerator for 1-2 days.

Banana Bread

Prep Time: 20 Mins, Cook Time: 35 Mins, Servings: 8, Serving Size: 1

Ingredients
- Salt: 1/4 tsp
- All-purpose flour: 3/4 cup
- Sour cream: 1/4 cup
- 2 bananas, (ripe)
- Baking soda: 1/4 tsp
- Granulated sugar: 1/2 cup
- Vegetable oil: 1/4 cup
- Chopped walnuts: 1/2 cup
- Vanilla extract: 1/2 tsp
- 1 egg

Instructions
- Combine baking soda, flour, and salt in a mixing bowl.
- In a bowl, mash the bananas with a fork.
- Combine the egg, oil, vanilla, sugar, and sour cream in a mixing bowl. Mix thoroughly.
- Combine the dry and wet ingredients in a mixing bowl. Don't overmix the ingredients.
- Fold walnuts into the mixture.
- Pour the batter into a microwave-safe pan that has been thoroughly sprayed with oil and placed into the air fryer.
- Cook for 35 to 37 Mins at 310 degrees Fahrenheit.
- Before serving, allow it to cool.

Nutrition Value
Calories: 245 Kcal, Carb: 21 g, Protein: 3 g, Fat: 7 g
Storage Suggestion: You can store it in the refrigerator for 5-6 days.

Easy Air Fryer Chocolate Chip Cookies

Prep Time: 10 Mins, Cook Time: 8 mins Servings: 10 Serving Size: 2

Ingredients
- Softened butter 8 tbsp
- Granulated sugar 1/3 cup
- Light brown sugar (packed) 1/3 cup
- Egg 1 large
- Vanilla extract 1 tsp
- Squeezed lemon juice 1/8 tsp
- Flour 1 cup
- Rolled oats ¼ cup.
- Baking soda 1/2 tsp
- Salt 1/2 tsp
- Cinnamon ¼ tsp
- Sweet chocolate chips 1 1/2 cups
- Chopped walnuts 1/2 cup.

Instructions
- Combine the sugar, brown sugar, and butter in a mixing bowl.
- Blend for thirty seconds with the mixer after adding the vanilla, lemon juice, and egg. Then, scraping down the bowl, mix on medium for a few Mins or until light and fluffy.
- Combine flour, baking soda, oats, salt, and cinnamon in a blender and mix for 45 seconds. It's important not to overmix it.
- Combine the chocolate chips and walnuts in a mixing bowl.
- Bakery release paper should be used to line the basket of an air fryer. Scoop the cookie dough into balls and place them 1 1/2 to 2 inches apart in a basket. Flatten the tops of your cookies with moistened palms.
- At 300 degrees, air fried for 6 to 8 Mins.
- Remove the cookies from the air fryer basket and let them cool for five Mins before removing them.
- Place the cookies on a wire rack to cool for another ten Mins.

Nutrition Value
Calories: 235 Kcal, Carb: 34 g, Protein: 10.2 g, Fat: 4.2 g

Storage Suggestion: You can store it in the refrigerator for 1-2 days.

Easy Air Fryer Cherry Turnovers

Prep Time: 10 Mins, Cook Time: 10 mins, Servings: 8, Serving Size: 1

Ingredients
- Puff pastry four sheets, package 17 oz
- Cherry pie filling 10 oz can
- Beaten egg 1.
- Water 2 tbsp
- Cooking oil

Instructions
- Arrange the puff pastry sheets on a flat surface.
- Fold each piece of puff pastry dough in half. Cut each sheet into four squares, for a total of eight squares.
- To prepare the egg wash, whisk the egg with the water in a mixing bowl.
- Brush the edges of each square with an egg wash using the cooking brush.
- Fill each square sheet with one tbsp of cherry pie filling.
- To construct the triangle, fold the dough diagonally and seal it. To cover the open edges of each turnover, use the back of the fork to drive lines into them.
- To vent your turnovers, cut three slits on the top crust.
- Brush the tops of each turnover with the egg wash.
- Drizzle frying oil into the air fryer basket and add the turnovers. Please make sure they don't touch the turnovers and don't stack them.
- For eight Mins, air fried at 370°F.
- Allow 2 to 3 Mins for your pastries to cool before removing them from the air fryer.

Nutrition Value
Calories: 301 Kcal, Carb: 38.1 g, Protein: 18.3 g, Fat: 15.2 g

Storage Suggestion: You can store it in the refrigerator for 4-5 days.

Easy Air Fryer Lemon Cake

Prep Time: 20 Mins, Cook Time: 35 mins, Servings: 6, Serving Size: 2

Ingredients
- All-purpose flour 1 1/2 cup
- Salt 1/2 tsp
- Baking powder 1 tsp
- Unsalted butter 1/2 cup
- Sweetener 1 cup
- Lemon zest 1 tbsp
- Squeezed lemon juice 2 tbsp
- Eggs 4
- Plain Greek yogurt 2/3 cup
- Vanilla extract 1 tsp

Instructions
- Using a six-cup Bundt pan, butter, and flour it.
- Combine the salt, baking powder, and flour in a medium mixing bowl.
- In a mixing dish, combine the butter and sweetener. Also, cream the butter using your mixer. Stir until the mixture is creamy.
- Two eggs should be added and whisked together with a hand mixer. Mix in the eggs that were left over.
- Combine the lemon zest, dry flour mix, yoghurt, vanilla, and lemon juice in a mixing dish. Blend until the batter is completely smooth.
- Fill a Bundt pan halfway with batter.
- Wrap foil around a Bundt pan. At 320 degrees, air fried for about fifteen Mins.
- Remove the foil from your air fryer and open it. Cook for another 15 to 20 Mins in the air fryer.
- Allow ten Mins for the cake to cool.
- Place the cake stand on top of the Bundt pan and spin it to release the cake.

Nutrition Value
Calories: 351 Kcal, Carb: 38.1 g, Protein: 24.2 g, Fat: 12.1 g

Storage Suggestion: You can store it in the refrigerator for 5-6 days.

5-mins Air Fryer Sugar Doughnut

Prep Time: 5 Mins, Cook Time: 5 mins, Servings: 2, Serving Size: 1

Ingredients
- Big Pillsbury biscuits one can
- Sugar 1/2 cup
- Cinnamon 1/2 tbsp
- Butter 5 tbsp

Instructions
- Preheat the air fryer to 330 degrees.
- Combine the sugar and cinnamon in a medium mixing bowl.
- Cut the center out of each biscuit by opening the can.
- Place the bigger section of the exterior in the air fryer.
- Run it at 330 degrees for 4 to 7 Mins.

Nutrition Value
Calories: 259 Kcal, Carb: 24.1 g, Protein: 15.8 g, Fat: 11.2 g
Storage Suggestion: You can store it in the refrigerator for 3-4 days.

Brazilian Grilled Pineapple

Prep Time: 5 Mins, Cook Time: 10 mins, Servings: 4, Serving Size: 1

Ingredients
- (Cut into spears) peeled & cored pineapple 1.
- Brown sugar 1/2 cup
- Ground cinnamon 2 tsp
- Melted butter 3 tbsp

Instructions
- Combine the cinnamon and brown sugar in a mixing bowl.
- Softened butter should be used to coat the pineapple spears. Drizzle cinnamon sugar over the spears and carefully push it in to ensure it sticks.
- Place your spears in a single layer in an air fryer basket. Preheat the air fryer to 400°F and set the timer for 10 Mins for the first batch. Brush with any remaining butter halfway through.
- Once the pineapples are cooked through and the sugar bubble, they are done.

Nutrition Value
Calories: 364 Kcal, Carb: 24.2 g, Protein: 9.3 g, Fat: 7.1 g
Storage Suggestion: You can store it in the refrigerator for 2-3 days.

Fruit Hand Pies

Prep Time: 10 Mins, Cook Time: 35 mins, Servings: 2, Serving Size: 2

Ingredients

For the crust
- All-purpose flour (187.5 g) 1.5 cups
- Kosher salt 1/2 tsp
- Shortening ¼ cup
- Butter ¼ cup
- Coldwater 62.5 g

For the fruit filling
- Egg 1 large
- Water 1 tbsp
- Coarse sugar 1 tsp

Instructions
- The air fryer had been preheated to 320 degrees F.
- Trace a six-inch circular frying pan on an 8 1/2 × 11-inch sheet of paper. Cut off the circle.
- Combine the flour and salt in a medium mixing bowl. Cut in shortening and butter using a pastry blender. Drizzle 1 tbsp cold water over a portion of the flour mixture. With a fork, toss the ingredients together. Place the wet pastry on one of the bowl's sides. Repeat with the remaining flour and 1 tbsp water until everything is wet. Fold the flour mixture into the ball and knead it well.
- Flatten the pastry slightly, then roll it out into a thirteen-inch circle on a lightly floured board from center to edge. Place a design on one of the pastry's edges. Cut a six-inch circle out of the pastry with a delicate knife. Make two circles by repeating this procedure. Discard the dough leftovers.
- Fill half of a pastry circle with fruit filling, leaving a 14-inch border. Brush a bare edge with water. Place an empty pastry half on the filling and fold it in half. To cover the pastry edge, use a fork to push around it. With the fork, poke a top in a few places. Rep with the remaining filling and pastry.
- Combine the egg and water in a mixing bowl. Drizzle coarse sugar over the pies and brush over the tops.
- Place the pies in an air fryer basket and cook for 35 Mins, or until golden brown on top.
- Allow pies to cool for 20 Mins on a wire rack before serving.

Nutrition Value
Calories: 403 Kcal, Carb: 34.2 g, Protein: 17.8 g, Fat: 12.9 g
Storage Suggestion: You can store it in the refrigerator for 5-6 days.

Air-fryer Mini-Nutella Doughnut Holes

Prep Time: 5 Mins, Cook Time: 5 mins, Servings: 32, Serving Size: 2

Ingredients
- Egg 1 large
- Water 1 tbsp
- Big refrigerated flaky biscuits one tube
- Nutella 2/3 cup
- Oil to deep-fat fry
- Sugar (confectioners)

Instructions
- Preheat your air fryer to 300 degrees. Using water, beat the egg. Roll each biscuit into a six-inch round. Make a circle on a lightly floured surface and cut each into four wedges. Brush each wedge with a thin layer of egg mixture and a tsp of Nutella. Carry the corners up over the filling and firmly crimp the edges to close.
- In batches, arrange biscuits in a single layer on the tray in an air-fryer basket. Cook for 8 to 10 Mins, turning once until the color turns golden brown. Serve immediately after brushing with confectioners' sugar.

Nutrition Value

Calories: 315 Kcal, Carb: 27.1 g, Protein: 16.3 g, Fat: 10.2 g
Storage Suggestion: You can store it in the refrigerator for 1-2 days.

Air-Fryer Bread Pudding

Prep Time: 10 Mins, Cook Time: 15 mins, Servings: 2, Serving Size: 1

Ingredients

- Chopped semisweet chocolate 2 ounces.
- Half-&-half cream 1/2 cup
- Sugar 2/3 cup
- Milk 1/2 cup
- Egg 1 large
- Vanilla extract 1 tsp
- Salt ¼ tsp
- (Crusts removed & sliced into cubes) day-old bread four slices.

Instructions

- In a microwave-safe dish, melt the chocolate and stir until smooth. Add the cream and put it aside.
- Stir together the milk, sugar, egg, salt, and vanilla in a mixing dish. Combine it with a chocolate concoction. Toss in the bread cubes to coat. Allow for fifteen Mins of resting time.
- Preheat the air fryer to 325 degrees. Fill the two oiled 8-ounce ramekins halfway with the bread mixture. In an air-fryer basket, place on a tray. Cook until a knife stabbed in the center emerges clean.
- Top with whipped cream and confectioners' sugar if desired.

Nutrition Value

Calories: 274 Kcal, Carb: 28 g, Protein: 17.2 g, Fat: 10.3 g
Storage Suggestion: You can store it in the refrigerator for 1-2 days.

Air-Fryer Caribbean Wontons

Prep Time: 5 Mins, Cook Time: 10 mins, Servings: 2, Serving Size: 1

Ingredients

- Softened cream cheese 4 ounces
- Sweetened shredded coconut ¼ cup
- Mashed ripe banana ¼ cup.
- Chopped walnuts 2 tbsp
- Canned chopped pineapple 2 tbsp
- Marshmallow crème 1 cup
- Wonton wrappers 24
- Cooking spray
- Sauce:
- Hulled fresh strawberries 1 lb.
- Sugar ¼ cup
- Cornstarch 1 tsp
- Ground cinnamon & confectioners' sugar

Instructions

- Preheat the air fryer to 350 degrees. Cream the cream cheese in a mixing bowl until it is very smooth. Combine the banana, coconut, walnuts, and pineapple in a large mixing bowl. Combine it with the marshmallow crème and fold it in.
- Place one tip of the wonton wrapper toward you. Cover the remaining wrappers with a moist paper towel until ready to use. Fill the center of the wrapper with two tsp of filling. Moisten the edges with water; fold the other side corners of the filling together and press to cover. Rep this procedure with the remaining wrappers and filling.
- In batches, place the wontons in a single layer on an oiled tray in an air-fryer basket and spray with cooking spray. Cook for ten to twelve Mins, or until golden brown and crisp.
- As a result, place the strawberries in a food processor, cover, and purée until smooth. Combine sugar and cornstarch in a pot. In a separate bowl, purée the strawberries. Bring to a boil, then cook and stir for two Mins, or until the sauce has thickened. If desired, drain the mixture, preserve the sauce, and discard the seeds. Drizzle the confectioners' sugar and cinnamon over the wontons. Serve it with a dipping sauce.

Nutrition Value

Calories: 251 Kcal, Carb: 24.1 g, Protein: 17.4 g, Fat: 18.2 g
Storage Suggestion: You can store it in the refrigerator for 2-3 days.

Air-Fryer Apple Fritters

Prep Time: 5 Mins, Cook Time: 8 Mins, Servings: 15, Serving Size: 2

Ingredients

- Cooking spray
- All-purpose flour 1-1/2 c
- Sugar ¼ cup
- Ground cinnamon 1-1/2 tsp
- Salt 1/2 tsp
- Milk 2/3 cup
- Baking powder 2 tsp
- Eggs 2 large
- Lemon juice 1 tbsp
- Divided vanilla extract 1-1/2 tsp
- Peeled & chopped Honeycrisp apples two
- Butter ¼ cup
- Confectioners' sugar 1 cup
- Milk 1 tbsp

Instructions

- The parchment should be used to line the air-fryer basket. Spray the pan with cooking spray. Preheat the air fryer to 410 degrees.
- Combine the sugar, baking powder, flour, cinnamon, and salt in a mixing bowl. Whisk together the eggs, milk, lemon juice, and 1 tsp of vanilla essence. Apples should be folded in.
- In batches, drop ¼ cup of dough into the air-fryer basket. Cooking spray should be used. Cook for five to six Mins, or until the color turns golden brown. Turn the fritters and air-fry for 1 to 2 Mins, or until golden brown.
- In a medium-high-heat pot, melt the butter. Cook for five Mins, or until the butter starts to brown and froth. Remove it from the fire and allow it to cool somewhat. 1 tbsp milk, confectioners' sugar, and any remaining vanilla essence should be stirred into the browned butter until smooth. Sprinkle on fritters just before serving.

Nutrition Value
Calories: 216 Kcal, Carb: 34 g, Protein: 10.1 g, Fat: 8.5 g
Storage Suggestion: You can store it in the refrigerator for 1-2 days.

Air-Fryer Carrot Coffee Cake

Prep Time: 20 Mins, Cook Time: 35 mins, Servings: 6, Serving Size: 1

Ingredients

- Lightly beaten egg one large
- Buttermilk 1/2 cup
- Sugar1/3 cup + sugar 2 tbsp
- Canola oil 3 tbsp
- Dark brown sugar 2 tbsp
- grated orange zest 1 tsp
- Vanilla extract 1 tsp
- All-purpose flour 2/3 cup
- Wheat flour (white whole)1/3 cup
- Baking powder 1 tsp
- Pumpkin pie spice 2 tsp
- Baking soda ¼ tsp
- Salt ¼ tsp
- Shredded carrots 1 cup
- Dried cranberries ¼ cup
- Toasted chopped walnuts 1/3 cup.

Instructions

- Preheat the air fryer at 350 deg F, then Oil & flour in a 6" round frying pan. Stir together the egg, sugar, buttermilk, oil, orange zest, vanilla, and brown sugar in a mixing dish. Combine baking soda, flours, baking powder, 1 tsp pie pumpkin spice, and salt in a separate bowl. Slowly incorporate into the egg mixture. Combine the carrots & dried cranberries in a mixing bowl. Place in the pan that has been prepared.
- Combine walnuts, the remaining 1 tsp pumpkin spice, and the remaining two tbsp sugar in a mixing bowl. Drizzle over the batter in a layer. Place the pan within the air fryer basket with care.
- Cook for 35 to 40 Mins unless the toothpick inserted comes out clear. If the top becomes too black, cover it tightly with foil and chill it in the pan for 10 Mins before removing it from the pan. Warm the dish before serving.

Nutrition Value
Calories: 142 Kcal, Carb: 23 g, Protein: 10.2 g, Fat: 8.5 g
Storage Suggestion: You can store it in the refrigerator for 4-5 days.

French Toast Cups with Raspberries (Air-fryer)

Prep Time: 10 Mins, Cook Time: 20 mins, Servings: 2, Serving Size: 1

Ingredients

- (Cut into 1/2-inch cubes) Italian bread two slices.
- Fresh/frozen raspberries 1/2 cup
- Cream cheese 2 ounces
- Eggs 2 large
- Milk 1/2 cup
- Maple syrup 1 tbsp

Raspberry syrup

- Cornstarch 2 tsp
- Water 1/3 cup
- Fresh/frozen raspberries 2 cups
- Lemon juice 1 tbsp
- Maple syrup 1 tbsp
- Grated lemon zest 1/2 tsp

Instructions

- Between two oiled custard cups, split half bread pieces (8-oz). Cream cheese and raspberries are sprinkled on top. Top with the bread that was left over. Whisk together the milk, syrup, and eggs; pour over the bread. Refrigerate for one hr after covering.
- Preheat the air fryer to 325 degrees. In an air-fryer basket, place custard cups on the tray. Cook for 12 to 15 Mins, or until golden brown and puffy.
- As a result, whisk together the water and cornstarch until smooth in a saucepan. Bring 1.5 cup raspberries, syrup, lemon zest, and lemon juice to a simmer; reduce heat to low. Cook and stir for two Mins, or until the sauce has thickened. Remove the seeds and strain the liquid; refrigerate it slightly.
- Stir together the remaining 1/2 cup berries and the syrup in a separate bowl. If desired, drink cinnamon on the French toast cups; serve with the syrup.

Nutrition Value
Calories: 127 Kcal, Carb: 17.2 g, Protein: 8.9 g, Fat: 6.7 g
Storage Suggestion: You can store it in the refrigerator for 8-10 days.

Chapter 18: Vegetarian Recipes

Air Fryer Simple Grilled American Cheese Sandwich

Prep Time: 5 Mins, Cook Time: 8 mins, Servings: 1, Serving Size: 1

Ingredients
- Sandwich Bread 2 slices
- Cheddar Cheese 2-3 slices
- Butter or Mayonnaise 2 tsp

Instructions
- Place the cheese in the middle of both bread pieces and the butter on the exterior.
- Cook for 8 Mins at 370 degrees in an air fryer. Halfway through, flip the coin.

Nutrition Value
Calories: 251 Kcal, Carb: 39.2 g, Protein: 12.2 g, Fat: 13.1 g
Storage Suggestion: You can store it in the refrigerator for 2-3 days.

Air Fryer Simply Seasoned Chickpeas

Prep Time: 10 Mins, Cook Time: 16 mins, Servings: 2, Serving Size: 2

Ingredients
- Garbanzo beans drained 1 16-ounce can.
- Olive oil 1 tbsp
- Garlic powder ½ tsp
- Salt & pepper

Instructions
- Drain the Garbanzo beans from the can.
- Combine the garbanzo beans, garlic powder, salt, olive oil, and pepper in a medium mixing bowl and toss to coat.
- Do not preheat the oven. Simply place it in an air fryer basket. Preheat oven to 400°F and bake for 8 Mins. Remove the basket from the air fryer, toss gently, and cook for another 8 Mins at 400 degrees.
- Remove the fries from the fryer and set them aside to cool. Serve right away, or store in an airtight jar for up to a week.

Nutrition Value
Calories: 198 Kcal, Carb: 27.4 g, Protein: 7.3 g, Fat: 11.8 g
Storage Suggestion: You can store it in the refrigerator for 4-5 days.

Air Fryer Tacos

Prep Time: 15 Mins, Cook Time: 30 mins, Servings: 6, Serving Size: 2

Ingredients
- Small russet potatoes 4-5 (about 1 lb)
- Mini corn tortillas 24
- Grapeseed oil 2 tbsp, or preferred oil
- Ground cumin ½ tsp
- Smoked paprika ½ tsp (*optional)
- Granulated garlic ½ tsp
- Salt & pepper
- Long toothpicks 24

Instructions
- Place the potatoes in a medium/large saucepan and fill with cold water. Bring to a boil over high heat, then reduce to medium-high heat and simmer for about 15-20 Mins. Drain and cool slightly before peeling.
- Toss the peeled potatoes with the spices in a large mixing dish. Mash until the mixture is smooth. The lumps are just right. Season with salt and pepper to taste and add more if required. (If the mash is too dry to taste, add a couple of tbsp of non-dairy milk, sour cream, or butter.)
- In a large pan, heat the tortillas until they are warm and malleable. As the remaining tortillas heat up, cover with a cloth.
- 1 tbsp mash, spread over half of a tortilla to seal the top, fold the paper firmly and thread a toothpick through it.
- Brush each side of the tacos lightly with oil. Often, a little coat of oil will be enough. Please place them in the basket of a standing air fryer (stagger them, so there is a little room for each). Cook for 12-15 Mins at 390°F until crispy.

Nutrition Value
Calories: 147 Kcal, Carb: 23.2 g, Protein: 10.6 g, Fat: 5.3 g
Storage Suggestion: You can store it in the refrigerator for 5-6 days.

Weight Watchers Air Fryer Mozzarella Cheese Sticks

Prep Time: 5 Mins, Cook Time: 10 mins, Servings: 2, Serving Size: 2

Ingredients
- Sargento Light String Cheese 1 package
- Italian breadcrumbs 1 cup
- Egg 1
- Flour 1/2 cup
- Marinara sauce 1 cup (for dipping, optional)
- Salt & pepper

Instructions
- In a mixing dish, season the breadcrumbs with salt and pepper.
- In one bowl, combine flour, breadcrumbs, and eggs; in another bowl, combine flour, breadcrumbs, and eggs.
- Dip the cheese sticks in flour, then in the egg and breadcrumbs.
- Freeze cheese sticks for about an hr if you want them to firm up.
- Preheat the Air Fryer to 400°F. Add the cheese sticks to the fryer.
- Cook for 4 Mins before flipping. Cook for a further 4 Mins.

Nutrition Value
Calories: 174 Kcal, Carb: 19.2 g, Protein: 6.9 g, Fat: 3.3 g
Storage Suggestion: You can store it in the refrigerator for 2-3 days.

Zucchini-Parmesan Chips

Prep Time: 10 Mins, Cook Time: 15 mins, Servings: 2, Serving Size: 1

Ingredients
- Zucchini 2 medium
- Salt 1 tbsp
- Italian-seasoned Breadcrumbs ½ cup
- Freshly grated Parmesan cheese ½ cup
- Egg 1 large, beaten.
- Cooking spray Canola oil
- Kosher salt & black pepper freshly ground.

Instructions
- Slice the zucchini into little discs using a mandolin slicer or as thinly as possible with a knife. Toss the zucchini slices with the salt and soak in a colander for 30 Mins. Scrub well with cold water to remove any excess salt. After that, place the zucchini slices on paper towels and pat them dry.
- In a small dish, combine the breadcrumbs and Parmesan cheese.
- Dip the zucchini slices in the egg, then coat them fully with breadcrumbs on both sides. Spray both sides with canola oil.
- In the air fryer basket, place the slices. Make sure they don't cross each other. At 3900 F, fry air in batches until crispy, about 10 Mins. Season with salt and pepper to taste.

Nutrition Value
Calories: 203 Kcal, Carb: 29.3 g, Protein: 4.6 g, Fat: 8.5 g
Storage Suggestion: You can store it in the refrigerator for 6-7 days.

Breakfast Puffed Egg Tarts

Prep Time: 10 Mins, Cook Time: 20 mins, Servings: 4, Serving Size: 2

Ingredients
- All-purpose flour
- Frozen puff pastry 1 sheet half a 17.3-oz/490 grams package, thawed.
- Shredded cheese 3/4 cup such as Gruyère, Monterey Jack or Cheddar, divided
- Eggs 4 large
- Minced fresh parsley/chives 1 tbsp optional.

Instructions
- 390 degrees Fahrenheit Preheat the air fryer to 350°F.
- On a lightly floured surface, unfold the pastry sheet. Cut into four squares.
- Place two squares in the air fryer basket, spacing them apart. Air-fry for 10 Mins, or until the pastry is medium golden brown.
- Using a metal spoon, push each square center down to make an indentation in the basket. 3 tbsp cheese in each depression, then carefully break the egg in the center of each croissant.
- Air-fry for 7-11 Mins, or until the eggs are done to your liking. Allow cooling for 5 Mins on a wire rack over waxed paper. Sprinkle with half of the parsley if desired. Serve it with a side of sugar.
- Rep steps 2-4 with the left pastry squares, eggs, cheese, and parsley.

Nutrition Value
Calories: 272 Kcal, Carb: 42.6 g, Protein: 13.6 g, Fat: 9.2 g
Storage Suggestion: You can store it in the refrigerator for 3-4 days.

Air Fryer Mac and Cheese

Prep Time: 15 Mins, Cook Time: 20 mins, Servings: 4, Serving Size: 2

Ingredients
- Elbow macaroni 1 ½ cup
- Water 1 cup
- Heavy cream ½ cup
- Sharp cheddar cheese 8 oz shredded & separated.
- Dry mustard 1 tsp
- Kosher salt ½ tsp
- Black pepper ½ tsp
- Garlic powder ¼ tsp

Instructions
- Combine the elbow macaroni, heavy cream, water, 34% cheese, dry mustard, black pepper, kosher salt, and garlic powder in a 7" pan big enough to hold all ingredients. To combine the ingredients, stir them together.
- Preheat the Air Fryer to 360 degrees Fahrenheit and place it in the Air Fryer basket. Set the timer for 18-20 Mins and start the Air Fryer. Open the Air Fryer basket halfway through cooking and toss in the remaining cheese. Close it and continue to cook.
- When the cooking is finished, remove the lid from the Air Fryer and mix in the macaroni and cheese. Remove the pan from the basket and set it aside to cool for 5-10 Mins. The mac & cheese may thicken as it cools. Serve and have fun.

Nutrition Value
Calories: 280 Kcal, Carb: 23.9 g, Protein: 10.2 g, Fat: 15.3 g
Storage Suggestion: You can store it in the refrigerator for 4-5 days.

Air Fryer Sweet Potato with Hot Honey Butter

Prep Time: 20 Mins, Cook Time: 35 mins, Servings: 2, Serving Size: 1

Ingredients
- Sweet potatoes 1-4 scrubbed clean & patted dry.
- Oil 1 tsp
- Honey Butter
- Unsalted butter 4 Tbsp
- Honey 1 Tbsp
- Hot sauce 2 tsp
- Salt ¼ tsp

Instructions
- Coat the sweet potatoes with oil and place them in the air fryer basket.
- Cook at 400 degrees Fahrenheit for 35-40 Mins, or until the sweet potatoes are soft on the interior.

Honey Butter
- While the sweet potatoes are cooking, whisk the butter, spicy sauce, honey, and salt in a mixing bowl until smooth.

- Break the sweet potato apart, fluff the insides slightly, and then top with butter.

Nutrition Value
Calories: 238 Kcal, Carb: 25.8 g, Protein: 15.3 g, Fat: 3.2 g
Storage Suggestion: You can store it in the refrigerator for 1-2 days.

Air Fryer Parmesan Truffle Oil Fries

Prep Time: 20 Mins, Cook Time: 40 mins, Servings: 6, Serving Size: 2

Ingredients
- Russet potatoes 3 large peeled & cut lengthwise.
- White truffle oil 2 tbsp
- Parmesan shredded 2 tbsp
- Paprika 1 tsp
- Salt & pepper
- Parsley chopped 1 tbsp

Instructions
- In a large mixing bowl, layer the sliced potatoes with cold water.
- Allow the potatoes to soak in the water for at least 30 Mins, preferably an hr.
- Scatter the fries on a level surface and thoroughly dry them with paper towels. Season them with salt, pepper, and 1 tbsp of white truffle oil.
- Half fries should be added to the Air Fryer basket. Reduce the heat to 380 degrees Fahrenheit and cook for 15-20 Mins. Set a 10-Min timer and shake the basket once at the 10-Min mark.
- Allow more time to cook the fries if you want them to be crispier. If the fries are crisp before 15 Mins, remove them.
- Start cooking the second half as soon as the first half is done.
- Add the remaining truffle oil and parmesan to the fries as soon as they come out of the Air Fryer.
- On top, shredded parsley. Serve.

Nutrition Value
Calories: 256 Kcal, Carb: 47.3 g, Protein: 4 g, Fat: 1.2 g
Storage Suggestion: You can store it in the refrigerator for 5-6 days.

Easy Air Fryer Crispy Crunchy Sweet Potato Fries

Prep Time: 20 Mins, Cook Time: 25 mins, Servings: 6, Serving Size: 1

Ingredients
- Sweet potatoes 2 large peeled & cut lengthwise.
- Cornstarch 1 1/2 tbsp
- Paprika 2 tsp
- Garlic powder 2 tsp
- Salt & pepper
- Olive oil 1 tbsp

Instructions
- Sweet potatoes are sliced and put in a large dish with cold water. Allow the sweet potatoes to soak in the water for an hr.
- Remove the sweet potatoes from the water and pat them dry. Cornstarch should be sprinkled all over it.
- Sprinkle with paprika, salt, garlic powder, and pepper.
- Place the fries in the air fryer basket and sprinkle them with olive oil. Also, don't overcrowd the basket. Cook in batches as necessary. If there are white areas of cornstarch visible on the fries, spray the area with olive oil.
- Preheat the oven to 380 degrees Fahrenheit and cook for 23 to 25 Mins. Set a 10-Min timer, stop at the 10-Min mark, and shake the basket once. If you want crispy fries, cook them longer and check them often.
- Serve.

Nutrition Value
Calories: 210 Kcal, Carb: 28.9 g, Protein: 10.3 g, Fat: 12.3 g
Storage Suggestion: You can store it in the refrigerator for 3-4 days.

Air Fryer Sweet Potato Hash

Prep Time: 20 Mins, Cook Time: 15 mins, Servings: 6, Serving Size: 2

Ingredients
- Sweet potato 2 large, in small cubes
- Bacon 2 slices, in small pieces
- Olive oil 2 tbsp
- Smoked paprika 1 tbsp
- Sea salt 1 tsp
- Ground black pepper 1 tsp
- Dried dill weed 1 tsp

Instructions
- Preheat the air fryer oven to 400 degrees F. Prepare the air fryer by preheating it.
- Whisk together the sweet potato, bacon, paprika, salt, pepper, olive oil, and dill in a large mixing bowl. Place the mixture in a hot air fryer. Cook for 12 to 16 Mins. After 10 Mins, check and stir until crispy and golden, then every 3 Mins.

Nutrition Value
Calories: 104 Kcal, Carb: 12.2 g, Protein: 2 g, Fat: 1 g
Storage Suggestion: You can store it in the refrigerator for 3-4 days.

Crispy Avocado Fries

Prep Time: 5 Mins, Cook Time: 10 mins, Servings 4, Serving Size: 2

Ingredients
- Panko breadcrumbs 1 cup
- Garlic powder 1 tsp
- Paprika 1 tsp
- All-purpose flour 1 cup
- Eggs 2 large
- Avocados 2, sliced.
- For serving Ranch (optional)

Instructions
- Combine the panko, garlic powder, and paprika in a mixing bowl. Place the flour in a separate bowl, and then beat the eggs in a shallow bowl.
- Avocado slices are dipped in flour. One at a time, coat with egg, then Panko mixture till completely covered.
- Cook for 10 Mins at 400 degrees in an air fryer.
- If desired, serve with ranch dressing.

Nutrition Value

Calories: 115 Kcal, Carb: 16.4 g, Protein: 5 g, Fat: 3.2 g
Storage Suggestion: You can store it in the refrigerator for 5-6 days.

Bob Harper's Air-Fried French Fries

Prep Time: 10 Mins, Cook Time: 25 mins, Servings: 4, Serving Size: 2

Ingredients

- Fingerling potatoes 1 lb.
- Olive oil 1 tbsp or one (5- to 6-sec) spray olive oil cooking spray
- Salt & pepper

Instructions

- Preheat your air fryer at 390° F.
- Boil your potatoes for around 10 mins. Drain and set aside to cool. Season with salt and pepper and drizzle using olive oil. Cut in half lengthwise.
- In the air fryer, cook potatoes for 12 to 15 Mins. Open the fryer, shake the potatoes, and return them to the air fryer for another 10 to 12 Mins.

Nutrition Value

Calories: 67 Kcal, Carb: 8 g, Protein: 2.8 g, Fat: 1.4 g
Storage Suggestion: You can store it in the refrigerator for 2-3 days.

Air-Fryer Pickles

Prep Time: 10 Mins, Cook Time: 15 mins, Servings: 32, Serving Size: 2

Ingredients

- Dill pickle slices 32
- All-purpose flour 1/2 cup
- Salt 1/2 tsp
- Eggs 3 large, lightly beaten.
- Dill pickle juice 2 tbsp
- Cayenne pepper 1/2 tsp
- Garlic powder 1/2 tsp
- Panko breadcrumbs 2 cups
- Snipped fresh dill 2 tbsp
- Cooking spray
- Optional ranch salad dressing

Instructions

- Preheat the air fryer oven to 400 degrees Fahrenheit. Allow the pickles to sit on the paper towel for about 15 Mins, or until the liquid has almost completely evaporated.
- In a separate bowl, combine the flour and salt. Whisk together the eggs, cayenne, pickle juice, and garlic powder in a separate small bowl. Combine the panko and dill in a third bowl.
- Shake off the excess flour after dipping the pickles in the flour mixture on both sides. Dip in the egg mixture, then pat in the crumb mixture to help the coating adhere. In batches, place pickles on an oiled tray in the air-fryer basket. Cook for 7-10 Mins, or until golden and crispy. Turn the pickles sprinkle with cooking oil spray. Cook for another 7-10 Mins, or until crispy and golden brown. Serve right away. If desired, top with ranch dressing.

Nutrition Value

Calories: 79 Kcal, Carb: 11.3 g, Protein: 3.4 g, Fat: 1.9 g
Storage Suggestion: You can store it in the refrigerator for 4-5 days.

Tostones (twice air-fried plantains)

Prep Time: 10 Mins, Cook Time: 20 mins, Servings: 2, Serving Size: 1

Ingredients

- Green plantain 1 large, ends trimmed & peeled (6 oz after)
- Water 1 cup
- Olive oil spray
- Kosher salt 1 tsp
- Garlic powder ¾ tsp

Instructions

- Cut the plantain into 1-inch pieces for a total of 8 pieces.
- Combine the water, garlic powder, and salt in a mixing dish.
- Preheat the air fryer to 400 degrees Fahrenheit.
- When ready, do it in two batches, drizzle with olive oil, sprinkle with plantain, and fry for 6 Mins.
- When they're heated, remove them from the air fryer and flatten them with a tostonera/jar bottom/measuring cup.
- Dip them in seasoned water and set them aside.
- Preheat the air fryer to 400°F and cook the plantains in batches for 5 Minutes, brushing both sides with olive oil.
- When they're finished, give them another spray of oil and season with salt. Eat as soon as possible.

Nutrition Value

Calories: 154 Kcal, Carb: 15.6 g, Protein: 4 g, Fat: 2.6 g
Storage Suggestion: You can store it in the refrigerator for 5-6 days.

Salad Green

Prep Time: 15 Mins, Cook Time: 10 Mins, Servings: 8, Serving Size: 2

Ingredients

- Cucumber: 2 cups, diced
- One Romaine heart
- Green olives: 1/2 cup, chopped
- Leafy lettuce: 5 cups
- Red pepper flakes: ¼ tsp
- Cherry tomatoes: 1/2 cup

Instructions

- All veggies should be chopped and diced. Combine the two.
- Season with kosher salt and pepper, as well as chili flakes.
- If desired, drizzle with any Italian dressing.
- Serve with any lean protein of your choice.

Nutrition Value

Calories: 49 Kcal, Carb: 2.2 g, Protein: 1.5 g, Fat: 7 g
Storage Suggestion: You can store it in the refrigerator for 3-4 days.

Ranch Seasoned Air Fryer Chickpeas

Prep Time: 5 Mins, Cook Time: 17 Mins, Servings: 8, Serving Size: 2

Ingredients
- Lemon juice: 1 tbsp
- One can of chickpea (not rinsed but drained) saves the liquid from the can
- Olive oil: 1 tbsp
- Garlic powder: 2 tsp
- Onion powder: 2 tsp
- Dried dill: 4 tsp
- Sea salt: ¾ tsp

Instructions
- Add one tbsp of chickpea liquid to a mixing bowl. At 400 degrees F, air fried for 12 Mins.
- Then, combine the fried chickpeas, olive oil, lemon juice, onion powder, dill, salt, and garlic powder in a mixing bowl, and toss well to coat the chickpeas.
- Return the chickpeas to the air fryer and cook for another five Mins at 350°F.
- Serve warm or chilled.

Nutrition Value
Calories: 113.2 Kcal, Carb: 9.1 g, Protein: 16 g, Fat: 2 g

Storage Suggestion: You can store it in the refrigerator for 3-4 days.

Air Fryer Spanakopita Bites

Prep Time: 10 Mins, Cook Time: 15 Mins, Servings: 4, Serving Size: 2

Ingredients
- 4 sheets phyllo dough
- Baby spinach leaves: 2 cups
- Grated Parmesan cheese: 2 tbsp
- Low-fat cottage cheese: ¼ cup
- Dried oregano: 1 tsp
- Feta cheese: 6 tbsp crumbled
- Water: 2 tbsp
- One egg white only
- Lemon zest: 1 tsp
- Cayenne pepper: 1/8 tsp
- Olive oil: 1 tbsp
- Kosher salt and freshly ground black pepper: ¼ tsp, each

Instructions
- Add water and spinach to a saucepan over high heat and simmer until wilted.
- Drain it and set it aside to cool for 10 Mins. Excess moisture should be squeezed out.
- Cottage cheese, Parmesan cheese, oregano, salt, cayenne pepper, egg white, freshly crushed black pepper, feta cheese, spinach, and zest should all be combined in a mixing bowl. It may be mixed well or processed in a food processor.
- On a level surface, place one phyllo sheet. Oil is sprayed over the surface. Spray the second layer of phyllo on top of the first. Add a total of four oiled sheets to the mix.
- From the four greased sheets, cut 16 strips. Fill one strip with one tbsp of filling. It should be rolled around the filling.
- Using a spray bottle, coat the air fryer basket with oil. Spray the basket with oil and place eight bites in it. Cook for 12 Mins at 375°F until golden brown and crispy. Halfway through, flip the page.
- Serve with a leaner protein.

Nutrition Value
Calories: 82 Kcal, Carb: 7 g, Protein: 4 g, Fat: 4 g

Storage Suggestion: You can store it in the refrigerator for 3-4 days.

Chapter 19: Vegan Recipes

Pumpkin Muffins

Prep Time: 15 Mins, Cook Time: 20 Mins, Servings: 20, Serving Size: 2

Ingredients
- 1 tsp powdered baking soda
- 2 eggs
- 1 tsp bicarbonate of soda
- 2 tsp ground cinnamon
- 1 tsp ground nutmeg
- 1 lb of sugar
- 12 cups of flour
- flaxseed meal (four tbsp)
- 1 cup pureed pumpkin
- 12 cup melted butter (Vegan)

Instructions
- Combine the butter, pumpkin puree, and egg in a small mixing dish and mix well.
- In a large mixing bowl, combine flour, flaxseed meal, nutmeg, baking soda, sugar, baking powder, and cinnamon.
- Preheat the oven to 350°F and bake the muffins in a muffin tin that fits your fryer for 15 Mins.
- As a snack, serve the muffins cold. Have a blast!

Nutrition Value
Calories: 205 Kcal, Carb: 25.3 g, Protein: 3.4 g, Fat: 7 g

Storage Suggestion: You can store it in the refrigerator for 1-2 days.

Apple Snack from Mexico

Prep Time: 15 Mins, Cook Time: 10 Mins, Servings: 5, Serving Size: 2

Ingredients
- 1 cup caramel sauce (clean)
- 1 cup chocolate chips (dark)
- 12 cup chopped pecans
- 1 tbsp lemon juice
- 6 broad apples, peeled, cored, and cubed

Instructions
- Combine the apples and lemon juice in a small bowl, whisk well, and transfer to an air fryer-safe pan.
- Toss in the pecans and chocolate chips, sprinkle with caramel sauce, mix well, and steam for about 5 Mins at 320°F in the fryer.
- Rotate gently, then break into tiny bowls and serve as a snack right away. Have a blast!

Nutrition Value
Calories: 165 Kcal, Carb: 20.2 g, Protein: 8 g, Fat: 12 g

Storage Suggestion: You can store it in the refrigerator for 3-4 days.

Potato Compote

Prep Time: 15 Mins, Cook Time: 15 Mins, Servings: 15, Serving Size: 3

Ingredients
- White pepper and a pinch of salt
- 4 tbsp of Water
- 1 tsp cumin powder
- 6 minced garlic cloves
- 3 tbsp extra virgin olive oil
- 4 tbsp lemon juice
- 12 cup tahini
- 2 cups peeled and chopped sweet potatoes
- 20 ounces drained canned garbanzo beans

Instructions
- Cook the potatoes for 15 Mins at 360 degrees F in the basket of your air fryer. Allow them to cool before peeling and putting them in your food processor. Pitching, as well as bowling
- Combine the sesame paste, ginger, beans, lemon juice, cumin, water, and oil in a mixing dish.
- Season with salt and pepper, then divide into small bowls and serve. Have a blast!

Nutrition Value
Calories: 127 Kcal, Carb: 8.6 g, Protein: 5.3 g, Fat: 3 g

Storage Suggestion: You can store it in the refrigerator for 6-7 days.

Banana Snack

Prep Time: 15 Mins, Cook Time: 10 Mins, Servings: 10, Serving Size: 2

Ingredients
- 2 tsp vegetable oil
- 2 peeled and sliced bananas (16 bits each)
- 1 cup cocoa powder
- 1 lb peanut butter
- Crust for 18 baking cups

Instructions
- Place the chocolate chips and heat over medium heat in a small jar, constantly stirring until the chocolate melts. Remove from the heat.
- Stir together the peanut butter and coconut oil in a cup.
- Combine 1 tsp chocolate mix, 1 slice banana, and 1 tsp butter mix in a cup.
- Repeat with the remaining cups, putting them all in a dish that fits your air fryer, frying for 5 Mins at 320 degrees F, then chilling until ready to serve as a snack. Have a blast!

Nutrition Value
Calories: 148 Kcal, Carb: 13.2 g, Protein: 7.9 g, Fat: 3.2 g

Storage Suggestion: You can store it in the refrigerator for 7-8 days.

Apple Chips

Prep Time: 15 Mins, Cook Time: 15 Mins, Servings: 4, Serving Size: 2

Ingredients
- 2 tsp white sugar
- 1 tsp powdered cinnamon
- a grain of salt
- 2 cored and sliced apples

Instructions
- Combine the salt, apple slices, sugar, and cinnamon in a saucepan and mix thoroughly. Cook for around 10 Mins at 390 degrees F, flipping once in the basket of your air fryer.
- Cut the bowls of apple chips in half to serve as a party snack. Have a blast!

Nutrition Value
Calories: 79 Kcal, Carb: 6.1 g, Protein: 4.7 g, Fat: 2.4 g
Storage Suggestion: You can store it in the refrigerator for 5-6 days.

Sweet Popcorn

Prep Time: 10 Mins, Cook Time:15 Mins, Servings: 6, Serving Size: 2

Ingredients
- 3 tbsp brown sugar
- 3 and 12 tbsp butter
- 4 tbsp corn kernels

Instructions
- Cook the corn kernels for approximately 6 Mins at 400 degrees F in an air fryer pan. Place in a serving dish, sprinkle and put away for the time being.
- On low heat, melt the butter on a dish, then add the sugar and whisk until it is completely dissolved.
- Toss in the popcorn, turn to thoroughly cover, remove from the heat, and sprinkle again on the dish.
- Allow chilling until ready to eat, divide into bowls and serve as a snack or lunch. Have a blast!

Nutrition Value
Calories: 94 Kcal, Carb: 17.3 g, Protein: 5.6 g, Fat: 8.9 g
Storage Suggestion: You can store it in the refrigerator for 4-5 days.

Chickpeas Snack

Prep Time: 12 Mins, Cook Time: 12 Mins, Servings: 6, Serving Size: 2

Ingredients
- Season with salt and black pepper to taste.
- 2 tsp of paprika (smoked)
- 2 tbsp extra virgin olive oil
- 1 tsp cumin powder
- 17 ounces drained canned chickpeas

Instructions
- Toss the chickpeas in a pan with the cumin, oil, salt, paprika, and pepper to coat, then transfer to the fryer basket and cook at 390°F for approximately 10 Mins.

- Serve as a snack by cutting into tiny bowls. Have a blast!

Nutrition Value
Calories: 68 Kcal, Carb: 14.2 g, Protein: 7.3 g, Fat: 3.8 g
Storage Suggestion: You can store it in the refrigerator for 5-6 days.

Crispy Radish Chips

Prep Time: 15 Mins, Cook Time:15 Mins, Servings: 5, Serving Size: 2

Ingredients
- 2 tbsp chopped chives
- Season with salt and black pepper to taste.
- 18 sliced radishes
- Spray for cooking

Instructions
- Arrange radish slices in the basket of your air fryer, drizzle with cooking oil, season to taste with salt and black pepper, and cook for about 10 Mins at 350 degrees F, flipping midway through.
- Serve in dishes with a sprinkling of chives on top. Have a blast!

Nutrition Value
Calories: 102 Kcal, Carb: 14.3 g, Protein: 9.7 g, Fat: 7.1 g
Storage Suggestion: You can store it in the refrigerator for 3-4 days.

Zucchini Cakes

Prep Time: 15 Mins, Cook Time:15 Mins, Servings: 5, Serving Size: 2

Ingredients
- 4 grated zucchinis
- 4 minced garlic cloves
- 2 chopped yellow onions
- Season with salt and black pepper to taste.
- 1 cup flour (whole wheat)
- 2 eggs
- 1 cup chopped dill
- Spray for cooking

Instructions
- Combine zucchini, onion, garlic, salt, flour, egg, pepper, and dill in a small mixing bowl and whisk well. Form tiny patties out of the mixture, coat with cooking spray,

put on an air fryer pan, and cook for 6 Mins on each side at 370 degrees F.
- Serve them as soon as possible as a snack. Have a blast!

Nutrition Value
Calories: 47 Kcal, Carb: 5 g, Protein: 2 g, Fat: 1.4 g
Storage Suggestion: You can store it in the refrigerator for 5-6 days.

Banana Chips

Prep Time: 15 Mins, Cook Time: 20 Mins, Servings: 5, Serving Size: 2

Ingredients
- 2 tsp extra virgin olive oil
- 1 tsp masala chat
- 1 tsp powdered turmeric
- a grain of salt
- 6 peeled and cut bananas

Instructions
- Combine banana slices, turmeric, salt, chat masala, and oil in a small bowl; stir well and let aside for about 10 Mins.
- Place banana slices in an air fryer preheated to 360 degrees F and cook for 15 Mins, turning once.
- As a light snack, serve. Have a blast!

Nutrition Value
Calories: 64 Kcal, Carb: 14.3 g, Protein: 9.7 g, Fat: 15.3 g
Storage Suggestion: You can store it in the refrigerator for 5-6 days.

Zucchini Chips

Prep Time: 15 Mins, Cook Time: 1 hr and 20 Mins, Servings: 8, Serving Size: 2

Ingredients
- 4 tbsp of balsamic vinaigrette
- 4 tbsp of extra virgin olive oil
- Season with salt and black pepper to taste.
- 6 thinly sliced zucchinis

Instructions
- Whisk together the salt, vinegar, oil, and pepper in a small cup.
- In your air fryer, toss the zucchini slices in the batter, coat

thoroughly, and cook for 1 hr at 200 degrees F.
- As a snack, serve chilled zucchini chips. Have a blast!

Nutrition Value
Calories: 74 Kcal, Carb: 17.2 g, Protein: 8.1 g, Fat: 4.8 g
Storage Suggestion: You can store it in the refrigerator for 4-5 days.

Grapefruit, Broiled in the Air Fryer

Prep Time: 10 Mins, Cook Time: 16 Mins, Servings: 2, Serving Size: 2

Ingredients
- 1 refrigerated red grapefruit
- 1 tbsp butter that has been softened
- 1 tbsp Brown sugar is a type of sugar that is used
- 2 tbsp Brown sugar is a type of sugar that is used
- Foil made of aluminum
- 12 tsp Cinnamon powder

Instructions
- Preheat your air fryer to 400°F (200°C) before using it.
- Cut the grapefruit in half crosswise and slice a tiny sliver from the bottom of each side if it isn't resting flat. Cut the grapefruit along the outer edge and between each segment using a sharp paring knife to make it easier to consume before it's cooked.
- 1 tbsp melted butter 1 tbsp brown sugar in a small bowl. Fill each half of a grapefruit with the mixture. The rest of the brown sugar should be sprinkled on top.
- Place each grapefruit half on two 5-inch pieces of Al foil and fold up the edges to catch any juices. Place in the basket of an air fryer.
- The sugar mixture should be bubbling after 6–7 Mins in the air fryer. Sprinkle the fruit with cinnamon until ready to serve.

Nutrition Value
Calories: 105 Kcal, Carb: 18.3 g, Protein: 10.4 g, Fat: 8.2 g
Storage Suggestion: You can store it in the refrigerator for 3-4 days.

Apples with Brown Sugar and Pecans Roasted

Prep Time: 10Mins, Cook Time: 20 Mins, Servings: 2, Serving Size: 2

Ingredients
- 2 tbsp pecans, coarsely chopped
- 1 tbsp sugar (brown)
- 1 tbsp flour (all-purpose)
- 14 tbsp apple pie seasoning
- 2 mid apples, peeled and cored, cut into small half moons
- 1 tbsp melted butter

Instructions
- Preheat to 360°F (180°C) before using.
- In a small mixing bowl, mix the sugar, flour, pecans, and apple pie powder. Toss apple wedges with butter in a mid mixing dish and toss to coat. Lay down the apples in a single layer in the air fryer basket and top with the pecan mixture.
- In a preheated air fryer, cook until apples are soft, about 11 to 16 Mins.

Nutrition Value
Calories: 61 Kcal, Carb: 13.5 g, Protein: 6.3 g, Fat: 10.8 g
Storage Suggestion: You can store it in the refrigerator for 2-3 days.

Air Fryer Cinnamon-Sugar Doughnuts

Prep Time: 10 Mins, Cook Time:10 Mins, Servings: 8, Serving Size: 2

Ingredients
- 14 cup melted butter
- 12 cup sugar (white)
- a quarter cup of brown sugar
- 1 tbsp cinnamon powder
- 14 tsp nutmeg powder (Optional)
- 16.3 ounces package flaky biscuit dough refrigerated

Instructions
- Melt the butter in a mixing bowl. Combine white sugar, brown sugar, cinnamon, and nutmeg in a separate cup.
- To make a doughnut shape, divide the biscuit dough into separate biscuits and cut out the centers using a biscuit cutter (or the bottom of a piping tip). In the air fryer basket, place the doughnuts.
- Before golden browning, bake for 4 to 6 Mins at 350 degrees F (175 degrees C). After rotating the doughnuts, cook for a further 1 to 3 Mins.
- Take the doughnuts out of the air fryer and set them aside. Dip the doughnut in melted butter (covering the top, bottom, and sides), then in the sugar-cinnamon mixture until thoroughly coated. Serve immediately.

Nutrition Value
Calories: 58 Kcal, Carb: 8 g, Protein: 2.5 g, Fat: 4.1 g
Storage Suggestion: You can store it in the refrigerator for 5-6 days.

Air Fryer Roasted Bananas

Prep Time: 2 Mins, Cook Time: 7 Mins, Servings: 1, Serving Size: 2

Ingredients
- 1 banana, sliced diagonally in 1/8" thick slices
- avocado oil (for cooking spray)

Instructions
- Line your air fryer basket with parchment paper.
- Preheat your air fryer to 375 degrees Fahrenheit (190 degrees C).
- Put banana slices in the basket, ensure they don't touch and cook in batches if feasible. Banana slices should be coated with avocado oil.
- In the air fryer, cook for 5 Mins. Remove the banana slices from the basket and turn them over gently (they will be soft). Cook for another 2 to 3 Mins, or until the banana slices have caramelized and are browning. Carefully remove from the basket.

Nutrition Value
Calories: 84 Kcal, Carb: 15.2 g, Protein: 18.5 g, Fat: 8.5 g
Storage Suggestion: You can store it in the refrigerator for 3-4 days.

Pesto Crackers

Prep Time: 15 Mins, Cook Time: 20 Mins, Servings: 5, Serving Size: 2

Ingredients
- 4 tsp unsalted butter
- 4 tbsp pesto (basil)
- 2 minced garlic cloves
- 1/2 tsp of dried basil
- a cup and a half of flour
- Season with salt and black pepper to taste.
- 1 tsp powdered baking soda

Instructions
- Combine the pepper, salt, flour, baking powder, cayenne, garlic, pesto, basil, and butter in a mixing bowl and stir until the dough is firm.
- Preheat the oven to 325 degrees F and bake the dough for 17 Mins on a prepared baking sheet that fits your air fryer.
- Allow crackers to cool before breaking and eating as a snack or meal. Have a blast!

Nutrition Value
Calories: 48 Kcal, Carb: 8.1 g, Protein: 3.8 g, Fat: 4.1 g
Storage Suggestion: You can store it in the refrigerator for 3-4 days.

Veggie Toast

Prep Time:15 Mins, Cook Time: 20 Mins, Servings: 5, Serving Size: 2

Ingredients
- 1 cup crumbled goat cheese
- 4 tbsp of softened butter
- 5 slices of bread
- 2 tbsp extra virgin olive oil
- 4 sliced green onions
- 2 chopped yellow squash
- 2 cup sliced crème mushrooms
- 2 red bell peppers, thinly sliced

Instructions
- Combine the red bell pepper, mushrooms, green onions, squash, and oil in a mixing dish. Transfer to the air fryer and cook for 10 Mins at 350 degrees F, shaking the fryer once before transferring to a bowl.
- Spread the butter on the bread pieces and cook for 5 Mins at 350 degrees F in an air fryer.
- Fill each bread slice with the vegetable mixture, sprinkle with crumbled cheese, and consume for lunch. Have a blast!

Nutrition Value
Calories: 59.3 Kcal, Carb: 5 g, Protein: 12.4 g, Fat: 2 g
Storage Suggestion: You can store it in the refrigerator for 4-5 days.

Stuffed Mushrooms

Prep Time:15 Mins, Cook Time: 25 Mins, Servings: 5, Serving Size: 2

Ingredients
- 1 tsp rosemary, finely chopped
- a third of a cup of breadcrumbs
- 2 cups broken spinach
- 7 tsp grated parmesan
- (1/2 cup) Ricotta cheese
- 2 tbsp extra virgin olive oil
- 5 Portobello mushroom caps, large

Instructions
- Brush the mushroom caps with a little oil, place them in the air fryer dish, and cook at 350 degrees F for approximately 2 Mins.
- Meanwhile, combine half of the parmesan cheese, ricotta, spinach, breadcrumbs, and rosemary in a mixing dish.
- Fill the mushrooms with the mixture, sprinkle with the remaining parmesan, and cook for approximately 10 Mins at 350 degrees F in the air fryer basket.
- Divide them onto plates and serve with a side salad of your choice for lunch. Have a blast!

Nutrition Value
Calories: 138 Kcal, Carb: 21.8 g, Protein: 13.1 g, Fat: 19.4 g
Storage Suggestion: You can store it in the refrigerator for 4-5 days.

Air Fryer Blooming Onion

Prep Time: 20 Mins, Cook Time: 30 mins, Servings: 4, Serving Size: 2

Ingredients
For the onion
- Large yellow onion 1
- Large eggs 3
- Breadcrumbs 1 cup
- Paprika 2 tsp
- Garlic powder 1 tsp
- Onion powder 1 tsp
- Kosher salt 1 tsp
- Extra-virgin olive oil 3 tbsp

For the sauce
- Kosher salt
- Mayonnaise 2/3 cup
- Ketchup 2 tbsp
- Horseradish 1 tsp
- Paprika 1/2 tsp
- Garlic powder 1/2 tsp
- Dried oregano ¼ tsp

Instructions
- Remove the onion's stem and put the onion on the flat side. Cut an inch down from the root into 12 - 16 portions, taking care not to cut all the way through. Turn the onion over and gently pull off portions to separate the petals.
- In a separate dish, whisk together 1 tbsp water and the eggs. In a separate small dish, combine the breadcrumbs and seasonings. Dip the onion in the egg wash, then dredge it in the breadcrumb mixture before coating it completely. Drizzle some oil over the onion.
- Place the onion in the air fryer basket and cook for 20 to 25 Mins at 375 degrees until soft. More oil may be drizzled as required.
- Combine the mayonnaise, horseradish, paprika, ketchup, garlic powder, and dried oregano in a medium mixing bowl. Season it with salt and pepper.
- Serve the onion with sauce for dipping.

Nutrition Value

Calories: 68.1 Kcal, Carb: 13.1 g, Protein: 8.3 g, Fat: 5 g
Storage Suggestion: You can store it in the refrigerator for 3-4 days.

The Ultimate Air Fryer Veggie Burgers

Prep Time: 20 Mins, Cook Time: 25 mins, Servings: 6, Serving Size: 2

Ingredients
- Sweet Potato 500 g
- Cauliflower 800 g
- Carrots 190 g
- Chickpeas 1 Cup
- Whole meal Breadcrumbs 2 Cups
- Grated Mozzarella Cheese 1 Cup
- Mixed Herbs 1 Tbsp
- Basil 1 Tbsp
- Salt & Pepper

Instructions
- Vegetables should be peeled and sliced before being placed in the Instant Pot's bottom. 1 cup heated water in the Instant Pot Cover the Instant Pot, close the valve and cook for 10 Mins manually.
- Drain the veggies and squeeze out any excess moisture with a tea towel until they are completely dry.
- After the chickpeas have been added, the veggies have been mashed.
- Blend in the breadcrumbs thoroughly.
- Seasoning is added, and the mixture is formed into the shape of a vegetable burger.
- Roll the grated cheese until it is completely covered with cheese.
- Cook the vegetable burgers in an air fryer for 10 Mins at 180°C/360°F. Follow this recipe at 200°C/400°F for more than 5 Mins to create a crusty vegetable burger appearance.
- Serve hot with a salad or bread buns (or both).

Nutrition Value
Calories: 78 Kcal, Carb: 13.9 g, Protein: 7.5 g, Fat: 3.7 g
Storage Suggestion: You can store it in the refrigerator for 5-6 days.

Air Fried Asparagus with Garlic and Parmesan

Prep Time: 5 Mins, Cook Time: 8 mins, Servings: 4, Serving Size: 2

Ingredients
- Asparagus 1 bundle
- Olive oil 1 tsp
- Garlic salt 1/8 tsp
- Parmesan cheese 1 Tbsp (grated or powdered)
- Pepper

Instructions
- Clean and dry the asparagus. Cut 1" off the bottom of the woody stalks to remove them.
- Arrange the asparagus in a single layer in an air fryer and spray with oil.
- Garlic salt should be evenly distributed over the asparagus. Season with salt and pepper, then top with Parmesan cheese.
- Cook at 400 degrees for 7-10 Mins. Cooking thinner asparagus might be faster.
- After the asparagus has been withdrawn from the air fryer, top it with Parmesan cheese.
- Enjoy.

Nutrition Value
Calories: 86 Kcal, Carb: 8.9 g, Protein: 3 g, Fat: 1 g
Storage Suggestion: You can store it in the refrigerator for 1-2 days.

Air Fryer Corn on The Cob

Prep Time: 5 Mins, Cook Time: 8 mins, Servings: 1-2, Serving Size: 2

Ingredients
- Corn
- Cilantro
- Salt & pepper
- Butter

Optional toppings
- Sriracha
- Basil & parmesan cheese
- Bacon

Instructions
- Remove and trim the husk if necessary. In an air fryer, put the corncobs flat in one layer.
- Spray corn with your preferred cooking spray and bake for 10-15 Mins at 400 degrees until lightly roasted.
- Microwave the butter, salt, and pepper in a cup until the butter has melted.
- Garnish with cilantro and a dollop of butter on top of the corn.

Nutrition Value
Calories: 58 Kcal, Carb: 5.9 g, Protein: 2.5 g, Fat: 1 g
Storage Suggestion: You can store it in the refrigerator for 4-5 days.

Air Fryer Sweet Potato

Prep Time: 20 Mins, Cook Time: 35 mins, Servings: 3, Serving Size: 1

Ingredients
- Sweet potatoes 3
- Olive oil 1 tbsp
- Kosher salt 1-2 tsp

Instructions
- Clean the sweet potatoes, then poke holes in them with a fork to allow air to escape.
- Rub the potatoes with olive oil and salt in an equal layer.
- Set the potatoes in the Air Fryer basket and place them in the machine if they are coated.
- Cook the potatoes at 392°F for 35-40 Mins, or until fork tender.
- Finish with your favorites.

Nutrition Value
Calories: 94 Kcal, Carb: 10.2 g, Protein: 8.9 g, Fat: 3.6 g
Storage Suggestion: You can store it in the refrigerator for 2-3 days.

Air Fryer Eggplant

Prep Time: 15 Mins, Cook Time: 20 mins, Servings: 1-2, Serving Size: 2

Ingredients
- Olive oil 2 tbsp
- Garlic powder 1 tsp
- Red pepper 1/2 tsp
- Sweet paprika 1 tsp optional
- Italian seasoning 1/2 tsp
- Eggplant 1 cut into 1" pieces.

Instructions

- Toss all ingredients together until the eggplant pieces are coated with spices and olive oil. Place the eggplant in the air fryer basket.
- The eggplant is air fried for 20 Mins at 375°F, shaking the basket halfway through.

Nutrition Value
Calories: 58 Kcal, Carb: 7 g, Protein: 3 g, Fat: 1.7 g
Storage Suggestion: You can store it in the refrigerator for 5-6 days.

Air Fryer Bacon Wrapped Asparagus

Prep Time: 10 Mins, Cook Time: 20 mins, Servings: 6, Serving Size: 2

Ingredients
- Bacon 1 lb cut in half.
- Asparagus 1 lb trimmed.
- Salt, pepper, & Creole seasoning/seasoned salt to taste
- Olive oil 1 tbsp

Instructions
- The asparagus ends are cut, and the bacon is sliced in half.
- Drizzle olive oil over the asparagus. Season with salt, pepper, and Creole spice. Toss to coat evenly.
- Two asparagus stalks are wrapped in a half piece of bacon.
- Cook for 10 minutes in an air fryer, then switch and cook for another ten minutes. Depending on how crispy you prefer your bacon, you may cook it for less time.
- Serve right away or keep in an airtight container for up to a week.

Nutrition Value
Calories: 79 Kcal, Carb: 5 g, Protein: 8.6 g, Fat: 3.4 g
Storage Suggestion: You can store it in the refrigerator for 5-6 days.

Air Fryer Cajun Sweet Potato Fries

Prep Time: 10 Mins, Cook Time: 30 mins, Servings: 2, Serving Size: 1

Ingredients
- Sweet Potato Yam 1 med
- Cajun Seasoning 1 tsp
- Cornstarch 2 tbsp
- Olive oil 3 tbsp
- Cajun mayo
- Hellman's mayonnaise 1 cup
- Dijon Mustard 2 tbsp
- Lime 1
- Cajun Seasoning 1/2 tsp
- Cayenne pinch

Instructions
- On a large chopping board, cut the yam into 14" fries.
- Soak them in water in a large mixing dish.
- Soak for at least 30 Mins, then drain and transfer to a new bowl.
- Toss it in some cornstarch to coat it.
- Season with salt and pepper and drizzle with olive oil.
- Preheat oven to 400 degrees Fahrenheit and bake for 30 Mins.
- While the bacon is cooking, make the spicy mayo and eat it with the bacon.

Nutrition Value
Calories: 71 Kcal, Carb: 14.7 g, Protein: 6.2 g, Fat: 12.8 g
Storage Suggestion: You can store it in the refrigerator for 7-8 days.

Roasted Rainbow Vegetables in the Air Fryer

Prep Time: 10 Mins, Cook Time: 20 mins, Servings: 4, Serving Size: 1

Ingredient
- Red bell pepper 1, seeded & cut into 1" pieces.
- Yellow summer squash 1, cut into 1" pieces.
- Zucchini 1 cut into 1" pieces.
- Fresh mushrooms 4 ounces cleaned & halved.
- Sweet onion ½, cut into 1" wedges.
- Extra-virgin olive oil 1 tbsp
- Salt & pepper

Instructions
- Preheat your air fryer according to the manufacturer's instructions.
- Combine the red bell pepper, zucchini, mushrooms, summer squash, and onion in a large mixing bowl. Shake together the olive oil, black pepper, and salt.
- Arrange the veggies in a single layer in the air fryer basket. Air-fry the veggies until they are roasted, about 20 Mins, tossing halfway through.

Nutrition Value
Calories: 58 Kcal, Carb: 6 g, Protein: 2 g, Fat: 0.7 g
Storage Suggestion: You can store it in the refrigerator for 5-6 days.

Air Fryer Roasted Cauliflower

Prep Time: 10 Mins, Cook Time: 12 mins, Servings: 4, Serving Size: 1

Ingredients
- Chopped cauliflower 4 cups.
- Olive oil 1 tbsp
- Parsley 1 tsp
- Thyme 1 tsp
- Minced Garlic 1 tsp
- Salt 1 tsp
- Parmesan cheese ¼ cup
- Salt & pepper

Instructions
- Combine the cauliflower, olive oil, parsley, chopped garlic, thyme, and salt in a large mixing bowl.
- Toss to combine, and the cauliflower is evenly distributed.
- Place the cauliflower in an air-fryer basket. Preheat oven to 400 degrees for 20 Mins.
- After 10 Mins, combine the cauliflower and parmesan cheese in a mixing bowl.
- Season to taste with salt and pepper and serve right away.

Nutrition Value
Calories: 108 Kcal, Carb: 17.9 g, Protein: 10.3 g, Fat: 8.7 g
Storage Suggestion: You can store it in the refrigerator for 4-5 days.

Sweet and Spicy Air Fryer Brussels Sprouts

Prep Time: 10 Mins, Cook Time: 20 mins, Servings: 4, Serving Size: 1

Ingredients
- Brussels sprouts 1 lb cut in half.

- Honey 2 tbsp
- Vegetable oil 1 1/2 tbsp
- Gochujang 1 tbsp
- Salt 1/2 tsp

Instructions
- Stir together the honey, gochujang, vegetable oil, and salt in a mixing dish. Set aside about 1 tbsp of the sauce. Toss the sprouts into the bowl and toss until they are evenly covered.
- Place the Brussels sprouts in the Air Fryer, making sure they don't overlap, and fry for 15 Mins at 360°F, shaking the bucket halfway through. Remove the dish from the table.
- After 15 Mins, increase the temperature to 390 ° F and cook for another five Mins. When the sprouts are done, place them in a bowl and top with the remaining sauce, stirring to combine. Enjoy.

Nutrition Value
Calories: 147 Kcal, Carb: 18.8 g, Protein: 14.9 g, Fat: 7.2 g
Storage Suggestion: You can store it in the refrigerator for 6-7 days.

Air Fryer Green Beans

Prep Time: 5 Mins, Cook Time: 10 mins, Servings: 4, Serving Size: 1

Ingredients
- Green beans 2 cup
- Oil ½ tsp

Instructions
- Wash the green beans and, if required, trim the ends. Toss the beans in the oil.
- In an air fryer, cook the beans. Cook at 390°F for 10 Mins.
- Enjoy.

Nutrition Value
Calories: 86 Kcal, Carb: 17.3 g, Protein: 11.9 g, Fat: 7.1 g
Storage Suggestion: You can store it in the refrigerator for 4-5 days.

Chapter 20: Lean and Green Recipes

Air Fryer Sweet & Sour Chicken

Prep Time: 5 Mins, Cook Time: 10 Mins, Servings: 2, Serving Size: 1

Ingredients

Chicken
- 4 cups chicken breasts /thighs: cut into one-inch pieces
- Cornstarch: 2 tbsp

Sweet & Sour Sauce
- Cornstarch: 2 tbsp
- Pineapple juice: 1 cup
- Water: 2 tbsp
- Honey: 1/2 cup
- Soy sauce: 1 tbsp
- Rice wine vinegar: 3 tbsp
- Ground ginger: ¼ tsp

Optional
- ¼ cup pineapple chunks
- 3-4 drops of red food coloring (for traditional orange look)

Instructions
- Preheat your air fryer to 400°F.
- Coat the chicken with cornstarch until it is fully covered.
- Place the chicken in the air fryer and cook for 7 Mins and 9 Mins. Remove from the air fryer
- Meanwhile, simmer pineapple juice, ginger, brown sugar, soy sauce, and rice wine vinegar in a pot. Allow for a five-Min simmer.
- Prepare a cornstarch slurry and whisk it into the sauce. Allow for one Min of simmering.
- Serve with steamed veggies and a coating of cooked chicken pieces.

Nutrition Value
Calories: 302 Kcal, Carb: 18 g, Protein: 22 g, Fat: 8 g
Storage Suggestion: You can store it in the refrigerator for 4-5 days.

Air Fryer Buffalo Cauliflower

Prep Time: 5 Mins, Cook Time:15 Mins, Servings: 4, Serving Size: 1

Ingredients
- Homemade buffalo sauce: 1/2 cup
- One head of cauliflower, cut bite-size pieces
- Butter melted: 1 tbsp
- Olive oil
- Kosher salt & pepper, to taste

Instructions
- Spray your air fryer basket with cooking oil.
- Combine buffalo sauce, melted butter, pepper, and salt in a mixing bowl. Mix thoroughly.
- Spray the cauliflower parts with olive oil and place them in the air fryer. Cook for 7 Mins at 400 degrees Fahrenheit.
- Take the cauliflower from the air fryer and combine it with the sauce. Coat the cauliflower in a thick layer of oil.
- Return the cauliflower to the air fryer when it has been covered with sauce.
- Cook for 7-8 Mins at 400 degrees F, or until crispy.
- Take the air fryer out of the oven and serve with a leaner protein.

Nutrition Value
Calories: 101 Kcal, Carb: 4 g, Protein: 3 g, Fat: 7 g
Storage Suggestion: You can store it in the refrigerator for 3-4 days.

Low Carb Air-Fried Calzones

Prep Time: 15 Mins, Cook Time: 27 Mins, Servings: 2, Serving Size: 1

Ingredients
- Cooked chicken breast: 1/3 cup(shredded)
- 1 tsp olive oil
- Spinach leaves(baby): 3 cups
- Whole-wheat pizza dough, freshly prepared
- Marinara sauce: 1/3 cup (lower sodium)
- Diced red onion: ¼ cup
- Skim mozzarella cheese: 6 Tbsp
- Cooking spray

Instructions
- Add oil and onions to a medium pan over medium heat. Sauté until the vegetables are tender. After that, add the spinach leaves and simmer until they are wilted. Remove the pan from the heat and stir in the chicken and marinara sauce.
- Divide the dough into two halves.
- Place a quarter of the spinach mixture on each round of dough.
- Top with shredded skim cheese. Crimp the edges and fold the dough over.
- Using cooking spray, coat the calzones.
- Place the calzones in the air fryer to cook. Cook at 325°F for 12 Mins, or until the dough is lightly golden. Cook for another eight Mins after flipping the calzone.

Nutrition Value
Calories: 348 Kcal, Carb: 18 g, Protein: 21 g, Fat: 12 g
Storage Suggestion: You can store it in the refrigerator for 4 days.

Air Fryer Low Carb Chicken Bites

Prep Time: 10 Mins, Cook Time:10 Mins, Servings: 3, Serving Size: 1

Ingredients
- Chicken breast: 2 cups
- Kosher salt& pepper to taste
- Smashed potatoes: one cup
- Scallions: ¼ cup
- One Egg beat
- Whole wheat breadcrumbs: 1 cup

Instructions
- Cook the chicken until it is tender.
- With the assistance of a fork, shred the chicken.

- Toss the shredded chicken with crushed potatoes and onions. Season with kosher salt and freshly ground black pepper.
- Coat in beaten egg, then breadcrumbs.
- Cook for 8 Mins at 380 degrees Fahrenheit in an air fryer. Alternatively, cook till golden brown.
- Warm the dish before serving.

Nutrition Value
Calories: 234 Kcal, Carb: 15 g, Protein: 25 g, Fat: 19 g
Storage Suggestion: You can store it in the refrigerator for 4-5 days.

Air Fryer Popcorn Chicken

Prep Time: 10 Mins, Cook Time: 20 Mins, Servings: 2, Serving Size: 1

Ingredients

For Marinade
- 8 cups, chicken tenders, cut into bite-size pieces
- Freshly ground black pepper: 1/2 tsp
- Almond milk: 2 cups
- Salt: 1 tsp
- paprika: 1/2 tsp

Dry Mix
- Salt: 3 tsp
- Flour: 3 cups
- Paprika: 2 tsp
- Oil spray
- Freshly ground black pepper: 2 tsp

Instructions
- Combine all of the marinade ingredients, as well as the chicken, in a mixing bowl. Mix thoroughly, then place in a Ziploc bag and chill for at least two hrs, or up to six hrs.
- Combine all of the dry ingredients in a large mixing bowl.
- Toss the marinated chicken with the dry ingredients. Back into the marinade, then into the dry mixture for the second time.
- Using olive oil to spray the air fryer basket, arrange the breaded chicken pieces in a single layer. Spray the chicken pieces with oil as well.
- Cook for 10 Mins at 370 degrees, tossing halfway through.
- Serve with salad leaves or a dipping sauce right away.

Nutrition Value
Calories: 340 Kcal, Carb: 14 g, Protein: 20 g, Fat: 14 g
Storage Suggestion: You can store it in the refrigerator for 4-5 days.

Air Fried Cheesy Chicken Omelet

Prep Time: 5 Mins, Cook Time: 18 Mins, Servings: 2, Serving Size: 1

Ingredients
- Cooked Chicken Breast: 1/2 cup(diced)divided
- Four eggs
- Onion powder: ¼ tsp, divided
- Salt: 1/2 tsp, divided
- Pepper: ¼ tsp, divided
- Shredded cheese: 2 tbsp divided
- Granulated garlic: ¼ tsp, divided

Instructions
- Grease 2 ramekins with olive oil and set aside.
- In each ramekin, crack two eggs. Season cheese with salt and pepper.
- To mix, use a blender. Top with 1/4 cup cooked chicken.
- Cook in an air fryer at 330°F for 14-18 Mins, or until thoroughly done.

Nutrition Value
Calories: 185 Kcal, Carb: 10 g, Protein: 20 g, Fat: 5 g
Storage Suggestion: You can store it in the refrigerator for 6-7 days.

Air-Fried Tortilla Hawaiian Pizza

Prep Time: 10 Mins, Cook Time: 20 Mins, Servings: 1, Serving Size: 1

Ingredients
- Mozzarella Cheese
- Tortilla wrap
- Tomato sauce: 1 tbsp
- Toppings
- Cooked chicken shredded or hotdog: 2 tbsp
- Pineapple pieces: 3 tbsp
- Ham: half slice, cut into pieces
- Cheese slice cut into pieces

Instructions
- Spread tomato sauce over a tortilla that has been laid flat on a dish.
- Toss in some shredded mozzarella and your favorite toppings. Serve with cheese slices on top.
- Cook for five to ten Mins at 160 degrees Celsius in an air fryer.
- Remove the chicken from the air fryer and slice it. Serve with baby spinach on the side.

Nutrition Value
Calories: 178 Kcal, Carb: 15 g, Protein: 21 g, Fat: 15 g
Storage Suggestion: You can store it in the refrigerator for 4-5 days.

Air Fryer Personal Mini Pizza

Prep Time: 2 Mins, Cook Time: 5 Mins, Servings: 1, Serving Size: 1

Ingredients
- Sliced olives: ¼ cup
- One pita bread
- One tomato
- Shredded cheese: 1/2 cup

Instructions
- Preheat your air fryer to 350 degrees Fahrenheit.
- Place the pita on a platter and flatten it out. Toss in the cheese, tomato pieces, and olives.
- Preheat oven to 350°F and bake for 5 Mins.
- Take the pizza out of the air fryer and set it aside.
- Cut it up and eat it.

Nutrition Value
Calories: 344 Kcal, Carb: 37 g, Protein: 18 g, Fat: 13 g
Storage Suggestion: You can store it in the refrigerator for 6-7 days.

Air Fryer Party Meatballs

Prep Time: 5 Mins, Cook Time: 15 Mins, Servings: 4, Serving Size: 1

Ingredients

- Worcester Sauce: 2 ½ Tbsp
- Lean Mince Beef: 4 cups
- Dry Mustard: 1/2 tsp
- Tabasco: 1 Tbsp
- Brown Sugar; 1/2 cup
- Vinegar: ¼ Cup
- Tomato Ketchup: ¾ Cup
- Lemon Juice: 1 Tbsp
- Three crushed Gingersnaps

Instructions

- In a large mixing bowl, combine allspice ingredients and stir thoroughly.
- After that, add the minced meat and stir thoroughly.
- Form them into medium-sized balls with your palms.
- Place them in the air fryer and cook for 15 Mins at 375°F, or until fully done.
- Before serving, take them out and put sticks to them.

Nutrition Value

Calories: 383 Kcal, Carb: 25 g, Protein: 22 g, Fat: 13 g
Storage Suggestion: You can store it in the refrigerator for 4-5 days.

Air Fryer Chicken Nuggets

Prep Time: 15 Mins, Cook Time:15 Mins, Servings: 4, Serving Size: 1

Ingredients

- Olive oil spray
- Skinless boneless: 2 chicken breasts, cut into bite pieces
- 1/2 tsp of kosher salt& freshly ground black pepper, to taste
- Grated parmesan cheese: 2 tbsp
- Italian seasoned breadcrumbs: 6 tbsp (whole wheat)
- Whole wheat breadcrumbs: 2 tbsp
- olive oil: 2 tsp

Instructions

- Preheat your air fryer to 400 degrees Fahrenheit for 8 Mins.
- Mix panko, parmesan cheese, and breadcrumbs in a large mixing bowl.
- Season the chicken with kosher salt and pepper, then toss olive oil.
- Using a fork, immerse a few chicken pieces into the breadcrumb's mixture.
- Spray these pieces with olive oil and place them in an air fryer.
- Cook for 8 Mins, flipping halfway.
- Serve with kale chips.

Nutrition Value

Calories: 188 Kcal, Carb: 8 g, Protein: 25 g, Fat: 4.5 g
Storage Suggestion: You can store it in the refrigerator for 5-6 days.

5-Ingredient Air Fryer Lemon Chicken

Prep Time: 5 Mins, Cook Time: 15 Mins, Servings: 4, Serving Size: 1

Ingredients

- Whole-wheat crumbs: 1 and 1/2 cups
- Six pieces of chicken tenderloins
- Two eggs
- Two half lemons and lemon slices
- Kosher salt to taste

Instructions

- Whisk your eggs in a bowl.
- Place the breadcrumbs in a separate dish.
- Coat the chicken with egg and then wrap it in breadcrumbs.
- In the air fryer, place the breaded chicken.
- Cook the chicken for 14 Mins at 400 degrees F, flipping halfway through.
- Remove from the air fryer and pour lemon juice over the top before serving with lemon slices and kosher salt.

Nutrition Value

Calories: 240 Kcal, Carb: 12 g, Protein: 27 g, Fat: 12 g
Storage Suggestion: You can store it in the refrigerator for 6-7 days.

Low Carb Chicken Tenders

Prep Time: 10 Mins, Cook Time: 20 Mins, Servings: 3, Serving Size: 1

Ingredients

- Chicken tenderloins: 4 cups
- Eggs: one
- Superfine Almond Flour: ½ cup
- Powdered Parmesan cheese: ½ cup
- Kosher Sea salt: ½ tsp
- (1-tsp) freshly ground black pepper
- (1/2 tsp) Cajun seasoning,

Instructions

- Pour your beaten egg onto a small platter.
- In a zip lock bag, combine all of the ingredients for the cheese. Almond flour, kosher salt, freshly ground black pepper, and additional ingredients
- Using an oil spray, coat the air fryer.
- Breading and egg are used to prevent clumpy fingers. For the egg and the breading, use separate hands. Dip each tender in the egg, then in the breadcrumbs, until all of them are breaded.
- Place one tender at a time with a fork. Place it in a zip lock bag and shake it vigorously. Ensure that the tenders are completely coated in the almond mixture.
- Remove the tender with a fork and set it in the air fryer basket.
- Tenders should be sprayed with oil.
- Cook for 12 Mins at 350°F, or until an internal temperature of 160°F is reached. Raise the temperature to 400°F for 3 Mins to shade the surface.
- Serve with a side of sauce.

Nutrition Value

Calories: 280 Kcal, Carb: 6 g, Protein: 20 g, Fat: 10 g
Storage Suggestion: You can store it in the refrigerator for 5-6 days.

Cheesy Cauliflower Tots

Prep Time: 15 Mins, Cook Time: 12 Mins, Servings: 4, Serving Size: 2

Ingredients

- 1 large head cauliflower
- 1 cup shredded mozzarella cheese
- 1/2 cup grated Parmesan cheese
- 1 large egg
- ¼ tsp garlic powder

- ¼ tsp dried parsley
- 1/8 tsp onion powder

Instructions

- Fill a large saucepan with 2 cups of water on the burner, then place a steamer in the oven. Put the bath on the stove to boil.
- Break the cauliflower into flowers and set on a steamer box, then cover with a lid and cover the pot.
- Allow the cauliflower to steam for 7 Mins, or until fork tender. Allow cooling in the cheesecloth or kitchen towel from the steamer basket.
- To remove as much additional humidity as possible, press down on the sink. The mixture will be too soft to mold into tots if not all moisture is removed.
- With a blade, mash to a smooth consistency.
- Combine the garlic powder, parmesan, egg, cauliflower, mozzarella, parsley, & onion powder in a mixing bowl. Remove until everything is fully blended. The mixture should be smooth yet moldable.
- To make a tot, take 2 tsp of the mixture and roll it into a ball. Rep with the remaining mixture. In the air fryer, place the basket.
- Preheat the oven to 320 degrees Fahrenheit and set the timer for 12 Mins.
- Halfway through the cooking time, turn the tots.
- When thoroughly cooked, cauliflower tots should be golden. Warm the dish before serving.

Nutrition Value

Calories: 181 Kcal, Carb: 6.6 g, Protein: 13.5 g, Fat: 9.5 g

Storage Suggestion: You can store it in the refrigerator for 5-6 days.

Air Fryer Turkey Fajitas Platter

Prep Time: 5 Mins, Cook Time: 20 Mins, Servings: 2, Serving Size: 1

Ingredients

- Cooked Turkey Breast: ¼ cup
- Six Tortilla Wraps
- One Avocado
- One Yellow Pepper
- One Red Pepper
- Half Red Onion
- Soft Cheese: 5 Tbsp
- Mexican Seasoning: 2 Tbsp
- Cumin: 1 Tsp
- Kosher salt& Pepper
- Cajun Spice: 3 Tbsp
- Fresh Coriander

Instructions

- Prepare the avocado by chopping it up and slicing the veggies.
- Turkey breast should be diced into little bite-size pieces.
- Combine onions, turkey, soft cheese, and peppers in a bowl with spices. Mix everything up well.
- Wrap it in foil and place it in the air fryer.
- Cook at 200°C for 20 Mins.
- Serve immediately.

Nutrition Value

Calories: 379 Kcal, Carb: 84 g, Protein: 30 g, Fat: 39 g

Storage Suggestion: You can store it in the refrigerator for 7-8 days.

Air Fryer Tenderloin Turkey Breast

Prep Time: 5 Mins, Cook Time: 25 Mins, Servings: 3, Serving Size: 1

Ingredients

- Turkey breast tenderloin: one-piece
- Thyme: 1/2 tsp
- Sage: 1/2 tsp
- Paprika: 1/2 tsp
- Pink salt: 1/2 tsp
- Freshly ground black pepper: 1/2 tsp

Instructions

- Preheat your air fryer to 350 degrees Fahrenheit.
- Combine all spices and herbs in a dish and massage all over the turkey.
- Spray the air fryer basket with oil. Place the turkey in the air fryer and cook for 25 Mins at 350 degrees F, flipping halfway through.
- Serve with a salad of micro greens.

Nutrition Value

Calories: 162 Kcal, Carb: 1 g, Protein: 13 g, Fat: 1 g

Storage Suggestion: You can store it in the refrigerator for 3-4 days.

Chapter 21: Holiday Specials Recipes

Churros with Chocolate Sauce (Air Fryer)

Prep Time: 20 Mins, Cook Time: 30 mins, Servings: 12, Serving Size: 4

Ingredients
- Water 1/2 cup
- Kosher salt ¼ tsp
- Unsalted butter ¼ cup, + 1/2 cup (2 1/8 oz.) divided 2 Tbsp All-purpose flour
- Large eggs 2
- Granulated sugar 1/3 cup
- Ground cinnamon 2 tsp
- Bittersweet baking chocolate 4 ounces
- Heavy cream 3 tbsp
- Vanilla kefir 2 tbsp

Instructions
- Bring the water, salt, and butter (¼ cup) to a boil in a saucepan over med high. Reduce the heat to medium-low; stir in the flour with a wooden spoon for about 30 seconds, or until the dough is smooth. Cook, often stirring, until the dough begins to break away from the edges of the pan and a film form on the bottom of the pan, about 2 to 3 Mins. Move the dough into a med bowl. Stir continuously for around 1 min till slightly cooled. 1 egg at a time, constantly whisking after each addition until completely smooth. Fill a piping bag with the mixture and a medium star tip. Allow 30 Mins for chilling.
- In a basket of air fryers, pipe 6 (3" long) pieces in a layer. Cook at 380°F for about 10 Mins, or until golden. Rep with the remaining dough.
- Combine the sugar and cinnamon in a medium mixing bowl. Brush the remaining 2 tbsp melted butter over the fried churros before coating them in the sugar mixture.
- In a small microwave-safe dish, combine the cream and chocolate. For about 30 seconds, Microwave on HIGH for 15 seconds, stirring after 15 seconds, until melted and smooth. Stir in the kefir. Serve the churros with a chocolate sauce.

Nutrition Value
Calories: 207 Kcal, Carb: 36 g, Protein: 28.6 g, Fat: 10.8 g
Storage Suggestion: You can store it in the refrigerator for 5-6 days.

Air Fryer Party Meatballs

Prep Time: 25 Mins, Cook Time: 30 mins, Servings: 2, Serving Size: 1

Ingredients
- Mince Beef 1 lb
- Tomato Ketchup ¾ Cup
- Tabasco 1 Tbsp
- Worcester Sauce 2 1/2 Tbsp
- Vinegar ¼ Cup
- Lemon Juice 1 Tbsp
- Brown Sugar ½ Cup
- Dry Mustard ½ Tsp
- Gingersnaps crushed 3.

Instructions
- In a large mixing bowl, combine the ingredients and stir until evenly covered.
- Add the mince to the mixing bowl and thoroughly combine.
- Make medium-sized meatballs and fry them in the Air Fryer.
- Preheat oven to 375°F and bake for 15 Mins.
- Place them on sticks before serving.

Nutrition Value
Calories: 119 Kcal, Carb: 18.6 g, Protein: 14.9 g, Fat: 10.9 g
Storage Suggestion: You can store it in the refrigerator for 4-5 days.

Air-Fryer Ground Beef Wellington

Prep Time: 10 Mins, Cook Time: 20 mins, Servings: 2, Serving Size: 3

Ingredients
- Butter 1 tbsp
- Minced fresh mushrooms 1/2 cup.
- All-purpose flour 2 tsp
- Pepper ¼ tsp, divided.
- Half-&-half cream 1/2 cup
- Large egg yolk 1
- Finely chopped onion 2 tbsp
- Salt ¼ tsp
- Ground beef 1/2 lb
- refrigerated crescent rolls 1 tube (4 ounces)
- Large egg 1, lightly beaten optional.
- Dried parsley flakes 1 tsp

Instructions
- Preheat the oven to 300 degrees Fahrenheit. In a pot, melt the butter over mid heat. Cook and stir the mushrooms for 5-6 Mins, or until they are tender. Combine the flour and 10% tsp pepper in a mixing bowl. Gradually pour in the cream. Make it boil, then simmer and mix for 2 Mins, or until the sauce has thickened. Take away from the heat and put aside.
- In a bowl, whisk together the egg yolk, 2 tbsp mushroom sauce, onion, salt, and 1/8 tsp pepper. Crumble the meat into the mixture and thoroughly mix it in. Make two loaves out of the dough. Unroll the crescent dough and cut it into two rectangles, pressing the holes shut. Place the meatloaf in each rectangle. Bring the edges together and squeeze to close. If desired, brush with beaten egg.
- Arrange the Wellingtons in a single ground on the greased tray in the fryer basket. Cook for 18-22 Mins, until a thermometer

inserted into the meatloaf registers 160 degrees or until golden brown.
- Meanwhile, boil the remaining sauce over low heat and stir in the parsley. Serve the sauce with the Wellingtons.

Nutrition Value
Calories: 99 Kcal, Carb: 13.8 g, Protein: 9 g, Fat: 6.2 g
Storage Suggestion: You can store it in the refrigerator for 6-8 days.

Air-Fryer Steak Fajitas

Prep Time: 15 Mins, Cook Time: 25 mins, Servings: 6, Serving Size: 1

Ingredients
- Large tomatoes 2, seeded & chopped.
- Diced red onion 1/2 cup.
- Lime juice ¼ cup
- Jalapeno pepper 1, seeded & minced.
- Minced fresh cilantro 3 tbsp
- Ground cumin 2 tsp, divided.
- Salt ¾ tsp, divided.
- Flank steak 1 beef (1-1/2 lb)
- Onion 1 large halved & sliced.
- Whole wheat tortillas 6 (8"), warmed.
- Sliced avocado & lime wedges optional.

Instructions
- To make the salsa, combine the first five ingredients in a dish and whisk in 1 tsp cumin and 1/4 tsp salt. Allow it to rest until ready to serve.
- Preheat the oven to 400 degrees Fahrenheit. Season the meat with the remaining cumin and salt. Place the air-fryer basket on a plate that has been greased. Cook for 6 to 8 Mins on each side, or until the flesh reaches the desired thickness (a thermometer should register 135° for med-rare, 140° for medium, and 145° for med-well). Remove the pan from the heat and set it aside for 5 Mins.
- Meanwhile, place the onion on the plate in the air-fryer basket. Cook, stirring once or twice, until crisp-tender, about 2-3 Mins. Thinly slice the steak against the grain and serve tortillas with onion and salsa. If desired, garnish with avocado and lime wedges.

Nutrition Value
Calories: 198 Kcal, Carb: 15.9 g, Protein: 23.3 g, Fat: 12.5 g
Storage Suggestion: You can store it in the refrigerator for 7-8 days.

Air-Fryer Sweet and Sour Pork

Prep Time: 10 Mins, Cook Time: 15 mins, Servings: 2, Serving Size: 1

Ingredients
- Unsweetened crushed pineapple 1/2 cup, undrained.
- Cider vinegar 1/2 cup
- Sugar ¼ cup
- Packed dark brown sugar ¼ cup.
- Ketchup ¼ cup
- Reduced-sodium soy sauce 1 tbsp
- Dijon mustard 1-1/2 tsp
- Garlic powder 1/2 tsp
- Pork tenderloin 1 (¾ lb), halved.
- Salt 1/8 tsp
- Pepper 1/8 tsp
- Optional sliced green onions
- Cooking spray

Instructions
- In a saucepan, combine the first 8 ingredients. Bring it to a boil, then reduce the heat. Cook, uncovered, for 6 to 8 Mins, or until thickened, stirring occasionally.
- Preheat the oven to 350 degrees Fahrenheit. Season the pork with salt and pepper. Spray the pork with cooking spray and place it in the air-fryer basket on a greased tray. Cook for 7-8 Mins, or until the pork browns on the edges. Place two tbsp of sauce on top of the meat. Cook for another 10 to 12 Mins, or until a thermometer inserted into the pork registers at least 145°F. Allow 5 Mins for the pork to rest before slicing. Serve with the remaining sauce. If desired, garnish with chopped green onions.

Nutrition Value
Calories: 218 Kcal, Carb: 19.4 g, Protein: 13.1 g, Fat: 14.8 g
Storage Suggestion: You can store it in the refrigerator for 4-6 days.

Air-Fryer Keto Meatballs

Prep Time: 5 Mins, Cook Time: 10 mins, Servings: 4, Serving Size: 2

Ingredients
- Grated Parmesan cheese 1/2 cup
- Shredded mozzarella cheese 1/2 cup
- Large egg 1, lightly beaten.
- Heavy whipping cream 2 tbsp
- Garlic clove 1, minced.
- Lean ground beef 1 lb (90% lean)

Sauce
- Tomato sauce with garlic, basil, and oregano 1 can (8 ounces)
- Prepared pesto 2 tbsp
- Heavy whipping cream ¼ cup

Instructions
- In a saucepan, mix the first eight ingredients. Bring to a boil, then reduce to low heat. Cook, occasionally stirring, until the sauce has thickened, about 6 to 8 Mins.
- Preheat the oven to 350 degrees Fahrenheit and the fryer to 400 degrees Fahrenheit. On the pork, season with salt and pepper. Place the pork in an air fryer basket on a prepared baking sheet and spritz with cooking spray. Cook for 7-8 Mins, or until the edges of the pork begin to brown. Toss the pork with two tbsp of sauce. Cook for another 10 to 12 Mins, or until a thermometer inserted into the pork registers a temperature of at least 145 degrees Fahrenheit. Allow 5 Mins for the pork to rest before cutting. With the remaining sauce, serve. If desired, sprinkle with chopped green onions.

Nutrition Value
Calories: 227 Kcal, Carb: 38.2 g, Protein: 18.5 g, Fat: 13.2 g
Storage Suggestion: You can store it in the refrigerator for 6-7 days.

Air-Fryer Quinoa Arancini

Prep Time: 25 mins, Cook Time: 30 Mins, Servings: 3, Serving Size: 1

Ingredients

- Ready-to-serve quinoa 1 package (9 ounces)/cooked quinoa 1-¾ cups.
- Large eggs 2, lightly beaten.
- Seasoned breadcrumbs 1 cup, divided.
- Shredded Parmesan cheese ¼ cup
- Olive oil 1 tbsp
- Minced fresh basil 2 tbsp or dried basil 2 tsp
- Garlic powder 1/2 tsp
- Salt 1/2 tsp
- Pepper 1/8 tsp
- Mozzarella cheese 6 cubes part-skim (¾ inch each)
- Cooking spray
- Optional Warmed pasta sauce

Instructions

- Preheat the air fryer oven to 375 degrees Fahrenheit. Prepare the quinoa according to the package recommendations. 1 egg, 1/2 cup breadcrumbs, parmesan cheese, basil, oil, and spices
- It should be divided into 6 pieces. Form each portion into a ball by wrapping it around a cheese cube.
- Combine the remaining egg and 1/2 cup of breadcrumbs in separate small dishes. Roll the quinoa balls in breadcrumbs after dipping them in the egg. Place on an oiled tray in the air-fryer basket and spray with cooking mist. Cook for 6-8 Mins, or until brown. If desired, top with spaghetti sauce.

Nutrition Value

Calories: 137 Kcal, Carb: 18.3 g, Protein: 10.7 g, Fat: 7.9 g

Storage Suggestion: You can store it in the refrigerator for 8-10 days.

Air Fryer Grilled Cheese Sandwich

Prep Time: 5 Mins, Cook Time: 5 mins, Servings: 1, Serving Size: 1

Ingredients

- Bread 2 slices
- Butter 1 tsp
- Cheddar cheese 2 slices
- Turkey 2 slices (optional)

Instructions

- The air fryer has been preheated to 350°F.
- Spread the butter on the edge of the bread. If using, top with cheese and turkey, then top with another buttered bread slice.
- Place the sandwich into the Air Fryer. Set a timer for 5 Mins. This is the halfway point.
- The sandwich should have the appearance of a toasted, melting cheese sandwich.

Nutrition Value

Calories: 129 Kcal, Carb: 17.9 g, Protein: 12.7 g, Fat: 9.1 g

Storage Suggestion: You can store it in the refrigerator for 5-6 days.

Air Fryer Vegan Veggie Balls

Prep Time: 10 Mins, Cook Time: 12 mins, Servings: 4, Serving Size: 2

Ingredients

- Cauliflower 200 g
- Sweet Potato 100 g
- Carrot 70 g
- Parsnips 90 g
- Garlic Puree 2 Tsp
- Chives 1 Tsp
- Paprika 1 Tsp
- Mixed Spice 1 Tsp
- Oregano 2 Tsp
- Desiccated Coconut ½ Cup
- Gluten-Free Oats 1 Cup
- Salt and Pepper

Instructions

- Place the cooked veggies in a clean tea towel and squeeze off the excess water.
- In a mixing dish, arrange them and season them. Blend well and roll into medium-sized balls.
- Place them in the fridge for 2 hrs to allow them to firm up a bit.
- Combine the coconut and gluten-free oats and blitz until it resembles hard flour in a mixer. Pour it into a bowl.
- Roll the vegetable balls in the mixture and place them on the air fryer's grill plate.
- Cook for 10 Mins at 200°C/400°F. Cook for another 2 Mins at the same temperature on the other side.
- Serve.

Nutrition Value

Calories: 127 Kcal, Carb: 16.2 g, Protein: 26.8 g, Fat: 4.9 g

Storage Suggestion: You can store it in the refrigerator for 5-6 days.

Air Fryer Jamaican Jerk Meatballs

Prep Time: 10 Mins, Cook Time: 14, mins Servings: 4, Serving Size: 1

Ingredients

- Jerk dry rub 1 tbsp
- Chicken mince 1 kg
- Breadcrumbs 100 g
- Jamaican Sauce Ingredients:
- Jerk dry rub 1 tsp
- Honey 4 tbsp
- Soy sauce 1 tbsp

Instructions

- Combine the chicken, breadcrumbs, and jerk spice in a mixing dish and stir well. Make meatballs using a meatball press or meatball shapes.
- Place the meatballs in the air fryer and cook for 14 Mins at 180°C/360°F.
- Combine the honey, soy sauce, and the remaining jerk dry rub in a mixing bowl. Make a thorough mix.
- Toss them in the sauce and serve them on sticks when the meatballs are done.

Nutrition Value

Calories: 194 Kcal, Carb: 29.8 g, Protein: 10.4 g, Fat: 6.9 g

Storage Suggestion: You can store it in the refrigerator for 5-6 days.

Crispy Air Fryer Eggplant Parmesan

Prep Time: 10 Mins, Cook Time: 25 mins, Servings: 4, Serving Size: 2

Ingredients
- Eggplant 1 large
- Whole wheat breadcrumbs 1/2 cup
- Finely grated parmesan cheese 3 tbsp
- Salt
- Italian seasoning mix 1 tsp
- Whole wheat flour 3 tbsp
- Water 1 tbsp + egg 1
- Olive oil spray
- Marinara sauce 1 cup
- Grated mozzarella cheese ¼ cup
- Fresh parsley/basil to garnish

Instructions
- Cut the eggplant into 1/2" thick slices. Rub some salt on both sides of the slices and set aside for at least 10-15 Mins.
- Whisk together the egg, water, and flour to form the batter in a separate dish.
- In a shallow medium plate, combine breadcrumbs, Italian seasoning blend, parmesan cheese, and salt. Mix thoroughly.
- Now, evenly distribute the batter among the eggplant slices. Drop the battered slices into the breadcrumb mixture to coat them evenly on both sides.
- Place breaded eggplant slices on a clean, dry flat dish and drizzle with oil.
- Preheat the Air Fryer to 360°F. Then arrange the eggplant slices on the wire mesh and cook for about 8 Mins.
- Top the pieces with about 1 tbsp marinara sauce and a sprinkling of fresh mozzarella cheese. Cook for another 1-2 Mins, or until the cheese has melted.
- Serve warm with your favorite pasta.

Nutrition Value
Calories: 247 Kcal, Carb: 10.2 g, Protein: 17.8 g, Fat: 4.2 g
Storage Suggestion: You can store it in the refrigerator for 4-5 days.

Air fryer Falafel Burger

Prep Time: 10 Mins, Cook Time: 15 mins, Servings: 2 Serving Size: 1

Ingredients
- Canned Chickpeas 400 g
- Red Onion 1 Small
- Lemon 1 Small
- Gluten-Free Oats 140 g
- Cheese 28 g
- Feta Cheese 28 g
- Greek Yoghurt 3 Tbsp
- Soft Cheese 4 Tbsp
- Garlic Puree 1 Tbsp
- Coriander 1 Tbsp
- Oregano 1 Tbsp
- Parsley 1 Tbsp
- Salt & Pepper

Instructions
- Combine all ingredients in a food processor or blender, including the lemon rind, garlic, drained chickpeas, and red onion. Whiz them up until they're rough but not too rough.
- In a mixing bowl, combine all of them with 12 hard pieces of cheese, tiny cheeses, and feta.
- Combine all of the ingredients to make a burger.
- Roll them all in gluten-free oats until there's no more chicken mixture visible.
- Place them in an Air fryer baking sheet and cook for eight Mins at 180°C/360°F.
- Combine the remaining Greek yogurt, soft cheese, and the extra pepper and salt for the burger sauce in a mixing bowl. Combine all of the ingredients until they are frothy and delicious. Mix in the lemon juice one by one.
- Place the falafel burger and toppings into the prepared buns. Toss in some burger sauce.

Nutrition Value
Calories: 291 Kcal, Carb: 38.2 g, Protein: 24 g, Fat: 17 g
Storage Suggestion: You can store it in the refrigerator for 5-6 days.

Easy Air Fryer Crispy Crunchy Sweet Potato Fries

Prep Time: 10 Mins, Cook Time: 25 mins, Servings: 6, Serving Size: 2

Ingredients
- Large, sweet potatoes peeled & cut lengthwise 2.
- Cornstarch 1 1/2 tbsp
- Paprika 2 tsp
- Garlic powder 2 tsp
- Salt & pepper
- Olive oil 1 tbsp

Instructions
- Combine the sliced sweet potatoes and cold water in a large mixing bowl. Allow the sweet potatoes to soak in the water for an hr.
- Remove them from the water and let them dry. Cornstarch should be sprinkled all over it.
- paprika, salt, garlic powder, and pepper to taste
- Place the fries in the air fryer basket and sprinkle them with olive oil. Also, don't overfill the basket. Cook in batches as required. If there are white patches of cornstarch on the fries, spray them with olive oil.
- Preheat the oven to 380 degrees Fahrenheit and cook for 23-25 Mins. Set a timer for 10 Mins, then come to a halt and shake the basket (once).
- If you want crispy fries, cook them longer and watch them.

Nutrition Value
Calories: 129 Kcal, Carb: 9.2 g, Protein: 7.9 g, Fat: 3.9 g
Storage Suggestion: You can store it in the refrigerator for 5-7 days.

Easy Air Fryer Pepperoni Pizza

Prep Time: 5 Mins, Cook Time: 8 mins, Servings: 1, Serving Size: 1

Ingredients
- Whole wheat pita 1
- Pizza sauce/marinara 2 tbsp
- Mozzarella cheese shredded 1/8th cup.
- Cheddar cheese 1/8th cup, shredded.
- Pepperoni 8 slices
- Olive oil spray
- Chopped parsley 1 tbsp, optional.

Instructions
- Drizzle some sauce over pita bread, & pile on the pepperoni & shredded cheese.
- Spray the pizza using olive oil.
- Preheat Air Fryer oven to 400°F and bake for 8 Mins. Check the pizza after 6-7 Mins to ensure it hasn't overcooked.
- Remove the pizza from the Air Fryer. Serve.

Nutrition Value
Calories: 218 Kcal, Carb: 28 g, Protein: 18.9 g, Fat: 12.4 g
Storage Suggestion: You can store it in the refrigerator for 4-5 days.

Sweet Potatoes Au Gratin
Prep Time: 35 Mins, Cook Time: 1 hr 5 mins, Servings: 6, Serving Size: 2

Ingredients
- Sweet potatoes 2 lb sliced in ¼-½" rounds.
- Butter 1 tbsp
- Garlic cloves 2 minced.
- Cream cheese 4 oz
- Heavy whipping cream ¼ cup
- Shredded cheddar cheese 1 cup divided ½ cup portions.
- Shredded parmesan Reggiano cheese ¼ cup
- Onion powder 1 tsp
- Salt & pepper
- Shredded mozzarella cheese ½ cup

Instructions
- Preheat the air fryer oven to 350 degrees Fahrenheit.
- Heat a saucepan over medium heat and add the butter.
- When the butter has melted, add the garlic and simmer for a few Mins, until aromatic.
- Combine the whipped cream, Parmesan Reggiano, cream cheese, and ½ cup shredded cheddar cheese. Stir. Toss in the onion powder, pepper, and salt to taste. Taste the sauce several times and adjust the seasoning as needed.
- Stir constantly until the cheese has melted.
- Remove the pan from the heat and put it aside.
- Arrange sliced sweet potatoes in a 9/13 baking dish in a line. Drizzle the cheese sauce over the top.
- Add the remaining shredded cheddar (½ cup) and mozzarella to the platter.
- Cover with foil and bake for 30 Mins.
- Remove the foil and bake for another 25 Mins, or until the sweet potatoes are tender.
- Switch on the oven's broil option a few Mins before the dish is done baking if you want a crisp top. Broil for 1-3 Mins, or until the tip is crispy.
- Serve.

Nutrition Value
Calories: 158 Kcal, Carb: 16.2 g, Protein: 19.9 g, Fat: 8.3 g
Storage Suggestion: You can store it in the refrigerator for 6-7 days.

- Combine tomato paste, garlic, pepper, salt, basil, spinach, and scallops in a mixing bowl.
- Adjust the air fryer to 350°F for ten Mins, or until the scallops have reached an internal temperature of 135°F and the sauce is hot and bubbling. Serve right away.

Nutrition Value
Calories: 87 Kcal, Carb: 7 g, Protein: 8 g, Fat: 3 g
Storage Suggestion: You can store it in the refrigerator for 5-6 days.

Chapter 22: Pizza Recipes

Perfect Personal Pizzas in an Air Fryer

Prep Time: 5 Mins, Cook Time: 5 Mins, Servings: 1, Serving Size: 1

Ingredients
- Stonegate Mini Naan
- 2 tbsp of Jarred pizza sauce
- 2 tbsp of Shredded pizza cheese
- 6 /7 Mini Pepperoni

Instructions
- Pizza sauce in a circle, small pepperoni, and shredded pizza cheese will be topped on little naan.
- Place the topping pizza in the air fryer basket.
- Preheat the air fryer to roughly 375 degrees Fahrenheit.
- "Fry" the pizza for about five to seven Mins, or until the cheese melts and the crust begins to brown. Serve right away.

Nutrition Value
Calories: 149 Kcal, Carb: 4.2 g, Protein: 7.1 g, Fat: 6.9 g
Storage Suggestion: You can store it in the refrigerator for 2-3 days.

Optavia Biscuit Pizza

Prep Time: 15 min, Cook Time: 20 Mins, Servings: 3, Serving Size: 1

Ingredients
- Buttermilk Cheddar & Herb Biscuit 1 sachet
- Water 2 Tbsp
- Tomato sauce 1 Tbsp
- Shredded cheese lower fat 1 Tbsp

Instructions
- Preheat the air fryer to 350 degrees Fahrenheit.
- In a mixing dish, combine biscuits and water, spread into a circle on parchment paper, and bake for approximately 10 Minutes.
- After adding the tomato sauce and shredded cheese, bake for a few Mins more until the cheese has melted.

Nutrition Value
Calories: 58 Kcal, Carb: 5 g, Protein: 1.2 g, Fat: 0.6 g
Storage Suggestion: You can store it in the refrigerator for 5-6 days.

Air Fryer Margherita Pizza

Prep Time: 15 mins, Cook Time: 10 Mins, Servings: 1, Serving Size: 1

Ingredients
- The thin crust baked pizza crust 1
- Pizza sauce 3 tbsp
- Thinly sliced Campari tomato 1
- Fresh mozzarella 5 Slices
- Fresh basil few
- Olive oil 1 tsp

Instructions
- On the pizza dough, spread the sauce (pizza sauce). Uniformly arrange the tomato slices on the crust. Place the fresh mozzarella in between the tomato pieces.
- Cook for 5-8 Mins at 350°F in the air fryer basket, or until the cheese has melted.
- Remove the pizza from the oven and sprinkle with olive oil and fresh basil. Begin serving as soon as possible.

Nutrition Value
Calories: 74 Kcal, Carb: 8 g, Protein: 6 g, Fat: 3 g
Storage Suggestion: You can store it in the refrigerator for 2-3 days.

Air Fryer Pizza Pockets

Prep Time: 10 mins, Cook Time: 20 Mins, Servings: 4, Serving Size: 1

Ingredients
- Olive oil Extra virgin 2 tsp
- Finely chopped red capsicum 1/2
- Sliced Button mushrooms, 100g (6)
- Baby spinach 120g
- Leg ham Lean, finely chopped 50 g
- Fetta crumbled 80 g
- Fresh basil leaves, torn ¼ cup
- Dried oregano ½ tsp
- Helga's Traditional White Wraps 4
- Tomato pastes 1/3 cup
- Olive oil spray
- Green salad, to serve

Instructions
- Heat the oil in a frying pan over medium heat. Cook for 5 Mins, or until the capsicum softens. Add the mushrooms and mix well. Cook for another 5 Mins, or until the mushrooms are brown and the liquid in the pan has evaporated. In a mixing bowl, combine all of the ingredients. Allow for a cooling time of 10 Mins.
- In the meanwhile, place the spinach in a heatproof dish. Half-fill the pot with boiling water. Allow 1 Min or until the leaves are completely wilted. Drain all of the water. Allow for a cooling time of 10 Mins.
- Squeeze the spinach to remove any leftover moisture before blending it with the capsicum mixture. Combine the ham, fetta, basil, and oregano in a mixing dish. Season with salt and pepper to taste. To combine, whisk everything together.
- A single wrap should be placed on a flat surface. 14 of the capsicum mix should go on top of 1 tbsp tomato paste in the middle of the wrap. Roll up the wrap and fold in the ends to enclose the filling to form a package. Rep the technique with the remaining wrappers, tomato paste, and capsicum mixture to produce four packages. Oil may be sprayed on the tops.
- Preheat the air fryer to 180°C (350°F). In two pans, cook for 6 to 10 Mins, seam-side down, or until brown and crisp. Serve with a salad.

Nutrition Value
Calories: 83 Kcal, Carb: 16 g, Protein: 6 g, Fat: 3 g
Storage Suggestion: You can store it in the refrigerator for 5-6 days.

Air Fryer Mexican Pizza

Prep Time: 30 mins, Cook Time: 25 Mins, Servings: 4, Serving Size: 1

Ingredients
- Lean ground turkey 12oz
- Cumin ½ tsp
- Gum powder ½ tsp
- Cumin powder ½ tsp
- Cilantro, chopped 1 tbsp
- Green onion, chopped 1
- Mexican cheese reduced fat 1 cup
- Spinach, chopped handful
- Avocado sliced 1/2
- Salsa ¼ cup
- Whole wheat tortilla, 6" or fajita sized 4

Instructions
- In a small skillet, cook the turkey until it is no longer pink.
- Combine cumin, green onion, garlic powder, cilantro, and chili powder in a large mixing bowl.
- Preheat the air fryer to 350 degrees Fahrenheit.
- Grease the air fryer tray and place the tortilla in it. Approximately 2 oz. To each tortilla, add ground turkey, a bit of spinach, and roughly a quarter cup of cheese. Bake for 5-10 Mins, or until the cheese has melted completely.
- On each tortilla, spread 1 tbsp salsa and 1 tbsp avocado.
- Keep in mind that the fryers cook in a variety of ways. Before trying these recipes, please read the manufacturer's safety instructions that came with your air fryer.

Nutrition Value
Calories: 39 Kcal, Carb: 5 g, Protein: 1 g, Fat: 1 g
Storage Suggestion: You can store it in the refrigerator for 4-5 days.

Pizzas for a Quick Lunch
Prep Time:15 Mins, Cook Time: 10 Mins, Servings: 5, Serving Size: 1

Ingredients
- 2 cup sliced grape tomatoes
- 4 cups grated mozzarella
- 4 chopped green onions
- 1 tsp dried basil
- 5 oz. sliced jarred mushrooms
- 1 pizza sauce cup
- 2 tbsp extra virgin olive oil
- 5 pita bread

Instructions
- On each pita bread, spread some pizza sauce, top with green basil and onions, chop the mushrooms, and top with cheese.
- Cook for 7 Mins at 400 degrees F after filling the air fryer halfway with pita pizzas.
- Serve each pizza with tomato slices on top, divided across plates. Have a blast!

Nutrition Value
Calories: 69 Kcal, Carb: 9.2 g, Protein: 6.2 g, Fat: 2.3 g
Storage Suggestion: You can store it in the refrigerator for 2-3 days.

APPENDIX

Measurement Conversion Chart & Cooking Chart

Pan Size Equivalents

9-by-13-inches baking dish	22-by-33-centimeter baking dish
8-by-8-inches baking dish	20-by-20-centimeter baking dish
9-by-5-inches loaf pan	23-by-12-centimeter loaf pan (=8 cups or 2 liters in capacity)
10-inch tart or cake pan	25-centimeter tart or cake pan
9-inch cake pan	22-centimeter cake pan

US to Metric Conversions

1/5 teaspoon	1 ml (ml stands for milliliter, one thousandth of a liter)
1 teaspoon	5 ml
1 tablespoon	15 ml
1 fluid oz	30 ml
1/5 cup	50 ml
1 cup	240 ml
2 cups (1 pint)	470 ml
4 cups (1 quart)	.95 liter
4 quarts (1 gal.)	3.8 liters
1 oz	28 grams
1 pound	454 grams

Metric to US Conversions

1 milliliter	1/5 teaspoon
5 ml	1 teaspoon
15 ml	1 tablespoon
30 ml	1 fluid oz.
100 ml	3.4 fluid oz.
240 ml	1 cup
1 liter	34 fluid oz.
1 liter	4.2 cups
1 liter	2.1 pints
1 liter	1.06 quarts
1 liter	.26 gallon
1 gram	.035 ounce
100 grams	3.5 ounces
500 grams	1.10 pounds
1 kilogram	2.205 pounds
1 kilogram	35 oz.

Measurements Conversion Chart

US Dry Volume Measurements

MEASURE	EQUIVALENT
1/16 teaspoon	dash
1/8 teaspoon	a pinch
3 teaspoons	1 Tablespoon
1/8 cup	2 tablespoons (= 1 standard coffee scoop)
1/4 cup	4 Tablespoons
1/3 cup	5 Tablespoons plus 1 teaspoon
1/2 cup	8 Tablespoons
3/4 cup	12 Tablespoons
1 cup	16 Tablespoons
1 Pound	16 ounces

US liquid volume measurements

8 Fluid ounces	1 Cup
1 Pint	2 Cups (= 16 fluid ounces)
1 Quart	2 Pints (= 4 cups)
1 Gallon	4 Quarts (= 16 cups)

Farenheit	Celsius	Gas Mark
275° F	140° C	gas mark 1-cool
300° F	150° C	gas mark 2
325° F	165° C	gas mark 3-very moderate
350° F	180° C	gas mark 4-moderate
375° F	190° C	gas mark 5
400° F	200° C	gas mark 6-moderately hot
425° F	220° C	gas mark 7- hot
450° F	230° C	gas mark 9
475° F	240° C	gas mark 10- very hot

Made in the USA
Monee, IL
06 May 2022

96021603R00085